THE CAMBRIDGE COMPANION T[?]
TRAVEL W[?]

The Cambridge Companion to Postcolo[?] [?]rs an
insight into the scope and range of perspec[?] [?] in this field
of writing. Encompassing a diverse range o[?] [?], performances and
forms, postcolonial travel writing recounts jo[?] [?]ndertaken through places,
cultures, and communities that are simultaneously living within, through, and
after colonialism in its various guises. *The Companion* is organized into three
parts. Part I, "Departures," addresses key theoretical issues, topics, and themes;
Part II, "Performances," examines a range of conventional and emerging travel
performances and styles in postcolonial travel writing; and Part III,
"Peripheries," continues to shift the analysis of travel writing from the
traditional focus on Eurocentric contexts. This *Companion* provides a
comprehensive overview of developments in the field, appealing to students
and teachers of travel writing and postcolonial studies.

DR. ROBERT CLARKE is Senior Lecturer in the English Studies Program,
School of Humanities, and Co-Director of the Centre for Colonialism and its
Aftermath, University of Tasmania, Australia. He is author of *Travel Writing
from Black Australia: Utopia, Melancholia, and Aboriginality* (2016) and editor
of *Celebrity Colonialism: Fame, Power and Representation in Colonial and
Postcolonial Cultures* (2009). He has been a guest editor for special issues on
travel writing for *Postcolonial Studies* and *Studies in Travel Writing*.

THE CAMBRIDGE
COMPANION TO
POSTCOLONIAL
TRAVEL WRITING

EDITED BY
ROBERT CLARKE
University of Tasmania

CAMBRIDGE
UNIVERSITY PRESS

CAMBRIDGE
UNIVERSITY PRESS

University Printing House, Cambridge CB2 8BS, United Kingdom

One Liberty Plaza, 20th Floor, New York, NY 10006, USA

477 Williamstown Road, Port Melbourne, VIC 3207, Australia

314–321, 3rd Floor, Plot 3, Splendor Forum, Jasola District Centre, New Delhi – 110025, India

79 Anson Road, #06–04/06, Singapore 079906

Cambridge University Press is part of the University of Cambridge.

It furthers the University's mission by disseminating knowledge in the pursuit of education, learning, and research at the highest international levels of excellence.

www.cambridge.org
Information on this title: www.cambridge.org/9781107153394
DOI: 10.1017/9781316597712

© Cambridge University Press 2018

First published 2018

Printed in the United Kingdom by Clays, St Ives plc.

A catalogue record for this publication is available from the British Library.

Library of Congress Cataloging-in-Publication Data
NAMES: Clarke, Robert, 1968- editor.
TITLE: The Cambridge companion to postcolonial travel writing / edited by Robert Clarke.
DESCRIPTION: New York: Cambridge University Press, 2018. | Series: Cambridge companions to literature | Includes bibliographical references and index.
IDENTIFIERS: LCCN 2017032442 | ISBN 9781107153394 (hardback)
SUBJECTS: LCSH: Travelers' writings–History and criticism. | Postcolonialism in literature. | Travel writing–History. | Travel in literature. | BISAC: LITERARY CRITICISM / Semiotics & Theory.
CLASSIFICATION: LCC PN56.T7 C36 2018 | DDC 809/.93327–dc23
LC record available at https://lccn.loc.gov/2017032442

ISBN 978-1-107-15339-4 Hardback
ISBN 978-1-316-60729-9 Paperback

In memory of Anthony Carrigan (1980–2016)

CONTENTS

ILLUSTRATIONS

NOTES ON CONTRIBUTORS

ROBERT CLARKE is Senior Lecturer in the English Studies Program, School of Humanities, and Co-Director of the Centre for Colonialism and its Aftermath (CAIA) at the University of Tasmania. He is author of *Travel Writing from Black Australia: Utopia, Melancholia, and Aboriginality* (2016), and editor of *Celebrity Colonialism: Fame, Power and Representation in Colonial and Postcolonial Cultures* (2009). He has been a guest editor for special issues on travel writing for *Postcolonial Studies* and *Studies in Travel Writing*.

BRIAN CREECH is Assistant Professor of Journalism at Temple University in Philadelphia, PA. His research uses critical and cultural theory to interrogate journalism's modes of representation, new media technologies, and international media forms. Recent articles have appeared in *Journalism*; *Communication, Culture, and Critique*; and the *Communication Review*, among other journals.

JILL DIDUR is Professor of English at Concordia University in Montreal. Her research addresses critical concerns in globalization studies, the environmental humanities, postcolonial and diasporic theory, critical posthumanism, and literature and media. She is author of *Unsettling Partition: Literature, Gender, Memory* (2006), and coeditor of *Global Ecologies and the Environmental Humanities: Postcolonial Approaches* (with Elizabeth DeLoughrey and Anthony Carrigan, 2015).

JUSTIN D. EDWARDS is Professor in the Division of Literature and Languages at the University of Stirling, Scotland. He is coauthor of *Mobility at Large: Globalisation, Textuality and Innovative Travel Writing* (with Rune Graulund, 2012), and coeditor of *Postcolonial Travel Writing: Critical Explorations* (with Rune Graulund, 2010) as well as *Other Routes: 1500 Years of Asian and African Travel Writing* (with Tabish Khair, Martin Leer, and Hanna Ziadeh, 2006).

CHARLES FORSDICK is James Barrow Professor of French at the University of Liverpool in England, and Arts & Humanities Research Council Theme Leadership Fellow for "Translating Cultures." He is a member of the Academy of Europe. His monographs include *Travel in Twentieth-Century French and Francophone Cultures* (2005), and he is coeditor of *Postcolonial Thought in the French-Speaking*

World (with David Murphy, 2009), *Travel Writing: Critical Concepts in Literary and Cultural Studies* (with Tim Youngs, 2012), and *Travel and Ethics: Theory and Practice* (with Corinne Fowler and Ludmilla Kostova, 2013).

ANNA JOHNSTON is Australian Research Council Future Fellow with the Institute of Advanced Studies in the Humanities, and Associate Professor in English Literature at the University of Queensland in Brisbane, Australia. Her publications include *Missionary Writing and Empire, 1800–1860* (Cambridge University Press, 2003) and *Traveling Home:* Walkabout Magazine *and Mid-Twentieth-Century Australia* (2016, with Mitchell Rolls).

CHRISTOPHER M. KEIRSTEAD is Professor of English at Auburn University in Alabama, USA. His book *Victorian Poetry, Europe, and the Challenge of Cosmopolitanism* was published in 2011. Recent and forthcoming work includes a chapter on travel and poetry for the *Cambridge History of Travel Writing* and articles in *Studies in Travel Writing, Genre,* and *Victorian Periodicals Review.*

EVA-MARIE KRÖLLER is Professor in the English Department at the University of British Columbia in Vancouver, Canada. She is author of *Canadian Travellers in Europe* (1987), editor of the *Cambridge Companion to Canadian Literature* (2004, 2nd edn forthcoming 2017), and of *The Cambridge History of Canadian Literature* (with Coral Ann Howells, 2009). Currently, she is completing a study of life-writing and the imperial network.

STEPHEN M. LEVIN is Associate Professor of English at Clark University in Worcester, MA. He specializes in contemporary British and postcolonial literature, transnational cultural studies, and critical and literary theory. He is author of *The Contemporary Anglophone Travel Novel: The Aesthetics of Self-Fashioning in the Era of Globalization* (2008).

MARY LOUISE PRATT is Silver Professor and Professor Emerita of Social and Cultural Analysis, Spanish and Portuguese Languages and Literatures at New York University, NY, and Olive H. Palmer Professor of Humanities (emerita) at Stanford University. She has published extensively on modern Latin American literature, language and politics, and culture and imperialism. Amongst her many works, she is author of *Imperial Eyes: Travel Writing and Transculturation* (1992; revised edition 2008). Her recent publications include "Language and the aftermaths of empire," *PMLA* (2015) and "Is this Guantanamo or Club Med?" *American Quarterly* (2016).

SRILATA RAVI is Professor of French at the University of Alberta (Faculté Saint-Jean). Her publications include *Translating the Postcolonial in Multilingual Contexts* (2017, co-edited with Judith Misrahi-Barak); *Autour de l'œuvre de Gérard Bouchard. Histoire sociale, sociologie historique, imaginaires collectifs et politiques publiques* (2015, coedited with Claude Couture); *Rethinking Global Mauritius: Critical Essays on Mauritian Literatures and Cultures* (2013); *Ecritures mauriciennes au féminin: penser l'altérité* (coedited with Véronique Bragard, 2011); and *Rainbow Colors-Literary Ethno-topographies of Mauritius* (2007).

ASHA SEN is Professor of Postcolonial Studies at the University of Wisconsin-Eau Claire in the United States. From 2013 to 2016, she served as Director of the university's Women's Studies program. Her most recent publication is *Postcolonial Yearning: Reshaping Spiritual and Secular Discourses in Contemporary Literature* (2013). Her current research focuses on intersections between postcolonial and indigenous feminist thought.

APRIL SHEMAK is Associate Professor of English at Sam Houston State University in Huntsville, TX. Her book *Asylum Speakers: Caribbean Refugees and Testimonial Discourse* was published in 2011. She is an associate editor of the *Encyclopedia of Postcolonial Studies* (2016).

TIM YOUNGS is Professor of English and Travel Studies at Nottingham Trent University in England, where he is Director of the Centre for Travel Writing Studies. He is founding editor of the journal *Studies in Travel Writing* and is the author or editor of several books on travel writing. Among these are *The Cambridge Companion to Travel Writing* (co-edited with Peter Hulme, 2002) and *The Cambridge Introduction to Travel Writing* (2013).

ACKNOWLEDGMENTS

This *Companion* is dedicated to Dr. Anthony Carrigan who died in early 2016. Dr. Carrigan's research and scholarship broke new ground exploring the intersection of postcolonial studies, travel writing, and eco-criticism. Dr. Carrigan was to contribute a chapter to this volume. I am very grateful for the encouragement he provided me toward the development of this *Companion*.

I wish to thank also Ms. Erin Hortle for her diligent research and editorial support. Substantial work on this *Companion* was undertaken during study leave in 2016 that I was granted by the University of Tasmania and I acknowledge the support of the School of Humanities and the research committee of the Faculty of Arts, as well as the Centre for Colonialism and its Aftermath (CAIA). I also wish to express my gratitude to my colleagues in the English Program of the School of Humanities for their continuing support, advice, and encouragement. And for their patience and love, I thank my children, Ava, Daniel, and Julian.

CHRONOLOGY: 1899–2016

The creation of a time-line for any field of scholarly endeavor is always a risky business. There will inevitably be questions raised about starting points, key dates and events, inclusions, and omissions. Admitting such is not intended to forestall or deflect criticism or debate – quite the opposite. It is to recognize, however, that the Chronology assembled here is intended to be provisional and indicative. The Chronology has been organized into two columns. The right-hand column includes notable works of colonial and postcolonial travel writing texts. The left-hand column mixes events from world and national histories, and also mentions significant works of postcolonial literature and criticism. The year 1899 has been selected as a starting point, although as contributions to the *Companion* have made clear, the genealogy of postcolonial travel writing could be lengthened to include works that precede this year. The choice of that year coincides with the initial publication of Joseph Conrad's *Heart of Darkness*, a work of fiction that holds a key place in the development of postcolonial travel writing.

1899	Second Anglo-Boer War (to 1902) Rudyard Kipling, "The White Man's Burden"	Joseph Conrad, *Heart of Darkness* (book published 1902)
1900	Relief of Mafeking from Boer Siege Yihetuan Movement (Boxer Rebellion) in China (anti-Western uprising)	
1901	Queen Victoria dies Australian Federation Rudyard Kipling, *Kim* First transatlantic radio signal	

1902	Land grant in Kenyan highlands begins large-scale white settlement	Euclides da Cunha, *Rebellion in the Backlands (Os Sertões)*
	J. A. Hobson, *Imperialism: A Study*	
	US passes the Chinese Exclusion Act	
	Rudyard Kipling, *Just So Stories*	
1904	Namibia: uprising of Herero and Nama against German rule (until 1907)	Ham Mukasa, *Uganda's Katikiro in England: Being the Official Account of His Visit to the Coronation of His Majesty Kind Edward VII*
	East Indies: revolt by Achenese in Sumatra forcibly put down	
	The Casement Report: Roger Casement details abuses in the Congo Free State	
	Sigmund Freud, *The Psychopathology of Everyday Life*	
1905	Japan defeats Russia in the Russo-Japanese War; attempted Russian Revolution	
	India: launch of *swadeshi* ("of our own country") protesting British partition of Bengal	
1906	Muslim League established in India	Percy Falcke Martin, *Through Five Republics (of South America): A Critical Description of Argentina, Brazil, Chile, Uruguay and Venezuela in 1905*
	Self-government restored to the Transvaal and Orange Free Colony	
1907	New Zealand attains dominion status	Gertrude Bell, *The Desert and the Sown: Travels in Palestine and Syria*
	Mahatma Gandhi commences nonviolent resistance campaign in South Africa	Wilfred Scawen Blunt, *Secret History of the English Occupation of Egypt*
	Anglo-Russian entente	
	Baden-Powell forms the Scouts	
1908	Oil discovered in Persia	
	Congo Free State becomes the Belgian Congo	
	Arnold van Gennep, *The Rites*	

of Passage – sociological study of the crossing of frontiers
Sven Hedin explores Persia and Tibet

1909		A.B.C. Merriman-Labor, *Britons through Negro Spectacles; or A Negro on Britons*
1910	Union of South Africa becomes a dominion Japan annexes Korea Mexican Revolution against dictatorship of Porfirio Diaz	Gertrude Bell, *Amurath to Amurath*
1911	Mexico: Diaz regime falls, liberal reformer Francisco Madero assumes presidency Italo-Turkish War (until 1912); Italy occupies Libya China: revolution ends imperial regime King George V attends Great Dehli Durbar	Charlotte Mansfield, *Via Rhodesia: A Journey through Southern Africa*
1912	Cuba: uprising led by Independent Movement of People of Color, forcibly put down with the assistance of USA The Putumayo Report: Roger Casement details atrocities committed Peru's Putumayo Indians Robert Falcon Scott dies on return from the South Pole African National Congress forms in South Africa	Matthew Henson, *A Negro Explorer at the North Pole*
1913	Mexico: Madero deposed, then murdered; Pancho Villa resumes guerrilla campaign South Africa: Native Land Act Leonard Woolf, *A Village in the Jungle*	

1914   First World War (until 1918)
        Opening of the Panama Canal
1915   Ceylon: Sinhala anti-Muslim
        riots; colonial government
        declares martial law
        J. G. Frazer, *The Golden Bough*
1916   Ireland: Easter Rising
1917   Russian Revolution
        Balfour Declaration: promises a
        "national home" for Jews in
        Palestine and protection of civil
        and religious rights of non-Jews
        in the territory
        V. I. Lenin, *Imperialism: The
        Highest State of Capitalism*
1918   Declaration of the Irish Republic
        End of First World War
1919   Anglo-Irish War (to 1921)
        First Palestinian National
        Congress rejects Balfour
        Declaration
        India: Amritsar massacre
        Peace Conference, Versailles:
        League of Nations created;
        German colonies in Africa
        transferred to Britain, France
        and Belgium
1920   Gandhi wins control of Indian
        Congress
        Government of Ireland Act
1921   Civil War in Ireland (to 1923)
        Morocco: resistance to French/
        Spanish rule, led by Abd al-
        Karim (to 1926)
1922   Declaration of the Irish Free
        State
        James Joyce, *Ulysses*
        Britain receives League of
        Nations mandate for Palestine

	Kingdom of Egypt becomes independent of Britain	
1923	Ceylon: general strike, militant fusion of nationalist and class-based demands	D. H. Lawrence, *Kangaroo*
1924	India: violence between Hindus and Muslims; Gandhi begins hunger strike as a "penance and a prayer" E. M. Forster, *A Passage to India*	
1925	Syria: Druze revolt (to 1927)	
1926	Indonesia: riots in Java and Sumatra, forcibly put down by Dutch	T. E. Lawrence, *Seven Pillars of Wisdom*
1927	International Conference Against Imperialism and Colonial Oppression, Brussels Bolivia: massive revolt of indigenous people against government Mohandas K. Gandhi, *The Story of My Experiments with Truth*	Alexander David-Neel, *My Voyage to Lhasa* Andre Gide, *Voyage au Congo*
1929	Wall Street Crash Nigeria: Aba Women's Riots, or Women's War, against extension of colonial powers Palestine: riots sparked by founding of the Jewish Agency; several hundred killed, many by British soldiers Geneva Convention signed, regulating the treatment of prisoners of war	Rabindrinath Tagore, *Jatri*
1930	India: Gandhi launches Civil Disobedience Movement Brazil: military coup	
1931	Japan invades Manchuria Gandhi leads the Salt March	

1932

J. R. Ackerley, *Hindoo Holiday*
Freya Stark, *Baghdad Sketches: Journeys through Iraq*

1933   Hitler comes to power in Germany

Peter Fleming, *Brazilian Adventure*

1934   Italy establishes the colony of Italian Libya

George Orwell, *Burmese Days*
Freya Stark, *The Valley of the Assassins: And Other Persian Travels*
Evelyn Waugh, *Ninety-Two Days*

1935   Italy invades Abyssinia
Japan seizes Beijing, sets up a puppet regime in the North
Mulk Raj Anand, *Untouchable*

Vivienne de Watteville, *Speak to the Earth*

1936   Spanish Civil War (to 1939)
Paraguay: military coup, fascist regime installed
Palestine: Arab revolt (to 1939), protesting British rule
Jawaharlal Nehru, *An Autobiography*

Aina Kofoworola Moore, "The Story of Aina Kofoworola Moore" (in *Ten Africans*, Margery Perham ed.)
Parmenas Mockerie, "The Story of Parmenas Mockerie" (in *Ten Africans*, Margery Perham ed.)
George Orwell, "Shooting an Elephant"
Evelyn Waugh, *Waugh in Abyssinia*

1937   China: Shanghai falls to Japanese; Nanking sacked
Jamaica: riots against British rule
Trinidad: riots against British rule

Karen Blixen (aka Isak Dinesen), *Out of Africa*
Robert Byron, *The Road to Oxiana*
Claude McKay, *A Long Way from Home*
Ousmane Socé Diop, *Mirages de Paris*

1938   Munich Agreement: the appeasement of Hitler over German invasion of Czechoslovakia
C. L. R. James, *The Black*

Jacobins – history of the Haitian Revolution

Raja Rao, *Kanthapura*

1939	German invasion of Poland; outbreak of Second World War (until 1945)	Graeme Greene, *The Lawless Roads*

Aimé Césaire, *Return to My Native Land*

1940 Fall of France to Nazi forces
Fernando Ortiz, *Cuban Counterpoint: Sugar and Tobacco*

1941 Development of the jet engine
Japan bombs Pearl Harbor; US enters war
Japan captures Cambodia, Vietnam, Thailand; in response, Ho Chi Minh launches Viet Minh independence movement

1942 Kingdom of Ethiopia gains independence from Italy
Albert Camus, *The Stranger*

1945 USA drops atomic bombs on Hiroshima and Nagasaki; Japan surrenders
Proclamation of Indonesian Independence, commences period of diplomatic and armed resistance against the Netherlands
Algeria: French repression of nationalists; major uprising follows
Revolution in Vietnam brings Ho Chi Minh to power; French forces attempt to recapture colonial power; war ensues (to 1954)
Syria, Lebanon gain independence

1946 First Assembly of the United
Nations

1947 India gains Independence
The partition of India; creation
of Pakistan
Nuremberg trials
Palestine: UN announces plan
for partition, granting bulk of
land to Jewish population

1948 *Apartheid* implemented in South   Charles Mountford, *Brown Men*
Africa (until 1994)   *and Red Sand: Journeyings in*
Burma, Sri Lanka (Ceylon) gain   *Wild Australia*
independence
India: Gandhi assassinated
UN adopts Declaration of
Human Rights
Partition of Palestine; First
Arab-Israeli War
The Malay Emergency (to 1960)

1949 People's Republic of China   Paul Bowles, *The Sheltering Sky*
proclaimed after Communist
takeover
Indonesia, Laos gain
independence
V. S. Reid, *New Day*

1950 Korean War (to 1953)   Patrick Leigh Fermor, *The*
China invades Tibet   *Traveller's Tree: Island Hopping*
Aimé Césaire, *Discourse on*   *through the Caribbean Islands*
Colonialism

1951 Libya becomes an independent
kingdom

1952 Mau Mau resistance in Kenya;   Norman Lewis, *Golden Earth:*
state of emergency declared   *Travels in Burma*
Franz Fanon, *Black Skins, White*
Masks

1953 George Lamming, *In the Castle*   Sybille Bedford, *The Sudden*
of My Skin   *View: A Mexican Journey*

1954 Beginnings of nationalist   Elspeth Huxley, *Four Guineas:*
uprising in Algeria; war of   *A Journey through West Africa*
independence (to 1962)   Richard Wright, *Black Power:*

	Vietnamese army defeats French forces	*A Record of Reactions in a Land of Pathos*
1955	Bandung conference of independent African and Asian countries; declaration upholds principles of national sovereignty, human rights, equality among nations	Claude Lévi-Strauss, *Tristes Tropiques*
	Vietnam: outbreak of civil war in the South	
1956	Suez Crisis: defeat of British and French invasion of Egypt after Gamal Abdel Nasser nationalizes the Suez Canal	Édouard Glissant, *Soleil de la Conscience (The Sun of Consciousness)*
	Cuba: Castro initiates revolution Sudan, Tunisia and Morocco gain independence	Langston Hughes, *I Wonder As I Wander: An Autobiographical Journey*
	Naguib Mahfouz, *Palace Walk*	
1957	Ghana and Malaysia (Malaya) gain independence	Peter Abrahams, *Jamaica: An Island Mosaic*
	Algeria: Battle of Algiers	Lawrence Durrell, *Bitter Lemons of Cyprus*
	Kwame Nkrumah, *The Autobiography of Kwame Nkrumah*	James Morris, *The Market of Seleukia*
	Patrick White, *Voss*	
1958	Sri Lanka: anti-Tamil riots	Edgar Mittelhözer, *With a Carib Eye*
	Chinua Achebe, *Things Fall Apart*	James Morris, *South African Winter*
1959	Fidel Castro comes to power in Cuba	Nirad Chaudhuri, *A Passage to England*
		Bernard Dadié, *Un Nègre à Paris (An African in Paris)*
		Elspeth Huxley, *The Flame Trees of Thika: Memories of an African Childhood*
1960	Wilson Harris, *Palace of the Peacock*	Amiri Baraka/LeRoi Jones, "Cuba Libre"
		George Lamming, *The Pleasures of Exile*

1961 Building of Berlin Wall begins
USA-sponsored Bay of Pigs
invasion of Cuba thwarted
Franz Fanon, *The Wretched of
the Earth*
V. S. Naipaul, *A House for Mr
Biswas*

C. Wright Mills, *Listen, Yankee:
The Revolution in Cuba*
Philippa Duke Schuyler,
Adventures in Black and White
Peter Matthiessen, *The Cloud
Forest: A Chronicle of the South
American Wilderness*
Arnold Toynbee, *Between Oxus
and Jumna*

1962 Algeria, Jamaica, Rwanda,
Trinidad and Tobago, Uganda
gain independence
Cuban Missile Crisis

Albert Luthuli, *Let My People
Go*
V. S. Naipaul, *The Middle
Passage: Impressions of Five
Societies – British, French and
Dutch – in the West Indies and
South America*

1963 Kenya gains independence
Organization of African Unity
established

Vincent Massey, *What's Past Is
Prologue: The Memoirs of the
Right Honourable Vincent
Massey*

1964 Vietnam: "Gulf of Tonkin
Resolution," US escalates its
military campaign; war breaks
out (to 1973)
Albert Memmi, *The Colonizer
and the Colonized*

John Pepper Clark, *America,
Their America*
V. S. Naipaul, *An Area of
Darkness*

1965 Che Guevara in Congo (until
1966)
Central African Republic: Jean
Bedel Bokassa takes power in
coup; crowned "Emperor"
(dictatorship until 1979)
White Rhodesian government
declares unilateral independence
from Britain
Singapore breaks from Malaysia
and becomes separate state
Elizabeth Bishop, *Questions of*

Nirad Chaudhuri, *The
Continent of Circe*
Nat Nakasa, "Mr Nakasa Goes
to Harlem"

Travel

Wole Soyinka, *The Road*

1966	United Nations revokes South Africa's mandate to govern Namibia, sparking the Namibian War of Independence (to 1990) Zimbabwe: armed struggle launched Barbados, Botswana, Guyana, Lesotho gain independence First Tricontinental Conference, Havana Jean Rhys, *Wide Sargasso Sea* Gillo Pontecorvo (dir.), *La battaglia di Algeri (The Battle of Algiers)*	Amiri Baraka/LeRoi Jones, *Home: Social Essays*
1967	Secession of Biafra and outbreak of Nigerian civil war (to 1970) Six-Day War between Israel and neighboring Arab states Che Guevara captured and killed in Bolivia Establishment of ASEAN (Association of South East Asian Nations) Gabriel García Márquez, *One Hundred Years of Solitude*	Elias Canneti, *Die Stimmen von Marrakesch (The Voices of Marrakesh)*
1968	USA: Martin Luther King assassinated Student-led uprising world-wide, especially France, Mexico, USA Czechoslovakia: "Prague Spring" Vietnam: "Tet Offensive"	
1969	Britain sends troops to Northern Ireland to quell rioting Cambodia: US begins extensive secret bombing campaign	V. S. Naipaul, *The Loss of El Dorado: A Colonial History* N. Scott Momaday, *The Way to Rainy Mountain*

Muammar Gaddafi comes to
power in Libya
1970   Fiji, Tonga gain independence   Margaret Bacon, *Journey to*
Cambodia: Prince Sihanouk   *Guyana*
overthrown in right-wing coup   Emily Hahn, *No Hurry to Get*
Kwame Nkrumah,   *Home*
Consciencism   Freya Stark, *The Minaret of*
Jam: An Excursion in
Afghanistan
1971   Civil war in East Pakistan   Geoffrey Moorehouse, *Calcutta*
following declaration of
Bangladeshi independence;
India-Pakistan War, resulting in
defeat of the latter
Uganda: Idi Amin comes to
power in coup (dictatorship
until 1979)
1972   Northern Ireland: "Bloody
Sunday"; British paratroops kill
thirteen marchers in Derry; IRA
retaliates; direct rule imposed
Philippines: rebellion by Filipino
Muslims
1973   Chile: Salvador Allende   Huey P. Newton, *Revolutionary*
assassinated in coup led by   *Suicide*
General Augusto Pinochet, with   Lester Pearson, *Memoirs,*
assistance of the CIA (Pinochet   *1897–1948: Through*
dictatorship until 1990)   *Diplomacy to Politics*
Bahamas gain independence   Buchi Emcheta, *Second-Class*
Edward Kaumau Braithwaite,   *Citizen*
The Arrivants
Patrick White, *A Fringe of*
Leaves
1974   The Carnation Revolution,   Charles Ritchie, *The Siren Years:*
Portugal   *A Canadian Diplomat Abroad,*
Turkey invades Cyprus   *1937–1945*
1975   Vietnam War ends with defeat
of US
Cambodia: Pol Pot and Khmer
Rouge seize power

Angola, Mozambique gain
independence; civil wars
continue in both states
Portugal withdraws from East
Timor; Indonesia invades and
occupies East Timor
Sheikh Mujibur Raham, first
Prime Minister of Bangladesh,
murdered in military coup
resulting in two decades of
military dictatorship; strong
evidence of CIA involvement
Sam Selvon, *Moses Ascending*
Pramoedya Ananta Toer, *The
Earth of Mankind*

1976   Argentina: Isabel Peron ousted
in military coup; General
Roberto Videla takes power,
inaugurates "dirty war" against
leftists

Ryszard Kapucinski, *Another
Day of Life*

1977   South African activist Steve Biko
dies in police custody
Cambodian-Vietnam War
Anwar Sadat visits Israel as part
of a treaty mission.

V. S. Naipaul, *India:
A Wounded Civilization*
Charles Ritchie, *An Appetite for
Life: The Education of a Young
Diarist 1924–1927*
Bruce Chatwin, *In Patagonia*

1978   Vietnamese forces invade
Cambodia in attempt to oust Pol
Pot's Khmer Rouge
Afghanistan: Soviet backed
military coup
Edward Said, *Orientalism*

Ryszard Kapucinski, *The
Emperor: Downfall of an
Autocrat*
Shiva Naipaul, *North of South:
An African Journey*

1979   Cambodia: Khmer Rouge
toppled; guerrilla activity
continues (to 1989)
Soviet invasion of Afghanistan
Uganda: Idi Amin ousted from
power
Nicaragua: popular uprising
overthrows Somoza

Martha Gellhorn: *Travels with
Myself and Another: A Memoir*
Gita Mehta, *Karma Cola:
Marketing the Mystic East*
V.S. Naipaul, *A Bend in the
River*

dictatorship, brings Sandinista National Liberation Front to power
Randolph Stowe, *The Visitants*
Qurratulain Hyder, *Fireflies in the Mist*

1980	Zimbabwe gains independence; Robert Mugabe elected to power Salman Rushdie, *Midnight's Children* J. M. Coetzee, *Waiting for the Barbarians* J. M. G. Le Clézio, *Desert*	Robyn Davidson, *Tracks*
1981	Assignation of Egyptian President Anwar Sadat Toxteth Race Riots, Liverpool Iran-Contra Affair	Tété-Michel Kpomassie, *L'Africain de Groenland (An African in Greenland)* Charles Ritchie, *Diplomatic Passport: More Undiplomatic Diaries, 1946–1962*
1982	Falklands/Malvinas war between UK and Argentina Nicaragua: counter-revolutionary attack on Sandinista forces, armed and sponsored by US (war continues until 1990)	William Least Heat-Moon, *Blue Highways* Michael Ondaatje, *Running in the Family*
1983	Sri Lanka: violence against Tamils; armed resistance of LTTE ("Tamil Tigers") escalates in response Argentina: election of Raul Alfonsin ends eight years of military dictatorship Salman Rushdie, *Shame*	Joan Didion, *Salvador* Vikram Seth, *From Heaven Lake: Travels through Sinkiang and Tibet*
1984	Brunei gains independence Uruguay: massive protests and general strike topple military dictatorship	Krim Benterrak, Stephen Muecke and Paddy Roe, *Reading the Country: Introduction to Nomadology* V.S. Naipaul, *Finding the Centre*
1985		

Brazil: return to civilian government after twenty years of military dictatorship
Gabriel García Márquez, *Love in the Time of Cholera*
Jamaica Kincaid, *Annie John*
Cormac McCarthy, *Blood Meridian, or The Evening Redness in the West*
Keri Hulme, *The Bone People*

Patrick Marnham, *So Far from God: Journey to Central America*
George Ignatieff, *Making of a Peacemonger*
Benedict Allen, *Mad White Giant*

1986 Philippines: "People Power Revolution" topples Marcos dictatorship
Haiti: dictatorship of Jean-Claude Duvalier overthrown

Mark Abley, *Beyond Forget: Rediscovering the Prairies*
J.M.G. Le Clézio, *Voyage à Rodrigues*

1987 The First Intifada, Palestinian uprising against the Israeli occupation of the West Bank and Gaza (to 1993)
Gayatri Chakravorty Spivak, *In Other Worlds: Essays in Cultural Politics*

Bruce Chatwin, *The Songlines*
Nick Danzinger, *Danzinger's Travels: Beyond Forbidden Frontiers*
Jan Goodwin, *Caught in the Crossfire*
Caryl Phillips, *The European Tribe*
Salman Rushdie, *The Jaguar Smile*

1988 Australia: Bicentenary celebrations boycotted and wide scale protests led by Aboriginal activists
Afghanistan: withdrawal of Soviet troops; civil war ensues
Tsitsi Dangaremba, *Nervous Conditions*
Salman Rushdie, *The Satanic Verses*

Ferdinand Dennis, *Behind the Frontlines: Journey into Afro-Britain*
Christopher Hope, *White Boy Running*
Pico Iyer, *Video Night in Kathmandu: And Other Reports from the Not-So-Far-East*
Jamaica Kincaid, *A Small Place*
Jan Morris, *Hong Kong: Epilogue to an Empire*

1989 Fall of the Berlin Wall; collapse of Soviet Union and Eastern European communist states

William Dalrymple, *In Xanadu: A Quest*

China: Tiananmen Square
Massacre
Indigenous and Tribal Peoples
Convention adopted by the
International Labour
Organisation (ILO Convention
169)
Erna Brodber, *Myal*
Bill Ashcroft, Gareth Griffiths,
and Helen Tiffin, *The Empire
Writes Back: Theory and
Practice in Post-Colonial
Literature*

Stuart Stevens, *Malaria Dreams:
An African Adventure*

1990 Nelson Mandela freed from
prison in South Africa
Haiti: Jean Bertrand Aristide
overthrown in bloody coup
Namibia gains independence
Nicaragua: Sandinista
Government defeated in election
by US-sponsored coalition
Derek Walcott, *Omeros*
Robert J.C. Young, *White
Mythologies: Writing History
and the West*
Ariel Dorfman, *Death and the
Maiden*

Charles Glass, *Tribes with Flags:
A Journey Curtailed*
Rian Malan, *My Traitor's
Heart: Blood and Bad Dreams:
A South African Explores the
Madness in His Country, His
Tribe and Himself.*
Karen Tei Yamashita, *Through
the Arc of the Rainforest*
Radosław Sikorski, *Dust of the
Saints: A Journey to Herat in
Time of War*

1991 First Gulf War
East Timor: massacre of
unarmed Timorese by
Indonesian military in Santa
Cruz church
India: Rajiv Gandhi assassinated
by Tamil Tiger militants
Somalia: President Siad Barre
overthrown; civil war ensues
Ben Okri, *The Famished Road*
Sara Suleri, *Meatless Days*
Jean-Marie G. Le Clézio,
Onitsha

Jerry Ellis, *Walking the Trail of
Tears: One Man's Journey
along the Cherokee Trail of
Tears*
P. F. Kluge, *The Edge of
Paradise: America in Micronesia*
Pico Iyer, *The Lady and the
Monk: Four Seasons in Kyoto*
Gavin Young, *In Search of
Conrad*

1992	Algeria: Islamic party (FIS) poised to win national elections; huge anti-Islamic demonstrations; elections cancelled; President Boudiaf assassinated; State of Emergency declared Somalia: UN-sanctioned intervention to restore order and save victims of famine Mozambique: peace treaty signed between President Chissano and South African-backed Renamo forces Australia: *Mabo v Queensland;* High Court rejects the notion of terra nullius, recognizes existence of native title Mary Louise Pratt, *Imperial Eyes: Travel Writing and Transculturation*	Ferdinand Dennis, *Back to Africa* Amitav Ghosh, *In an Antique Land* Eddy L. Harris, *Native Stranger: A Blackamerican's Journey into the Heart of Africa* Doris Lessing, *African Laughter: Four Visits to Zimbabwe* Christopher Ondaatje, *The Man-Eater of Punanai* Paul Theroux, *Happy Isles of Oceania: Paddling the Pacific*
1993	Edward Said, *Culture and Imperialism* David Malouf, *Remembering Babylon*	William Dalrymple, *City of Djinns: A Year in Delhi* Janet Campbell Hale, *Bloodlines: Odyssey of a Native Daughter* Eddy L. Harris, *South of Haunted Dreams: A Ride through Slavery's Old Back Yard* Ryszard Kapuscinski, *Imperium* Daphne Marlatt, *Ghost Works* Rehman Rashid, *A Malaysian Journey* Dervla Murphy, *The Ukimwi Road*
1994	Genocide in Rwanda Abolition of Apartheid in South Africa; Nelson Mandela elected as President IRA ceasefire announced:	Caroline Alexander, *The Way to Xanadu* Jean Hatzfeld, *Life Laid Bare: The Survivors in Rwanda Speak* Barry Hill, *The Rock*

beginning of peace process in Northern Ireland
The North American Free Trade Agreement takes effect
Homi K. Bhabha, *The Location of Culture*

Stephen Minta, *Aguirre: The Recreation of a Sixteenth-Century Journey across South America*

1995 World Trade Organization established
Amazon Cooperation Treaty Organization established
Third Taiwan Straits Crisis
Paul Gilroy, *The Black Atlantic: Modernity and Double Consciousness*

Isabelle Eberhardt, *Prisoner of Dunes: Selected Writings*
Kim Lefèvre, *Retour à la saison des pluies*
Pankaj Mishra, *Butter Chicken in Ludhiana: Travels in Small Town India* Charles Nicholl, *The Creature in the Map: A Journey to El Dorado*
Luis Sepúlveda, *Patagonia Express*
(English translation 1996)
Feargal Keane, *Season of Blood: A Rwandan Journey*
Tahir Shah, *Beyond the Devil's Teeth*

1996 Truth and Reconciliation Commission in South Africa
Afghanistan: Taliban take power
Guatemala: peace pact signed

Justin Cartwright, *Not Yet Home: A South African Journey*
Eva de Carvalho Chipenda, *The Visitor: An African Woman's Story of Travel and Discovery*
Doris Pilkington-Garimara, *Follow the Rabbit Proof Fence*
Dany Laferrière, *Pays sans chapeau (Down Among the Dead Men)*

1997 Britain returns Hong Kong to China
Australia: The Human Rights and Equal Opportunity Commission releases "Bringing Them Home," the report into the "Stolen Generations"
Arundhati Roy, *The God of Small Things*

Mark Jenkins, *To Timbuktu: A Journey Down the Niger*
Elaine Lee (ed.), *Go Girl! The Black Woman's Book of Travel and Adventure*
Sekai Nzenza-Shand, *Songs to an African Sunset*

1998   General Pinochet, former Chilean dictator, arrested in London on human rights charges filed in Spain; British government transfers Pinochet back to Chile; precedent set for indicting those charged with human rights crimes
Indonesia: Suharto dictatorship overturned after thirty-two years

Philip Gourevitch, *We Wish to Inform You That Tomorrow We Will Be Killed with Our Families*
Rory Maclean, *Under the Dragon: Travels in a Betrayed Land*
Wilfred Thesiger, *Among the Mountains: Travels through Asia*
Ariel Dorfman, *Heading South, Looking North: A Bilingual Journey*
Amitav Ghosh, *Dancing in Cambodia and at Large in Burma*

1999   UN involvement in Kosovo
Indonesian troops withdraw from East Timor
Gayatri Chakravorty Spivak, *A Critique of Postcolonial Reason: Toward a History of a Vanishing Present*
J. M. Coetzee, *Disgrace*

Leila Ahmed, *A Border Passage: From Cairo to America – A Woman's Journey*
Adrian Giménez Hutton, *La Patagonia de Chatwin*
Leila Marmon Silko, *Gardens of the Dunes*
Gary Younge, *No Place Like Home: A Black Briton's Journey through the American South*
Peter Chilson, *Riding the Demon Road: On the Road in West Africa*

2000   Second Intifada (to 2005)
Ahmadou Kourouma, *Allah Is Not Obliged*

Caryl Phillips, *The Atlantic Sound*
Jeffrey Tayler, *Facing the Congo: A Modern-Day Journey into the Heart of Darkness*
Michaela Wong, *In the Footsteps of Mr. Kurtz: Living on the Brink of Disaster in Mobutu's Congo*

2001   "9/11": terrorist attacks on New York and Washington
US declares "War on Terror";

Pico Iyer, *The Global Soul: Jet Lag, Shopping Malls, and the Search for Home*

invades Afghanistan and overthrows ruling Taliban
Romuald Fonkoua, *Les Discours de voyages: Afrique-Antilles* V. S. Naipaul wins Nobel Prize for Literature

Fatema Mernissi, *Scheherazade Goes West: Different Cultures, Different Harems*
V. S. Naipaul, *Half a Life*
Ricardo Orizio, *Lost White Tribes: Journeys among the Forgotten*
Andres Ruggeri, *américa en bicicleta (America by Bicycle)*
Alma Guillermoprieto, *Looking for History: Dispatches from Latin America*
Rubén Martínez, *Crossing Over: A Mexican Family on the Migrant Trail*

2002   International Year of Ecotourism
The Angolan Civil War ends after twenty-six years of conflict
The International Criminal Court is established
Establishment of Timor Leste

Edwidge Danticat, *After the Dance: A Walk Through Carnival in Jacmel, Haiti*
Tony Horwitz, *Blue Latitudes: Boldly Going Where Captain Cook Has Gone Before*
Nicholas Jose, *Black Sheep: Journey to Borroloola*

2003   Invasion and occupation of Iraq by coalition dominated by US forces
Sudan: war breaks out in the Darfur region over the government's treatment of the non-Arab population
Aravind Adiga, *The White Tiger*

Louise Erdrich, *Books and Islands in Ojibwe Country: Traveling Through the Land of My Ancestors*
Che Guevara, *The Motorcycle Diaries: Notes on a Latin American Journey*
Annemarie Schwarzenbach, *Tod in Persien (Death in Persia,* English translation 2013)
Paul Theroux, *Dark Star Safari: Overland from Cairo to Cape Town*

2004   Haiti: coup d'état; Jean-Bertrand Aristide resigns as president
Cyprus: Annan Plan to reunite the island does not pass a

Suketu Mehta, *Maximum City: Bombay Lost and Found*
Pankaj Mishra, *An End to Suffering: The Buddha in the*

referendum.
Expansion of NATO to include
several Eastern European
nations
Indian Ocean: earthquake and
tsunami on December 24 off the
coast of Indonesia devastates
communities, approx.
230–280,000 lose their lives.
Roberto Balaño, *2666*

World
Kira Salak, *Cruelest Journey: Six
Hundred Miles To Timbuktu*
Charles Montgomery, *The
Shark God: Encounters with
Ghosts and Ancestors in the
South Pacific*

2005 Australia: "Cronulla Riots,"
violent clash between Sydney's
Lebanese and white populations
London bombings: coordinated
suicide-bomb attacks
Paul Gilroy, *Postcolonial
Melancholia*
Kate Grenville, *The Secret River*

Alexander Elder, *Straying from
the Flock: Travels in New
Zealand*
Ekow Eshun, *Black Gold of the
Sun: Searching for Home in
Africa and Beyond*
Jamaica Kinkaid, *Among
Flowers: A Walk in the
Himalaya*
Emma Larkin, *Finding George
Orwell in Burma*

2006 United Nations Human rights
council established
Kiran Desai, *The Inheritance of
Loss*

Cees Nooteboom, *Nomad's
Hotel: Travels in Time and
Space*

2007 United Nations Declaration on
the Rights of Indigenous People
Global Financial Crisis

Sadiya Hartman, *Lose Your
Mother: A Journey along the
Atlantic Slave Route*
Jean Hatzfeld, *The Strategy of
Antelopes: Living in Rwanda
after the Genocide*
Michèle Rakotoson, *Juillet, au
pays-Chroniques d'un retour à
Madagascar*
Fran Sandham, *Traversa: A Solo
Walk across Africa, from the
Skeleton Coasts to the Indian
Ocean*

2008 Australia: Prime Minister, Kevin
Rudd, apologizes to the Stolen

Tim Butcher, *Blood River:
A Journey to Africa's Broken*

Generations, those Aboriginal people who were removed from their families during the twentieth century
US: House of Representatives apologizes to African-Americans for slavery and Jim Crow laws
Canada: Prime Minister Stephen Harper apologizes to former students of Indian residential schools

Heart
Christina Thompson, *Come on Shore and We Will Kill and Eat You All: A New Zealand Story*
M. G. Vassanji, *A Place Within: Rediscovering India*

2009 International Year of Reconciliation
Chile: court decision made use of ILO 169; considered a landmark case in indigenous rights

Jocab Dlamini, *Native Nostalgia*
Roger Douglas, *The Last Resort: A Memoir of Zimbabwe*
Ian Thomson, *The Dead Yard: Tales of Modern Jamaica*
Sam Miller, *Delhi: Adventures in a Megacity*

2010 Arab Spring: revolutionary wave of demonstrations and protests (both violent and nonviolent) in the Arab world (until 2012); rulers forced from power in Tunisia, Egypt, Libya, Yemen; civil uprisings in Bahrain, Syria; major protests in Algeria, Iraq, Jordan, Kuwait, Morocco, Sudan

Dany Laferrière, *L'énigme du retour (The Return)*

2011 Osama bin Laden founder and leader of al-Qaeda is killed in a US military operation in Pakistan
India and Bangladesh end forty-year border dispute
Libyan dictator Muammar Gaddafi is killed
Neil Lazarus, *The Postcolonial Unconscious*

John Gimlette, *Wild Coast: Travels on South America's Untamed Edge*
Arundhati Roy, "Walking with Comrades" in *Broken Republic: Three Essays*

2012 Queen Elizabeth II celebrates her Diamond Jubilee and sixty years

Katherine Boo, *Behind the Beautiful Forevers; Life, Death*

as head of state of New Zealand, Australia, and Canada
Iran Oil embargo
Terrorist attack US embassy in Benghazi, Libya and kill the ambassador J. Christopher Stevens

and Hope in a Mumbai Undercity
Michael Jacobs, *The Robber of Memories: A River Journey through Colombia*
Maureen Klovers, *In the Shadow of the Volcano: One Ex-Intelligence Official's Journey through Slums, Prisons, and Leper Colonies to the Heart of South America*
Noo Saro-Wiwa, *Looking for Transwonderland: Travels in Nigeria*

2013 USA: Boston Marathon bombing
Syria: regime of Bashar al-Assad accused of using chemical weapons on civilians
Nelson Mandela dies aged 95

Tom Chesshyre, *A Tourist in the Arab Spring*
Alain Mabanckou, *Lumières de Pointe-Noire*
Tony Wheeler, *Dark Lands*

2014 Ukraine: fighting breaks out on the Crimean Peninsula, led by Russian nationalists
Israel: "Operation Protective Edge"
Syria and Iraq: rise of Islamic State
US: violent riots after the police shooting of unarmed African American teen, Michael Brown
Nigeria: 276 female students kidnapped from their school global social media campaign #bringbackourgirls spearheaded by US First Lady Michelle Obama

Julia Cooke, *The Other Side of Paradise: Life in the New Cuba*
Carl Hoffman, *Savage Harvest: A Tale of Cannibals, Colonialism, and Michael Rockefeller's Tragic Quest for Primitive Art*
Pico Iyer, *The Art of Stillness*
M. G. Vassanji, *And Home Was Kariakoo: A Memoir of East Africa*
Gaia Vince, *Adventures in the Anthropocene*

2015 France: coordinated terrorist attacks in Paris including the offices of satirical magazine Charlie Hebdo

Anna Badkhen, *Walking with Abel: Journeys with the Nomads of the African Savannah*

Humanitarian crisis in Syria leads to mass exodus of refugees into Europe
US and Cuba agree to open embassies in each other's countries
Marlon James, *A Brief History of Seven Killings*

2016 Brexit: The United Kingdom votes to leave the European Union
The ISIS terrorist group claims responsibility for a bomb attack on the Atatürk Airport, Istanbul
Donald J. Trump is elected President of the United States of America
400th anniversary of the death of William Shakespeare
Fidel Castro dies
Boxer Muhammed Ali dies

Ian Burnet, *Archipelago: A Journey across Indonesia*

Laura Elkin, *Flâneuse: Women Walk the City in Paris, New York, Tokyo, Venice and London*
MariNaomi, *Turning Japanese: A Graphic Memoir*
Tim Judah, *In Wartime: Stories from the Ukraine*
Hisham Matar, *The Return: Fathers, Sons, and the Land in Between* Teju Cole, *Known and Strange Things*

I

ROBERT CLARKE

Toward a Genealogy of Postcolonial Travel Writing

An Introduction

Bearing witness to encounters of people and cultures across historical, social, geographical, and ethnic divides, travel writing holds a special place in the literatures of the world. Scholars of literature, culture, and history find in travel writing a rich repository of material for understanding how individuals use their journeys near and far as events for understanding the world in which they live, of how it came to be, and the directions in which it appears to be headed. As well as appreciating its aesthetic and other qualities, readers of travel writing – academic and nonacademic – have been interested in the way travel writing has been influenced by the experience of European colonial and imperial enterprises since the Renaissance. Indeed, it has become almost axiomatic for some readers that travel writing has been deeply implicated in naturalizing and celebrating the ethos of European hegemony over the last 500 years. Yet, a close inspection of travel literature shows that there have always been critical and oppositional perspectives circulating within this field of writing. Moreover, especially in the twentieth and twenty-first centuries, socially and politically engaged travelers have used their accounts as vehicles to critique the persistence of colonialism and imperialism. Evident through a range of forms, this field of writing can be broadly termed postcolonial travel writing.

Neither a genre (a variety of writing) nor a sub-branch of the literary field (a "social space" of moral, political, and intellectual contest), postcolonial travel writing describes an eclectic and expansive corpus of journey literature, and a transnational collection of authors and readers attuned to the legacy and persistence of past forms of colonialism and imperialism, as well as the emergence of new modes of cultural, economic, and political dominance in the era of globalization. *The Cambridge Companion to Postcolonial Travel Writing* offers readers an insight into the scope and range of perspectives that one encounters in this field of writing.

I

Embarking: 1988, or Thereabouts

In the Chronology, I have chosen 1899 as a starting point for a time-line of postcolonial travel writing. That was the year of the initial publication, in serial form, of Joseph Conrad's *Heart of Darkness*; a text that has a very important place and influence within postcolonial travel writing. Choosing any year to commence a time-line is always a tricky proposition because of the inevitable omissions and biases that underlie such decisions. Chronologies are always provisional and open to revision. For the purposes of this Introduction, however, I want to select a much more recent year from which to commence a consideration of postcolonial travel writing specifically as a field of scholarly interest. The year 1988 was a good year for "postcolonial travel writing," even if the term had yet to be invented. In a humorous example of the "Empire writing back," Afghani author Idries Shah undertook a "study" of the "natives" of Britain. Meanwhile, Welsh writer Jan Morris courted imperialist nostalgia with her descriptions of the faded glories of a far-flung outpost of the British Empire. Pico Iyer, a young "hyphenated" cosmopolitan – "British subject, ... American resident and ... Indian citizen"[1] – explored the weird Asian fusions of West and East; Jamaican-born Ferdinand Dennis ventured behind the frontlines of the British African diaspora; New York-based Antiguan Jamaica Kincaid scandalized readers with fictionalized insights into the corruption of her island nation; and white expatriate South African Christopher Hope journeyed to his homeland after a decade's absence to confront the endurance of apartheid.[2] Different works and styles, addressing divergent journeys, places, peoples, histories, and contexts, these books speak to experiences and sensibilities broadly understood as postcolonial, through the most mercurial of literary forms, travel writing.

One could choose other years from which to orient a genealogy of postcolonial travel writing: 1988 certainly does not inaugurate this field of literature, as the Chronology indicates. Yet the publication record for this year does illustrate a number of things about this topic to be kept in mind when embarking on the kind of tour presented in this *Companion*. First, what is now termed "postcolonial travel writing" is in one sense an invention of the academy. By 1988 postcolonialism and travel writing were increasingly attracting the attention of academics in the humanities, especially those in literary studies. The intersection of these fields is exemplified in Edward Said's *Orientalism* (1978),[3] one of the foundational texts of postcolonial studies, and a book deeply concerned with nineteenth-century travel literature's role in crafting European notions of cultural Otherness. Said's use of the methodologies of Michel Foucault as tools of literary/cultural analysis would influence Anglophone scholars throughout the 1980s and beyond. After the publication of Bill Ashcroft, Gareth Griffiths, and Helen Tiffin's *The Empire Writes Back* in 1989, the field of postcolonial literary studies expanded rapidly.[4] With their concern for marginalized authors and texts, as much as for the complicity of genre with power, humanities scholars were particularly challenged by travel literature's role in (post) colonial cultures. This intellectual project gained momentum in the early 1990s with the publication of a number of foundational texts including Mary Louise Pratt's *Imperial Eyes: Travel Writing and Transculturation* (1992), David Spurr's *The Rhetoric of Empire: Colonial Discourse in Journalism, Travel Writing, and Imperial Administration* (1993), and Ali Behdad's *Belated Travellers: Orientalism in the Age of Colonial Dissolution* (1994).[5]

Of course, postcolonial travel writing is not simply a figment of the scholarly imagination. By the late 1980s, postcolonial writing – especially fiction – had become very popular with transnational readerships, and postcolonial travel writing was enjoying a privileged place for readers of travel writing.[6] Travel books have been popular with readers since the days of Marco Polo. Colonial travel writing was a hugely popular enterprise from the eighteenth to the twentieth centuries. Empires offer boundless opportunities for journeys of all kinds for those at the center of power; they provide an elsewhere to roam and explore. For those at the margins of power, and for those dominated by imperialism, empires provide very different, and often quite distressing, travel experiences. Though, as bell hooks writes, "[t]ravel is not a word that can be easily evoked to talk about the Middle Passage [or] the Trail of Tears,"[7] or for the hazardous sea voyages of recent asylum seekers, the records of such journeys demand attention. It is not surprising, then, that during the twentieth century books by metropolitan Europeans and North Americans chronicling journeys taken in former colonies would remain popular. Nor is it surprising that citizens of former colonies would produce travel narratives: of their "home" nations; of Europe; of other former colonies; sometimes relying on indigenous models of journey writing, at times imitating, appropriating, and subverting European conventions of travel discourse and hence their worldviews. While many such works of the former category notably express a sense of belatedness, nostalgia, and even melancholia, many of those of the latter draw attention to inequalities of development, and to disparities in race and class relations.

By the 1980s the tone, style, and content of mainstream travel writing was shifting. Encouraged by rapid developments in global transportation networks after the 1970s, new classes of travelers helped to usher in a boom time for travel publishing, reinvigorating a genre many had considered conservative, complacent, and moribund. Seasoned observers of travel literature like Colin Thubron sensed a more subjective and reflective attitude, along with an "awakened social consciousness," defining the kind of travel discourse one found in the middlebrow "travel book."[8] Narratives of journeys into places actively struggling with the legacies of colonialism and imperialism were notable for the way such processes became a key theme of the journey itself. Although it was not recognized as "postcolonial travel writing," it is clear that by the end of the 1980s – as the Chronology accompanying this *Companion* shows – a sizeable body of journey literature had emerged distinguished by the way it explored the nature of what may be simplistically called the "postcolonial condition," and to – if at times ambivalently and problematically, and by no means exclusively – reflect on and critique the history of colonialism and its aftermaths. Such texts risked reiterating a banal form of global village ideology, celebrating the relative ease and safety with which Western bourgeois travelers could explore and appropriate the exotica of the postcolonial world. Alternatively, the critiques of imperialism that these texts engaged in were often brought into proximity with assessments of contemporary forms of economic, political, and military domination. Furthermore, despite its power to illustrate the inequities of contemporary social relations, this was a body of work that enjoyed a profitable position in an ever-expanding global cultural marketplace eager to exploit the vogue in cultural difference.

So 1988 – or thereabouts – provides a convenient departure point for an examination of postcolonial travel writing and of the body of scholarship that has engaged with it. How postcolonial travel writing has developed over the last three decades, as a field of academic inquiry and as a publishing commodity, explains the need for the present volume. Still a number of questions need to be asked: How should we define this seemingly disparate body of writing? How does it differ from other understandings of travel writing? How do attempts at definition intersect with the principal themes of "postcolonial" and "travel writing" studies, respectively? The following section addresses these questions.

Defining the Field

The books from 1988 mentioned above are in many respects conventional examples of travel literature. They fit a formal definition of travel writing as first-person nonfictional prose about a journey undertaken by an identifiable author-narrator.[9] They are works that expect the reader to take the traveler on trust. They "[feature] human movement through culturally conceived space, normally undertaken with at least some expectation of an eventual return to the place of origin."[10] In this respect they accord with an understanding of the genre that Peter Hulme terms "exclusivist."[11] I will suggest below that the study of postcolonial travel writing has led to more expansive and inclusive understandings of travel writing. That is because, in many respects, the exclusivist definition reflects the Eurocentric and colonialist values that postcolonial literature *sui generis* takes as a target of critique. For now I want to consider some attempts to define postcolonial travel writing along the lines suggested by the exclusivist definition because they reveal a set of tensions that continue to energize scholarship in this field.[12]

While it has been in use for over twenty years, the term "postcolonial travel writing" retains a sense of novelty and ambiguity. In 1994, Patrick Holland, among the first to provide an overview of the field, identified four key journey types worth considering for "the specific interests of postcoloniality": "imperial travel ... mainly written during the nineteenth century," represented by works by British authors who traveled the Empire; "inter-commonwealth travel" involving "a traveller/writer from one country or region [who] visits and offers commentary upon another"; "return travel" in which a migrant journeys back to their "home"; and "within-the-country travel" in which travelers explore their own – specifically – national communities.[13] It is important to note the perspectival quality of Holland's approach: postcolonial travel writing encompasses those forms of the textualization of travel that are of "specific interests [to] postcoloniality." This imperative remains and demands an expansive understanding of "travel writing" *per se*.

Holland's definition situates postcolonial travel writing as a branch of postcolonial literature. In doing so, the definition betrays ambivalence about the meanings of the terms "postcolonial" and "travel writing." Holland's take on the postcolonial, for example, reflects a number of familiar tensions, the first being in relation to the sense of history implied by the concept. As writers like Neil Lazarus and Ato Quayson note the word "post(-)colonial" appeared in print a number of times before the 1980s. When it did, the word was used in a temporal sense: "To describe a literary work or a writer as 'postcolonial' was to name a period, a discrete historical moment, not a project or a politics."[14] By the early 1980s, however, scholars began to use the term primarily in a nontemporal sense. As postcolonial literary studies grew so too did its field of vision. Considering postcolonial literature in 2009, Quayson describes a broad academic consensus when he writes:

as the sign of a critical orientation towards colonialism and its legacies, post-colonial literature [...] designates the representation of experiences of various

5

kinds including those of slavery, migration, oppression and resistance, difference, race, gender, space and place, and the responses to the discourses of
imperial Europe. It is conventionally assumed that postcolonial literature is as
much a reflection on conditions under imperialism and colonialism proper as
about conditions coming after the historical end of empires.[15]

The spirit of Quayson's formulation is evident in Holland's early definition
of postcolonial travel writing. Yet, Holland's overview reflects a persistent
bias toward Anglophone writing evident in much criticism on travel literature.[16] This bias tends to exclude, or at least fails to acknowledge, the large
corpus of works on trans-imperial travel, or travel writings from non-British
cultures (Francophone, Hispanic, Lusophone, indigenous), or those narratives that speak to "internal" colonialisms. Moreover, while for the most
part Holland's definition presumes the "exclusivist" definition of the genre,
the limitations of that definition from a postcolonial perspective are reflected
in Holland's references to fictional and "fictionalized" texts by authors like
Alice Munro, Margaret Attwood, V. S. Naipaul, Michael Ondaatje, Jamaica
Kincaid, and Bruce Chatwin. On the one hand, this is indicative of the gray
area between "fiction" and "non-fiction" that has perennially concerned
scholars of travel literature.[17] On the other hand, it suggests that examining
travel writing from the perspective of the postcolonial invites a broader
purview, and that a postcolonial approach toward travel writing can potentially decolonize the genre. For Holland, postcolonial travel writing carries
the potential to unsettle readers' expectations of the postcolonial condition
as much as the conventions of travel literature: that "travel literature can
help to modify the massively Eurocentric structures of travel and coloniality
by insisting on specificity (of history, setting, motivation)."[18]

While Holland's definition was adopted by later writers, such as Barbara
Korte,[19] it would be expanded in Holland's collaboration with Graham
Huggan, *Tourists with Typewriter* (1998), in ways that not only address
some of the issues noted above, but which also introduce further complications. Holland and Huggan, while primarily focused on Anglophone
writing, are attune to the different qualities of ambivalence – of ambivalence
as a trope – evident in postcolonial travel narrative. For example, of a writer
like V. S. Naipaul they observe "[his] travel writings straddle the gap
between an unwanted colonial inheritance and an ambiguous postcolonial
present that is neither fully accepted nor understood."[20] Naipaul's melancholic journeys evoke a sense of placelessness that threaten a crisis of identity
in the narrator who cannot belong anywhere. This melancholic sense of an
identity stuck between "a past he [Naipaul] cannot accept and a future he
cannot countenance" (42–43) contrasts with the sensibility of a writer like

Pico Iyer who enjoys the freedom that postcoloniality and globalization apparently afford to shift across borders and identities. Yet, as in Naipaul's writing, Holland and Huggan detect a deep ambivalence in Iyer's work that qualifies and potentially undercuts an otherwise explicit critique of imperialism.

Politics and Genre

It has often been remarked that travel writing receives short shrift from postcolonial critics. Wimal Dissanayake and Carmen Wickramagemage's *Self and Colonial Desire: Travel Writings of V.S. Naipaul* (1993) is an early case in point. Drawing upon the insights into nineteenth-century colonial travel discourse that were emerging at the time from scholars like Mary Louise Pratt, Dissanayake and Wickramagemage's book positions late twentieth-century Anglophone travel writing as conservative and reactionary.[21] Such arguments were reasonably easy to apply in relation to British and North American authors such as Bruce Chatwin, Jan Morris, and Paul Theroux–white, middle-class, professional writers – as well as *emigrés* like Naipaul, whose journeys frequently took them into territories marked by imperialist intrusions past and present.[22] Their work became targets for postcolonial critics sensitive to renascent forms of imperialism. And they became emblematic of a style of travel writing that was championed by journals such as *National Geographic* magazine, the literary journal *Granta*, and annual series such as *Best American Travel Writing*.[23] While some critics were celebrating and even embracing the nomadic potentials of such travel discourse,[24] others were becoming increasingly concerned about the European concept of "travel" as inherently phallocentric, Eurocentric, and colonizing.[25]

Arguments about the conservatism of travel writing and travel *per se* became problematic as more writers from the margins of imperium gained prominence. If it is fair to say that writers like Theroux, Morris, and Chatwin came to emblematize a dominant Eurocentric form of travel writing that frequently took postcolonial – that is, non-European – people and places as their subjects, then it is also fair to say that for a time figures like Naipaul and Iyer, along with Caryl Phillips, Jamaica Kincaid, Amitav Ghosh, Vikram Seth, and Salman Rushdie were positioned as representative "postcolonial travel writers" who took as their subjects those people and spaces of the South as much as the North. In practice, both groups are of interest from the perspective of postcolonial studies and the emerging field of postcolonial travel writing. Moreover, the actual distinctions between such groups in terms of class and cultural backgrounds are by no means clear cut.

Nevertheless, one of the assumptions held about the second set of writers is that the critique of imperialism is a signal feature of their travel writing.

Holland and Huggan argue, however, that while this may be so, such critique is always ambivalent, and tells us much of the instability of the term "postcolonial." They characterize postcolonial travel narratives by authors like Naipaul, Iyer, and Philips as variously "antiracist," "resistant," "counter-Orientalist," and "anti-imperialist."[26] They label them as *counter*narratives in so far as they "pit themselves against the various forms of Western cultural imperialism still dominant within the genre [of travel writing]," while nevertheless "seeking alternatives to European models, different ways of seeing the world that combat centuries of European prejudice" (64, 65). At the same time these books reflect the "reality" of these writers: "a diasporic world ... of global differences and disjunctures" (64). Yet Holland and Huggan caution that such narratives are symptomatic of a globalized culture that readily commodifies cultural difference in its myriad forms under the sign of the exotic (65). This leaves postcolonial travel writers in an "embattled" state, "struggle[ing] to match their political views with a genre that is in many ways antithetical to them – a genre that manufactures 'otherness' even as it claims to demystify it, and that is reliant ... on the most familiar of Western myths" (65) even as it estranges them.

The question of the authenticity and effectivity of the anti-imperialism that is attributed to postcolonial travel writing remains unresolved. For example, Maria Lourdes Lopez Ropero and Debbie Lisle both adopt a functionalist approach to their treatments of travel writing, insofar as they are primarily concerned with the roles that travel writing plays in articulating cultural differences in a globalizing/transnational world. Yet they arrive at different conclusions about the political functions of the genre. For Ropero, writing on Caryl Phillips, the postcolonial "travelogue" reflects an explicitly ethical and political sensibility: "No longer an instrument of imperial expansion, travel writing has become a powerful vehicle of cultural critique, particularly in the hands of special-interest groups such as 'postcolonial' authors."[27]

For those like Ropero, postcolonial travel writing is an example of "engaged literature"[28]: explicitly anti-colonial and anti-imperial. For Lisle, however, contemporary travel writing is a reactionary genre and "embedded in the cosmopolitan vision of many travel writers [postcolonial or otherwise] is a reconstructed framework of colonialism and patriarchy."[29] Lisle is particularly concerned with "the tropes of power, control and exclusion at work in the [postcolonial travel] text" (4) and how they correspond with hegemonic discourses and social structures. For Lisle travel writing *per se* exemplifies how, "[a]cts of writing and speaking are given meaning through prevailing discourses and actually *do violence* to the world because they are

8

an imposition of ordered meaning on an otherwise ambiguous reality" (12). Travel writing "organises the world through a number of prevailing discourses, and sediments that world into a seemingly incontrovertible reality. Travelogues are politically interesting texts because they mask that process of discursive ordering and offer their observations as neutral documentations of a stable, single and ordered reality" (13). Arguments like those presented by Ropero and Lisle raise fundamental questions about the agency of texts as much of travelers that go beyond the present discussion but that the reading of postcolonial travel writing constantly provokes. They articulate critical perspectives to which contributions in this *Companion* return.

Between the "utopianism" of Ropero and the "dystopianism" of Lisle, other scholars seek a middle way in their approach to postcolonial travel writing. Gareth Griffiths, for example, acknowledges the liberationist potential of postcolonial travel writing, but is anxious that the essential conservatism of travel writing confounds such potential. He cautions that "travel writing itself may now have become so deeply imbricated with the idea of the colonial that even the most oppositional texts [remain] deeply problematic."[30] Griffiths advises a cautious approach to the politics of the genre. Yet in his analyses, and those of Lisle and Ropero, and Holland and Huggan, and more recently Claire Lindsay,[31] we are brought back again to questions of the nature of the postcolonial and of travel writing.

Emerging Trends

Much has taken place since Patrick Holland's 1994 overview of postcolonial travel writing. Individually, the fields of postcolonial studies and travel writing studies have consolidated institutional status for themselves within the Anglophone academy. While the latter worked toward the development of theories and could now be said to enjoy a fertile eclecticism, the former has been the stage for almost constant debate. Those debates have frequently been characterized by tensions between, on the one hand, theories and criticism that adopt an "essentially textualist account of culture" – represented by the work of Homi K. Bhabha and Gayatri Chakravorty Spivak – and, on the other, a materialist perspective that emphasizes "historically grounded directions and [attention to the] material impulses to colonialism, its appropriation of physical resources, exploitation of human labour and institutional repression."[32] Those debates are perhaps subsiding, as Lazarus suggests, although postcolonial studies seems to be a field within the humanities that is fixated on "rerouting," "transiting," "reconstructing," and "moving beyond" itself if reference to recent scholarly titles is anything to go by.[33]

Nevertheless, it is clear that despite repeated reference to the redundancy, inadequacy, and futility of the term "postcolonial," postcolonial studies remains strong insofar as it is understood as "[a] certain kind of interdisciplinary political, theoretical and historical academic work that sets out to serve as a transnational forum for studies grounded in the historical context of colonialism, as well as in the political context of contemporary problems of globalization."[34] Part of that strength has to do with the way postcolonial studies has intersected fruitfully with travel writing studies. Indeed, travel writing – and more broadly speaking studies of traveling cultures – has provided a productive space for the exploration of ideas and processes that have become synonymous with postcolonial studies: hybridity and syncretism, transculturalism and transnationalism, counter-hegemony/discourse/narrative, alterity, and subalternity.

For Justin D. Edwards and Rune Graulund the critical aspect of postcolonial travel writing is not simply the manner in which it presents counter-narratives and enacts oppositionality toward imperialism past and present, but rather its potential to explore experiences, ontologies, and "frames of reference that exist outside the boundaries of European knowledge production."[35] Postcolonial travel writing, they assert, is infused with self-reflexivity: the text cannot escape being implicated in colonialist rhetoric, but nevertheless "deploys travel discourse in a manner that subverts both colonial claims to truth making, as well as the nexus between travel and domination" (3). For them, postcolonial travel writing promises "to merge the ideas of Empire with the material conditions of the places in which the writer travels [to effect] a convergence – and interlocking – of the conceptual and the material" (8). Acknowledging the complicity of the genre with colonialism, they champion the potential in what they call "innovative" travel writing to enable transformative possibilities for cross-cultural dialogue and understanding: "Postcolonial travel texts ... foreground new ways of encountering the world, thus bypassing exploitative and hierarchical relations by seeking out new stylistics, new grammars, fresh vocabularies and innovative narrative structures for experiencing and writing travel."[36]

Edwards and Graulund argue for a broadening of the "exclusivist" definition of travel writing to encompass "new" forms of travel discourse. Others argue that an examination of travel writing from a postcolonial perspective demands looking at the way travel narrative appears in writing by subaltern subjects in forms that we don't immediately recognize as travel writing from a Eurocentric perspective. Writing of Francophone African travel narrative, Aedín Ní Loingsigh states that "our recognition that we live in a world of generalized travel has not led ... to a sufficiently radical reassessment of twentieth-century developments in the representation of travel."[37]

Ní Loingsigh examines the rich legacy of African journey writing that appears in a range of forms. Understanding the significance of such journeys demands engagement with the textualization of subjectivity and mobility that have become the staple themes of postcolonial criticism. It also involves accounting for the historical determinants that conditioned displacement and hence make postcolonial journeys so politically and morally significant for travelers and their readers. In this manner, critics like Ní Loingsigh seek to "untie travel writing from its Western moorings and to open up a space" (3) for the examination of non-Western forms of journey literature.[38]

The more expansive examination of travel literature that postcolonial studies invites challenges some of the most central ideas that have developed in relation to colonial and postcolonial travel writing in the last two decades. These include the proclivity of many critics to view all instances of exoticism as necessarily linked to discourses of appropriation and commodification: as Charles Forsdick puts it, "a cultural or imaginative procedure akin to physical colonization and domestication."[39] While it is necessary to recognize the dangers inherent in exoticism as a discursive tool, Forsdick asserts that "there exists a more anxious, less categorical exoticism that has the capacity to 'articulate important ambiguities that both define colonialism's culture and hold the capacity to dismantle it'" (x).[40]

Untying travel writing from its Western moorings seems like a good mission statement for postcolonial travel writing. If we develop that idea, it might lead us into interesting places, while nevertheless keeping true to the fundamental qualities of travel literature. In this regard, Carl Thompson's assertion remains as valid as ever, namely that "travel involves an encounter between self and other that is brought about by the movement through space, [and] all travel writing is at some level a record or product of this encounter, and of the negotiation between similarity and difference that it entailed."[41]

In 2002, reviewing four key texts for the study of postcolonial travel writing, Sara Mills noted that while travel writing studies had benefited through its engagement with postcolonial theory, the crisis in postcolonial theory that was apparent in the early 2000s forced scholars of travel writing to rethink their methodologies and approaches. She wrote:

> It is no longer possible simply to continue to do 'Orientalist' readings of particular travel texts; instead it has become necessary to question what elements in travel texts are the result of colonialism and what are not. This has opened up the field of research in travel writing to the analysis of pre-colonial texts and contemporary texts rather than the restrictive focus on the 19th century. And whilst early travel texts have always been the subject of

analysis to the extent that they could be seen as prefiguring colonialism, the relation between contemporary travel writing and colonialism is a new departure. Gone too is the focus on generalisations about travel writing as a whole, women travellers, men travellers or colonial discourse; instead there are specific studies which are located in time and space and it is the specificity of context which is of interest.[42]

The trends that Mills detected in 2002 have developed in the years since, and are evident in the chapters that follow. A focus on analytical and contextual specificity; on contemporary works and emergent and renascent forms of colonialism and imperialism; on non-Anglophone and nonmetropolitan travel discourses; on travel writing that bears witness to involuntary and coercive mobilities; and on textualizations of travel that go beyond the conventions of the "first person non-fictional travel book": these are among the elements that are coming to define the field of study of postcolonial travel writing, as the contributions to this *Companion* show.

Overview of the *Companion*

The *Companion* is organized into three sections: "Departures," "Performances," and "Peripheries." The chapters in Part I, "Departures," address key issues, topics, and themes in postcolonial travel writing. Justin D. Edwards considers dominant theoretical trends in relation to the study of postcolonial travel writing, and the way travel writing challenges key theoretical assumptions of postcolonial literary and cultural studies. Jill Didur examines the engagement with nature and the environment in postcolonial travel writing. I examine how postcolonial travel writing necessarily provokes a reappraisal of the past and a confrontation with history, memory, and mourning. The chapters in this part, read alongside the present chapter, work to orient readers to the primary theoretical preoccupations of the field of postcolonial travel writing studies and emerging concerns and questions.

The chapters in Part II, "Performances," foreground a range of conventional and emerging travel performances and styles in postcolonial travel writing. "Performances" is used here to emphasize the way that postcolonial travel writing is characterized by a range of travel tropes, itineraries, and styles, and to recognize the function of travel discourse as a form of postcolonial performativity whereby subjectivities of travelers and travelees are framed in terms of complicity with, or resistance to, modes of colonial and imperial power. Srilata Ravi examines the journeys to imagined homelands of diasporic returnees in francophone postcolonial travel writing. Eva-Marie Kröller uses the wartime diaries of Canadian diplomat travelers as case studies on the writings of emissaries. Charles Forsdick investigates provincial and regional francophone travelers journeying to the metropoles of the (former) colonial center. Tim Youngs considers African American travel writing as postcolonial engagements with colonial spaces. Asha Sen analyses the writings of travelers in search of the spiritual and sacred. And Christopher Keirstead investigates contemporary travelers following in the footsteps of colonial travelers.

The chapters in Part III, "Peripheries," continue the collection's aim of shifting the analysis of travel writing from the traditional focus on Eurocentric forms and contexts. The chapters in this section cover a range of topics. Brian Creech explores the ways that travel journalism and new media are evolving as significant sites of travel discourse. Anna Johnston looks at the role that travel magazines have played – and continue to play – in settler (post)colonialism. April Shemak considers refugee and asylum seeker narratives as forms of postcolonial travel writing. And Stephen M. Levin examines representations of tourists in postcolonial fiction.

The *Companion* is concluded with an afterword by Mary Louise Pratt, whose groundbreaking 1992 work, *Imperial Eyes: Travel Writing and Transculturation*, remains a pivotal and energizing text within the field of postcolonial travel writing studies. Looking back over the time since the publication of *Imperial Eyes*, as well as the contributions to this volume, Pratt generously identifies a set of vital questions and issues that continue to invigorate this field of scholarship.

NOTES

1 Pico Iyer, *Video Night in Kathmandu* (London; Black Swan, [1988] 1992), 24.
2 The texts referenced here are: Idries Shah, *The Natives Are Restless*; Jan Morris, *Hong Kong*; Pico Iyer, *Video Night in Kathmandu*; Ferdinand Dennis, *Behind the Frontlines: Journey into Afro-Britain*; Jamaica Kincaid, *A Small Place*.
3 Edward Said, *Orientalism* (London: Penguin, 1978).
4 Bill Ashcroft, Gareth Griffiths, and Helen Tiffin, *The Empire Writes Back* (London: Routledge, 1989).
5 Mary Louise Pratt, *Imperial Eyes: Travel Writing and Transculturation* (London: Routledge, 1992); David Spurr, *The Rhetoric of Empire: Colonial Discourse in Journalism, Travel Writing, and Imperial Administration* (Durham: Duke University Press, 1993); Ali Behdad, *Belated Travellers: Orientalism in the Age of Colonial Dissolution* (Durham: Duke University Press, 1994).
6 See Robert Clarke, "Travel and Celebrity Culture," *Postcolonial Studies* 12, no. 2 (2009): 145–52.
7 bell hooks, "Representing Whiteness in the Black Imagination," in *Cultural Studies*, eds. Lawrence Grossberg, Cary Nelson, and Paula Treichler (New York: Routledge, 1992), 338–46 (343).

8 Colin Thubron, "Travel Writing Today: Its Rise and Its Dilemma," *Essays by Divers Hands: Being the Transactions of the Royal Society of Literature of the United Kingdom* 44 (1984): 167–81 (179).

9 Tim Youngs, *The Cambridge Introduction to Travel Writing* (Cambridge: Cambridge University Press, 2013), 3.

10 Helen Gilbert and Anna Johnston, "Introduction," in *In Transit: Travel, Text, Empire*, eds. Helen Gilbert and Anna Johnston (New York: Peter Lang, 2002), 1–20 (5).

11 *Talking about Travel Writing: A Conversation between Peter Hulme and Tim Youngs* (Leicester: The English Association, 2007), 3; cited in Youngs, *Cambridge Introduction to Travel Writing*, 4.

12 For a full discussion concerning debates relating to travel writing as a genre, see Youngs, *Cambridge Introduction to Travel Writing*, 1–16.

13 Patrick Holland, "Travel Literature (Overview)," in *The Encyclopedia of Post-Colonial Literatures in English*, ed. Eugene Benson and L. W. Conolly, vol. 2 (London: Routledge, 1994), 1586–89 (1586).

14 Neil Lazarus, *The Postcolonial Unconscious* (Cambridge: Cambridge University Press, 2011), 10–11.

15 Ato Quayson, "Postcolonial Literature in a Changing Historical Frame," in *The Cambridge History of Postcolonial Literature*, ed. Ato Quayson (Cambridge: Cambridge University Press, 2012), 1–29 (6).

16 See Claire Lindsay, "Travel Writing and Postcolonial Studies," in *The Routledge Companion to Travel Writing*, ed. Carl Thompson (London: Routledge, 2016), 25–34 (32).

17 See Youngs, *Cambridge Introduction to Travel Writing*, 3–4.

18 Holland, "Travel Literature," 1559.

19 Barbara Korte, *English Travel Writing: From Pilgrimages to Postcolonial Explorations* (London: MacMillan, 2000).

20 Patrick Holland and Graham Huggan, *Tourists with Typewriters: Critical Reflections on Contemporary Travel Writing* (Ann Arbor: University of Michigan Press, 1998), 43.

21 Wimal Dissanayake and Carmen Wickramagemage, *Self and Colonial Desire: Travel Writings of V.S. Naipaul* (New York: Peter Lang, 1993).

22 See for example, Ruth Brown, "*The Songlines* and the Empire that Never Happened," *Kunapipi* 13, no. 3 (1991): 5–13; and, Tim Youngs, "Punctuating Travel: Paul Theroux and Bruce Chatwin," *Literature and History* 6, no. 2 (1997): 73–88. For feminist critiques of mainstream travel discourse, see also Sara Mills, *Discourses of Difference: An Analysis of Women's Travel Writing and Colonialism* (London: Routledge, 1991); and, Sidonie Smith, *Moving Lives: Twentieth-Century Women's Travel Writing* (Minneapolis: University of Minneapolis Press, 2001).

23 See Catherine A. Lutz and Jane Collins, *Reading National Geographic* (Chicago: University of Chicago Press, 1993); Charles Sugnet, "Vile Bodies, Vile Places: Traveling with *Granta*," *Transition* 51 (1991): 70–85; Carla Almeida Santos, "Cultural Politics in Contemporary Travel Writing," *Annals of Tourism Research* 33, no. 3 (2006): 624–44.

24 See, for example, Iain Chambers, *Migrancy, Culture, Identity* (London, Verso, 1994), 95.

25 Caren Kaplan, *Questions of Travel: Postmodern Discourses of Displacement* (Durham: Duke University Press, 1996); Janet Wolff, "On the Road Again: Metaphors of Travel in Cultural Criticism," *Cultural Studies* 7 (1993): 224–40 (230).

26 Holland and Huggan, *Tourists with Typewriters*, 65.

27 Maria Lourdes Lopez Ropero, "Travel Writing and Postcoloniality: Caryl Phillips's *The Atlantic Sound*," *Atlantis* 25, no. 1 (2003): 51–62 (51).

28 Jean Paul Sartre, *What Is Literature?*, trans. Bernard Frechtman (New York: Philosophical Library, 1949): "The 'engaged' writer knows that words are action [and] that to reveal is to change and that one can reveal only by planning to change" (23).

29 Debbie Lisle, *Global Politics of Contemporary Travel Writing* (Cambridge: Cambridge University Press), 70.

30 Gareth Griffiths, "Postcolonial Travel Writing," in *The Cambridge History of Postcolonial Literature*, ed. Ato Qayson (Cambridge: Cambridge University Press, 2012), 58–80 (77).

31 Lindsay, "Travel Writing and Postcolonial Studies."

32 Benita Parry, *Postcolonial Studies: A Materialist Critique* (London: Routledge, 2004), 3.

33 See for example, Janet Wilson, Cristina Sandru, and Sarah Lawson Welsh, eds., *Rerouting the Postcolonial: New Directions for the New Millennium* (London: Routledge, 2010); Ania Loomba, Suvir Kaul, Matti Bunzil, Antoinette Burton, and Jed Esty, eds., *Postcolonial Studies and Beyond* (Durham: Duke University Press, 2005); Joel Kuortti and Jopi Nyman, eds., *Reconstructing Hybridity: Post-Colonial Studies in Transition* (Amsterdam: Rodopi, 2007).

34 Robert J. C. Young, "Editorial: Ideologies of the Postcolonial," *Interventions* 1, no. 1 (1998): 4–8 (4).

35 Justin D. Edwards and Rune Graulund, "Reading Postcolonial Travel Writing," in *Postcolonial Travel Writing: Critical Explorations*, ed. Justin D. Edwards and Rune Graulund (Basingstoke: Palgrave Macmillan, 2010), 3.

36 Justin D. Edwards and Rune Graulund, *Mobility at Large: Globalization, Textuality and Innovative Travel Writing* (Liverpool: Liverpool University Press, 2012), 9–10.

37 Aedín Ní Loingsigh, *Postcolonial Eyes: Intercontinental Travel in Francophone African Literature* (Liverpool: Liverpool University Press, 2009), 2.

38 This is something I have attempted in my own work on Australian Aboriginal travel writing: see, Robert Clarke, *Travel Writing from Black Australia*, (New York: Routledge, 2016) 115–37.

39 Charles Forsdick, *Travel in Twentieth-Century French and Francophone Cultures: The Persistence of Diversity* (Oxford: Oxford University Press, 2005), x.

40 Forsdick quotes Edward Hughes, *Writing Marginality in Modern French Literature: From Loti to Genet* (Cambridge: Cambridge University Press, 2001), 170.

41 Carl Thompson, *Travel Writing* (London: Routledge, 2010), 10.

42 Sara Mills, "Postcolonialism and Travel Writing," *Journal of Commonwealth and Postcolonial Studies* 9, no. 2 (2002): 151–61 (151–52). The texts that Mills reviews in this essay are: Steve Clark, ed., *Travel Writing and Empire: Postcolonial Theory in Transit* (London: Zed, 1999); Helen Gilbert and Anna Johnston, eds., *In Transit: Travel, Text, Empire* (New York: Peter Lang, 2002); Holland and Huggan, *Tourists with Typewriters*; and, Liselotte Glage, ed., *Being/s in Transit: Traveling, Migration, Dislocation.* (Amsterdam: Rodopi, 2000).

I

Departures

2

JUSTIN D. EDWARDS

Postcolonial Travel Writing and Postcolonial Theory

In recent scholarship, the convergence of the words "postcolonial," "travel," and "writing" has led to a series of debates that revolve around, but are not limited to, the representation of otherness, the power of speaking of and for a foreign culture, as well as the hierarchies embedded in discourses of difference. For some theorists and critics, travel writing is a genre that can never truly free itself from its colonial heritage and, from this perspective, it will always remain a neocolonial mode that reproduces a dominant North Atlantic idea of "civilization" from which travel writers continue to consolidate a privileged position by classifying, evaluating, and passing judgment on other parts of the world. For other postcolonial writers and theorists, the genre of travel writing has the potential to embrace revisionist, critical, and subversive narratives, political positions, and innovative modes of representation. From this perspective, travel texts can convey accounts that defy colonial discourses and challenge the politics of empire by approaching the experience of travel from a postcolonial angle and embracing new ways of telling the story of travel to foreign locations. Following this narrative trajectory, some of the innovative texts produced by postcolonial travel writers enable us to rethink the nature of the genre as well as its political, aesthetic, and ethical potential. This chapter examines these debates by exploring the major scholarly work on travel writing by postcolonial theorists and literary critics. But it also examines several postcolonial travel texts to reflect on how the traveler and his or her discourses have contributed to the debates in postcolonial studies.

Edward Said, Orientalism and Being Out of Place

Soon after he was diagnosed with leukemia, the postcolonial theorist Edward Said published *Out of Place* (1999), a text that merges the generic forms of the memoir and the travel narrative. As his death approaches, Said pieces together a series of distant memories and combines these with descriptions of a life of travel. Exiled from Palestine in 1948, the young Said and his family were forced to emigrate and, as a result, the text focuses on the many journeys of his life, thus articulating a personal disruption and a politics of identity that ties the narrator to a community of displaced Palestinians. His experiences of traveling engender myriad responses: His descriptions of the "social vacancy" of Middle America are juxtaposed with the rich, teeming, and historically dense metropolises of Jerusalem and Cairo.[1] The vibrant and busy streets of Manhattan are contrasted with the family's quiet and secluded summerhouse in Dhour el Schweir. The winding lanes of London's West End reverberate with memories of the Talbiyah, the Arab section of West Jerusalem where Said spent parts of his childhood. Each of these descriptions is tied to a different motivation for travel: travel for holidays, travel for education, travel for work, travel for health, travel for family, travel for politics, and travel for exile. In all of these forms, travel does not reinscribe or reconfirm the narrator's sense of self through reflections on the nuances of sameness and difference. Nor is travel considered to be a form of cultural capital that might lead, at least in a humanist sense, to a holistic and well-rounded self within the world. Instead, travel is part of the narrator's imagination of a Palestinian polity based on mobility, travel, diversity, and contingency.

Travel for Said is a way of life. In the final paragraph, for instance, he highlights a series of physical and figurative movements that foreground a sense of being "at home" in movement. Said writes,

> I occasionally experience myself as a cluster of flowing currents. I prefer this to the idea of a solid self, the identity to which so many attach so much significance. These currents, like the themes of one's life, flow during the waking hours, and at their best they require no reconciling, no harmonizing. They are "off" and may be out of place, but at least they are always in motion, in time, in place, in the form of all kinds of strange combinations moving about, not necessarily forward, sometimes against each other, contrapuntally yet without one central theme. (295)

In this passage, the "cluster of flowing currents" combines with motions in time and place that produce unique combinations of identity: He is Arab and Christian, Palestinian and American, the Anglophone "Edward" and the Arabic "Said." This identificatory complexity is interwoven with the physical mobility of continuous travel between Cairo and New York, Beirut and London, Jerusalem and Boston, Dhour and Paris. These movements are not necessarily chronological or teleological but include various discordant tensions alongside harmonious cadences. We might read these numerous flows as an embodied form of diversity, and the celebration of a heterogeneous sense of self that is never easily defined.

The innovative form of *Out of Place* – with its merger of memoir and travel writing – contributes to crosscultural communication between the Middle East, Europe, and the United States, and explores the complexities of cultural mobility across these regions and nations. This leads to transcultural sensitivities that are culturally, socially, and politically progressive. The text also highlights an awareness that representations of travel have often relied upon a "seeing I" to construct visions of otherness: Even in the more inclusive contemporary manifestations of travel writing the gaze of the traveler still requires a coherent subject position "capable of describing, organizing, and translating difference."[2] Even "a writer as gifted as Salman Rushdie," writes the international relations scholar Debbie Lisle, is helpless in the face of travel writing, a genre that inevitably shackles writers into producing works exhibiting a spectacular "lack of multiplicity," for it is a textual form that is caught up in the rhetoric of Empire.[3]

How does Said reconcile this tension? The answer, I suggest, lies in the relationship between form and content. For rather than dismissing the entire genre as simply continuing a colonial enterprise, Said engages in a progressive politics of mobility whereby the traveler/writer is self-reflexive about his participation in the genre and responds through a series of experimentations in form and style. For instance, Said circumvents the politically problematic gaze of the travel writer by negating the coherent subject position of the traveler: He uses quotation marks to mark out the name "Edward" and thus "Said" becomes "Edward's" Other, "the person for whom *Out of Place* provides a journey of discovery and recovery."[4] Moreover, the quotation marks around "Edward" articulate the unique subject position of the traveler by focusing on the self as a discursive subject. This articulates the paradoxical continuity of a traveler who is not only multiply located but also multidirectional. Said thus strives to represent the multivalence of identity through the places in which he travels and, in turn, complicate the powerful gaze of the traveler who is grounded in a coherent sense of self and clearly delineates "home" from "abroad."

This experimentation in form combines with a politically charged position that foregrounds the displacement Said and his family experienced after the creation of the state of Israel in 1948. The combination of innovative writing techniques and political content distinguishes *Out of Place* from travel writing that is associated with colonization. Indeed, in his seminal *Orientalism* (1978), Said points to how European travel writing by writers such as Gertrude Bell often disseminates political, social, and cultural hierarchies to assert control over the societies and peoples who inhabit the places of Asia,

North Africa, and the Middle East.[5] The views expressed by Bell, T. E. Lawrence, and others are consistent with European discursive finality wherein the traveler believes he or she has solved the problem of definition of the "Oriental" and the "East." For Bell, writing in *The Desert and the Sown*, "[t]he Oriental is like a very old child [whose] utility is not ours,"[6] thus invoking significant discourses of difference and presenting the Arab as a single, unchanging figure with, as Said puts it, "centuries of experience and no wisdom."[7] For Bell "No one who does not know the East can realize how it all hangs together."[8]

It was Said's *Orientalism*, one of the most influential works of postcolonial theory, which first linked travel writing to the colonial project. Drawing on the scholarship of Michel Foucault, Said theorized orientalism as a complex cultural and ideological discourse, "a Western style for dominating, restricting, and having authority over the Orient."[9] Travel writing was vital for supporting the Orientalist project and became an increasingly popular genre for audiences back home who wanted to read about how European colonial powers were engaging in "discoveries," missionary projects, military conflict, and trade. These travel narratives included seemingly objective accounts of "other" places and peoples that constructed distinctions between "the Orient" and "the Occident," which supported imperialist expansion through depictions of "the East" as inferior. As a result, these texts were linked to socioeconomic and political structures that sought to justify colonization and garner institutional support for imperial expansion.

Claire Lindsay correctly asserts that the "influence of Said's book on postcolonial studies and on the analysis of travel accounts (which are always representations of the cultural 'other') has been huge."[10] She notes that the limitations of Said's primary corpus pose the risk of generalization (a critique anticipated by Said) and that the methodology of *Orientalism* includes the risk of narrowing the conception of "the East" as a place that was "acted upon" by various forms of imperialism. Yet Lindsay also demonstrates how critics of travel writing – notably Ali Behdad and David Spurr – avoid these pitfalls by recognizing the potentially essentializing conception of Orientalism and drawing on other postcolonial theorists such as Homi Bhabha and Gayatri Spivak. For instance, in *The Rhetoric of Empire: Colonial Discourse in Journalism, Travel Writing, and Imperial Administration* (1993), David Spurr explores how Western journalists, travel writers, and government bureaucrats represent the non-Western world. He identifies twelve rhetorical modes through which "the Other" was and continues to be constructed (surveillance, appropriation, aestheticization, classification, debasement, negation, affirmation, idealization, insubstantialization, naturalization, eroticization, and resistance) and he examines how these constructions work in texts that depict otherness and difference. Similarly, Ali Behdad's *Belated Travelers: Orientalism in the Age of Colonial Dissolution* (1994) begins by asserting that "there is no 'outside' to the language of empire" and thus the postcolonial critic must be aware of his or her "parasitic" dependence upon the imperial "system of power."[11] In fact, Behdad's study of travel writing reflects on how the late-twentieth-century critic of Orientalism bears an uncanny resemblance to the belated Orientalist of the previous century. The project of the one cannot be simply extricated from that of the other. This is because the critic is contained within "the discourse of Orientalism" and "to write about the Orient inevitably involves an intertextual relation in which the 'new' text necessarily depends for its representational economy on an earlier text," for both are situated within (historically different configurations of) the same limits (6). Given this complicitous situation, the political and aesthetic agenda of today's postcolonial critic can no longer be simply one of transgressing these limits but of recording, with an ever-greater degree of self-consciousness, the fluctuating "micropractices" that make them possible: For Behdad, "one can only engage in a shifting and indeterminate practice of deconstruction, describing the ideological complexities and political strategies of Orientalism in order to expose their limitations and problems," and registering the extent to which the "noise of contestation" produced by the critic serves not only to trouble the orientalist "discursive system" but also to reinforce it, enabling a "continual process of transformation and restructuration that ensures [the] discourse of power its cultural hegemony" (137).

Politics and Travel: Identities in the Contact Zone

Many feminist critics and theorists have criticized Said's *Orientalism* for its lack of attention to gender. This has not tempered Said's influence on, for instance, the work of Mary Louise Pratt, Reina Lewis, and Sara Mills, but these critics have engaged in sustained analyses of women's travel writing as a corrective to Said's gender-neutral approach to texts. A significant example of this is Sara Mills's *Discourses of Difference: An Analysis of Women's Travel Writing and Colonialism* (1993), which is concerned with analyzing gender as an important variable in the construction of colonial and imperial discourses. Focusing on British women travel writing from the mid-nineteenth century onward, Mills argues that travel writers such as Mary Kingsley and Alexandra David-Neel "were unable to adopt the imperial voice with the ease with which male writers did" and were more cautious and less likely to adopt and disseminate the "truths" of British rule without reflection, consideration, and qualification.[12] Women like Kingsley and

David-Neel, Mills argues, sometimes convey unease about the tensions between empire and gender and, as a result, their texts include counter-hegemonic discourses within the colonial project. Drawing on Foucault's definition of discourse, Mills provides a significant theoretical paradigm that focuses on the question of subject "agency" – the extent to which subjects can use discourses or are constituted by them. With this in mind, it is important for Mills to identify the ways in which interpretive and conceptual schemas delimit understandings, and the gender politics involved in the intentional deployment of concepts and categories to achieve specific political goals. For while many British women travel writers have been involved in anti-imperialist and antiracist activities, it does not necessarily follow that the more personal voice of a white, class-privileged woman will engender a critique of colonialism.

The decolonization of knowledge as it relates to race, ethnicity, nationality, gender, religion, and class is central to the theoretical underpinning of Mary Louise Pratt's *Imperial Eyes: Travel Writing and Transculturation* (1992/2008).[13] Pratt's book begins with the premise that travel writing by Europeans (for European readers) produced knowledge about non-European places and supported expansionist politics by fashioning a domestic subject of European imperialism. Thus, Pratt seeks to de-center the Western eye and reconceptualize the relationship between center and periphery by theorizing spaces (contact zones) alongside colonial power relations (transculturation) as well as European critiques of imperialism (anti-conquest). The influence of the theoretical foundations of Pratt's book is widespread: These terms are now widely used in geography, anthropology, philosophy, history, and cultural and literary studies. Nevertheless, some scholars have pointed to the lack of specificity in the idea of the "contact zone," questioning how it is delimited and how it can incorporate or distinguish regional differences in economic, cultural, or environmental terms. Where is the contact zone? Where does it begin? Where does it end? And if some scholars find the notion to be too abstract and expansive, then for others it is too reductive. They argue that the contact zone is temporally problematic because of its confinement to a historical period in the past; it thus fails to take into account the politics of recent re-readings of the experiences of, and in, such territories. In this, the contact zone does not lie in the annals of history, but is still acting to influence people in the continuing politics of colonial encounters.

Transculturation is a theoretical term that Pratt adopts from Latin American scholars such as Fernando Ortiz and Ángel Rama,[14] who use the word to describe a process arising out of the colonial encounter wherein intercultural and bidirectional dynamics are part of a two-way flow of information, knowledge, and cultural products. This process merges the acquisition of another culture (acculturation) with the uprooting of a previous culture (deculturation) to engender new cultural phenomena. Transculturation often arises out of colonial conquest and subjugation, particularly in a postcolonial era when indigenous cultures articulate historical and political injustices while also struggling to regain a sense of cultural identity. This gives the power of transformative cultural agency to the colonized subject by transforming, appropriating, adapting, and "rewriting" the modes and genres from the North Atlantic, sometimes engendering texts of resistance by revising models for articulating local experience and culture. However, if the contact zone lacks the nuance of cultural and political specificity, then Pratt's use of transculturation becomes an amorphous concept and, as a result, can be conceived too easily as a one-way process wherein the periphery has a profound impact on the metropolis. Specificity would have arisen out of particular examples, but because Pratt does not include empirical evidence she opens herself up to the claim that her use of transculturation is as monolithic a term as the contact zone.

A potential theoretical pitfall arising out of Pratt's work is the preoccupation with a reading practice that only focuses on "imperial eyes" and overlooks other complex dimensions of multilayered and structurally sophisticated travel texts. Within this paradigm, travel and travel writing can be reduced to the gaze of power, and this has blinded scholars to "the chronotope of the random" and how those imperial eyes were "mediated through prolix, irregular texts."[15] In *The Global Politics of Contemporary Travel Writing* (2006), for instance, Debbie Lisle asserts "that the cosmopolitan vision embedded in contemporary travel writing [...] is not as emancipatory as it claims to be; rather, it is underscored by the remnants of Orientalism, colonialism and Empire."[16] While it is undisputable that some of the texts in her case studies reinscribe the dichotomies of civilized/uncivilized or safe/dangerous, Lisle's theoretical footing is based on the claim that all contemporary writers participating in the genre "fail to address the intricate and ambiguous power relations" in the territories and borders they cross (9). "There may be good travelogues and bad travelogues," writes Lisle, "but as a whole, the genre encourages a particularly conservative political outlook that extends to its vision of global politics. This is frustrating because travel writing has the *potential* to re-imagine the world in ways that do not simply regurgitate the status quo or repeat a nostalgic longing for Empire" (xi, emphasis added). Such an assertion relegates the entire genre of travel writing to a Eurocentric and colonizing form and, in fact, early in her study Lisle makes the problematic claim that all travel writers conform to a North Atlantic perspective and "seek to jettison their colonial heritage" (4). Lisle adopts a conventional and Eurocentric view of travel writing, an under-standing of the genre that is not entirely suitable for reading non–North Atlantic and postcolonial travel texts. In fact, by assuming that all travel narratives conform to a European or North American tradition, Lisle ignores the large body of non-European travel writings, but she also silences non-Western voices and limits possibilities for constructive discussions about other traditions of travel writing.

The blind spots arising out of this theoretical paradigm help to explain how the movements of some (non-European) peoples have been effectively frozen under that narrative gaze. This blinkered perspective also helps to explain why the presence of non-European travelers has often been over-looked when they appear in European travel accounts: Tabish Khair and other scholars observe that eighteenth- and nineteenth-century European travel writing about Ghana, Sudan Libya, and Egypt includes many refer-ences to Asian and African travelers, but these have been largely ignored by North Atlantic researchers fixated on encoding the colonizing gaze of the European traveler.[17] Such an erasure creates the perception of travel as European(ized) travel and negates centuries of travel by non-Europeans, many of whom left behind detailed and rich accounts of their journeys (11). This has resulted in a critical trajectory on travel writing that conflates travel with European modernity, thus negating both travel and modernity from the world outside of Europe. Writing in 2006, Khair notes that

> academic interest in travel writing over the past ten years has been dominated by critical readings of the accounts of white men (and, less often, white women) from Europe traveling through the world. [...] Such has been the centrality of later European Self-Other perception that even obvious facts—like the porous borders between Asia, Africa and Europe from prehistory through the Greek civilization and the Moorish era in Spain to the present times—have been overlooked outside of specialist circles. (15)

In attempting to reveal the imperial eyes of European travel texts, scholars of travel writing have reinscribed European centrality by looking through a limited lens that does not register Asian and African travelers or their texts. Travel writers such as, among many others, Al-Abdari, Ibn Battuta, Al-Amraoui, Dean Mahomed, and B. M. Malabari are mostly overlooked in scholarly debates because they do not fit the European imperial eyes para-digm or they focus on cultural transactions between Asia and Africa that did not require the bridge of European colonization.

This long tradition of Asian and African travel writing informs contem-porary postcolonial writers who choose to engage in the genre. And these travel texts do not necessarily engage in an orientalist project that separates

26

the West from the rest by imposing hierarchies and casting the non-European as the exotic other. For instance, the Indian writer Pankaj Mishra asserts that in his travel texts he is not interested in engaging in "exoticism or complete 'Otherness'" but instead seeks a "degree of familiarity between the reader and the page": "I suppose," he states, "it is another aspect of the self-exploration that travel writing is for me, that as someone journeying out of ignorance I can't pretend to superior ethnographic knowledge for the sake of the reader. And the awareness and disclosure of my own assumptions is part of the process."[18] Here, Mishra articulates the self-reflection and self-awareness that characterizes many postcolonial travel texts: He is mindful of his physical and conceptual proximity to his subject; he is conscious of his political position as a traveler with an Indian passport; and he articulates his experiences of the world as a citizen who is not from a North Atlantic country.

Reflexivity and the Transnational Traveler

Self-awareness about travel and travel writing has led to innovative forms in postcolonial travel texts. In Michael Ondaatje's *Running in the Family* (1983), for example, self-reflection engenders narrative fragmentation so that the text remains open to the plurality of stories and the rejection of metanarrative.[19] Similarly, M. G. Vassanji's *A Place Within* (2008) includes new organizing principles for narration by drawing on a poetics of place and ethnicity based on a synchronous foreignicity that embraces antithesis, polarity, and confusion.[20] Caryl Phillips's *Atlantic Sound* (2000) questions notions of home by articulating different forms of travel and highlighting disjunctions while also using montage and juxtaposition to convey a single position in multiple places, thus representing the world as multidimensional and presenting the self within that multiplicity.[21] Whatever textual strategy is employed, the postcolonial travel writer highlights his or her presence within the construction of the text and actively negotiates the multivalence of their lives. In this, the distinction between the reader and the writer falls away because knowledge is rethought as experience throughout the text. Rather than representing a subject's travels from one point to another, these texts embrace fragmentation and disruption.

A salient example of this is Amitav Ghosh's *At Large in Burma* (1996), a travel narrative that interlaces family reminiscences, political activism, as well as colonial and postcolonial history.[22] Ghosh's text, like so many works of postcolonial travel writing, demonstrates a reflexive awareness of the postcolonial travel market and a recognition that the travel writer is always in some way complicit in the travel industry and the forms of exoticization of postcolonial subjects and cultures. The text begins with Ghosh's stories of his aunt and uncle's expatriate life in Burma before WWII. For his Indian uncle, Burma was "a golden land" during the British colonial period, a time when many merchants and moneylenders from India settled in Burma and held government posts (a situation that, as Ghosh points out, fueled Burmese nationalism and led to anti-Indian riots) (67). During his first visit to Rangoon, Ghosh finds the Spark Street Temple where his family spent much of their time, and he traces his uncle's connection to the place alongside the political history of Burmese independence, the assassination of Aung San, and the rise of Ne Win's military rule. Here, the trace of a retrospective narrative looks back to the past as it articulates the present and projects into the future. This "looking back" structures this section of *At Large in Burma*, but it is also caught up in tracing the mobility that is the subject of retro-spection: The trace is, after all, a track, a path, a mark, wherein the narrator traces the paths that take him from one place to another, marking out the various territories he moves through in this foreign and familiar land.

Traces of the past are also present in the text's representation of political activism. Before visiting Aung San Suu Kyi (who is under house arrest in Rangoon), Ghosh recalls first meeting her in 1980 in Oxford, where he was a graduate student. He harks back to her "life of quiet, exiled domesticity on a leafy street in North Oxford" and reflects on the political voice she found in Burma in the late 1980s and early 1990s (75). During his trip, Ghosh interviews her and describes the gateside meetings where she speaks to her local followers as well as foreign tourists, travelers, and journalists. Throughout the interview, Ghosh glimpses the complexity of Burma's colo-nial and postcolonial history with the internal tensions that arise out of its ethnic, religious, and ideological diversity. This inspires him to partake in a dangerous journey: He travels to the mountainous frontier of eastern Burma to meet the Karenni insurgents, a guerrilla network that has been engaged in an armed struggle for independence since 1946. He seeks answers to ques-tions about what it means to fight for so long and what "freedom" means for the Karenni people.

But in this remote place, Ghosh finds sameness, not difference. When he arrives at a base camp "deep inside the forest," Ghosh meets a commander who asks, "Are you Indian?" in spoken English that sounds eerily similar to his own (87, 88). The Karenni commander is Burmese but of Indian descent – his mother Hindu, his father Sikh – and had been part of the Indian business community in Burma established under British colonial rule. Ghosh reflects on the fact that "our relatives had [probably] known one another once in Burma" and he is confronted with the happenstance of fate: "each of us," he writes, "could have been in the other's place" (89). Here, as he searches for knowledge about freedom, independence, and armed struggles, Ghosh encounters his own sense of self through a random twist of history that delineates what he is and what he might have been. In this, the sense of place in the text moves beyond the discourses of difference associated with the limited paradigms of us and them, here and there, home and abroad. The multivalent perspectives and shifting points of view do not assert a single authoritative voice that is stable, normative, or incontestable. Consequently, the text does not simply reduce the world to a single set of prevailing discourses or perspectives to represent a seemingly incontrovertible reality. Nor does the text veil the processes of discursive ordering by providing observations as neutral documentations of a stable, single, and ordered reality. Rather, the competing narrative modes, and different conceptions of home and belonging, engender an interstitial place in between difference and sameness that unmasks their own discursive ordering as well as conventional conceptions of travel, place, and identity. This is not to say that the text includes a postmodern disavowal of political positioning; instead, it betrays awareness that in order to take a stand – to demarcate what constitutes home and self to *us* – we must first be attentive to the claims of others and register familiarity within the foreign.

For critics such as Inderpal Grewal and Sam Knowles, the theoretical paradigm of transnationalism is appropriate for reading postcolonial travel texts by Ghosh and his contemporaries. For Knowles, transnationalism opens up the possibility of reading these texts as a "reshaping of the national and as a response to the idea of modernity" wherein transnationality challenges binary divisions of space (home and abroad, foreign and familiar) and allows minority communities to negotiate their collective identifications.[23] Likewise, for Grewal, transnational associations formed by contemporary diasporic communities engender postcolonial histories, and literary and aesthetic productions that circulate forms of knowledge that bypass metropolitan centers.[24] To put it simply, transnationalism is a social phenomenon and a theoretical paradigm for cultural research that has grown out of the heightened interconnectivity between people and the receding economic and social significance of boundaries among nation states. Most importantly, transnationalism raises the question of borders, which is at the heart of any adequate definition of otherness and the nation-state. Theories of transnationalism thus offer insights into a postcolonial travel writer's complex personal, textual, and geopolitical relationships to the places where she travels, and her links to multiple homelands or senses of belonging. Transnational movement engenders an erosion of clear-cut national affiliations and this, in turn, has a profound impact on the ways in which the traveler experiences and represents the place where she travels.

Transnationalism opens up the possibility of shifting away from hierarchical and asymmetrical power relations in travel and travel writing. This arises out of sensitivity to "transversal" movements of culture that allow for the emergence of networks that circumvent the North Atlantic centers of European imperialism. Understanding transnationalism in terms of cultural transversalism rather than vertical relations between center and margin is fruitful for analyzing contemporary travel writing because it complicates the dated notions of hybridity central to the construction of North Atlantic locales as privileged sites of plurality. By distinguishing between "global" and "transnational," Françoise Lionnet and Shu-mei Shih suggest that "the logic of globalization [...] assumes a global universal core or norm, which spreads out across the world while pulling into its vortex other forms of culture to be tested by its norm [...] with all the attendant problems of Eurocentric universalism."[25] By contrast, the transnational works in a less centripetal fashion, for it "can be conceived as a space of exchange and participation [...] where it is still possible for cultures to be produced and performed without necessary mediation by the center" (5). Within postcolonial travel writing, the transnational imagination presents a prospect for transgressing fixed national spaces/identities of political allegiance and economic control. This is done by circumventing North Atlantic top-down power and by exploring imagined communities of modernity that challenge macropolitical (global) dominance and turn to micropolitical (cultural) experiences of everyday life.

Conclusion

The convergence of travel writing and postcolonial theory contributes to an understanding of cultural difference as unstable, in flux, and how the history of racialization contributes to the formation of subjectivities, but not a unified subject position. In other words, by composing postcolonial travel texts that are in process, multiple, collective, and disruptive, the genre allows writers to compose the traveling subject as a possible site for active cultural and ideological struggle. These are particularly critical issues in the context of postcolonial politics and the colonial legacy of the genre. At a moment when cultural plurality, cultural mobility, and hybridity have challenged the metanarratives of cultural nationalism, not only are postcolonial travel writers able to experiment with new forms of expression, but they also enter into dialogue with political debates raised in postcolonial theory, particularly about cultural, racial, ethnic, and national difference in the varying historical contexts of travel practice. Moreover, the unique strand of self-conscious textuality foregrounded by these writers is extremely pertinent as a wide range of writers and theorists continue to insist on new diverse cultural performances while, at the same time, maintaining a critical context of articulation within the border pressures of globalization. In fact, questions about cultural mobility and the narrating (traveling) subject are especially important now, after two decades of increasing global connectivity and the decline of nation-based power. There is more than ever a need to find new ways of expressing a sense of belonging and exclusion that takes into account the flows of global mobility and disrupts center-periphery conceptions of space and place.

NOTES

1 Edward Said, *Out of Place: A Memoir* (London: Granta, 1999), 235.
2 Debbie Lisle, *The Global Politics of Contemporary Travel Writing* (Cambridge: Cambridge University Press, 2006), 132.
3 Lisle, *Global Politics of Contemporary Travel Writing*, 49; David Spurr, *The Rhetoric of Empire: Colonial Discourse in Journalism, Travel Writing, and Imperial Administration* (Durham: Duke University Press, 1993), 9–12.
4 Bryan Turner, "Edward Said and the Exilic Ethnic: On Being Out of Place," *Theory, Culture and Society* 17, no. 6 (2000): 125–29 (127).
5 Edward Said, *Orientalism* (New York: Vintage, [1978] 2003), 229–31.
6 Gertrude Bell, *The Desert and the Sown: Travels in Palestine and Syria* (London: William Heinemann, 1907), ix.
7 Said, *Orientalism*, 230.
8 Gertrude Bell, *From Her Personal Papers, 1889–1914*, ed. Elizabeth Burgoyne (London: Ernest Benn, 1958), 204; quoted in Said, *Orientalism*, 229.
9 Said, *Orientalism*, 3.
10 Claire Lindsay, "Travel Writing and Postcolonial Studies," in *The Routledge Companion to Travel Writing*, ed. Carl Thompson (London: Routledge, 2016), 25–34 (27).
11 Ali Behdad, *Belated Travelers: Orientalism in the Age of Colonial Dissolution* (Durham: Duke University Press, 1994), 5–6.
12 Sara Mills, *Discourses of Difference: An Analysis of Women's Travel Writing and Colonialism* (New York: Routledge, 1993), 3.
13 Mary Louise Pratt, *Imperial Eyes: Travel Writing and Transculturation*, 2nd edn. (London: Routledge, [1992] 2008).
14 Fernando Ortiz, *Cuban Counterpoint: Tobacco and Sugar*, trans. Harriet de Onís (Durham: Duke University Press, [1940] 1995), 13; Ángel Rama, *Transculturación narrativa en América Latina* (Buenos Aires: Ediciones El Adariego, 1982), 21.
15 Ina Ferris, "Mobile Words: Romantic Travel Writing and Print Anxiety," *Modern Language Quarterly* 60, no. 4 (1999): 451–68 (458).
16 Lisle, *Global Politics of Contemporary Travel Writing*, 5.
17 Tabish Khair, "African and Asian Texts in the Light of Europe," in *Other Routes: 1500 Years of African and Asian Travel Writing*, ed. Tabish Khair,

Martin Leer, Justin D. Edwards, and Hanna Ziadeh (Oxford: Signal Books, 2006), 1–27 (7).

18 Quoted in Tabish Khair, "An Interview with William Dalrymple and Pankaj Mishra," in *Postcolonial Travel Writing: Critical Explorations*, ed. Justin D. Edwards and Rune Graulund (Basingstoke: Palgrave Macmillan, 2010), 173–84 (175, 178).

19 Michael Ondaatje, *Running in the Family* (London: Picador, 1983).

20 M. G. Vassanji, *A Place Within: Rediscovering India* (Toronto: Doubleday Canada, 2008). The poet and scholar Fred Wah defines, "synchronous foreignicity" as "the ability to remain within an ambivalence without succumbing to the pull of any single culture (resolution, cadence, closure)": Fred Wah, "Half-Bred Poetics," in *Faking It: Poetics and Hybridity* (Edmonton: NeWest, 2000), 71–96 (83).

21 Caryl Phillips, *The Atlantic Sound* (New York: Vintage, 2000).

22 Amitav Ghosh, *At Large in Burma* (Delhi: Ravi Dayal, [1996] 1998).

23 Sam Knowles, *Travel Writing and the Transnational Author* (Basingstoke: Palgrave, 2014), 16.

24 Inderpal Grewal, "Amitav Ghosh: Cosmopolitanisms, Literature, Transnationalisms," in *The Postcolonial and the Global*, ed. Revathi Krishnaswamy and John C. Hawley (Minneapolis: University of Minnesota Press, 2008), 178–90 (181).

25 Françoise Lionnet and Shu-mei Shih, "Introduction: Thinking through the Minor, Transnationally," in *Minor Transnationalism*, ed. Françoise Lionnet and Shu-Mei Shih (Durham: Duke University Press, 2005), 1–23 (5).

3

JILL DIDUR

Walk This Way

Postcolonial Travel Writing of the Environment

The relationship between travel writing and the environment has preoccupied postcolonial studies for some time. Historical studies such as Alfred Crosby's *Ecological Imperialism* (1985), John MacKenzie's *Empire of Nature* (1988), and Richard Grove's *Green Imperialism* (1995) have underscored the entanglement of empire and environment throughout the history of European mercantile and colonial expansion.[1] As Grove argues, the drive for European expansionism during the Renaissance period was partly underpinned by "the search for an eastern-derived Eden," as well as "the pursuit of gold and profits, the settlement of distant island colonies, the garnering of botanical knowledge and, increasingly, the lure of India and China and their riches."[2] "Paradoxically," as Grove points out, "the full flowering of what one might term the Edenic island discourse during the seventeenth century closely coincided with the realization that the economic demands of colonial rule on previously uninhabited oceanic island colonies threatened their imminent and comprehensive degradation" (5). Postcolonial studies has examined the history of this contradictory pull between colonialism and conservation in travel writing, and tracked how contemporary writers appropriate, subvert, and reinvent the genre for decolonizing purposes. Recent work in the environmental humanities also foregrounds postcolonial studies' role in bringing attention to the history of empire in shaping the environment and environmental discourse, with travel writing as a key genre in exploring this intersection.[3]

Postcolonial writers' ability to subvert a colonial genre like travel writing has been subject to debate. As David Arnold observes, "to represent the experience of travel, it is necessary to inhabit the European imagination, even if it is then still possible to tweak it."[4] The degree to which contemporary postcolonial and eco-travel writers are able to "'tweak' the legacies of 'ecological imperialism'" is something Graham Huggan explores. Acknowledging that much contemporary eco-travel writing can be associated with "human-centred" rather than "ecocentric" perspectives, Huggan nevertheless argues that it is short sighted to dismiss the "ideological work performed by eco-travel writers in [...] critically analyzing contemporary instances of human exploitation and environmental abuse."[5] Despite the fact that eco-travel writing "exists in almost constant tension with travel writing's traditional counterimpulses toward entertaining fabulation and self-glorifying myth," Huggan sees potential in its emphasis on "the social construction of 'nature,' providing an antidote to those less considered forms of nature writing" (53–54). With a clear focus on the co-implication of human and environmental issues, Huggan also views eco-travel writing as "reconfirming the usefulness of travel writing as an instrument of social and cross-cultural critique" (54).

My work with Elizabeth DeLoughrey and Anthony Carrigan examines how European genres like travel writing and critical approaches such as ecocriticism have been reoriented by postcolonial writers and critics who are conscious of how Enlightenment views of the natural world contribute to our current environmental crisis. This work reflects a generally uneasy relationship between postcolonial studies and the field of ecocriticism, a theoretical approach that postcolonial scholars view as unwittingly anchored in an American studies context and a sometimes parochial view of environmental history.[6] Instead of trying to "[diversify] the canon" to address blind spots in ecocritical approaches to literary study, however, postcolonial scholars and writers call for thorough "reimagining [of] the prevailing paradigms" that inform our study of the environment in the wake of empire.[7] Most prominent among postcolonial scholars engaged in this "reimagining" is Dipesh Chakrabarty, whose work on the Anthropocene articulates a view of history where the separation of human and natural history is no longer tenable, and where humans are instead understood as "a force of nature in the geological sense."[8] Chakrabarty calls on scholars in the environmental humanities and postcolonial studies to begin the fraught, but necessary, process of accounting for the entanglement of human and natural history that has informed both colonizing and decolonizing movements alike (208).

As I argue with DeLoughrey and Carrigan, "due to the ways in which the histories of colonialism have displaced and alienated people from the land, the imaginative and material act of ecological recuperation" in postcolonial writing

> is often deeply fraught. Consequently, far from any idealized notions of harmony and balance, postcolonial environmental representations often engage in the legacies of violent material, environmental, and cultural transformation. In an effort to recuperate history that colonial narratives sought to suppress, they might take on the authoritative voices of historians or [...] the adaptation of an 'official' journalistic voice (and its parody).[9]

The adaptation of a journalistic voice and the representation of the legacies of violent material, environmental, and cultural transformation are defining characteristics of Arundhati Roy's "Walking with the Comrades." Roy's essay is postcolonial travel writing of the environment, a "generic negoti-ation" that offers an "incisive critique of how mainstream environmental narratives are framed, drawing attention to the power relations and struc-tural inequalities they all too frequently occlude" (5). Roy's work fore-grounds the material and spatial experience of traveling in the forests of Central India under the unique guidance of the adivasi[10] and Maoist guer-rillas, and contributes to "the creation of alternative modes of articulation and analysis in line with the tradition of postcolonial thought and writing" (5). In the third part of this chapter, I consider how Roy takes up the colonial genre of travel writing, tweaks its underlying "European imagination," and unearths the co-implication of empire and the environment in the Danda-karanya forest of Central India, thus appropriating the genre for her activist and decolonizing ends.

Emergent Materialities, Travel Writing, and the Environment

As well as challenging the binary opposition of nature and culture, recent work in the environmental humanities examines the extent to which writing about the environment is "involved in the creative modelling and remodeling of (literary) environments."[11] Noting that first-wave ecocritical scholarship favored referential, mimetic, or didactic dimensions of literary texts concerned with the environment, critics have called for attention to the "transformative role of aesthetics itself" (3) and how this bears on our understanding of materiality. Critics such as Donna Haraway, Anna Lowenhaupt Tsing, Bruno Latour, and N. Katherine Hayles have long challenged the "boundaries between human semiotic processes, knowledge practices, and the very material world itself,"[12] offering approaches that highlight how aesthetics and discourse play a role in shaping "emergent materialities" (6). Materiality in this context is best understood as "an emergent property created through dynamic interactions between physical characteristics and signifying strategies" (28), but it also resonates with indigenous and non-Western worldviews that are central to the field of postcolonial studies.[13] Where postcolonial travel writing and the environ-ment is concerned, however, it is useful to consider how this materialist approach is largely anticipated in the study of empire and travel that under-pins Mary Louise Pratt's seminal work, *Imperial Eyes: Travel Writing and Transculturation*. Pratt's work on travel writing, I argue, helps us to see the foundational way in which the history of empire has shaped our understanding of the environment, the way this continues to reverberate in contemporary postcolonial writing about travel, and the way that this becomes an important resource for decolonizing interventions in this area.

Pratt's book appeared at a moment when, as she notes, "the text of Euroimperialism" and its "power to constitute the everyday with neutrality, spontaneity, [and] numbing repetition" had become the focus of "a large-scale effort to decolonize knowledge."[14] While it has been twenty-five years since Pratt's intervention, the text of Euroimperialism that is the focal point of *Imperial Eyes* has shown itself to be more resilient than imagined, and the task of dismantling it more complex than expected. Pratt's departure point for her study is the juncture where this intimate relationship between text and materiality intensified: the publication of Carl Linné's *System Naturae* in 1735, a text that outlines "a classificatory system designed to categorize all plant forms on the planet known or unknown to Europeans" (16), and early examples of internationally supported scientific explorations of continental interiors (such as the La Condamine expedition in 1735). Described by Pratt as a "new version" of "planetary consciousness," she argues that Europe became oriented "toward interior exploration and the construction of global-scale meaning through the descriptive apparatuses of natural history" (15). Common to both these events in the eighteenth century is the production of a multitude of texts that documented this interior exploration, including "[o]ral texts, written texts, lost texts, secret texts, texts appropriated, abridged, translated, anthologized, and plagiarized; letters, reports, survival tales, civic description, navigational narrative, monsters, and marvels, medicinal treatises, academic polemics, old myths replayed and reversed" (23). Not only did this deluge of texts signal a shift away from writing about the natural world as a secondary or marginal aspect of travel, but also, as Pratt contends, "[w]ith the founding of the global classificatory project [...] the observing and cataloguing of nature itself became narratable. It could constitute a sequence of events, or even produce a plot" (27–28). Pratt demonstrates the role of Euroimperialism in producing interior exploration and the manner in which writing about natural history in related travel accounts transforms our relationship to the nonhuman.

Placing nature at the center of narratives of travel from the mid-seventeenth century onward played an important role in shaping the materiality of the environments about which they were written. Pratt's account of this period and its long-term impact on the environment are clear in this regard; she argues that natural history, as it is articulated within travel writing, not only frames our way of looking at the nonhuman, it is also "more directly transformative" of its ontological status: "It extracts all the things of the world and redeploys them into a new knowledge formation whose value lies precisely in its difference from the chaotic original. Here the naming, the representing, and the claiming are all one, the naming *brings the reality of order* into being" (33, emphasis added). Pointing out that Foucault's analysis of natural history in *The Order of Things* stops short of underscoring natural history's "transformative and appropriative dimensions," Pratt emphasizes how European naturalists extracted specimens and resources from their place of origin, gave them new names, and then circulated them within a new so-called universal system of meaning. Referring to this as a practice of "global resemaniticizing," Pratt stresses how "[n]atural history extracted specimens not only from their organic or ecological relationships with each other, but also from their places in other people's economies, history, social and symbolic systems" (31). This effectively renarrativized nature and disrupted already "*existing networks* of historical and material relations among people, plants and animals wherever it applied itself" (32, emphasis added). The implications of such all-encompassing claims about how Euroimperialism transformed the more-than-human and substituted for ways in which the earth was *previously* endowed with stories (though significantly, without the same planetary ambitions), is worth considering here (and I will return to this later in my discussion of Roy's "Walking with the Comrades").

Picking up on Pratt's notion of the "seeing man [...] whose imperial eyes passively look out at and possess" the landscape (7), David Arnold explains how *Imperial Eyes* "has effectively combined the Foucauldian paradigm of power/knowledge with imperial themes of travel and landscape, nature, art, and material and institutional form."[15] Arnold builds on Pratt's reference to Foucauldian notions of power/knowledge in relation to travel and the idea of the gaze as a form of surveillance as well as a tool for ordering in science, and coins the concept of "the traveling gaze" to describe how the traveler's way of looking both frames and imposes itself on the landscape with the idea of possessing and reforming it to his/her desires (28). Unlike the gaze associated with reforming the prisoner in Foucault's panopticon, however, Arnold understands "the traveling gaze" as mobile, and capable of challenging previous understandings of landscape and nature as an "objective fact" rather than "a social construction" (29). Thus Arnold's concept of "the traveling gaze" not only refers to "the process by which much of the observation and hence understanding of India was conducted through travel," but also the relationship this had to the appropriation and subordination of the Indian landscape to ideas of colonial "improvement" (27).

A more extensive understanding of the "directly transformative" relationship between travel writing and the environment (or what Oppermann refers to as the "narrative agency"[16] of texts) is something that Erik Mueggler has explored in his engagement with the archive of early twentieth-century colonial plant hunters in the Tibet/China border region. Mueggler's, *The Paper Road*, examines the social relations between British plant collectors, members of their local expedition teams, and what he describes as "the river of specimens, notes, diaries, letters, photographs, ritual texts, manuscripts, articles, and books that flowed from these collaborations."[17] This archive makes visible how "the body mediates between reading the book of the earth and writing it," and supports an understanding of landscape "as a social process of layering the earth with paper" (16). Playing on the image of plant hunters collecting botanical specimens in the field and pressing them between sheets of paper, Mueggler describes how "wandering botanists put the earth onto or between sheets of paper: collecting, writing, and photographing" (16), and adopts a material ecocritical approach to explain how this reshaped ideas of landscape and the environment.

The social relations that Mueggler identifies as critical to the production of landscape in the archive he is studying are both British and Chinese, but also human and nonhuman. His account of a "dialog" among these different constituents further illustrates the entanglement of "human semiotic processes, knowledge practices, and the very material world itself" in travel writing and its related archive.[18] In telling the story of a twenty-six-year conversation (1906–1932) between George Forrest and Zhao Chengzhang (his Chinese "assistant"), for example, Mueggler patiently unfolds how the historical archive of maps, letters, journals, photographs, and specimens (now largely housed in the Royal Botanic Garden Edinburgh and the Royal Botanic Gardens, Kew) are the product of an exchange of knowledge and different experiences of the landscape. Mueggler's focus on the autonomy and agency of the earth offers an understanding of human and nonhuman history as the result of a social relation. He also underscores that writing and texts are "among the accretions"[19] that have shaped the earth and the concept of landscape. "To think about the archival quality of a landscape," he explains, "is to reject the dogmatic version of representation: the world over there, images of the world over here, perceptions[,] the troubled link between" (16). Instead, Mueggler's project unearths a much more complicated and lively interrelation between text and matter, making visible not only how land becomes entangled with the project of colonial botanical exploration and its archive of written texts, but also the agency of the nonhuman in resisting that process.

Almost two hundred years separates the journey of Zhao and Forrest and those early examples of European interior exploration that Pratt reflects on in *Imperial Eyes*, but the relationality of text and earth, human and nonhuman, Europe and its Others, persists here. Also consistent between these two periods in history is the uneven quality of power relations that informed the colonial project and how this shaped the dialogue between these different participants. Interactions in the "contact zone" of colonialism, Pratt reminds us, usually involve "conditions of coercion, radical inequality, and intractable conflict" (6). Mueggler's account of Forrest's collaborations with Zhao, for example, establishes that the botanical insights Forrest gained into the Tibet/China border region involved a high level of unacknowledged "borrowings" (14), and the mutual transformation of the non-European and the colonial subjects begins to come into focus. As Paul Carter explains in his landmark work in this area, *The Road to Botany Bay: An Exploration of Landscape and History*, the historical significance of

> explorers' journals and the settlers' diaries, does not reside in any stylistic illusion of picturesque completeness [...] Quite the contrary, it is their open-endedness, their lack of finish, even their search for words, which is characteristic: for it is here, where forms and conventions break down, that we can discern the process of transforming space into place.[20]

In "Walking with the Comrades," Arundhati Roy begins her account of traveling with Maoist rebels in Central India with a healthy postcolonial suspicion of the claim that the landscape she is entering has ever been a *tabula rasa* or shaped by the culture of imperialism alone. Instead, she adopts an open-ended attitude to following her local guides down unfamiliar pathways, plays with language and vision, and actively acknowledges the "borrowings" her travel account involves. The slow methodical pace of their walking throughout her travel narrative slows down her observations, and allows her "body, hands and eyes" to move, as Mueggler suggests of his colonial explorers, "along lines etched in the earth and inscribed on paper."[21] With a focus on the archival quality of the Dandakaranya landscape, Roy's travel writing subverts the genre's reliance on an authoritative voice and instead offers a view of the landscape as charged with a joint human and nonhuman agency. Roy bends her way of walking, looking, and writing about the forests of Central India to accommodate "other ways of building social relations with the earth and its inhuman inhabitants" (18).

Postcolonial Travel Writing and the Environment

Roy's "Walking with the Comrades" might not be the most obvious example of postcolonial travel writing concerned with the environment, but it does conform to the basic qualities of a (eco)travel narrative while consciously "tweaking" colonial conventions in ways that reject self/Other binaries that extend to human and nonhuman concerns. Roy's essay first appeared in the March 29, 2010 issue of the Indian newsmagazine, *Outlook*, and was then anthologized a year later with two other related essays under the title *Broken Republic*.[22] The essay's central focus is on the activities of the Maoist-oriented People's Liberation Guerrilla Army (PLGA) in the Dandakaranya forests in response to what is popularly known as the Indian government's "Operation Green Hunt," a reference to the escalation of the state's military presence in the region since 2009 that many reports suggest is associated with an illegal use of force and human rights abuses against local adivasi communities. But "Walking with the Comrades" is also equally a travel account, where, as the title suggests, Roy shares her impressions of the weeks she spent traveling on foot through the heavily forested and highly contested region with the PLGA, gaining first-hand insight into their social, environmental, economic, political, and cultural concerns.

As the book's jacket summarizes, "[i]n *Walking with the Comrades*, Arundhati Roy chronicles the weeks she spent living with the forest guerrillas resisting [government] assaults, taking us to the front lines of a conflict over whether global capitalism will tolerate any societies existing outside of its colossal control."[23] The Dandakaranya forest region, as Roy portrays it, is a world where normal assumptions are "upside-down" and "inside-out" (38), a place where the Indian state and its representatives act in illegitimate ways, and where the guerrillas are considered the strongest allies of not only the local communities but also the forest itself. Roy's essay substantiates this inverted view of the relationship between the government and rebel forces by temporarily suspending the account of her trip into the forest to first provide a history of "tribal people's" resistance to the colonial and postcolonial state's claims to adivasi land and natural resources, and efforts to displace them from territories where they have longstanding ancestral lineages. As Roy explains, the Indian Constitution reinscribed the colonial policy of placing tribal homelands under the custodianship of the state, denied the tribals' traditional right to forest resources (and criminalized those who challenged this), and simultaneously undermined the community's dignity and livelihood (43). Roy's portrayal of the way in which the rights of tribal communities have been marginalized by the Indian state has much in common with her representation of the government's displacement of adivasi and Dalit communities in areas flooded by megadam projects in her earlier, well-known essay "The Greater Common Good."[24] The forced removal of adivasi communities from ancestral lands in the interest of the "greater common good" seems a common point of comparison in both contexts.

Roy emphasizes how large infrastructure projects like megadams have physically displaced the tribals as well as transformed the landscape. Analyzing the rhetorical strategies Roy deploys in her critique of the alliance between corporate and government agendas in India and its effects on adivasi and

Dalit groups, Nixon explains that "[i]f the idea of the modern nation-state is sustained by producing imagined communities, it also involves actively producing unimagined communities."[25] "Assaults on a nation's environmental resources," Nixon points out, "frequently entail not just the physical displacement of local communities, but their imaginative displacement as well, indeed on prior rhetorical and visual evacuation of those communities from the idea of the developing nation-state" (150). Roy's travel narrative counters this erasure of the adivasi community by the Indian state through a first-person account of her experience of "walking with the comrades" in the Dandakaranya forest, following counterintuitive pathways, learning new ways of looking, and reflecting on how her perspective is shaped by unexpected encounters with human and nonhuman companions along the way.

As Richard Kerridge has pointed out, both travel writing and nature writing share a similar colonial trope where "the traveler as heroic venturer" seeks out an "encounter with the exciting Other," "only [for the narrative] to edge its way around the opportunity and bring the traveller home, unscathed, unchanged."[26] Rather than rehearse what Kerridge refers to as this "trope of late-Romantic doubt" – "confrontation, climax, and recoil" – Roy's account of her experience of "walking with the comrades" revises the view of the PLGA as an unjustified armed response to state-sponsored military action. From the outset of the journey, Roy describes her PLGA contact in comic and disarming, rather than threatening or violent, terms, and proceeds to immerse herself in the company of the Other rather than look away and move on. In other words, Roy embraces rather than recoils from "the porousness of the self" (171) and engages with the members of the PLGA in an ongoing conversation that makes up the bulk of her narrative.

Where many of the media reports and government statements that demonize the PLGA refer to the region as a "jungle," and sometimes flippantly as "Pakistan" (51), Roy describes the landscape in Dandakaranya as a "forest," and in largely pastoral and inviting terms. Roy's preference for the word "forest" differs from early nineteenth-century travelers in India, who used the term "jungle" to refer to a wide variety of landscapes in India to convey significant connotations of backwardness and decay. As Arnold explains, "[t]he evidence of India's ruination lay not in deserted palaces and crumbling mausoleums; it was also inscribed in nature. Of all the many terms used by traveler and topographer to describe Indian terrain [...] none was more expressive than the word 'jungle.'"[27] Though the term "jungle" was frequently used in colonial travel writing about India, it was often applied to landscapes in what Arnold describes as "a bewildering variety of ways" (80). Arnold elaborates: "[t]here were 'wet' jungles as well as 'dry' ones, jungles of grass, thorn-shrub, and bamboo, 'low' jungles as well as 'tree jungles'" (80). What was consistent about all these different uses of the term jungle, however, was that it was usually invoked to suggest the primitive, disordered, decaying, diseased, and wild quality of a landscape, thus rendering it ripe for the "improvement" by the traveling gaze of colonial powers.

Roy's account of her travel with the PLGA reverses the relationship between the modern state and the natural world in Dandakaranya, setting up a contrast between the barbarous violence of the Indian police and military forces on the one hand, and the natural beauty of the forest (rather than "the jungle") and the mundane status of the PLGA members on the other. On the first day of her journey to meet the PLGA, for example, as she leaves the motorbike that has brought her to the edge of the forest and embarks on foot with her guide to their rendezvous point, she notes, "It was a beautiful day. The forest floor was a carpet of gold" (51). While Roy repeatedly offers loving descriptions of the natural world throughout her account of walking with the PLGA, it is far from "a stylistic illusion of picturesque completeness"[28] characteristic of colonial accounts of travel. Instead, Roy's narrative is alive to its spatial quality describing how, as she follows Mangtu across the riverbed to a zone that she has been told the police view as PLGA-controlled territory, she recalls that this is also the location where, as the police commissioner has previously told her, they "shoot to kill" (52). As she imagines herself and her guide "in a policeman's rifle-sights" (52), instead of pausing and retreating, "encountering otherness while avoiding its most disconcerting demands,"[29] Roy observes, "[b]ut Mangtu seemed quite unconcerned, and I took my cue from him" (52). Here as elsewhere the detached, faceless snipers of the Indian state are contrasted with the friendly and idiosyncratic members of the PLGA.

The inverted moral relationship between the state and the guerrillas is intensified when, after crossing the river that marks the border of the PLGA-controlled region, Roy switches the narration of her experience walking in the forest from past to present tense, and maintains this throughout the remainder of the essay. The transition to the present tense from this point onward in the essay gives the account of her sojourn in the Dandakaranya forest immediacy, positioning the reader alongside her on the trail. Like the archives associated with the spatial histories described by Carter and Mueggler above, Roy's in-time and on-the-spot account of her experiences reflects an "open-endedness" and "lack of finish," allowing the reader to witness "where [narrative] forms and conventions break down" and "discern the process of transforming space into place."[30] Roy's description of following Chandu through the forest is characterized by an awareness of her limited vision and heightened attention to isolated details. As the sun sets and Chandu continues to lead into the forest, Roy observes that he seems to be able to see in the dark. I have to use my torch. The crickets start up and soon there's an orchestra, a dome of sound over us. I long to look up at the night sky, but I dare not. I have to keep my eyes on the ground. One step at a time. Concentrate.

I hear dogs. But I can't tell how far away they are. The terrain flattens out. I steal a look at the sky. It makes me ecstatic. I hope we're going to stop soon. 'Soon' Chandu says. It turns out to be more than an hour. I see silhouettes of enormous trees. We arrive. (52–53)

I quote this passage at length because it exemplifies much of Roy's essay; she is conscious that her vision is constrained and her sense of time and space is unsettled. Despite this, Roy is pleasantly disoriented, conscious of the sound of animals and insects, and describes herself as "ecstatic" when finally she is able to catch a glimpse of the sky. The sense that she has entered a somewhat pastoral landscape is reinforced by her description of sounds as she drifts off to sleep: "I can hear cowbells, snuffling, shuffling, cattle-farting. All's well in the world. My eyes close" (53). Roy's depictions of scenes of local harmony recall colonial accounts of travel in India that frequently contrasted the experience of passing through "dangerous 'jungles'" with arrival in locations where they found "pleasing 'topes' of mango (and sometimes tamarinds) that had been planted to provide travelers with shade and villagers with fruit."[31] "Unlike the jungles, hurried through as quickly as possible," Arnold explains, "these were designated as 'groves' or even 'orchards,' and welcomed as pleasant spots at which to breakfast or camp" (81). Roy's picturesque rendering of her surroundings, Chandu's gentle demeanor, and the tribal community's harmonious way of life are, however, undercut by jarring images of menace and violence. When Roy and Chandu pause for a nap in a local "gazebo," Roy remarks on its "spare beauty," but also reports how her eye is drawn to a "stack of flattened, empty, corrugated cardboard boxes" that had previously contained high-powered explosives (54). These and other examples of Roy's contradictory observations about the human and nonhuman world she encounters during her time in the forest suggest that, though she is in awe of the natural beauty of the Dandakaranya forest and the PLGA's social and cultural values, she is equally aware that they are in an armed conflict with the Indian state and its corporate partners and that she is traveling in a war zone. Rather than flee, however, she "doubles down," describing how she further integrates herself into the ranks of her group, adopts their practice of "numbering off" like the rest of the comrades with whom she travels, and empathizes with their armed resistance in the face of the Indian state's refusal to acknowledge the tribals' alternative mode of belonging in the forest.

Other examples of Roy offering a seemingly benign rustic setting that is quickly shown to be laced with hints of violence to come (effectively

Image 1 "Sleeping Comrade" *Walking with the Comrades*, 41, photo credit Sanjay Kak 2010.

distancing her travel account from the colonial discourse of the picturesque), can be seen in the various photos that accompany the essay. In the first in a series of photographs scattered throughout the essay, Roy juxtaposes a pastoral image of the forest with a snapshot of "Sleeping Comrade," resting barefoot on a spare setting, but wearing a combat vest and rifle poised within reach [Image 1] Equally unnerving is the image of Roy's assigned companion, comrade Kamla, "show[ing] off" the fertile Janatana Sarkar fields with an arresting smile and a rifle casually draped over her shoulder (77). [Image 2].

Elsewhere Roy describes "girls and boys. In their teens and early twenties" who are "dressed in saris and lungis, some in frayed olive green fatigues" while "[e]very one of them has a muzzle loading rifle" (56). Typical of the way Roy portrays PLGA supporters, she describes the group as "full of fun and curiosity," and remarks how they "giggle" when explaining how "a crude mortar fashioned out of a heavy three-foot galvanized pipe [...] makes a big noise" that "scares the police" (56). [Image 3] More than just ruffling the smooth operation of the traveling gaze, Roy's image of the somewhat innocent gun-toting "young people," offers a troubling multigenerational spectacle of how the everyday lives of the tribals have been militarized in response to Operation Green Hunt, and keeps the reader on edge (56). The counter-pastoral aesthetic performed by the text and images in Roy's essay is typical of the deeply fraught "material act of ecological recuperation" found in postcolonial narratives where the "histories of colonialism have displaced and alienated people from the land."[32] Though Roy's account of her time traveling with the PLGA suggests the adivasi community lives in a more relational and sustainable

Image 2 "Comrade Kamla Shows Off Janatana Sarkar Fields" *Walking with the Comrades*, 77,
photo credit Sanjay Kak 2010.

Image 3 "Village Militia" *Walking with the Comrades,* photo credit Sanjay Kak 2010.

fashion with their environment, "Walking with the Comrades" is equally
concerned with "the legacies of violent material, environmental, and cultural
transformation" (5) that have resulted in the community's isolation and the
decline of the Dandakaranya forest. Both aspects of the narrative further
reinforce the "upside-down" and "inside-out" quality of the tribal community's relationship to mainstream Indian society (38, 49).

In addition, Roy's narrative is conscious of the way the nonhuman environment shapes her experience of "walking with the comrades." Midway through Roy's account, she offers a brief reflection on how the identity of the forest has been reinscribed over time. "Dandakaranya," Roy tells her readers, "is part of what the British, in their White Man's way, called Gondwana, land of the Gonds." (68). Despite the state's colonial and postcolonial history of neatly compartmentalizing the landscape for administrative and political advantage, the image "Walking with the Comrades" offers of Dandakaranya and the tribal community's relationship to the land is more complex and relational. Roy's description of the history of the region and her experience moving through the forest with the PLGA suggests that the identity and agency of the tribal community is defined outside of binary understandings of the human and nonhuman and in response to state repression, and instead expresses a fluid and social relationship with the land. Unlike colonial accounts of travel that erase the agency of the indigenous communities, animals, insects, rivers, mountains, and forests in depictions of landscape, Roy's travel account works to make these social relations with the land visible, and remains open to unfamiliar modes of living in its account of her journey.

Building on an earlier reference to her ecstatic glance at the stars on the first night of her journey, Roy comments how the location of the PLGA camp on her second night of the journey provides her with "the most beautiful room [...] My private suite in a thousand-star hotel" (57). Roy plays on the language of tourism, here, satirizing the culture of consumption that underpins contemporary travel and then redirects her experience of the natural world while walking with the PLGA in more serious directions. Reworking her earlier reference to the "star spangled banner" in the context of the PLGA's activities, Roy suggests a more authentic notion of liberty is at stake for the adivasi community and the Dandakaranya forest. When she later discovers a group of "ten kids" who are part of the "Young Communists Mobile school" has joined the camp, she observes that "they trail the PLGA with stars in their eyes, like groupies of a rock band" (88–89). The conflation of the extraterrestrial and terrestrial blurs the relationship between the social, political, cultural, human, and nonhuman influences that shape the Dandakaranya forest, and the military confrontation between the Indian government and the PLGA.

Although travel writing might be understood as a colonial genre emerging out of European ways of seeing, it is also a rich resource for postcolonial writers like Roy who seek to question binary representations of nature and culture and the literary and the material, as well as make visible the entanglement of empire and the environment in the history of imperialism. Roy's "Walking with the Comrades" rejects the stance of the "heroic adventurer"

Walk This Way

in favor of a fluid and self-reflexive mode of representing her experience that questions taken for granted views of the environment and highlights the social relation between the traveler and the landscape. Her account of traveling with Maoist rebels in the Dandakaranya forest calls for a revision of colonial ways of seeing the Other – both human and nonhuman – and anticipates and agitates for more equitable and sustainable relations with the Indian state, as well as the earth.

NOTES

1 Alfred W. Crosby, *Ecological Imperialism: The Biological Expansion of Europe, 900–1900* (Cambridge: Cambridge University Press, 1986); John M. MacKenzie, *The Empire of Nature: Hunting, Conservation and British Imperialism* (Manchester: Manchester University Press, 1997); and Grove Richard, *Green Imperialism: Colonial Expansion, Tropical Island Edens and the Origins of Environmentalism, 1600–1860* (Cambridge: Cambridge University Press, 1995).

2 Grove, *Green Imperialism*, 5, 23–24.

3 See for example: Helen Tiffin, *Five Emus to the King of Siam: Environment and Empire* (Amsterdam: Rodopi, 2007); Graham Huggan and Helen Tiffin, *Postcolonial Ecocriticism: Literature, Animals, Environment* (New York: Routledge, 2010); Rob Nixon, *Slow Violence and the Environmentalism of the Poor* (Cambridge: Harvard University Press, 2011); Elizabeth DeLoughrey and George Handley, *Postcolonial Ecologies: Literatures of the Environment* (New York: Oxford University Press, 2011); Elizabeth DeLoughrey, Jill Didur, and Anthony Carrigan, *Global Ecologies and the Environmental Humanities: Postcolonial Approaches* (New York: Routledge, 2015); Jill Didur, "Strange Joy: Plant-Hunting and Responsibility in Jamaica Kincaid's (Post)colonial Travel Writing," *Interventions: International Journal of Postcolonial Studies*, 13, no. 2 (2011): 236–55.

4 David Arnold, "Narrativizing Nature: India, Empire and the Environment," in *Global Ecologies*, ed. DeLoughrey, Didur and Carrigan, 35–50 (42).

5 Graham Huggan, *Extreme Pursuits: Travel/Writing in an Age of Globalization* (Ann Arbor: University of Michigan Press, 2009), 54.

6 For a fuller account of this dynamic in ecocritical scholarship, see Susie O'Brien, "'Back to the World': Reading Ecocriticism in a Postcolonial Context," in *Five Emus to the King of Siam: Environment and Empire*, ed. Helen Tiffin (Amsterdam: Rodopi Press, 2007), 177–200.

7 Rob Nixon, "Environmentalism and Postcolonialism," in *Postcolonial Studies and Beyond*, ed. Ania Loomba and Suvir Kaul (Durham: Duke University Press, 2005), 233–51 (246). See DeLoughrey, Didur, and Carrigan, "A Postcolonial Environmental Humanities," in *Global Ecologies and the Environmental Humanities*, where we argue that environmental concerns have been foundational to the early work by postcolonial writers and scholars (including Glissant, Said, Saro-Wiwa, Plumwood, and Spivak), and evident in their attention to the othering of indigenous, gendered, raced, queer subjects, and the nonhuman within the colonial context.

8 Dipesh Chakrabarty, "The Climate of History: Four Theses," *Critical Inquiry*, 35 (2009): 197–227 (204, 207).

47

9 DeLoughrey, Didur, and Carrigan, "A Postcolonial Environmental Humanities," in *Global Ecologies and the Environmental Humanities*, 1–32 (5).

10 The term "adivasi" refers to ethnic and tribal groups considered to be indigenous to South Asia.

11 Sonja Frenzel and Birgit Neumann, "Introduction: Literary Environments, Ecocritical Theories and Ethics in Anglophone Literatures," *Literary Environments: Ecocritical Theories and Ethics in Anglophone Literatures*, Special Issue of *anglistik & englischunterricht* 84 (forthcoming 2017): 1–19.

12 Serpil Oppermann, "From Ecological Postmodernism to Material Ecocriticism: Creative Materiality and Narrative Agency," in *Material Ecocriticism*, ed. Serenella Iovino and Serpil Oppermann (Bloomington: Indiana University Press, 2014), 2–36 (28).

13 For an analysis of how indigenous storytelling offers alternative ways of knowing the land and that challenge the transparency of legal and scientific discourse informed by Enlightenment philosophy and the anthropocentrism of settler culture, see J. Edward Chamberlin, *If This Is Your Land, Where Are Your Stories?: Finding Common Ground* (Toronto: Vintage Canada, 2004).

14 Mary Louise Pratt, *Imperial Eyes: Travel Writing and Transculturation* (London: Routledge, 1992), 2.

15 David Arnold, *The Tropics and the Traveling Gaze: India, Landscape, and Science, 1800–1856* (Seattle: University of Washington Press, 2011), 9.

16 Oppermann, "From Ecological Postmodernism," 28.

17 Erik Mueggler, *The Paper Road: Archive and Experience in the Botanical Exploration of West China and Tibet* (Berkeley: University of California Press, 2011), 17.

18 Oppermann, "From Ecological Postmodernism," 10, 30.

19 Mueggler, *Paper Road*, 16.

20 Paul Carter, *The Road to Botany Bay: An Exploration of Landscape and History* (Minneapolis: University of Minnesota Press, 2010), xxii–xxiii.

21 Mueggler, *Paper Road*, 17.

22 A paperback version of the collection was subsequently released under the title *Walking with the Comrades*.

23 Arundhati Roy, *Walking with the Comrades* (New York: Penguin, 2011). Further intext page references are to this text.

24 Arundhati Roy, "The Greater Common Good," in *The Cost of Living* (New York: Modern Library, 1999).

25 Nixon, *Slow Violence*, 150.

26 Richard Kerridge, "Ecologies of Desire: Travel Writing and Nature and Nature Writing as Travelogue," in *Travel Writing and Empire: Postcolonial Theory in Transit*, ed. Steve Clark. (London: Zed Books, 1999), 164–82 (165, 166).

27 Arnold, *Tropics and the Traveling Gaze*, 80.

28 Carter, *Road to Botany Bay*, xxii.

29 Kerridge, "Ecologies of Desire," 172.

30 Carter, *Road to Botany Bay*, xiii.

31 Arnold, *Tropics and the Traveling Gaze*, 81.

32 DeLoughrey, Didur and Carrigan, "Postcolonial Environmental Humanities," 5.

4

ROBERT CLARKE

History, Memory, and Trauma in Postcolonial Travel Writing

The Persistence of the Past

The postcolonial always involves an encounter with the past, and that encounter is perhaps nowhere more compelling than in travel writing. At stake in this encounter is the question of how the past inheres within the present, and how, in travel writing, the traveler, travelee, and reader are affected by and implicated in the persistence of the past. At its worst, postcolonial travel writing exploits nostalgic and sentimental versions of the past that legitimize the history of colonialism and reinforce social divisions that underlie the contemporary global order. Yet at its best, postcolonial travel writing bears witness to the enduring legacies of the past in ways that trouble contemporary certainties, and it performs the valuable political and moral work of reckoning with the past in the name of a just future.

In any travel narrative, time is a complicated feature of the journey as well as of the storytelling. There is the time of the journey, the time of the telling, and the inevitable lag between event and narration, mediated through processes of editing. There is also the time of reading, which influences how historical moments and agents are judged. There are the histories and collective memories of the places and peoples visited, and the way these are invoked, resisted, mourned, and forgotten. In addition, there are the personal memories of the traveler, most notable in narratives of return – when, say, a traveler returns to a home country or city after an absence – as well as those journeys in which the encounter with exotic places and people provides a context for the travelers' engagement with their personal past. All of this is to say that in postcolonial travel writing time takes on special significance for the way multiple temporal domains impinge upon the narration and reception of a given piece. Each factor influences our understanding of a travel text as a "window onto the past," as well as the historicity of the text: that is, how it constructs places and people as subjects *in* and *to* history.

Postcolonial travel writing addresses journeys undertaken in the aftermaths of colonialism; journeys through cultures and social landscapes that are in a sense post-traumatic. In the face of people and societies attempting to craft a renewed and positive transformation of the body politic, travelers also bear witness to, and are often complicit with, forces and processes that perpetuate colonial and neocolonial oppressions in the face of direct and clandestine resistance. Travelers are inevitably caught up in a consumerist culture that exploits the exotic aura of the past. This has been witnessed in recent years by, among other things, the rise of so-called dark tourism. Dark tourist sites are examples of how history and memory may be appropriated within travel discourse in ways that forestall the proper reckoning of the colonial past. Yet, at its best postcolonial travel writing reminds the reader of the inadequacy of reductive notions of the past: that the past was never simply colonial; that the present is not overdetermined by the logic of late capitalism and consumerism. The openness of time – the reinterpretability of the past, the refashioning of narratives for the future – provides a means of working through the traumas of colonialism.

Making/Selling Colonial History

For readers, as much as for critics, of colonial travel writing, imperial travelers and their texts can easily be (mis)taken for agents of history. Postcolonial critics of travel writing constantly question the nature of such agency and the discourse of history that it serves. Moreover, postcolonial travel writing betrays – and is in a sense defined by – an ambivalence about history: history as a source of truths and untruths; history as a source of inspiration as well as anxiety. History can be a motivator for postcolonial journeys. Yet, equally, history can provide a veneer of exoticism, encouraging a seductive form of nostalgia that buries the truth of the past, as it defines the value of spaces, cultures, and experiences as travel commodities.

It could be said that many colonial and imperial travelers helped to "make" history; others might properly be understood as onlookers. And while many European travel texts reflect the nexus between power and knowledge that characterizes colonial discourses, there is a substantial body of work that serves as witness to the excesses of European imperialism and questions the moral, political, and legal legitimacy of the expropriation of territory, and the impoverishment, enslavement, and extermination of indigenous populations. These include narratives as diverse as those of the sixteenth-century Spanish Dominican friar Batholomé de las Casas, and those of freed or escaped eighteenth-century African slaves such as Ouladah Equiano and Venture Smith, as well as the work of abolitionists like

Alexander Falconbridge.[1] In their anticolonial sentiments, these texts are precursors of postcolonial travel writing whereby a journey narrative is explicitly yoked to a critique or condemnation of imperial practices. Flora Tristan and Maria Calcott Graham in their early nineteenth-century Latin American travelogues;[2] Roger Casement in his inquiries into colonial excesses in the Congo and the Putumayo;[3] and George Orwell in his account of his experiences as a colonial officer in Burma:[4] each of these travelers provides material that scrutinizes the colonial order in a specific context in the nineteenth and twentieth centuries. We can also include here the accounts of visits to the imperial and metropolitan centers by figures like Ham Mukasa, Mohandas K. Gandhi, Rabindranath Tagore, and Bernard Dadier.[5] Such travelers and their accounts represent the way colonial travel writing could be deployed to criticize Europe's intrusions and even promote efforts for reform.

Yet, colonial and imperial travelers did not simply record history – in either a pro- or anticolonial vein. They also helped to fashion historical sensibilities. Through their particular ways of seeing, and the rhetoric they employed to translate such visions into words,[6] colonial travelers naturalized a set of relationships between the colonized and colonizer, space and time, that, among other things, shaped the European institution of "History." Indeed, the nexus of colonialism and history raises challenges for postcolonial travelers as much as for critics. As Bill Ashcroft, Gareth Griffiths, and Helen Tiffin write, "the emergence of history in European thought is coterminous with the rise of modern colonialism, which in its radical othering and violent annexation of the non-European world, found in history a prominent, if not *the* prominent, instrument for the control of subject peoples."[7] History is founded on a set of myths: "the myth of a value free, 'scientific' view of the past, the myth of the beauty of order, the myth of the story of history as a simple representation of the continuity of events" (317). Such myths "authorized nothing less than the construction of world reality" (317). For the postcolonial writer, then, the conventions of travel writing reflect the manner in which an imperial European historical vision has been yoked, so to speak, to modes of narrativity (318). As David Spurr argues, "colonial travel discourse played a central role in affirming colonialism."[8] The risk for postcolonial travelers, especially those who follow the familiar conventions of European travel narrative, is that explorations of the past can become affirmations of the moral and political legitimacy of the colonial past and apologies for the colonial present.

Colonial discourse creates a sense of past-ness that is particularly fraught for postcolonial writers. Take, for example, the kinds of narratives that feature United Kingdom or North American travelers exploring the vestiges of the British colonial world: journeys that examine the fates of imperial metropolises as in Geoffrey Moorhouse's *Calcutta* (1971), William Dalrymple's *City of Djinns* (1994), or Jan Morris's *Hong Kong: An Epilogue to Empire* (1988). Insofar as they seek out the past "glories" of Empire and enviable privileges afforded colonizers, they flirt with what Renato Rosaldo terms *imperialist nostalgia*, whereby the past is romanticized and sentimentalized, and consequently "racial domination appears innocent and pure."[9] This sense of nostalgia, in travel writing at least, gains momentum through the modern traveler's sense of belatedness[10] and their awareness that travel is in some ways implicated in the destruction of the past. For Rosaldo, imperialist nostalgia involves a metropolitan agent who mourns that which s/he is complicit in destroying. Complementing this sense of loss is "a peculiar sense of mission, the white man's burden, where civilized nations stand duty-bound to uplift so-called savage ones."[11] Imperialist nostalgia – even when it occurs alongside a repudiation of the colonial order – bears with it the vestiges of the cultural logic of nineteenth-century colonialism, namely the civilizing mission.

Geographer Derek Gregory identifies another kind of nostalgia that he refers to as "colonialist nostalgia," a "conspicuously *therapeutic* gesture that fuses two moments into a single constellation."[12] These moments involve "nostalgia *for colonialism itself*, a desire to re-create and recover the world of late Victorian and Edwardian colonialism as a culture of extraordinary confidence and conspicuous opulence" (140), and a colonial claim to knowledge and authority. Gregory contends that travelers have been complicit in the construction of *traditions* associated with particular places and territories, such as Egypt, that are represented as "space[s] of constructed visibility" (115) that conform to and accommodate a set of travel styles and expectations.

As well as telling stories of the past, history is employed in postcolonial travel writing to explain the pathos of the present. Much travel writing to postcolonial cultures is motivated by a desire to encounter the vestiges of the past that can account for the disjunctures between the West and the rest: that explain the underdevelopment of postcolonial societies, and in doing so potentially displace responsibility for the present onto agents located in another era. This can take different forms and it need not be a search for the colonial past *per se*. Nevertheless, despite the specific temporal concerns of the journey, the past of colonialism necessarily impinges on the consciousness of the writer and reader. And it does so because of the disjunctions that arise during a journey: of the clash between the temporalities of class, gender, and race.

History is evident in those works that explicitly engage with colonial spatial tropes such as "the middle passage," "the dark continent," migrancy, and exile. Caryl Phillips's *The Atlantic Sound* is a key text in this respect with its nuanced observations of and encounters with the spaces that came to define the north Atlantic slave trade. Explorations of displacement are key to accounts of the journeys of ordinary migrants from Empire's margins to its centers, like Ferdinand Dennis' *Behind the Frontlines: Journey into Afro-Britain*; or, more frequently, those from the center to the margins, as in Riccardo Orizio's *Lost White Tribes: The End of Privilege and the Last Colonials in Sri Lanka, Jamaica, Brazil, Haiti, Namibia, and Guadeloupe*,[13] or Linda Christmas's *The Ribbon and the Ragged Square: An Australian Journey*. At times flirting with nostalgia and melancholia, these works, quite apart from the hidden or subaltern histories uncovered, provide insights into the polymorphism, evolution, and hybridity of colonial space. They encourage a shift in understanding of colonial space from one that is governed by a Manichean logic of separation, to one that constantly negotiates, and frequently accommodates, difference. This moves toward understanding colonial spaces as "contact zones," "that is, social spaces where disparate cultures meet, clash, and grapple with each other, often in highly asymmetrical relations of domination and subordination."[14]

History is explicitly on display in those works that take as a key theme of their journey particular practices of European colonialism like slavery. Again, Phillips's *The Atlantic Sound* (2000) is a notable text in this regard, as is Ekow Eshun's *Black Gold of the Sun: Searching for Home in Africa and Beyond* (2005), and Saidiya Hartman's *Lose Your Mother: A Journey Across the Atlantic Slave Route* (2007). Often these works foreground the anachronous and disturbing consequences of remembering slavery. A case in point is Phillips's observations of the constructed traditions and rivalries among different African communities – indigenous and diasporic – with regard to the history of slavery and the spaces of its contemporary "touristic" commemoration. Another example is seen in Eshun's discovery that his ancestor was in fact a slave trader. Apart from the manner in which they challenge the production and reception of colonial history, these works deserve to be read in the light of contemporary slave narratives, for example, such as those detailed in books like Laura T. Murphy's *Survivors of Slavery: Modern-Day Slave Narratives* (2014), Mende Nazer and Damien Lewis's *Slave: My True Story* (2002), and Zana Muhsen's *Slave* (1991). The latter texts provide notable deployments of travel narratives even if they do not fit the exclusivist conventions of travel writing (see Chapter 1). Insofar as they direct our attention to modern forms of people trafficking, they resonate with the cultural memory of slavery and Empire, and of the legacy of antislavery movements and contemporary humanitarianism. Moreover, they invite contrapuntal readings of mainstream travel writing by shining a light on the intersection of slavery and those leisure pursuits associated with travel, from construction and fashion, to hospitality and sex work. These texts bear testimony to the history of human trafficking that was at the heart of the European colonial project, and to how such practices persist. In books like these we witness attempts to gain insights into the past that are orthogonal to official Eurocentric perspectives. They also speak to the way memory – personal as much as collective – is employed in postcolonial travel writing as a supplementary and disrupting discourse. Moreover, they teach us something about the nature of travel that has deep ramifications. The conventional European travel book is underpinned by an assumption of the voluntary nature of travel. Yet so much travel in the postcolonial context is involuntary; it takes place under conditions of necessity, reluctance, coercion, and deprivation. In its explorations of the past, postcolonial travel writing necessarily disrupts the Eurocentric fantasy of the liberty of the bourgeois (masculine) ego that colonial travel discourse so often champions.

Landscapes of Memory

As the discussion on nostalgia above suggests, in much postcolonial travel writing memory serves as a supplement to history. Indeed, memory can prove to be a "dangerous supplement," in Derrida's terms, in that it can "[add] only to replace. It intervenes or insinuates itself in-the-place-of; if it fills, it is as if one fills a void."[15] Memory can trouble the "truth" of history, just as much as history may call into question the veracity of memory. Yet putting aside the claims to truth of either memory or history, travel writing is a form of discourse that is valuable not only to understanding what happened, but also how individuals and societies remember the past, and how such remembering is shaped and altered over time.

Leela Gandhi positions the themes of history and memory squarely within the ambit of postcolonial studies. Gandhi suggests that "[t]he emergence of anti-colonial and 'independent' nation-States after colonialism is frequently accompanied by a desire to forget the colonial past," yet this desire to forget can lead to a form of "postcolonial amnesia."[16] Such amnesia may serve the imperatives of renewal and self-invention, but it can also involve the repression of the intimate and potentially complicit relationships between colonizer and colonized. For Gandhi postcolonialism provides "a theoretical resistance to the mystifying amnesia of the colonial aftermath" through an insistence on "revisiting, remembering and, crucially, interrogating the colonial past" (4). The process of returning to the colonial scene discloses a relationship of reciprocal antagonism and desire between colonizer and colonized. And it is in the unfolding of this troubled and troubling relationship that we start to discern the ambivalent prehistory of the postcolonial condition. If postcoloniality is to be reminded of its origins in colonial oppression, it must also be theoretically urged to recollect the compelling seductions of colonial power. The forgotten archive of the colonial encounter narrates multiple stories of contestation and its discomforting other, complicity (4). For Gandhi, postcolonialism calls for an at times painful remembrance and reckoning with the colonial past in all its complexity. For many critics, postcolonial travel writing provides a challenge to and a source of inspiration for the critical work of postcolonialism, particularly its memory work.

In a similar vein, Michael Rothberg notes that, while the disciplines of postcolonial studies and memory studies have developed in parallel since the 1980s without necessarily intercepting or impacting upon one another, "issues related to cultural memory make up some of the core concerns of postcolonial studies."[17] Rothberg notes that "the self-critical reflection of postcolonial studies on its own conditions of possibility, which has always accompanied the development of the field, has concerned above all that field's fundamental relation to the *disjunctive temporality* of colonial legacies – colonialism's ability to colonize not just space, but time as well" (360; italics in original). The appreciation of "disjunctive temporality" is something postcolonial studies shares with memory studies, focused as it is on "the relative weight and 'mixture' of past and present in a temporality beyond any notion of linearity or 'homogenous empty time'" (360). The exploration of "disjunctive temporality" could in fact be applied to much travel writing, indeed travel discourse, as a defining quality of its rhetoric. Violence is the theme that provides a compelling intersection for postcolonial and memory studies. It fascinates many postcolonial travelers as well as critics intrigued by "how violence fundamentally shapes the temporality of modern memory and how regimes of memory help propagate and potentially resist violence through the creation of unexpected solidarities" (361).

The exploration of memories, especially those concerned with violent pasts, for many travelers calls for a particular kind of journey, one that Michael Cronin usefully describes as "vertical" as opposed to "horizontal."[18] Horizontal travel, according to Cronin, reflects the more conventional understanding of travel as a linear progression from place to place, bounded by a fairly limited itinerary. Vertical travel involves temporary dwelling in a location for a period of time where the traveler begins to travel down into the particulars of place either in space (botany, studies of microclimate, exhaustive exploration of local landscape) or in time (local history, archaeology, folklore). As Catherine Mee suggests, these two categories do not necessarily imply a hierarchy of value. Both of them can lead to intense encounters between travelers and others.[19]

We can observe examples of the kinds of memory work pertinent to the postcolonial context outlined by Gandhi and Rothberg, and their intersection with different kinds of traveling – horizontal and vertical – in a range of travel texts from the 1990s on. In recounting the ways in which the past impacts upon the present, travel writers call upon memories: their own as well as those of those they encounter upon their journeys. Michael Jacob's *The Robber of Memories: A River Journey through Colombia* (2012), provides an example of an Anglophone traveler's encounters with a culture's way of remembering and forgetting its turbulent past, in particular its histories of *external* and *internal* colonialisms.[20] This book considers the way the history and memory of imperialism and its aftermath are suppressed and invoked as forces of resistance in Latin America. And it does so by relying on a conventional horizontal journey narrative.

The Robber of Memories presents an at times lyrical account of the author's journey along the River Magdalena in central Colombia. It is a narrative that employs tropes of remembering and forgetting, as the author struggles with his memories of his parents' experiences of dementia. As he sails upriver toward the river's source, Jacobs encounters and interviews ordinary Colombians dealing with the fall-out of the country's recent civil war; a war that the author witnesses firsthand in the mountains near the headwaters of the Magdalena. Jacobs notes too the phenomenon of the disappeared, a word that has entered the idiom of postcolonial nations from Argentina to Northern Ireland to Lebanon; one describing the victims of military and paramilitary squads on both sides of the nations' civil conflicts. Jacobs's book bears witness to the active forgetting on the part of ordinary Colombians as an act of survival in a still bitterly divided community, as well as tactical acts of remembering that ensure that memories of the civil war's victims are not lost.

Jacob Dlamini's *Native Nostalgia* (2009)[21] provides an example of a return narrative and one that draws upon the author's deep and personal engagement with a specific place. In Cronin's term, *Native Nostalgia* may be read as a work of vertical travel. A journalist and historian, Dlamini grew up under the apartheid regime in South Africa. In *Native Nostalgia*, Dlamini is concerned with the way history and memory is being fashioned in the post-apartheid era, particularly by the ruling African National Congress party. Dlamini begins by observing the nostalgia that many black South Africans have for the apartheid years. Employing Svetlana Boym's theories of nostalgia, Dlamini is keen to reappraise nostalgia in contrast to the kind of models assumed by either Rosaldo or Gregory. For Dlamini, nostalgia is not always already "a reactionary sentiment" (17). Following Boym, Dlamini recognizes two varieties of nostalgia: "reflective" and "restorative." The latter, "restorative" nostalgia, attempts a "transhistorical reconstruction of the lost home," whereas the former, "reflective" nostalgia, "dwells on the ambivalences of human longing and belonging and does not shy away from the contradictions of modernity."[22]

Dlamini is keen to throw into question the kind of postcolonial ideology that positions the colonized as essentially victim. He is concerned to reveal aspects of life under the colonial system in ways that deny that such life was overdetermined by colonialism, and in doing so to uncover those elements that gave sustenance to the struggle for social change. Nostalgia, in this sense, is not a repudiation of anticolonialism; it is a mode of respect for how the anticolonial struggle came into being. As such, Dlamini's text demonstrates Michael Walder's point that "[n]ot only is nostalgia deeply implicated in the political life of people, it is a part of their historical sense of themselves."[23] It is unwise to define the postcolonial as simply a state or condition that comes after colonialism. Likewise, Dlamini's book urges us not to assume that the post colonial is reducible to a set of experiences and values assumed by a transhistorical and universal understanding of colonialism. For Dlamini, memory and nostalgia are key to understanding the specificity of colonialism: of how colonialism was enacted and lived in a given place over a given period of time.

Like other cultural media, postcolonial travel writing can enable a conversion of history into heritage. The concept of heritage speaks to how narratives of the past are deployed in the present; and in turn the experience of heritage in the postcolonial context necessarily evokes a sense of dissonance as different groups attempt to use the past to different ends.[24] Australian travel writing of the last thirty years makes a useful case study in this respect. A book like Annie Caulfield's *The Winner's Enclosure* (1999), for example, makes much of the heritage craze in Australia in the late 1990s and how this could be interpreted as a strategy by mainly white settler Australians to shore up their sense of privilege and legitimacy in the face of Aboriginal demands for recognition and justice. On the other hand, works like Barry Hill's *The Rock* (1994), Kim Mahood's *Craft for a Dry Lake* (2000), and Nicholas Jose's *Black Sheep: Journey to Borroloola* (2003) recount journeys to uncover the hidden stories of the colonial national past, including those of interracial intimacy and solidarity, in the name of reconciliation between settler and indigenous communities. Other works that focus more keenly on Aboriginal subjects, like Krim Benterrak, Stephen Muecke, and Paddy Roe's *Reading the Country: Introduction to Nomadology* (1984), Ruby Langford Ginibi's *My Bundjalung People* (1994), and Kim Scott and Hazel Brown's *Kayang and Me* (2005), recover an Aboriginal perspective on Australia's colonial past and the dispossession of its first nation people. In many of these narratives the theme of violence, including the search for sites of massacre and stories of the removal of individuals and communities, is addressed through asymptotic journeys: journeys that detail a traveler's approach – literal and much as metaphorical – to significant sites of cultural memory in which arrival is in some sense always deferred and the impossibility of return foregrounded.[25]

Trauma: Dark Travel and Journeys of Reconciliation

Colonialism and imperialism are violent and traumatizing experiences. Anticolonial movements have also been marked by conflicts, upheavals, and displacements. The histories and memories of such events and their consequences for contemporary populations and cultures are irresistible subjects for many travel writers. Moreover, the way such histories and memories shape so-called dark tourism and dark travel has become an area of great critical concern in literary studies, as well as anthropology and sociology. How such violence and trauma is mediated through the narratives and representations of history and memory is a key concern for the reader of postcolonial travel writing.

Given the structural role of violence in colonialism, and the growth in psychoanalytic perspectives in postcolonial studies, it is not surprising that the aftermath of colonialism has been frequently viewed through the lens of trauma. Postcolonialism, particularly in its modernist-inflected moments, is committed to waking up from the nightmare of history, and that in turn can be a traumatizing experience. Indeed, it could be said that postcolonial studies has in no small way contributed to establishing trauma as the determining affect of our age.[26]

The theme of trauma is most obvious in works that take as their principal focus a particular tragic event or conflict. One example of this is the set of texts that have addressed the Rwandan genocide of the early 1990s. These works represent an archive of memory. They include books by Western eyewitnesses "on the ground," such as Romeo Dallaire's *Shake Hands with the Devil* (2003), James Orbinski's *An Imperfect Offering* (2008), and Feargal Keane's *Season of Blood: A Rwandan Journey* (1996); and narratives by those who entered the conflict zone after the event, such as Philip Gourevitch's *We Wish to Inform You That Tomorrow We Will Be Killed with Our Families* (1998) and Jean Hatzfeld's trilogy *Life Laid Bare: The Survivors in Rwanda Speak* (1994), *Machete Season: The Killers in Rwanda Speak* (2003), and *The Strategy of Antelopes: Living in Rwanda after the Genocide* (2007). Such narratives gain their strength and rhetorical power from the way they respond to firsthand accounts of victims, perpetrators, and other witnesses. They perform the role of mediating secondary and tertiary witnesses to the experiences of Rwandans on both sides of the conflict. They also provide a powerful means by which to draw attention to the actions – or lack thereof – of Western nations and their failures to enforce international laws and humanitarian principles.

Nevertheless, the focus on dark themes in travel and tourism discourse has led to criticism of the voyeuristic postcolonial gaze that commodifies suffering and sells it on to the morally dubious audiences of potential dark tourists. Dark tourism has acquired a great deal of currency in recent social science research. Philip Stone defines dark tourism as "tourist encounters with spaces of death or calamity that have perturbed the public conscious-ness, whereby actual and recreated places of the deceased, horror, atrocity, or depravity, are consumed through visitor experiences."[27] While dark tourism has acquired a deal of interest in social science research,[28] the idea of "dark travel" has been proposed as a more expansive term that pertains to cultural practices and discourse of travel on sites marked by traumatizing, disturbing, and unsettling histories. This broader term allows for the consid-eration of the activities of agents like travel writers whose relation to the industry of tourism can vary greatly, but who are necessarily implicated in debates about the uses of "dark spaces."[29]

In travel writing it would seem that the definition of places as dark – as "shadow zones," "badlands," or "traumascapes"[30] – depends to a large degree on the way the narrator engages with the history and collective memory of the place. For Gourevitch, in *We Wish to Inform You ...*,[31] for example, the Rwandan killing fields are dark spaces for the compara-tively recent events that occurred there. But those events are placed within a longer heritage of violence that stretches back centuries and that in various ways condition how the contemporary stories of these places are told. Traveling to dark spaces necessarily impacts upon travelers' sens-ibilities. Visiting dark places can be empowering but it can also be debilitating. While some like Jacqueline Wilson argue that visiting dark sites can have a powerful pedagogical effect,[32] it is also clear that travel-ing to such places necessarily involves a range of risks: physical, psycho-logical, and moral.

Sarah de Mul is correct when she writes that for many postcolonial travel writers "the colonial experience does not seem to pass, but, instead, insti-gates a compulsion to return."[33] The past frequently returns in postcolonial travel writing, either under the guise of history or collective memory. And while the past, even in its most traumatic form, can be used to gratuitously embellish travel accounts and provide them with an aura of the sensational and exotic, it may also be addressed in ways that look toward a more hopeful future. In the travel narratives of indigenous colonized peoples, for example, one can observe journeys undertaken in the spirit of resistance, resilience, and reconciliation. In such journeys, history and memory are utilized to not only question colonial versions of the past and affirm the identities and sovereignties of indigenous people but also to suggest ways in which postcolonial cultures might progress toward justice. Indeed, in the last thirty years the power of history and memory has been most keenly observed in postcolonizing cultures in relation to the discourse of reconciliation.

An example can be found in what I have termed elsewhere "journeys to Country" in Australian Aboriginal travel narratives.[34] While there are few Aboriginal travel books – understood in the traditional European sense of the term – travel narrative is ubiquitous in Indigenous Australian literature, both oral and written. One observes examples of journeys to Country in many works of Aboriginal life writing. Such journeys often entail an Aboriginal traveler undertaking a trip from their home, usually in an urban environment, toward the country or territory that they understand to be their "Home" Country. Frequently this is a place that they have never visited; yet one that is associated with their families' traditional and ancestral connections. More often than not, it is the site at which their families first encountered colonial intrusion and violence.

Reflecting Bart Moore-Gilbert's observations on the intersections of travel writing and autobiography in postcolonial writing,[35] one observes such journeys in iconic works of Australian Aboriginal literature such as Sally Morgan's *My Place* (1987), Ruby Langford Ginibi's *My Bundjalung People* (1994), and Scott and Brown's *Kayang and Me* (2005). These narratives can become affirmations of the indigenous traveler's sense of identity and survival in the face of colonialism. This sense is made all the more poignant when the traveler approaches places such as massacre sites where atrocities were committed against their ancestors. While such sites are easily appropriated within the melancholic discourses of dark tourism, postcolonial travelers can appropriate the sites as spaces of mourning: spaces in which the past is *re-presenced* as part of a history of colonization to be shared between the indigenous traveler narrator and the implied settler colonial reader. If the encounter with the past in postcolonial travel writing reminds us that the past was never fully colonial, then the journeys of reconciliation exemplify the way travel discourse may be mobilized as a call for justice in the name of a truly decolonized future.

NOTES

1 Batholomé de las Casas, *Brevísima relación de la destrucción de las Indias (A Brief Account of the Destruction of the Indies*, 1542); Ouladah Equiano, *The Interesting Narrative of the Life of Ouladah Equiano, Or Gustavus Vassus, The African* (1789); Venture Smith, *The Narrative of the Life and Adventures of Venture, a Native of Africa: But Resident Above Sixty Years in the United States of America, Related by Himself* (1798); Alexander Falconbridge, *An Account of the Slave Trade on the Coast of Africa* (1788).

2 Flora Tristan, *Peregrinations of a Pariah* (1838); Maria Calcott Graham, *Voyage to Brazil and Journal of a Residence in Chile* (1824). See Mary Louise Pratt, *Imperial Eyes: Travel Writing and Transculturation* 2nd edn. (London: Routledge, [1992] 2008), chapter 7.

3 See Robert M. Burroughs, *Travel Writing and Atrocities: Eyewitness Accounts of Colonialism in the Congo, Angola, and the Putumayo* (London: Routledge, 2011).

4 George Orwell "Shooting an Elephant," *Inside the Whale and Other Essays* (London: Victor Gollancz, [1936] 1940).

5 Ham Mukasa, *Uganda's Katikiro in England: Being the Official Account of His Visit to the Coronation of His Majesty Kind Edward VII* (1904); Rabindrinath Tagore, *Jatri* (1929); Bernard Dadié, *Un Nègre à Paris (An African in Paris)* (1959).

6 See, for example, Simon Ryan, *The Cartographic Eye: How Europeans Saw Australia* (Cambridge: Cambridge University Press, 1996).

7 Bill Ashcroft, Gareth Griffiths, and Helen Tiffin, *The Post-Colonial Studies Reader*, 2nd edn. (London: Routledge, 2006), 317.

8 David Spurr, *The Rhetoric of Empire: Colonial Discourse in Journalism, Travel Writing, and Imperial Administration* (Durham: Duke University Press, 1993), 110.

9 Renato Rosaldo, "Imperialist Nostalgia," *Representations*, 28 (1983): 107–22 (107).

10 For a discussion of this theme in contemporary travel writing, see Patrick Holland and Graham Huggan, *Tourists with Typewriters: Critical Reflections on Contemporary Travel Writing* (Ann Arbor: University of Michigan Press, 1998).

11 Rosaldo, "Imperialist Nostalgia," 108.

12 Derek Gregory, "Colonial Nostalgia and Cultures of Travel: Spaces of Constructed Visibility in Egypt," in *Consuming Tradition, Manufacturing Heritage: Global Norms and Urban Forms in the Age of Tourism*, ed. Nezar Alsayad (London: Routledge, [2001] 2013), 111–51 (140).

13 Also published as, *Lost White Tribes: Journeys Amongst the Forgotten*.

14 Pratt, *Imperial Eyes*, 7.

15 Jacques Derrida, *Of Grammatology*, trans. Gayatri Chakravorty Spivak (Baltimore: Johns Hopkins University Press), 145.

16 Leela Gandhi, *Postcolonial Theory: A Critical Introduction* (St Leonards, NSW: Allen & Unwin, 1998), 4.

17 Michael Rothberg, "Remembering Back: Cultural Memory, Colonial Legacies, and Postcolonial Studies," in *The Oxford Handbook of Postcolonial Studies*, ed. Graham Huggan (Oxford: Oxford University Press, 2013), 359–79 (360).

18 Michael Cronin, *Across the Lines: Travel, Language, Translation* (Cork: Cork University Press, 2000).

19 Catherine Mee, *Interpersonal Encounters in Contemporary Travel Writing: French and Italian Perspectives* (London: Anthem, 2015), 80.

20 Michael Jacobs, *The Robber of Memories: A River Journey through Colombia* (London: Granta, 2012).

21 Jacob Dlamini, *Native Nostalgia* (Auckland Park: Jacana Media, 2009).

22 Svetlana Boym, *The Future of Nostalgia* (New York: Basic Books, 2001).

23 David Walder, *Postcolonial Nostalgias: Writing, Representation and Memory* (New York: Routledge, 2011), 3.

24 J. E. Tunbridge and G. J. Ashworth, *Dissonant Heritage: The Management of the Past as a Resource in Conflict* (Chichester: John Wiley, 1996), 5–6, 20–21.

25 Robert Clarke, *Travel Writing from Black Australia: Utopia, Melancholia, and Aboriginality* (New York: Routledge, 2016), 153–61.

26 Didier Fassin and Richard Rechtman, *The Empire of Trauma: An Inquiry into the Condition of Victimhood* (Princeton: Princeton University Press, 2009).

27 Philip Stone, "Dark Tourism Scholarship: A Critical Review," *International Journal of Culture, Tourism and Hospitality Research*, 7, no. 3 (2013): 307–18 (307).

28 See Anthony Carrigan, "Dark Tourism and Postcolonial Studies: Critical Intersections," *Postcolonial Studies*, 17, no. 3 (2014): 236–50.

29 See Robert Clarke, Jacqueline Dutton, and Anna Johnston, "Shadow Zones: Dark Travel and Postcolonial Cultures," *Postcolonial Studies*, 17, no. 3 (2014): 221–35.

30 For discussion of these terms, see, respectively, Clarke, Dutton, and Johnston, "Shadow Zones"; Ross Gibson, *Seven Versions of an Australian Badland* (St. Lucia: University of Queensland Press, 2002); and Maria Tumarkin, *Traumascapes: The Power and Fate of Places Transformed by Tragedy* (Melbourne: Melbourne University Press, 2005).

31 Philip Gourevitch, *We Wish to Inform You That Tomorrow We Will Be Killed with Our Families* (London: Picador, [1998] 2015).

32 Jacqueline Wilson, "Dark Tourism and National Identity in the Australian History Curriculum: Unexamined Questions Regarding Educational Visits to Sites of Human Suffering," in *Tourism and National Identities: An International Perspective*, ed. Elspeth Frew and Leanne White (London: Routledge, 2011), 202–14 (203).

33 Sarah de Mul, *Colonial Memory: Contemporary Women's Travel Writing in Britain and the Netherlands* (Amsterdam: Amsterdam University Press, 2011), 10.

34 Clarke, *Travel Writing from Black Australia*, 153–61.

35 Bart Moore-Gilbert, *Postcolonial Life Writing: Culture, Politics and Self-Representation* (London: Routledge, 2009).

II
Performances

5

SRILATA RAVI

Diasporic Returnees and Francophone Travel Narratives

In the last fifty years, forced and unforced migrations have produced some of the greatest displacements seen in history. Refugees, economic migrants, and political exiles have moved from their geographical places of origin to settle in foreign places, carrying with them memories of their past, tensions in the present, and aspirations for their future. While such movements have often resulted in permanent dislocations, rapid developments in communication technologies and affordable transportation have provided some members of these dispersed communities the opportunity of "looking back" or returning (temporarily, repeatedly, or permanently) to their homelands – to places left behind in the course of their migration. Using selected postcolonial travel texts in French, this chapter examines how the affective consequences of such diasporic returns are textualized.

As a critique of movement questioning all forms of contemporary displacement, diaspora has been theorized from different points of departure and multiple points of arrival. Arguably, "diaspora" is transnationalist in that it is the consequence of postcolonial and transnational movements of information, capital, and commerce. However, in this chapter it will be appropriate to distinguish diaspora, which is foremost a lived phenomenon located in time(s) and space(s), and transnationalism, which refers to impersonal forces of global capitalism.[1] William Safran argues that diasporic subjects "[retain] memory of a cultural connection with and general orientation towards their homelands [...], they harbour doubts about being fully accepted by the host land ... and many have maintained a myth of return."[2] While transnationalism dissolves social distances between homeland and host land into a single hybrid arena of interactions, most migrants still operate within the affective framework of home.[3] Diasporic return as a form of postcolonial travelogue allows us, therefore, to ground the analyses in different locations of origin and different points of return to examine effectively how narratives of "looking back" unpack notions of home, homeland, and displacement.

Diasporic Bizarreness and Return Narratives in French

The yearning for home, or the sustaining of an ideology of a place of origin, or the myth of homeland as a fixed center, is experienced in various ways in the diaspora. Not all diasporic lives are experienced as a nostalgic separation from homeland. Diasporic populations construct hybrid identities and manifest multiple identifications across nations, cultures, and languages.[4] It is useful to follow the distinction Avtar Brah takes between "homing desire" and "homeland."[5] She notes that the territory-based home is subject to change in history and that the very idea of home as place of belonging is mediated by desire and memory. Brah's idea of "homing desire" translates the affective and fantasized aspects of return and suggests that the geographical idea of home as place of origin cannot exist since such a place can never correspond to the place(s) left behind in the memory of the diasporic subject. That being the case, what compels diasporic subjects to undertake physical return to their places of origin and how does the "homing desire" lived while away unfold when they actually set foot on what was once their "homeland"?

As much as diasporic attachment implies a connection to a diasporic center, it also implies a necessary distance: This dual feature of connection and disconnection encapsulates the problematic of return.[6] Following Lauren Wagner, the chapter uses the term "diasporic" to refer to distance through space that is "both spatial and temporal" (193). It considers the source of influence for a diasporic subject not in a specific point in geographical space but in a specific "distant" space. Wagner also points out that leaving home is about the failure of memory to make sense of the place one comes to inhabit resulting in the migrant body being "out of place" or dislocated in the host land (194). Thus, in leaving an American or European home (or a residence in a richer country) to visit home in the past as place "left behind," the postcolonial migrant bodies of diasporic visitors, already "out of place" in their host lands, continue to be "out of place" in their homeland. Furthermore, this unfathomable feeling is compounded by the fact that the diasporic returnee is also a traveler-tourist participating unconsciously in the tourism culture of the homeland (195). In other words, diasporic subjects who return are traveling to visit, observe, and collect as "foreigners" either because they possess different passports or because of their financial advantages as visitors from richer countries: Returnees, therefore, can never altogether be considered outside the framework of tourism. Like tourists, they also look forward to seeing locations that reflect representations (perceived familiarity with the place) that had inspired them to "look back" in the first place. These expectations clash with perceptions of locals (friends and relatives) who presume that returnees will follow scripted performances that distinguish them as tourists. While an archetypal tourist collects experiences at his destination to shape memories when he returns to his geographical home, a diasporic returnee-tourist *re-collects* home at his/her destination through memories shaped in the diaspora. These memories, the returnee-visitor soon realizes, are unreliable, thereby rendering the destination irretrievable and further exacerbating his/her sense of "diasporic bizarreness," the enigmatic problematic of "multiple distancing" (in time, space, and body) that underwrites the traveler's narrative of return. Wagner deploys "diasporic strangeness" to describe the "out of place" experience of the diasporic subject as tourist visiting home. The use of the term "bizarreness" in this chapter complicates this experience to show that the diasporic dislocation can occur erratically and unpredictably at multiple levels. Bizarreness introduces the idea of unpredictability to the notion of "odd" contained in "strangeness" (194).

This travel writing considered here was produced after 1980. As Siobhán Shilton and Charles Forsdick note, these texts have "moved beyond post-war narratives of 'incomplete metamorphosis,' demonstrating greater counter-discursive potential than mid-twentieth-century narratives through [their] focus on the relationship between fluid, interconnected cultures, and [their] foregrounding of the metaphor of travel as a way of understanding identity."[7] This chapter examines Alain Mabanckou's *Lumières de Pointe-Noire,*[8] Dany Laferrière's *L'énigme du retour,*[9] Michèle Rakotoson's *Juillet, au pays-Chroniques d'un retour à Madagascar,*[10] and Kim Lefèvre's *Retour à la saison des pluies.*[11] It also draws from J. M. G. Le Clézio's utopian return narrative *Voyage à Rodrigues*[12] and the epistolary exchange about diasporic return between Leila Sebbar and Nancy Huston in *Lettres parisiennes.*[13] These writers, currently residing in North America and Europe, hail from a range of homelands: Republic of Congo, Haiti, Madagascar, Vietnam, Mascarene Islands, and Algeria.

Given the ambiguities inherent in the experiences of diasporic visitor-travelers, it is unsurprising that narratives of return blur the frontiers between autobiographical displacements and fictionalized travel. Despite the variations in the geographical points of departure and arrival, and durations of absence from "home," there are several commonalities that characterize these texts. Returns, usually after long periods of voluntary distancing, are motivated by specific reasons, often the illness or death of a close relative. The account of the completion of the literal return journey is almost always accompanied by references to other completed journeys (literal, imagined, and metaphorical) to the same or other locations. On the other hand, the forms that these narrations take vary: Some accounts are chronological; others are iterative and fragmented. Some accounts are purely in prose; others include a mixture of narrative and poetic sequences. While some texts are interspersed with photographs of family members and places and reference specific dates and locations, other descriptions contain less precise details. The analyses of each of travel narratives here are shaped to answer the following questions pertaining to the principal focus on diasporic bizarreness: How is the dual temporality of return inscribed into these diasporic return narratives? How do these return journeys abort the notion of home? Can critical nostalgia help to accomplish diasporic return meaningfully?[14]

Traveling in Two Tempos: Time and the Diasporic Returnee

The diasporic travel writer is not contained within boundaries, nations, or languages.[15] James Clifford argues that diasporic discourse involves the idea of homeland not as something that is "left behind" but as a place of "mobile" attachment in "contrapuntal modernity,"[16] a diasporic consciousness in which different places overlap. However, during a homeland visit, return time in the present confronts departure time in the past, and diasporic distance lived as mobile attachment elsewhere gives way to the ambivalent sensation of diasporic bizarreness at the point of return. This bizarreness unfolds in the textualization of return as travel in two tempos. This dual temporality is the principle axis around which the narrative of return is structured in *Lumières de Pointe-Noire* and *L'énigme du retour*.

Alain Mabanckou, author of *Verre Cassé* and *Mémoire de porc-épic* among other celebrated works, teaches at UCLA. The autobiographical narrator of *Lumières de Pointe-Noire* leaves his native country to pursue higher studies in France. From his account, one learns that he has not returned to Pointe-Noire in the Republic of Congo for twenty-three years. Meantime his father, papa Roger, and his mother, maman Pauline, have passed. The returnee-writer accomplishes this "retour au bercail" ["home-coming"][17] to the city of his birth on the invitation of the French Institute. This gives him the opportunity to meet his relatives and tour his native city. The book is divided into "Première semaine" [First week]and "Dernière semaine" ["Last week"]. The idea of fixed duration contained in these titles is a counterpoint to the lived experience of diasporic distance as recurring anguish: "Chaque nuit de pleine lune, l'angoisse me saisit et me pousse dehors" ["Every full moon night, anguish seizes me and pushes me outside"] (18). The first section is introduced through the remembering of a favorite childhood fable of the woman in the moon, "La Femme aux miracles," and travels through the past of his childhood and adolescence via encounters

with his relatives in the present. The nostalgic evocation of a happy childhood, interspaced with old photographs and descriptions of relatives, is
juxtaposed against encounters with aunts, uncles, and cousins who perceive
the writer-traveler as a diasporic visitor from a land of plenty. The narrator,
faithful to the image of the returning tourist and uneasy about his financially
advantaged position, is eager to distribute his dollars. The second section has
a more self-reflexive mood as the reader is taken through the narrator's
favorite childhood haunts – the Cinema Rex, the Trois-Cents neighborhood,
lycée Victor Augagneur, and the narrator's favorite places along la Côte
Sauvage. If the fable of "La femme aux miracles" introduced the return
narrative, the chapters in the book are framed with titles that make direct or
indirect references to popular French and Hollywood films. This structural
enclosing effectively packages the narrator's memories of "[s]on royaume
d'enfance" ["[h]is childhood kingdom"] (277), together with his experiences
of return in the present within the "timeless" time-frame of fabulation
(traditional [fable] and modern [cinema] mythmaking). This textual framing
in mythical time reflects the narrator's observation that the past is neither
"une ligne droite ["a straight line"], nor "une onde immobile et insensible à
l'impetuosité des vents" ["a static wave insensitive to the turbulences of
time"] (181). The nostalgic memories are transposed on to the images of
his nieces and nephews in the present who become the contented children
of Louboulo neighborhood and will not give up their happiness for anything
in this world (138). The duality of the image in the past and in the present
lies in the narrator's remark that some accounts can never travel; they can
never be read outside the spaces where they were written (278). When
looking at the photograph of himself with papa Roger and maman Pauline,
and observing the significance of his mother's positioning, the returnee
observes the extent to which the photograph differs in meaning when viewed
in the present of geographical return from when it was viewed in diasporic
time away from the homeland (81). Yet, paradoxically the diasporic returnee's desire to forget that he had ever stepped foot in the kingdom of
childhood (277) is his nostalgic way of thinking that his memories can be
preserved in another time. A similar instance of self-contradiction or diasporic bizarreness is reflected in the narrator's lack of enthusiasm to visit the
tombs of his parents "[p]arceque papa Roger et maman Pauline sont venus
vers moi" ["Because papa Roger and Maman Pauline came to me"] (276).
The ambivalence of diasporic distance is encapsulated in the narrator's wish
to bring back his past and his memories of home with him through his travel
account.

Mabankou's return "in two tempos" exposes the fissures and confusions
between his present time as a celebrated diasporic returnee and the nostalgic

time of his childhood in Pointe-Noire. The violence of this disjuncture and the impossibility of return in time are reflected in the traveler's analogy of an anthropologist digging into the past with a spade corroded by the tears of regrets (184). The product of this memorial excavation is represented as Catoblépas, the deadly monster with a large and heavy head hanging down as if it were going to eat its own legs. The violence of diasporic rupture is inscribed in this cannibalistic metaphor suggesting the illogical possibility of the returning self in the present being devoured by the lamented self in the past (185).

If the confrontation of diasporic time and homeland time results in a mixture of cannibalistic violence and sweet regret in Mabanckou's travel account, this encounter of two temporalities or the "enigma of return" (the title of Laferrière's book) is transcribed as a feverish state endured between the dawn of departure and the dusk of return[18] in Laferrière's *L'énigme du retour*. While *Pays sans chapeau* was a narrative of fictional return to Haiti inspired by the news of the death of his grandmother,[19] *L'énigme* is a work bordering between fiction and nonfiction that was conceived during a trip to Haiti.[20] While Laferrière had previously returned to Haiti, in an interview he explains that the journey described in *L'énigme* was the first occasion he was in Port-au-Prince as a writer. Like the returnee-narrator in the novel, Dany Laferrière was twenty-three years old when he left Haiti, fleeing political persecution in the same way as his father did before him in 1976. In much the same way as Mabanckou, Laferrière in *L'énigme* "navigue dans deux temps" ["navigates in two rhythms"] as images in the past seek continually to superpose themselves onto the images in the present.[21] The book contains two distinct sections, "Lent préparatifs du depart" ["Slow preparations for a departure"] and "Le retour" ["The return"]. The affective notion of time is introduced in the titles, juxtaposing the slowness of diasporic time with the ineluctable but forever postponed time of encounter with the past. As in Mabanckou's narrative, it is the temporal distance, inscribed as the emotional distance that serves as the point of departure for writing travel. This estrangement in time is lived as "ce temps pourri qui peut pousser à la folie" ["this rotten time that can lead to madness"] (27), and the only measure of this rotten and frustrating distance is Laferrière's own image in an old photo given to him by his mother (28). Both Alain Mabanckou's account and *L'énigme* make references to the last time that the traveler-writers were present in front of their mothers, women resigned to losing their sons, not knowing when they would return.[22] As the narrator in *L'énigme* sets foot on his native soil he feels like a foreigner, "un étranger dans sa ville natale" ["a stranger in his native city"] (152), but it is in the perception of distance as it is mirrored in the faces of loved ones that the feeling of diasporic bizarreness is experienced. This uncanny sensation is experienced as the tense feeling of having to relearn upon return what one knows already, but that which one had to unlearn when one was away.[23] This strangeness comes through in the realization that diasporic distance is unfathomable. Laferrière's diasporic time cannot be measured because it is inscribed outside of his "gènes" ["genes"]:[24] Thus distance, as fissure, has no duration because the diasporic returnee is both out of body and out of place. This realization of the immeasurability of diasporic estrangement in time and in space is expressed as: "Et l'exil du temps et plus impitoyable que l'exil de l'espace. Mon enfance me manque plus cruellement que mon pays" ["And being exiled in time is more pitiless than being exiled in space. I miss my childhood more cruelly than my country"] (75).

While the sojourn away from homeland produces narratives of survival, only the geographical return can generate the impossible question about how one *lives* diasporic distance. It is the answer to this question that the narrator's mother would like to have. The answer, however, is not straightforward because it plunges the returnee-son into an unavoidable "chute" (57) of diasporic bizarreness. This disorientated feeling of being dropped into a diasporic abyss – "dans la geule du temps" ["in the jaws of time"] (82) – is *un*-scriptable and can only be experienced in delirium, in "la douce maladie du sommeil" ["the gentle sickness of sleep"] (82), between raging fever and deep sleep, and will thus remain forever "énigmatique" (276). Laferrière's fragmented polylogue, partly in verse and partly in prose, partly fiction and partly nonfiction, textually translates this "enigma of return."

Aborting Home: Place and the Diasporic Returnee

During the course of diasporic return, looking back conjures two opposing places at once – a utopian space grounded in the place one wishes to rediscover as home and another that is dystopian – the geographical place actually reached, which does not resemble home.[25] While in the return accounts of Mabanckou and Laferrière this disjuncture is mirrored in the image of the abandoned mother and becomes the face of an irrecoverable past, in Michèle Rakotoson's *Juillet au pays-Chroniques d'un retour à Madagascar*, the very act of returning is aborted several times over. Rakotoson, a key figure in Malagasy literature, fled to France with her family in 1983 to avoid persecution by President Didier Ratsiraka's regime. The bizarreness/"bizarrerie"[26] of her diasporic distance or the impossibility of return are contained in her question, "Quitte-t-on vraiment le lieu de son enfance?" ["Does one really leave the place of one's childhood?"].[27] The textual wandering between aborted returns covers five years, five Julys, (2002–7) with a "first" return in 2002 after twenty-five years and ends with a reference to the elections that brought President Marc Ravalomanana to power in that year. Rakotoson's accounts of aborted returns are prefaced by an overpowering sentiment of dismemberment described as the mutilation of the self ("mutilation de soi") and mutilation of memory (8). Rakotoson distinguishes between "chez moi" ("homeland") and "cette idée de chez moi" (29) ("homing desire") or what she calls her "boule de ouate" ["cotton wool bubble"], one in which she has cloistered herself as "l'éternelle voyageuse" ["the eternal traveler"] (29). The diasporic visitor doomed to travel eternally soon realizes that "rentrer" in effect is not to return home, but to "enter again," like entering for the first time. This means that one must "[s]'y remodeler" ["remodel oneself"] by putting together the mutilated body and the mutilated memories in order to "combler la rupture, les lignes de failles" ["fill the gap, the cracks"] (40). The diasporic returnee notes that the contradiction of such remodeling is that no return can ever be the same since the distances change between the fissures. Thus, every return generates a new story, "une histoire qui de toute façon ne sera plus la même" ["a story that, in any case, will never be the same"] (43) created "entre deux langues, deux rythmes, deux mémoires" ["between two languages, two rhythms and two memories"] (44). Paradoxically, in rewriting home through return, it becomes impossible to traverse diasporic time and diasporic distance, and consequently the narrator's "no man's land" further widens.[28] The island home thus remains "indicible" (47) ["*un*-scriptable"] and hidden forever between the interstices of languages, rhythms, and memories.[29]

As the traveler roams the city riddled by the guilt of a tourist from a rich country, she experiences the ambivalence of diaspora in her inability to reconcile her womanhood constructed elsewhere and the image of the city in ruins that presents itself to her like "une femme excisée" ["a mutilated woman"] (79). This external transposition of her own mutilated self is poignantly expressed in the following lines: "Pourquoi en moi cette impression étrange d'être dans et hors de l'histoire. Peut-être suis-je restée trop longtemps à l'étranger, tout en y cultivant l'image de chez moi." ["Why do I have this strange impression of being in and out of history? Perhaps I have remained too long abroad while still cultivating an image of home"] (116). Homeland as territorial connection and homing desire as an affective mode of being become conflated when created outside of history causing "cette impression étrange" ["this strange impression]" of being in and out of time (116). Lived continually as in and out of one's body, in the in-between time of "errance" ["wandering"] diasporic distance produces a permanent "sentiment d'éloignement," ["feeling of estrangement"] (79) such that all geographical returns to homeland become aborted, terminating in emptiness and disintegration.[30] The difficulty to translate the "truth" of return into words is what makes the returnee/traveler/writer declare that return cannot be written without deforming it.[31]

In this context, it is interesting to note that diasporic Algerian writer Leila Sebbar, writing in 1986 to her Canadian friend and novelist Nancy Huston, asserts that she could never write an account of her return (an account that Rakotoson nevertheless successfully publishes despite the agonizing pain caused by the exercise) for fear of not finding things as they were, for fear of being out of place. Sebbar has accepted the fact that home as a place is not eternal[32] and to overcome the fear of mutilation and hurt she has chosen to write fiction: "Et puis, pour moi la fiction c'est la suture qui masque la blessure, l'écart entre les deux rives" ["And then, for me fiction, it is the only suture that masks the hurt, the distance between the two shores."] (264). Sebbar feels the need to hold on to the emotional and physical divide between home and diaspora so as to feel less "hors de moi' ["outside of myself"] (261). Writing return makes both women, Sebbar and Rakotoson, physically disfigured and doubly dislocated because as women in patriarchal societies they have always had to construct their subjectivities apart, on the margins, and in perpetual inequality: "Je suis une femme dans l'exil, c'est-à-dire à la lisière, à l'écart, au bord toujours, d'un côté et de l'autre, en déséquilibre permanent" ["I am a woman in exile, on the edge, deviant, always on the border, on one side and the other, in permanent imbalance"] (258). The semi-autobiographical forms that the novels of diasporic return take reveal this nervous unease of "deforming" the reality of return that Rakotoson expresses in *Juillet au pays* and that Sebbar transforms into fictional journeys in her oeuvre.

Nostalgia and the Diasporic Returnee

During their return trips, politically secure and professionally successful postcolonial writers in exile confront the harsh truth of the economic distance that separates them from the people they have left behind: friends and relatives who have not had the same opportunities to better their material and emotional situations. As such, diasporic return narratives are fueled by the guilt and shame experienced in the course of these confrontations.[33] The inability to improve local conditions and customs that inevitably places these travelers in a position of complicity with neo-imperial forces invariably upsets the crucial homing desire experienced by returnees. In effect, this poignant paradox, literarily expressed as "diasporic bizarreness" or the enigmatic problematic of multiple distancing in time, space, and body in the travel narratives analyzed here, is a counterpoint to the "happy remittance narrative" of global capitalism, one which conveys the stories of oft-exploited overseas workers who dutifully send money home to their families. Existential disenchantment without homing desire and financial settlement without longing for physical return are two extreme ends of the spectrum of return stories: Not all returns are expressions of utter disenchantment, nor are they all uncritically fulfilling. This chapter would be incomplete without taking up the case of Kim Lefèvre's return from her anguished sense of being métisse to recuperating and reaffirming her biological métissage that is lived as multiple disconnections in time, space, gender, and race. *Métisse Blanche*, Lefèvre's autobiographical narrative of her métisse origins in Vietnam, was published in 1988.³⁴ This autobiographical narrative was quickly followed by an account of the author's geographical return to Vietnam in 1990, which appeared as *Retour à la saison des pluies*. Divided into two distinct parts, much like Laferrière's account, into "Le passé resurgi" that reconstructs the present of her diasporic subjectivity through meeting with old acquaintances in Paris, persons she had avoided before writing her autobiography, and "Le retour," which maps the past through her physical return to Vietnam and her visits to her family members, especially her mother and her sisters. In comparison to Rakotoson's narrative of "dark return,"³⁵ Lefèvre's narrative, while accepting the impossibility of return to a geographical home and the guilt of being a Westerner lost in a third world home (156), is a successful story of family reunion: "Elle n'a encore rien dit, rien raconté. Elle s'est contentée de nous écouter babiller, toute à son bonheur de nous voir ensemble" ["She (the narrator's mother) still didn't say anything, convey anything. She was content to hear us babbling, very happy to see us altogether"] (179). This narrative of Lefèvre's poignant encounter with loved ones left behind presents the emotional reconnection with her mother as the discovery of the writer-returnee's link to her Vietnamese past hitherto hidden and consciously removed from memory: "Elle est mon passé vivant, le trait d'union entre ce que j'étais et ce que je suis" ["She is my living past, the link between what I was and what I am"] (221). Diasporic estrangement is compounded in the case of Lefèvre in the racial alienation that she suffers as a "métisse blanche" ["white métisse"]. Born of a Vietnamese mother and a French father whom she does not know, Kim, despite being accepted by the man that her mother married and the daughters that she had with him, suffers from the anguish of being racially displaced. She voluntarily leaves for France to study in 1960, unlike many others who were forced to leave in 1975 following the country's reunification.

Diasporic distance as physical absence from homeland is compensated by the emotional power of reconciliation through collaborative storytelling in the present of diasporic return: "Nous parlons, nous parlons comme si nous composions une symphonie, tantôt chuchotant tantôt riant" ["We talked, we talked as if we were composing a symphony, sometimes whispering, sometimes laughing"] (155). *Retour à la saison des pluies* can be described as a "critically nostalgic" account of return in that the access to the past (temporal and spatial) allows the returnee to move forward in the present.[36] Nostalgia is not necessarily counterproductive, it can be both critical in the analytical sense of re-evaluating the present in terms of the past and also critical in the sense of being vital and becoming a catalyst for action. The narrator questions the fixity of a geographical home and the permanence of any form of territorial connection between culture and belonging. The narrative is also consciously gendered in its grounding of the recovery of the diasporic self within the affective ties that define the mother-daughter bond. Even if it translates the impossibility of return to a geographical home it keeps the possibility of an emotional home still alive in the rediscovered link between the narrator and her mother, thus providing a more hopeful resolution to the paradox of diasporic distance, one that is also strongly located in the power of writing: "Je ne peux le ressusciter autrement que sur le ce papier où j'écris" ["I can only resuscitate the past on the paper that I write"] (221).

In a way, J. M. G. Le Clézio's journey to the island of Rodrigues in the footsteps of his grandfather's legend mirrors Lefèvre's nostalgic rediscovery of her mother's love. Born of parents who hailed from the island of Mauritius and raised in France, Le Clézio set foot on his native island, his "cultural home," only when he was forty years old, but the Mascarene Islands are a foundational matrix of Le Clézio's oeuvre.[37] Despite self-conscious reflections on the ravages of time, dislocation in space and the loss of innocence, both Le Clézio and Lefèvre believe in the power of recovery of a lost past either through words in the case of the latter or in the transcendent beauty of nature in the case of the former. In *Voyage à Rodrigues*, a semi-autobiographical travel journal, the returnee-explorer physically traces the adventures of his grandfather looking for a pirate's treasure on the island of Rodrigues. The travelogue is the reaffirmation of the possibility of recovery of the self in the past through a utopian communion with the island. This past cannot be lost since it resides in the eternal sublime produced by "l'harmonie du monde" ["the harmony of the world"];[38] it is a "mystery" that the traveler-explorer discovers in the light, the wind, and the black rocks of the island of Rodrigues (77). In another autobiographical account of the past seen through the story of his father's life in Africa, Le Clézio describes nostalgia not as "a dereistic affliction" or "a simple partition" that separates the world of today and that of yesterday but something "of substance, of sensations, of the most logical part of [his] life."[39] Le Clézio's return to Rodrigues is not experienced as a sentimental recuperation of the past but a logical revitalization in the present.

In *Retour à la saison des pluies* and *Voyage à Rodrigues* the returning traveler is successful in locating the connection between the present and the past: a connection that is constructed neither through blood ties nor through memorial links, but where past and present are connected because they throw out the "same shadow" of mystery,[40] the mystery that the infinite, unfathomable sea offers to Le Clézio and the mystery in immortal wisdom of a mother's love that Lefèvre receives on her return.[41] Through their channeling of diasporic bizarreness, experienced briefly as nostalgia for lost innocence, out of the social immediacy of a diasporic present, these two accounts present an interesting counterpoint to the translation of the impossibility of recovering loss of home suggested in the chapter's examination of the returnee writings of Mabanckou, Laferrière, Rakotoson, and Sebbar.

Conclusion

The texts examined in this chapter exhibit a range of diasporic returns: from return as an exercise in futility, return as impossible homecoming, to return as recovery of wonderment. The course of return or "looking back," even if nostalgic in a sentimental sort of way, brings into view dislocation and disenchantment. The desire for something that no longer exists throws the fissures between attachment and disconnection into anguishing and violent contrast while also keeping alive hopes of retrieval and resumption. Travel narratives of diasporic return oscillate between the discomfort of the present and unreliable memories of a comforting past, between sorrowful regret and painful recovery, between unfulfilled belonging and anguishing connections. The return narrative as "transformative dialogue, one that is rooted in one place but that opens up to other places for the future"[42] contains tensions and stresses that produce the critical energy to investigate the postcolonial/diasporic condition of perpetual displacement. Postcolonial travel writers have effectively used the genre of travel writing to engage in cultural critique[43] and to explore a range of pressing concerns that we face in a world where globalization and cosmopolitanism call into question fixed notions of belonging and affiliation. The array of diasporic looking back narratives examined here exposes the complexities of postcolonial habitus[44] and foregrounds diasporic bizarreness as the "ineluctable impossibility" of return to a territorial location called home.

NOTES

1 On this point, see Jana Evans Braziel and Anita Mannur, ed., *Theorizing Diaspora: A Reader* (London: Blackwell Publishing, 2003), 8.

2 William Safran, "Deconstructing and Comparing Diasporas" in *Diaspora, Identity, and Religion: New Directions in Theory and Research*, ed. Waltraud Kokot, Khachig Tölöyan, and Carolin Alfonso (London: Routledge, 2004), 9–29 (10).

3 Iraida H. López, *Impossible Returns: Narratives of the Cuban Diaspora* (Gainesville: University Press of Florida, 2015), 1–34.

4 Paul Gilroy, *The Black Atlantic: Modernity and Double Consciousness* (London: Verso, 1993); Stuart Hall, "Cultural, Identity and Diaspora," in *Identity: Community, Culture, Difference*, ed. Jonathan Rutherford (London: Lawrence & Wishart, 1990), 222–37.

5 Avtar Brah, *Cartographies of Desire: Contesting Identities* (London: Routledge, 1996), 197.

6 Lauren Wagner, "Diasporic Visitor, Diasporic Tourist: Post-Migrant Generation Moroccans on Holiday at 'Home' in Morocco," *Civilisations* 57 (2008): 191–205 (193).

7 Siobhán Shilton and Charles Forsdick, "Travel Literature in French Colonial and Postcolonial Encounters," *Contemporary French & Francophone Studies* 10, no. 1 (2006): 73–84 (80).

8 Alain Mabanckou, *Lumières de Pointe-Noire* (Paris: Seuil, 2013).

9 Dany Laferrière, *L'énigme du retour* (Montréal: Boréal, 2010); *Pays sans chapeau: roman* (Outremont, Québec: Lanctôt, 1996).

10 Michele Rakotoson, *Juillet, au pays-Chroniques d'un retour à Madagascar* (Bordeaux: Elytis, 2007).

11 Kim Lefèvre, *Retour à la saison des pluies* (La Tour d'Aigues: Éditions de l'Aube, 1995).

12 J.M.G. Le Clézio, *Voyage à Rodrigues* (Paris: Gallimard, 1986).

13 Nancy Huston and Leïla Sebbar, "Lettres parisiennes," *Communications*, 43, no. 1 (1986): 249–65.

14 Translations from the original texts in French are mine.

15 Justin D. Edwards and Rune Graulund, *Postcolonial Travel Writing: Critical Explorations* (Basingstoke: Palgrave MacMillan, 2010), 6.

16 James Clifford, *Routes: Travel and Translation in the Late Twentieth Century* (London: Harvard University, 1997), 256.

17 "Homecoming," Mabanckou, *Lumières*, 18. Further page references are given in the text.

18 "[sur] mon front apaise la fièvre/Je somnole entre aube et crépuscule" ["(a)s the fever cools down on my forehead/I doze off between dawn and dusk], Laferrière, *L'énigme*, 286.

19 Dany Laferrière, *Pays sans chapeau roman* (Outremont, Québec: Lanctôt, 1996).

20 "The narrator never dies," accessed December 18, 2015, www.wordswithoutborders.org/dispatches/article/the-narrator-never-dies-an-interview-with-dany-laferriere.

21 Laferrière, *L'énigme*, 175. Further references provided in the text.

22 Mabanckou, *Lumières*, 34; Laferrière, *L'énigme*, 28.

23 "Je me trouve dans la situation de quelqu'un/qui doit réapprendre ce qu'il sait déjà /mais dont il a dû se défaire en chemin" ["I find myself in the situation of

someone/ who must relearn what he already knows/but that which had to unlearn on his way"], 123.

24 "Un temps hors du temps inscrit dans nos genes" ["Time that is outside of the time written in our genes"], 75.

25 Lopez, *Impossible Returns*, 22.

26 "Il faudrait que nous disions, l'une et l'autre, la bizarrerie qu'il y a à « rentrer chez soi » en touriste." ["We must talk to each other about the bizarreness of coming home as a tourist"]: Huston and Sebbar, *Lettres parisiennes*, 43.

27 Rakotoson, *Juillet*, 15. Further references provided in the text.

28 "Le non man's land intérieur a grandi" ["The internal no man's land has widened"], 60.

29 "L'entre-deux glissé dans toutes les interstices" ["The in-between slipped through all the interstices"], 46.

30 "Une sensation de vide et d'écartelement," 116.

31 "Avec quels mots le dire? Avec quels rythmes, quels accents pour ne pas le déformer?" ["With what words to narrate it? In which tempo, with which accents, so as not to deform it?"], 142.

32 Huston and Sebbar, *Lettres*, 263.

33 On this point see Srilata Ravi, "Home and the 'Failed' City in Postcolonial Narratives of 'Dark Return,'" *Postcolonial Studies*, 17, no. 3 (2014): 296–306.

34 Kim Lefèvre, *Métisse blanche* (La Tour d'Aigues: Éditions de l'Aube, 1989).

35 Ravi, "Home and the 'Failed' City," 296.

36 In his commentary on memory, Leo Spitzer provides a reformulation of nostalgia, one which has the potential to open up spaces for change in the present. See Leo Spitzer, "Nostalgic Memory and Critical Memory in a Refuge from Nazism," in *Acts of Memory. Cultural Recall in the Present*, ed. Mieke Bal, Jonathan Crewe, and Leo Spitzer (London: University Press of New England, 1999), 87–104.

37 Jacqueline Dutton, "Le Clézio L'Îlien, ou Comment J.M.G. Le Clézio s'est insularisé," *Contemporary French & Francophone Studies*, 19, no. 2 (2015): 194–204.

38 Le Clézio, *Voyage*, 76.

39 Le Clézio, *The African*, trans. C. Dickson (Boston: David Godine, 2013), 104.

40 Le Clézio, *Voyage*, 102

41 Lefevre, *Retour*, 147

42 Edwards and Graulund, 10.

43 Edwards and Graulund, 3.

44 Shilton and Forsdick, "Travel Literature," 81.

6

EVA-MARIE KRÖLLER

Diplomats as Postcolonial Travelers

Canadian Emissaries to London during World War II

On 26 June 1940, Charles Ritchie "[w]alked [...] along the Broad Walk through Kensington Gardens" and observed that "[i]t was thronged with soldiers, the remains of the shattered continental armies, Dutch, French and Norwegian. Then the Canadians who have become almost part of the London streetscape and the newly arrived New Zealanders including many Maoris ... Moving in this procession of soldiers of the nations I had the sense of swimming in the full tide of history."[1] When he wrote this entry in his diary, Ritchie had been working for the Canadian Department of External Affairs since 1934. In early 1939 he was posted to Canada House in London, joining a group of diplomats who already were, or were about to become, stars of their profession, including High Commissioner Vincent Massey, Lester Pearson, George Ignatieff, and Georges Vanier. Among them were a future prime minister and winner of the Nobel Peace Prize (Pearson) and two governors-general (Massey and Vanier). Canada had a legitimate role to play in this war, these men forcefully asserted, and it must join the rest of the Commonwealth in providing the "immovable object against which [Nazism would be] dashed to pieces" (54).

Like Ritchie's diaries, the memoirs of Massey, Pearson, and Ignatieff, and the letters of Vanier as related in his biographies, convey the Canadians' unstinting war efforts once their nation "became the second most important of Germany's enemies, after Britain" following "the fall of France in June 1940,"[2] the month when Ritchie wrote the entry that opens this chapter. However, the diplomats also describe their government's persistent reservations about its involvement in the European military conflict. As Prime Minister Mackenzie King was only too aware, the relationship of Francophone Canadians to the British Crown remained fraught even some 180 years after the defeat of the French at the Battle of the Plains of Abraham. Conscription in World War I had caused an acrimonious rift between Anglophone and Francophone citizens and threatened national unity. Mindful of this precedent, Canada "delayed [entry into the war] for almost a week" in 1939,[3] and this bicultural tension was strong enough to erupt even abroad in London when the Vaniers' strong emotional attachment to France caused a clash with the anglophile Masseys.

This chapter builds upon scholarship on colonial lives, specifically the highly mobile lives of colonial administrators,[4] and on the formulation – through diplomacy among other means – of national identity in settler nations, with travel as a recurrent exploratory medium.[5] The discussion begins with the difficulties of applying the descriptor of "postcolonial" to Canadian World War II diplomats, first by highlighting the almost complete absence of Canadian Aboriginal soldiers from the diplomats' accounts of wartime Europe, and second by discussing the paradoxical combination of privilege, conservatism, and rebellion against the status quo that is displayed in the life-writing and achievements of Massey, Pearson, Ritchie, Vanier, and Ignatieff. The final section will focus on the types of travel writing that are evident in these texts, with particular attention to their ability to help formulate national (and postcolonial) identity abroad and in times of global crisis. The chapter maintains that the backgrounds, personalities, and interactions of these diplomats have much to tell us about Canadian postcolonial nationhood and the role of travel as an effective catalyst in this process.

The Diplomats' Memoir as Travel Writing

George Egerton has described the political memoir as a "polygenre" that, among other nonfiction genres, "appropriates autobiography, biography, diary, history, political science, and pamphleteering."[6] Egerton omits travel writing from his list, but it too is a persistently recurring sub-genre in diplomats' life-writing, with "a pronounced tendency to underline the 'travel adventure' side of the diplomatic life."[7] The accounts of Ritchie, Massey, Ignatieff, and Vanier all involve travel, their own or that of others, all coordinated from their offices in London and, in Vanier's case, also from Paris and Algiers. As a result, the books by and about them include numerous micro-travelogues ranging from brief paragraphs to multi-page essays. For all of these men, writing was an important daily task because "[d]iplomacy [...] depended on written communication"[8] through a steady flow of telegrams, communiqués, and speeches.

In discussing the activities in diplomacy and intelligence of T. E. Lawrence, David Hogarth, Gertrude Bell, and Freya Stark in the Middle East, Billie Melman underscores that these authors' achievements as travel writers match their work as political mediators, and she warns against viewing their writing merely as "an epiphenomenon of late colonial diplomacy."[9] For Ritchie's diaries at least, composed by a novelist *manqué*, the warning could be reversed, and his work as diplomat is at times in danger of becoming "an epiphenomenon" of keeping his diary. Two of his favorite types of travelogue are the adventure story and the urban sketch. The thrills of his expedition to D-Day France, for example, are a slightly self-ironic sequel to the stories by Walter Scott, J. M. Barrie, Arthur Conan Doyle, and Rudyard Kipling that his mother read to him and his brother Roley (in later life a Judge of the Supreme Court of Canada) in the family library in Halifax.[10] By contrast, Ritchie's descriptions of London owe much to the modernist *flâneurisme* of Virginia Woolf, whom he repeatedly cites in his diaries, although he found "her reflected atmosphere [...] rather alarming."[11]

Like the political memoir, travel writing is a hybrid genre, and with two such mercurial genres coming together, it is impossible to determine a template that applies to all travelogues as they occur in diplomats' lifewriting. There are, however, a number of recurrent features in these particular texts that are provoked by the abnormal conditions of war. Despite the occasional lushness of Ritchie's prose, travel writing in these books is – in keeping with the extreme situations described – mostly stripped to its basic elements, including the insistent recurrence of the departure scene, the arrival scene, and the panoramic view to which Mary Louise Pratt refers, in allusion to William Cowper's poem "The Solitude of Alexander Selkirk," as the "monarch-of-all-I-survey" perspective.[12] All of these structural elements are radically modified by wartime conditions. Thus, Vincent and Alice Massey were in shock when they were confronted with the carnage after the Dieppe Raid, and they realized that the official courtesies of a High Commissioner's welcome to the wounded soldiers were inadequate to address the situation.[13] As described by Ritchie, troop movements during the Dunkirk Evacuation and on D-Day conflated the normally discrete scenes of departure and arrival into simultaneous processes of invasion, evacuation, repatriation, and imprisonment. The authoritative view from above was certainly transformed when a civilian surveyed a battle scene from a military aircraft, where, no matter how high his diplomatic rank, he was a barely tolerated passenger. The view was even more transformed from the perspective of "the German wounded [who] were swung from the decks of the ship by a crane [and who] lay in waxen immobility as if they were already dead" when a transport of POWs arrived in Dover after Dunkirk.[14]

In addition to the basic scenes of departure, arrival, and view from above, these travelogues are also preoccupied with the sheer logistics of travel. Although its diplomats were later criticized for the insufficiency of their work on behalf of Jewish refugees,[15] Canada House coordinated the transport of stranded civilians and refugees and, later, of prisoners of war and enemy aliens to Canada on "ships [...] headed empty across the Atlantic to pick up Canadian troops."[16] The dangers of wartime travel were immediately apparent. Thus, the *Athenia*, on which many Canadian tourists, for some of whom Canada House first had to search in Europe, hoped to return home, "was torpedoed within the week [of sailing] with heavy loss of life."[17]

Imperial Subjects

Canadian diplomats' wartime travels may not immediately spring to mind as falling under "postcolonial travel writing," if one is to judge by contemporary criticism of the subject.[18] Indeed, these particular men's understanding of "postcolonialism" was largely limited to the autonomy of Canada's white Anglophone and Francophone settler societies vis-à-vis their "mother-countries" and did not include consideration of the colonialism that these societies themselves had imposed on Aboriginal people. Ritchie's reference, in the opening quotation, to the Maori among the recently arrived troops from New Zealand is not duplicated by descriptions of Australian or Canadian Aboriginal soldiers in his diary. Although it is possible that the Maori were little more than a curiosity to him, it is more likely that the existence of a "separate Maori infantry battalion,"[19] comprising 7,000 troops, made them conspicuous enough for him to notice them. Six Maori were eventually appointed commanding officers out of a total of ten, and as a result they were more readily acknowledged as equals than their Canadian and Australian counterparts. Massey does describe the contribution of "the Indians of Old Crow in the far north-west corner of the Yukon," who collected $300 "to be given to boys and girls [in Britain] who had lost parents in the air raids,"[20] and he ensured that "[a]n Indian private soldier from a unit in our army" was in attendance when the Masseys presented gifts to children from Southwark, Lambeth, and Bermondsey purchased with the money (283). Descriptions of Canadian Aboriginal soldiers in Europe are, however, few and far between in these texts. More revealing is the paternalist attitude expressed in photos from Massey's and Vanier's post-war tenures as governors-general, showing them in Native garb to emphasize the inclusiveness of their office and their willingness to travel to remote areas in the service of the nation.

And yet, as Massey's invitation to "[a]n Indian private soldier" indicates, Canada House was aware of the presence of Native soldiers and provided the Canadian press with clippings from British papers that described the sensation caused by the arrival of the "Maginot Mohicans," when "[e]agle-nosed red Indians" were said to "pad [. . .] down the gangway in moccasins," preceded by a reputation for being "admirable snipers."[21] This fanciful arrival scene that changed "six Micmacs [. . .] in service boots"[22] into

Mohicans in moccasins is a remarkable combination of literary and cinematic stereotypes, perhaps further fueled by the successful performance career of Grey Owl, later discovered to be the Englishman Archie Belaney, who toured Britain in the 1930s to such popular acclaim that he was introduced to King George VI and his family. Numerous Canadian papers carried the article about the "Maginot Mohicans," but instead of taking offense at the clichéd description of Aboriginal soldiers, the commentators were outraged by the backward image that this scene presumably projected of Canada as a whole, including its white population: "Isn't Canada a land of Indians and wigwams? So here they are – in moccasins," a nettled commentator in Toronto's *Globe and Mail* remarked.[23] The association between Native regalia and Canadian nationalism is so fraught, however, that even contemporary observers can get it wrong. Thus, the Tate Britain exhibition "Artist and Empire" featured Yousuf Karsh's portrait of Lord Tweedsmuir (John Buchan), governor general 1935–1940, in a Kainawa war bonnet. In allusion to Tweedsmuir's speech in 1937 to The Canadian Institute of International Affairs, the catalogue interprets the photo not only as a visual expression of "a distinct national identity" but also as proof that Tweedsmuir supported "the freedom [of each racial group] to protect its inheritance."[24] Although some imperialist observers found Tweedsmuir's statement that "[a] Canadian's first loyalty is [. . .] to Canada and to Canada's King"[25] insufficiently supportive of the British Commonwealth, he did not say a word about multiculturalism and he certainly did not talk about Aboriginals' right to their heritage.

A British commentator would have applied the label of "backward" to Massey and his team at his own peril, but as a group they do to some degree reflect the social and ethnic diversity of the Canadian population. Massey came from a wealthy family of agricultural equipment manufacturers, was educated at Balliol in Oxford, had a large circle of titled friends, and was so devoted to Britain that by the age of twenty-seven "he had made twenty transatlantic trips."[26] Ritchie came from one of Nova Scotia's foremost families, though one frequently short of cash, and like Massey he had numerous impressive friends even if his tended to be a little more louche. Vanier's father, while hard-working and ambitious, was probably illiterate, but he built a prosperous real-estate business, and Georges Vanier began his career as a lawyer in Montreal and became a distinguished military man.[27] The family had deep roots in seventeenth-century Normandy, and both Vaniers maintained a "quasi-religious" attachment to France (150). When, after the liberation of Paris, they returned to France "in a Royal Canadian Air Force plane escorted by two Spitfires" and flew over Normandy, "Georges [. . .] was overwhelmed by the realization that [his forebear]

Guillaume Vanier had left this very shoreline for Canada three centuries earlier" (177). His education at Oxford compensated for Pearson's small-town background as the son of a Methodist minister, but until late in life he referred self-ironically to his social "limitations" that required him to learn "to balance [...] a champagne glass as though [he] had never been brought up in a Methodist parsonage."[28]

Ignatieff's trajectory initially went in the opposite direction to everyone else's. He was the son of an exiled Russian count and princess with little of their wealth and position left to them after the October Revolution. In his memoirs, he captures his various transformations in the wildly diverse nicknames that were applied to him over his lifetime. First, British fellow students suspected him of being a Bolshevik. Then, after the family's arrival in Canada, his fellow workers at a Canadian railway camp identified him with the "Bohunks" and "Douks" (that is, *Doukhobors*, descendants of a dissenter sect from Russia), the dismissive names then common in Canada for immigrants from Central Europe.[29] Despite his career as a diplomat and Provost of the University of Trinity College, Ignatieff continued to be occasionally labeled an "ethnic." Thus, a student from Quebec, whom he hired for practice in conversational French when he was ambassador to NATO in Paris, reminded Ignatieff not to meddle in the conflict "between the French and the English" in Canada: "You ethnics keep out of it" (215). Likewise, when Ignatieff was discussed in the press as a possible candidate for governor-general, his "ethnic" background was considered by some to be a deterrent despite his impressive achievements.[30]

The differences in their backgrounds notwithstanding, these men had been raised in admiration of Britain. In Halifax, Ritchie was brought up "in an atmosphere [...] in which everything British was Best"[31] and despite his keen sense of situational absurdity and his caustic tongue, he remained an unapologetic monarchist all of his life. He never missed an opportunity to report on his encounters with royalty, whether it was being "led in with the other Secretaries" when the Queen came to tea with the Masseys (97) or observing Princess Margaret at a postwar reception in Paris, "a cool little devil [...] [with] all the Commonwealth and French officials and their wives sweating around her."[32] Partly through his education at Balliol, Massey's connections with the British aristocracy were so wide-ranging and intimate that they had Prime Minister Mackenzie King suspect violation of the rank of precedence when he intended for "[t]he fierce light that beats upon a throne ... to illuminate only prime ministers."[33] Although passionately opposed to any efforts by Downing Street to draw Canada "back into the imperial framework,"[34] King too expressed his support of wartime Britain in, for example, a collection of radio broadcasts and speeches entitled

Canada at Britain's Side (1941). As for Pearson, he delivers an account of his role as "Gold Stick in Waiting" at the 1937 coronation of King George VI that is pure farce, but the humor is, as is characteristic of him, mostly directed against himself and his unfortunate Canadian companions at the ceremony rather than at the monarchy as an institution.[35] From his comments on the abdication crisis and the importance he ascribes to the dominions' involvement in responding to it, it is clear that he meant no disrespect. In contrast to Pearson, Ignatieff was annoyed even decades later by "Massey's extraordinary admiration of the British upper classes,"[36] but he did insist on drawing a distinction between this "snobbishness" and the respect that was due to average British citizens for their "tremendous bravery and quiet determination ... during those dark days of war" (63). On a two-year stay in Britain in the 1920s when Georges Vanier attended the Staff College in Camberley, the Vaniers had been irritated by the "snobbery" extended to them as "colonials,"[37] but Vanier served on the coronation committee in 1937 (115), and in 1947 the Vaniers' son Jean was "one of the officers aboard the *Vanguard* [...] that took King George VI [and his family] to South Africa," where Princess Elizabeth celebrated her twenty-first birthday and from where she broadcast her pledge to the Commonwealth to do her duty as future Queen (197). (Like the other Vanier children, Jean confirmed the difficulty of fitting his parents into a single social category by becoming founder of *L'Arche*, an international organization dedicated to the welfare of mentally challenged citizens.)

This ample proof of their loyalty to the British crown notwithstanding, their devotion to France created a complex situation for the Vaniers, especially Pauline. One famous clash between her and Alice Massey illustrates not only the division between English and French as it occasionally affected even the team at Canada House, but also the masculine perspective of these texts, and it is a pity that there do not appear to be parallel diaries and memoirs by the women to offer a corrective to the men's views.[38]

Formulating Nationalism

At first sight, the diplomats' emotional attachment to the British crown may suggest a dedication to the status quo, but "swimming in the full tide of history" in World War II London, Canada's representatives began to formulate Canada's future as a post-imperial nation more definitively than the Balfour Report on Inter-Imperial Relations (1926) and its result, the Statute of Westminster (1931), had accomplished after the Great War and Canada's coming-of-age at Vimy. Nobody summarized the situation more forcefully than Pearson: "Never have I been so glad to be a Canadian as in these last days – at least we are not responsible for this mess," he said as desperate refugees hoping to emigrate to North America thronged through Canada House as "the door of escape from hell,"[39] and he added "If this country makes peace I hope Canada will become a republic and that would be the end [. . .] of our duty to the Empire."[40] This is Ritchie citing Pearson, having him use blunt language rarely evident in Pearson's own memoirs, but he did use it. As Minister of Foreign Affairs, he demonstrated some sixteen years later during the Suez crisis that he no longer intended Canada to act as Britain's "colonial chore-boy."[41] His and Prime Minister Louis St. Laurent's heated defense of Canada's autonomy in international affairs lost the Liberals votes in the next election in 1957, but his work as mediator during the crisis was impressive enough to earn him the Nobel Prize. His love of the British upper classes notwithstanding, Massey was a nationalist who energetically and lavishly supported Canadian arts and letters, presided over the highly significant Royal Commission on National Developments in the Arts, Letters and Sciences (1949), and became Canada's first Canadian-born governor-general.

Ritchie wrote his diary, no matter how much it was edited before publication, in immediate response to events rather than as a memoir in retrospect. As a result, it is especially acerbic in its criticism of British condescension toward the colonials, and Ritchie frequently uses epigrammatic generalizations to make his point. He takes exception to the "not unkindly but ... sober ironic air"[42] that English soldiers level at the troops from the colonies, becomes irate about a "Patronising old Pecksniff" in the House of Lords who boasts about his hospitality to the "lads from the Dominions" (65), and admires the Australians for "serv[ing] notice that [they] will continue to be a member of the Club at [their] own price" (158–59). Charming as he found the Queen in person, Ritchie is less certain about the Royal Tour, undertaken in 1939 by King George VI and Queen Elizabeth in Canada and the United States, the first time a British monarch had visited one of the dominions. Ritchie admits that the Royal Tour was a triumph of public relations, "the occasion for an overpowering manifestation of at any rate some Canadians of a deep yearning towards the mother country" (96). As one might suspect from the oddly contradictory mix of qualifiers ("overpowering," "at any rate some Canadians," "deep yearning"), Ritchie suspects a pragmatic and self-serving subtext, "an example of the English genius for making use of people" (96), even if the Tour is now interestingly read as an important stepping stone toward Canadian cultural distinctiveness, especially in the role played by the recently constituted Canadian Broadcasting Corporation in recording the event.[43] Ritchie's frequent trips to Ireland to visit his lover, the Anglo-Irish novelist Elizabeth Bowen, further fuel his objections to imperialism and the class division supported by it. In the wake of the 1945 Labour victory, the couple notes with distaste the flight of wealthy Britons to Ireland and Kenya, where, "fearful of high taxation and the march of democracy," they hoped to recover the economic and social privileges that were slipping away from them.[44] Bowen and Ritchie's worried discussion about Ireland going "Kenya-type smart" took place in 1948, but even four years earlier Ritchie was repulsed by "the hatred of the more intelligent English upper classes for the age they live in" and he speculated that "the English do not care a pin about justice. What they like is seemliness."[45] These discussions hint at a subject that deserves separate investigation, namely the phenomenon of collective "travel" in the 1940s as not only comprising the movements across Europe and the Atlantic of displaced people who had lost everything they owned but also, in fewer numbers, the voluntary displacements within the Commonwealth of privileged citizens determined to keep their social position.

Ritchie's diaries do feature expeditions, to be discussed below, into the midst of military action, but his preferred pose is that of solitary *flâneur* who, after a hectic day at Canada House, strolls about London with a bunch of violets in one hand and a copy of Théophile Gautier's *Mademoiselle de Maupin* in the other – eloquent proof that, contrary to his assertion elsewhere in the diaries, some Canadians can quite competently "stomach the excessive [sic]."[46] Indeed, it could be argued that Ritchie's strenuous resistance to complying with the stereotype of Canadians as bland, rural, and docile was his particular rebellion against colonialism. Moreover, this resistance provides proof that – as is so often the case with these men – one attitude can coexist with another that apparently contradicts it, in this case his patriotism on the one hand and, on the other, his longing for Europe, "away from the mindless beauty of [Canadian] woods and lakes [and] a community where there is no attractive way of going to the bad" (55). Pearson's method of self-assertion, by contrast, is to play up the "Canadian primitive,"[47] by insistently referring to his "transatlantic accent and attitudes" (103) and claiming that his young son "kept [him] segregated from a too close contact with other parents" (103) at his British school. Pearson paces his sentences with calculated irony by building up to the qualifier at the end when he describes how he disgraced himself with his British hosts by throwing a stone at a grouse rather than shooting it: "they were very kind people, especially to Canadians" (104). On a complicated trip with Ritchie to observe the Dunkirk Evacuation, he congratulates himself on having taken along a companion who "spoke good Oxford English" because the military police became suspicious of Pearson's "transatlantic accent" (178).

Ritchie's frequent affectation is made tolerable by his characteristic ironic awareness of it and by the free admission that it is not patriotism that makes wartime London attractive to him but the city's decay. Both the pose and its self-exposure give him the authority to pillory the presumption of class-conscious applicants for evacuation to Canada, such as "Lady B., looking radiant" who wants her son's complete school transferred to Canada, or a high-ranking Spanish diplomat who requires transport "for his daughter, his mother and a troop of maids and governesses on board the next ship."[48] Notwithstanding these applicants' confidence that privilege will protect them in this crisis, Ritchie reads the unkempt and rubbish-strewn lawns in the parks, the leaves blown into the vestibule of the Ritz, and above all the piles of rubble left behind by the bombs as signals that "the dissolution of civilized society is overpowering," at least of "civilized society" as represented by Britain (60). The future, however, does not belong to this decadence but to the "friendly barbarians" who have come to the defense of the mother country, a term Ritchie is quick to identify as "[never] heard here" (96). His detailed ground-level observations and the conclusions he draws from them differ sharply from Vincent Massey's. Generally spare in detail about wartime London, Massey's diaries record a bird's eye view from the roof of the Dorchester Hotel, an exclusive environment even in these straightened circumstances. No matter how different their approaches to reportage, Ritchie and Massey were united in their affection for London. This becomes especially apparent when they describe places that they find unambiguously distasteful and menacing. During his posting in Bonn 1954–58, Ritchie is for some time unable to shake the feeling of "a persistent, sinister undertone,"[49] and he pours his energy into describing, with merciless detail, "the ugliness of the Cologne population" (80). When Massey visits Berlin and Nuremberg in 1946, he concentrates on the ruined Nazi architecture and, at the war criminals' trial, the startling sight of "one of Goering's neckties on a tray in the gallery outside the cells with his name on a card," but the unequivocal sense of "a brooding ugliness" is the same in both accounts.[50]

The strongest reassurance that the Allies were gaining the upper hand was obtained from a military plane or from the deck of a destroyer. Brigadier Harry Crerar authorized Massey to fly "towards Calais and Boulogne" to look at military operations from the air, and the pilot, a man "more daring than precise," was merely given the instruction to "'just keep away from flak'" (410). Not to be outdone by Massey's trip, Ritchie temporarily abandoned his activities as *flâneur* and became "unendurably restless and determined by hook or crook to get to the Normandy beach-head"[51] shortly after the landing of the Allies. Using the pretext of a message by Mackenzie King to the Canadian troops that Ritchie drafted himself and for which he persuaded Vincent Massey to obtain the Prime Minister's signature, Ritchie traveled by troop ship to the manmade port of Arromanches. He was the only man in civilian clothes on board and, not having obtained a military pass to legitimize his expedition, faced the possibility of "being taken up by the Military Police and shot on sight as a spy" (169). He even had a costume for his trip to Normandy: an old Burberry coat, with bottles of whisky "for use as bribes" clanking in its pockets, seemed the perfect disguise for a pretend-intelligence agent (169).

Despite the play-acting, Ritchie was aware of the historical importance and collective interest of this particular eye-witness account. In a travelogue that, at eight pages, is sustained well beyond the length of any other section in the wartime volume of his diaries, he slips back into the skin of the journalist that he was at the beginning of his career. He does this in order to craft an *aide-mémoire* for himself and, to share in his published diaries thirty years later, a detailed word picture for civilians who were unable to get anywhere near the scene. He adapts the standard methods of radio and newsreel reportage by efficiently dividing up an apparently chaotic scene into comprehensible portions and animating the panorama with helpfully calibrated enumerations, vivid analogies, and the verbal equivalents of wide-angle shots, close-ups, and sound effects: "[The port] was crowded with troopships, a variety of landing craft, tankers, munition and supply ships and small tugs in which are seated majors with megaphones who are supposed to have some control over the movement of the shipping. They dash about like sheepdogs" (171). Here too he inserts a national theme, in the description of a "Canadian-manned landing craft" that doubles as an allegory of the ship of state. It is "run ... in a peculiarly Canadian way – the lack of fuss and feathers, the humour and the horse-sense with which the whole business is handled" (171). As in his opening shot of the location, he begins with a panorama, by stipulating the meaning of "Canadian way." He is careful to zoom in on the young soldiers who implement the "Canadian way," by identifying them as "a French-Canadian, a Dukhobor [sic], a lumberjack, an ex-rumrunner, a Newfoundlander" (172). Ritchie abruptly loses interest in the whole expedition, however, when word reaches him that his younger brother Roley has been seriously wounded and hospitalized, and Ritchie is now just as "desperately anxious" to get back to Britain as he had been to get away from it (175).

Diplomats' Memoirs and Diaries: Their Cultural Significance

What then is the cultural significance of these diaries and memoirs? It is not merely the political facts and perspectives they offer, important as they are.

Literary analysis of these texts, using travel writing as the point of reference, permits us to trace the emergence of a national consciousness from the ground up. Here, the metaphor of "from the ground up" means a literally spatial process. An accomplished *flâneur* like Ritchie sifts through the evidence of decay in the streets of London and determines from it that the war has diminished Britain's claim to predominance within the Commonwealth. At the opposite end, the bird's-eye view from airplane and troopship instructs him and the other memoirists what the allies, including the Canadians, have accomplished in resisting fascism and what global responsibilities they have assumed as a result of their participation. Because they are officials as well as private citizens, their wartime travels assume, or are meant to assume, an exemplary role. To fill it, the writers use a variety of templates, trying on different personae and accents to suit their nation's increasingly independent status. These range from the "transatlantic primitive" to the cosmopolitan dandy, but in constructing their new identities, they retain elements of Canada's imperial history – such as the monarchy – to keep themselves distinct from other independent nations, in particular the United States and the Soviet Union. Travel writing in wartime is an apt medium through which to study the process of national identity-formation because it is predicated on mobility, and even the most ritualized elements of travel, such as the conventions of departure and arrival, are definitively disturbed and made over.

NOTES

1 Charles Ritchie, *The Siren Years: A Canadian Diplomat Abroad, 1937–1945* (Toronto: Macmillan, 1974), 59.

2 John Hilliker, *Canada's Department of External Affairs*, vol.1, *The Early Years, 1909–1946* (Montreal: McGill-Queen's University Press, 1990), 217.

3 Lorna Lloyd, *Diplomacy with a Difference: The Office of High Commissioner, 1880–2006. Diplomatic Studies* (Leiden: Martinus Nijhoff, 2007), 63.

4 See David Lambert and Alan Lester, eds., *Colonial Lives across the British Empire: Imperial Careering in the Long Nineteenth Century* (Cambridge: Cambridge University Press, 2006).

5 See David Goldsworthy, *Losing the Blanket: Australia and the End of Britain's Empire* (Melbourne: Melbourne University Press, 2002); Daniel Gorman, *The Emergence of International Society in the 1920s* (Cambridge: Cambridge University Press, 2012); Carl Bridge, Frank Bongiorno, and David Lee, eds., *The High Commissioners: Australia's Representatives in the United Kingdom, 1910–2010* (Canberra: Department of Foreign Affairs and Trade, 2010), 103–10.

6 George Egerton, "Politics and Autobiography: Political Memoir as Polygenre," *Biography*, 15, no. 3 (1992): 221–42 (223).

7 Valerie Cromwell, "'Married to Affairs of State': Memoirs of the Wives and Daughters of British Diplomats," in *Political Memoir: Essays on the Politics of Memory*, ed. George Egerton (London: Frank Cass, 1994), 207–24 (213).

8 Zara Steiner, "The Diplomatic Life: Reflections on Selected British Diplomatic Memoirs Written Before and After the Great War," in *Political Memoir*, ed. Egerton, 167–87 (169).

9 Billie Melman, "The Middle East/Arabia: 'The Cradle of Islam,'" in *The Cambridge Companion to Travel Writing*, ed. Peter Hulme and Tim Youngs (Cambridge: Cambridge University Press, 2001), 105–21 (114).

10 Charles Ritchie, *An Appetite for Life: The Education of a Young Diarist 1924–1927* (Toronto: Macmillan, 1977), 17.

11 Ritchie, *Siren Years*, 154.

12 Mary Louise Pratt, *Imperial Eyes: Travel Writing and Transculturation*, 2nd edn. (London: Routledge, [1992] 2008), 197.

13 George Ignatieff, with Sonja Sinclair, *The Making of a Peacemonger: The Memoirs of George Ignatieff* (Toronto: University of Toronto Press, 1985), 68; Vincent Massey, *What's Past Is Prologue: The Memoirs of the Right Honourable Vincent Massey* (London: Macmillan, 1963), 367.

14 Ritchie, *Siren Years*, 55.

15 Irving Abella and Harold Troper, *None Is Too Many: Canada and the Jews of Europe 1933–1948* (Toronto: Lester & Orpen Dennys, 1982).

16 Ignatieff, *Making of a Peacemonger*, 60.

17 Lester Pearson, *Memoirs, 1897–1948: Through Diplomacy to Politics* (London: Gollancz, 1973), 135.

18 For a review of this point see the Introduction to this volume.

19 Fred Gaffen, *Forgotten Soldiers* (Winnipeg: Canadian Defense Academy Press, 2008), 80–81.

20 Massey, *What's Past*, 283.

21 "Retter Radio Reception," *The Globe and Mail* 9 January, 1940, 6.

22 James Dempsey, "Alberta's Indians and the Second World War," in *For King and Country: Alberta in the Second World War*, ed. Kenneth W. Tingley (Edmonton: Provincial Museum of Alberta, 1995), 39–52 (42).

23 "Retter Radio Reception," 6. A full discussion of Aboriginal soldiers' participation in World War II exceeds the scope of this chapter. For further information, see, for example, Gaffen, *Forgotten Soldiers*; R. Scott Sheffield, *The Red Man's on the Warpath: The Image of the "Indian" and the Second World War* (Vancouver: University of British Columbia Press, 2014); and, P. Whitney Lackenbauer and Craig Leslie Mantle, ed., *Aboriginal Peoples and the Canadian Military: Historical Perspectives* (Winnipeg: Canadian Defence Academy Press, 2007). I acknowledge the assistance of Fiona Anthes, Military History Research Centre, Canadian War Museum.

24 Alison Smith, David Blayney Brown, and Carol Jokobi, eds., *Artist and Empire: Facing Britain's Imperial Past* (London: Tate Publishing, 2015), 148.

25 Lord Tweedsmuir, "Canada's Outlook on the World," in *Canadian Occasions* (Toronto: Musson, 1941), 80–81.

26 Claude Bissell, *The Young Vincent Massey* (Toronto: University of Toronto Press, 1981), 131.

27 Mary Frances Coady, *Georges and Pauline Vanier: Portrait of a Couple* (Montreal: McGill University Press, 2011), 6, 18f.

28 Pearson, *Memoirs*, 106.

29 Ignatieff, *Making of a Peacemonger*, 17.

EVA-MARIE KRÖLLER

30 Clive Baxter, "Will Michener Stay Longer or an 'Ethnic' Succeed Him?" Uniden-tified Clipping (Canada: Governors-General, Clippings File, Vancouver Public Library).

31 Ritchie, *Siren Years*, 8.

32 Charles Ritchie, *Diplomatic Passport: More Undiplomatic Diaries, 1946–1962* (Toronto: Macmillan, 1981), 41.

33 Pearson, *Memoirs*, 106.

34 Charles Ritchie, *Storm Signals: More Undiplomatic Diaries, 1962–1971* (Toronto: Macmillan, 1983), 89.

35 Pearson, *Memoirs*, 112–18.

36 Ignatieff, *Making of a Peacemonger*, 63.

37 Coady, *Georges and Pauline Vanier*, 75.

38 See, for example, Coady, *Georges and Pauline Vanier*, 151f.

39 Quoted in Ritchie, *Siren Years*, 59.

40 Quoted in Ritchie, *Siren Years*, 54, 57.

41 Quoted in John English, *The Worldly Years: The Life of Lester Pearson. vol 2: 1949–1972* (Toronto: Knopf, 1992), 142.

42 Ritchie, *Siren Years*, 81.

43 Mary Vipond, "The Royal Tour of 1939 as a Media Event," *Canadian Journal of Communication*, 35, no. 1 (2010): 149–72; Simon J. Potter, "The BBC, the CBC, and the 1939 Royal Tour of Canada," *Cultural and Social History*, 3, no. 4 (2006): 4–44.

44 Victoria Glendinning and Judith Robertson, ed., *Love's Civil War: Elizabeth Bowen and Charles Ritchie. Letters and Diaries, 1941–1973* (Toronto: McClel-land and Stewart, 2008), 122, fn133.

45 Ritchie, *Siren Years*, 177.

46 Ritchie, *Diplomatic Passport*, 68.

47 Pearson, *Memoir*, 117.

48 Ritchie, *Siren Years*, 59.

49 Ritchie, *Diplomatic Passport*, 84.

50 Massey, *What's Past*, 437, 436.

51 Ritchie, *Siren Years*, 167.

7

CHARLES FORSDICK

Francophone Postcolonial Travel Writing

The Emergence of a Tradition

When the second French edition of Tété-Michel Kpomassie's *Un Africain au Groenland* [*An African in Greenland*] appeared in 2015, thirty-five years after the first, its publisher, Arthaud, marketed the work as "the mythical narrative of the first African travel writer [*écrivain-voyageur*]."[1] The claim requires some unpacking: Not only is a genre customarily associated with documentary realism marketed here – in the light of its author's origins – via an explicit association with myth but also a Francophone text is granted a universal preeminence, suggesting that the emergence of a singularized African tradition of travel writing is a recent, postcolonial phenomenon. Discussions of the origins of travelogues by African authors or writers of African heritage are beyond the scope of this chapter, although the narratives of Ibn Baṭūṭah, the fourteenth-century Moroccan Muslim traveler and scholar, are clearly contenders for such an accolade, and recent research has demonstrated in addition that the circulation of travel writing in indigenous languages complements and challenges Western understandings of the genre.[2] The recent conscription of Kpomassie to the guild of *écrivains-voyageurs* represents, however, a considerable shift in contemporary understandings of travel writing, specifically in France and in the wider French-speaking world, a shift that for many would have been unimaginable when Kpomassie's text was first published.

As its author outlines in a new preface to the work, this autobiographical account of a Togolese traveler's desire to visit Greenland and to discover there the art of hunting has, since its first appearance in 1981, had a more complex history than any stable generic identification may seem to imply. The work was recompensed on publication with the *Prix littéraire francophone international*, awarded annually to the "best book written in French by a non-French author and on a subject of universal relevance," but was otherwise not associated with the rapid renewal of interest in travel writing in the 1980s. Despite the support of the leading French anthropologist Jean Malaurie, this distinctive postcolonial travelogue attracted little attention in

93

France and then fell out of print. A review in English in the *Times Literary Supplement* by the poet, translator, and travel writer James Kirkup (and then his subsequent English translation of the work) ensured its visibility as a work of travel writing. Kirkup claimed the book was "surely the most extraordinary book to come out of black Africa,"[3] and his translation created a wider readership outside France, consolidated in 1988 by a BBC documentary, *The African Eskimo*, and a popular *New York Review of Books* edition.[4]

The slow recognition and resurrection of *An African in Greenland* as a work of travel writing is symptomatic of wider processes of generic inclusion and exclusion, of expansion and contraction, that are the subject of this chapter. Travel writing often describes and indeed depends on asymmetries of power between traveler and "travelee," and as such has been read as one of the key forms of colonial literature. The genre has consequently played a major role in documenting (as well as filtering for public consumption) accounts of imperial expansionism, serving – as Edward Said and others have demonstrated – as an important vehicle, especially from the later nineteenth century onward, for the forging of colonial discourse. A major critical maneuver following decolonization has not only been the revelation of this complicity between literary practice and colonial ideology but also an attempt to diversify and then to decolonize the genre of travel writing itself – by seeking alternative voices embedded in earlier examples of the genre, as well as by identifying the ways in which the travelogue itself can "write back" (and often has "written back"), challenging the orthodoxies the genre previously perpetuated. Central to these efforts is the assemblage of a corpus of postcolonial travel writing, a process considerably more evident in the English-speaking than the French-speaking world, perhaps as a result of the substantial impact of a body of thought seen as "postcolonial" on the production and consumption of literature in English. Whereas a corpus of Anglophone postcolonial travel writing is now relatively well established, associated with authors such as V. S. Naipaul, Richard Wright, Jamaica Kincaid, Pankaj Mishra, and Amitav Ghosh, there is no easily identifiable grouping of Francophone postcolonial authors who might be seen as their equivalent, and it is striking that one of the most prominent examples of a travelogue from the French Caribbean, the Haitian-American writer Edwidge Danticat's *After the Dance*, was written in English and published in an Anglophone series (Crown Journeys, and then Vintage Departures) devoted to travel writing.[5]

There is a similar imbalance in critical literature, where there is an increasing body of scholarship on English-language material that has added ethnicity and cultural origin to the range of variables in the light of which understandings of travel writing are often guided, extending accordingly beyond an emphasis on work by Western, white, straight, educated, and male authors. Edward Said and Mary Louise Pratt were among the first to subject the travelogue to such sustained postcolonial criticism, and their emphases on alternative perspectives and on different voices encouraged other critics to seek, to anthologize, and finally to study a corpus of postcolonial travelogues that may be seen to sit in a contrapuntal relationship with the dominant European tradition. There have been attempts to describe a similar tradition in French writing, the most notable of which is Romuald Fonkoua's volume *Les Discours des voyages*,[6] but it is only really the Hiberno-Scottish critic Aedín Ní Loingsigh who has performed the serious critical work of understanding literature of mobility produced in French through the prism of travel writing and the construction of genre in her book *Postcolonial Eyes*.[7]

Ní Loingsigh notes that a significant theme in early criticism of Francophone writing was mobility. Madeleine Borgomano, for instance, describes precolonial Africa as a culture "en mouvement perpétuel" [in perpetual movement], and seeks as a result to challenge the ways in which many French representations of colonized people attempt to reduce them to a condition of sessility, a spatial counterpart to what Johannes Fabian has dubbed the "denial of coevalness."[8] Mildred Mortimer developed this analysis by exploring the ways in which the journey motif – as a function of the teleology embedded in the Western genre of the novel, but also as part of traditional narratives in which the quest is associated with self-knowledge and coming of age – is central to many foundational texts of Francophone literature, by authors as diverse as Camara Laye, Ferdinand Oyono, Mongo Beti, and Mariama Bâ.[9] Such approaches associate travel and mobility with fiction, autobiography, and the memoir, meaning that there has been little attempt to identify an alternative "Francophone" tradition of travel writing or to investigate the ways in which texts can – in translation, with changing readerships, or simply with the passage of time – shift between generic categories. The aim of this chapter is to identify and study the emergence and consolidation of a specific Francophone tradition of postcolonial travel writing, distinguishing this in particular from the Anglophone tradition to which significant attention has recently been paid. These distinctions are partly to do with institutional and disciplinary issues, and the ways different linguistic communities talk about literature. They are also linked to differing creative practices, and a clear policing of the boundaries of French-language travel writing (and indeed of French literature more generally).

Francophone Postcolonial Travel Writing: A Historical Overview

Notwithstanding acknowledgment of the persistent presence of mobility as a dominant if not foundational motif in Francophone postcolonial literature, travel writing has long proved impermeable to writers working in French from colonized contexts (and more recently from the Global South). The mechanisms of this policing require close scrutiny, and are associated with authorial choices in terms of form and genre as much as with the official institutions of literature (including publishing, marketing, prize cultures, festivals) – although the relationship in this case between the individual and the systemic remains undeniable. A clear illustration of these mechanisms is provided by the re-emergence of interest in travel writing in later twentieth-century France, a development closely linked to the context of a return to narratives of adventure (reflected in the re-release of titles from the colonial period as well as in traces of contemporary colonial nostalgia). Central to this resurgence of travel writing was Michel Le Bris, who launched in 1989 the journal *Gulliver* and in 1990 the now highly successful "Etonnants voyageurs" festival (still held annually in Saint Malo). This activity crystallized, in the activity of a loosely configured group of authors gathered under the banner "pour une littérature voyageuse" [for a traveling literature], the title of the manifesto (in the form of a series of essays) they coauthored in 1992.[10] Committed to the rediscovery of earlier travel writers (such as Victor Segalen) and to the recognition of modern travel classics (by authors such as Nicolas Bouvier and Jacques Lacarrière), the movement contributed, unwittingly or not, to the further policing of the boundaries of the travel writing genre in France, for the authors and texts promoted were exclusively metropolitan, for the most part written by male authors, and failed to include any work by writers from former colonies or the *outre-mer*.

Such exclusion was striking: not only did the 1980s see the publication of travel texts by postcolonial authors (with Kpomassie, cited above, being the most prominent example), but Francophone writers associated with the 'Etonnants voyageurs' festival had themselves contributed to the travel genre (notably the Martinican Edouard Glissant, one of whose first texts, *Soleil de la Conscience* [1956], was a poetic narrative of a journey from the French Caribbean to France).[11] At the same time, the selection of recovered "lost" travel classics complementing the publication of new travelogues perpetuated the guild identity evident in the membership of the "pour une littérature voyageuse" movement, and did not extend to key writers such as the Ivoirian Bernard Dadié, whose narratives of journeys to Paris, New York, and Rome from the late 1950s and early 1960s contributed significantly to a satirical strand of the travel genre that can be tracked back to Montesquieu and his

Persian Letters. It has been argued that this exclusive definition is linked to an imperial nostalgia evident in the work of some of the travel writers associated with this particular moment in the genre's recent history, as if those seen previously in a colonial context as "travelees" were not granted the right afforded by the travelogue to travel – and indeed write – back. This policing of a genre is all the more surprising given that the vehicles of the "pour une littérature voyageuse" movement – notably the festival and journal with which it was associated – in general welcomed postcolonial writers, but significantly as novelists and not as *écrivains-voyageurs.* Prominent French-language authors of the late twentieth century – such as Patrick Chamoiseau or Tahar Ben Jelloun, both of whose work was rewarded with major literary prizes – were accepted as contributors of postcolonial texts to imported categories such as "world fiction," but such categorization might be seen as a further act of generic containment. When this interest in "world fiction" was further Gallicized by authors gathered around Le Bris in 2007 in the concrete form of "littérature-monde" (a manifesto for which appeared in *Le Monde* in March of that year),[12] the emphasis among the diverse authors from across the Francosphere was again very much on the novel and not the travelogue. The "étonnants voyageurs" of the 1970s (Bouvier, Lacarrière, and others) are seen as key to the genealogy of this "world-literature in French," but the mobility-focused writings of many of the postcolonial authors among the signatories – Maryse Condé, Ananda Devi, Edouard Glissant, Dany Laferrière, Alain Mabanckou, Anna Moï, Gisèle Pineau, Boualem Sansal, Abdourahman A. Waberi, and others – were not given similar weight.

Despite the clear policing of the generic boundaries of French-language travel writing, it is evident that the Francophone postcolonial travelogue is increasingly visible. These contemporary manifestations of the genre are not only postcolonializing the form and revealing many of the previous ideological assumptions with which it was associated but also encouraging a re-historicization of the travel narrative and its expansion to include texts it previously failed to encompass. Such a literary historical approach can allow discernment of the genealogy of a Francophone tradition of postcolonial travel writing. As the work of scholars such as Mildred Mortimer (discussed above) makes clear, questions of mobility have always played a foundational role in Francophone writing, although the journeys these texts describe are often very different from the "travel" on which Francophone European examples of the genre (from Belgium, France, and Switzerland) depend. It is possible even to track these patterns of mobility back to early nineteenth-century Haitian literature, produced in the aftermath of independence in 1804, where one of the first plays published was Fligneau's *Haïtien expatrié,* a dramatization of the Danish exile of two Haitian characters whose return to independent Haiti allows them to see that it is the people of Europe who remain enslaved.[13] Some would argue that Toussaint Louverture's memoir, drafted while he was imprisoned at the Fort de Joux in France in 1802–03, also belongs to such a tradition as they focus in part on the displacement of the revolutionary leader's enforced exile in France from which he would never return.[14] The emergence of a tradition of the so-called Francophone travelogue is, however, more of an early twentieth-century phenomenon, triggered by a historical event (World War I) and a social phenomenon (colonial exhibitions) that would be responsible in different ways for the movement of large numbers of colonized peoples to metropolitan France.

Bakary Diallo was one of the first of the 134,000 sub-Saharan African troops involved in the World War I to produce an account of his own experience of the conflict. *Force-Bonté* is an autobiographical narrative of his journey from a remote village in Senegal to France, via service in Morocco.[15] Much of the critical attention paid to the work has involved discussion of authorship: It has been widely claimed that since Bakary was illiterate, he provided the raw material for a ghost writer to produce the text, creating from the outset of the corpus of modern Francophone travelogues questions around the status of colonial or postcolonial traveler as what Percy Adams called the "travel-liar."[16] This thesis of the ghost-written text is supported by the pro-colonial nature of the work, which questions neither the use of colonial soldiers in the conflict nor their treatment in its aftermath, and is often seen to present a sub-Saharan African voice to counter contemporary authors more critical of France such as the former *tirailleur* and activist Lamine Senghor. The narrative is divided into three parts: an account of the narrator's Peulh childhood; his experiences as a *tirailleur sénégalais*, including in Senegal, Morocco (where he takes part in the suppression of local resistance), and finally France at the Battle of the Marne; and then his efforts after the war to gain French citizenship and settle in France itself. Janós Riesz has studied the text closely, and argues for a significance and originality in the text that most other critics have denied.[17] What is clear is that the work explores the mobility of a sub-Saharan subject in ways that had previously depended on the ventriloquism of French voices, and also reflects on the complex motivations for "travel" of a *tirailleur sénégalais*, with reference to the deployment of colonial troops to suppress colonial insurrection as well as to the shifting attitudes to home that such journeys to Europe often generated. Even though a major strand of *Force-Bonté* refers to the narrator's progressive mastery of French, criticism of the work has nevertheless focused primarily on questions of authorship and narratorial trustworthiness, an approach that unwittingly draws the text into a travel writing tradition where such issues have long been prominent.

Shortly after the publication of *Force-Bonté*, another text appeared describing a different form of interwar migration, associated with the 1931 colonial exhibition at Vincennes. *Mirages de Paris*, by the Senegalese author Ousmane Socé Diop, is the account of the journey of the protagonist Fara to France, where he meets a French woman Jacqueline Bourciez who becomes the mother of his child.[18] Like *Force-Bonté*, *Mirages de Paris* is a fictionalized account of an African journey to France that would customarily have remained anonymous and certainly denied the status of featuring as a formal travel narrative. As Aedín Ní Loingsigh suggests, Socé's text shows a real geographical sensitivity, exploring the impact of colonialism on land-scape and culture in Fara's native Senegal, and the ways in which the protagonist's education – and in particular his acquisition of French – is central to his journey to France.[19] At the heart of the text is a critique of the slippage between the French rhetoric of republican equality and the actual and often racist treatment granted to sub-Saharan African travelers to France. Fara experiences a reverse exoticism, evident as he travels northward on the train to Paris, and the text contributes to a de-familiarization of France, no longer seen as the traveler's point of departure but instead as the African protagonist's destination. The "mirages" of the title captures, however, the dynamics of this process, for Paris is at once familiar (as freighted via colonial education), but at same time unrecognizable and even alienating. Although travel to the *exposition coloniale* is the motivation for Fara's journey, the exhibition features only briefly in the account, but Socé presents it as a site at which the stereotypes evident among the French about colonial cultures are confirmed and not challenged, where the version of sub-Saharan Africa presented in French metropolitan travel writing is stage-managed for the entertainment of the paying public. Fara's consciousness of the representational practices by which he is objectified, but with which he is ultimately complicit, transforms his journey into a form of exile from which there can be no return: the Paris he sought is revealed to be a mirage, and the protagonist becomes – in Ní Loingsigh's terms – a type of "anti-traveler," reflecting a figure who would become recurrent in many subsequent Francophone postcolonial travelogues (51).

Mirages de Paris ends with Fara's suicide in the waters of the Seine. The text subverts with tragedy the customary structure of the travelogue, which often depends on concluding settlement or return. While eschewing this dramatic outcome, two key Francophone travel narratives from the 1950s adopt the same trajectory described by Socé, bringing an educated colonial subject to metropolitan France. However, in the context of the rapid postwar reconfiguration of Empire, they deploy the resulting travel narrative to different ends. *Soleil de la conscience* (1956) is Edouard Glissant's first prose text, published at the end of his first decade in France. The text inaugurates a series of essays produced by Glissant, subsequently gathered under the title "Poétique," and exploits the generic indeterminacy of the form to explore his journey from Martinique to France and his experience of dwelling in the metropolitan "centre." As is the case with Socé's work, the text is rooted in an "exotisme à rebours" [reverse exoticism], a defamiliarization of France associated with, for instance, the author's account of his first experience of snow. Although Glissant casts himself as a "voyageur," *Soleil de la conscience* remains an unorthodox travel narrative, outlining a search for literary form by an author struggling to understand his relationship with the world in which he dwells. At much the same time, but in a more orthodox travelogue format, the Ivoirian author Bernard Dadié recounted in *Un nègre à Paris* (1959) the journey to Paris of his loosely fictionalized narrator, Tanhoe Bertin. This text was the first in a trio of travel narratives by Dadié, with two later works serving as narratives of journeys to Italy (*Patron de New York* [1964] and *La Ville où nul ne meurt* [1969]).[20]

Un nègre à Paris consciously adopted the dynamics of the reverse gaze, deployed in numerous French travel narratives since Montesquieu's *Persian Letters*, in order to present France itself – in the context of rapid decolonization – as a journey destination in its own right, with its inhabitants, the French, cast as sessile "travelees." Such an exoticizing maneuver was not uncommon, and was used to comic effect by Jean Rouch in his film *Petit à petit* (1970), where the protagonists of an earlier work, *Jaguar* (1967), travel to Paris and imitate white ethnographers as they study Parisians, measuring their skulls with calipers, making notes about clothes, diet, and everyday life. Dadié's satire tracks the protagonist's journey from his home to Dakar to Paris, underlining the slippage between an imagined France (freighted through colonial education and wider colonial culture) and the reality of the place he discovers. His account demonstrates the gap between the African traveler's self-perception (and associated belief that travel bestows a certain status) and the ways in which he is perceived, with this maneuver not only satirizing the ethnocentrism and solipsism of the conventional French travelogue to Africa, but also allowing a series of *faux naïf* reflections on contemporary France itself. Arrival on 14 July leads to a radical defamiliarization of French revolutionary history, and the two world wars are also presented as a version of intertribal struggle. Dadié's strategy is twofold: on the one hand, in observing for instance gender relations or the relationship of Parisians to their pets or the role of journalists in society, he seeks to understand French culture through an Ivoirian lens; on the other, as he travels, for example, in the metro, he treats Paris – as Barthes would Tokyo a decade later in *L'Empire des signes* (1970) – as untranslatable and beyond his understanding.

Underpinning the narrator's ethnographic observations is an unspoken awareness of context: Published in 1959, the travelogue is dated July–August 1956, and so is to be situated squarely in the context of French sub-Saharan African decolonization (achieved only two years later, in 1958). *Un nègre à Paris* deploys the devices of travel as both a critique of the assumptions and prejudices on which colonialism was based and as a means of reflecting on the relationships that might emerge between France and Africa in a post-colonial frame. A repeated interest in Parisian women parodies the ethno-pornographic focus on colonized women in French popular culture (and in ephemeral forms such as the postcard) as well as in (pseudo-)scientific journalism. At the same time, however, as Ní Loingsigh suggests, central to Dadié's travel texts is the "implication that Africa and Africans themselves are about to begin their own journey of discovery in which comparisons with other cultures will prove invaluable for determining future political, eco-nomic and cultural directions."[21] Michael Syrotinski goes on to relate this context directly to a form of generic critique, evident in Dadié's awareness of "the complicitous manner in which European travel writing served the ideology of colonial imperialism."[22] Central to this shift is the status of Dadié's protagonist as tourist, free to travel where he pleases (although often still subject to a persistent white gaze). In this capacity, from the exoticizing perspective of reverse ethnography, he provides a fresh account of the successes and failures of French history and culture. Looking forward in time, however, and dwelling on the implications of contemporary encoun-ters in the "contact zone" of travel, he focuses equally on the coming challenges, for both former colonizer and former colonized, in negotiating the afterlives of empire, in adjusting to new forms of postcolonial mobility, and in forging new political and social relationships in the shadow of the colonial past.

A Genre in Motion: Contemporary Diversification, Future Directions

Dadié's text – as was the case in the works of Bakary Diallo and Ousmane Socé – depends on a fictionalized narrator operating (to a greater or lesser extent) within the generic frame of documentary travel writing. The motiv-ations for this hybridization of form and voice are unclear, but undoubtedly relate to a significant degree to the (lack of) elasticity of the conventional travelogue, closed for much of the twentieth century to the voices of non-metropolitan writers who were expected to play the role of travelees. As has already been suggested, a clear exception to this tendency (discussed at the opening of this chapter) was Tété-Michel Kpomassie's *An African in Greenland*, a rare example of a postcolonial travelogue in French recognized as such. The multi-stage journey to the Arctic that this text recounts began in 1958, in the same chronological and political context as Dadié's account. There are two distinctive elements, however, to his text: the first is the clear coincidence of author and narrator, which grants Kpomassie the status of "écrivain-voyageur" (although the long time devoted to the journey itself, as well as the time lag between the journey and its writing, raises familiar questions about memory and the place of fictionalization in the travelogue); the second is the geography of the itinerary: Kpomassie's sixteen-month stay in Greenland (June 1965–October 1966) is preceded by an almost eight-year journey (September 1958–June 1965), recounted in the first part of the text, via various African and European locations where he stays to earn the money he needs to continue his travels. The centripetal dynamics of earlier travelers from French colonies, from "periphery" to "centre," are therefore replicated, but only partially, for Paris and France are no longer destinations in their own right, but serve as yet another stage on the journey to Greenland. Kpomassie's work is therefore disruptive in multiple ways: while prizing open a space within the French-language travelogue for a sub-Saharan African voice, it simultaneously undermines any expectations about the mode of travel such an author might adopt and the routes he might follow.

The motivations for the journey recounted in *An African in Greenland* diverge from those of previous itineraries discussed in this chapter (linked variously to war, education, and colonial exhibitions), and may be seen to converge with more conventional Western travelogues. Kpomassie's travels are in part triggered by another travelogue, Robert Gessain's *Les Esquimaux du Groenland à l'Alaska* (1947), not read at school by the narrator but purchased in the Protestant bookshop in Lomé.[23] What appears to draw him to the text are the competing meanings of the image on its cover: a hunter, whose activity is familiar, but whose clothing, trappings, and weapons are radically different; and although Gessain's text largely disappears from view once Kpomassie arrives in Greenland, it appears to leave him with an ethnographic interest in the culture he visits. Embedded in this mode of observation is both an auto-ethnographic impulse (Kpomassie is struck by the ways in which his striking physical differences mean that he as observer is often transformed into observed) and a tendency toward comparison (Togolese and Greenlandic cultures are both seen as radically altered by the impact of colonialism, and the shifts from "tradition" to "modernity" this entails). One of the motivations for the traveler's initial departure had been what Frances Bartkowski dubs "flight from paternal authority,"[24] following a traumatic incident during an initiation rite. The text concludes, however, with a positive desire to return home: The stay in Greenland leads to the accumulation of significant knowledge of the country and its people, a process that allows him to view his own culture of origin from a radically different perspective, while at the same time creating connections between origin and destination.

Kpomassie's text suggested not only the possibility of a generic diversification of Francophone postcolonial literature to include the travelogue within its purview but also the inscription within the literary corpus of journey narratives accounts dependent on vectors different from what Edward Said in *Culture and Imperialism* called the "voyage-in."[25] Whereas *An African in Greenland* describes an epic, iterative itinerary in which European cities are simply stages on the way to a radically different destination, a cluster of postcolonial travel narratives by diasporic authors focus on accounts of return. Although this sub-genre was in many ways initiated in the 1930s by the Negritude authors Aimé Césaire and Léon Gontran Damas, who deployed poetry and ethnographic documentary to recount their own travel in the interwar Black Atlantic (including journeys back, respectively, to Martinique and French Guiana), a cluster of texts adopting this approach has become particularly apparent in the recent postcolonial period as authors use the device of the journey to explore the changing dynamics of a former colonizing France with their own formerly colonized countries of origin. Kim Lefèvre is one of a number of Vietnamese writers who describes her journey back from France to her Vietnam in *Retour à la saison des pluies* (1990).[26] This theme is also relatively common, although with different emphases given their country's much longer postcolonial status, among writers of Haitian origin. Dany Laferrière's *L'Enigme du retour* (2009) recounts his own relationship to Haiti, a country he had been forced to leave during the Duvalier dictatorship, via a telling of his travel between Quebec and Port-au-Price, focused in particular on the journey back after his father's death.[27]

Despite its diverse origins, work by authors such as Laferrière and Lefèvre are similar to a long-established tradition of travel writing since the diasporic journeys they describe depend on clear axes and vectors, linking a stable home with their (or their parents') country of origin, and deploying travel as an interlude in which questions of identity are brought to the fore. The visibility of Francophone postcolonial travelogues impacts increasingly on travel writing in French, and these alternative tendencies are becoming increasingly apparent. Although the policing of the genre outlined at the beginning of this chapter may be seen to persist, the strategies of exclusion on which travel writing has long depended are under pressure as a combination of changing creative practices, publishing policies, and general literary appetite prize open understandings of what constitutes the genre. Recent years have also seen rapid evolution in the literatures of mobility, with work falling into this category also focusing on questions of motility that have traditionally been factored out of many travelogues as the privilege of the traveling narrator was taken as read.[28]

Central to these recent developments is a wider corpus, not necessarily recognized as traditional travel literature but sharing nevertheless the spaces such as the Mediterranean, on which journeys associated with that genre have often focused. These texts, recounting stories of contemporary migration, combine fiction and documentary reality; the blurring of the lines between these two modes returns the travelogue to questions regarding the "travel-liar" apparent since its emergence in a modern recognizable form. The hopes, fears, and often disastrous endings of clandestine itineraries undertaken by sub-Saharan African migrants are fictionalized by Abasse Ndione in *Mbëkë mi* (2008), a text whose subtitle – "à l'assaut des vagues de l'Atlantique" [out to conquer the Atlantic waves] – underlines the nature of the journeys they undertake.[29] Ndione's work opens with a brief, neutral account in his preface of an inaugural journey, from Senegal to the Canary Islands, of fifteen Senegalese fisherman "en pirogue" [in a canoe]. Their arrival in Tenerife and transfer to Madrid are reported to their parents, who thought them lost at sea. Their achievement is then transformed into the myth that *Mbëkë mi* explores: "The route of the extraordinary immigration of thousands of young African men, fleeing their country in peacetime and seeking a better future in Europe, had been opened [...]" (11). Ndione's text is a brief and subtly crafted one, describing the gathering of the group of migrants seeking to undertake the journey, the preparations of their boat and supplies, and their departure into the Atlantic. By focusing on individuals and their life stories, the aim is the re-humanization of narratives of contemporary migration, but a detail early in the text – the cart carrying belongings to the boat travels along the avenue Ousmane-Socé-Diop – seems to create a knowing connection to an earlier Senegalese travelogue, *Mirages de Paris*, and suggests that the hopes on which this journey is founded are equally hallucinatory. Travel by sea is described in detail, in part from the perspective of the characters for whom this is a first journey by boat. Initial conditions are good, and the crossing begins without incident, but a week after their departure, there is a sudden deterioration in the weather, accompanied by mechanical failure, a loss overboard of passengers and a breakdown of order onboard. The text concludes with the survivors being collected by a Spanish Red Cross vessel, by which point their individuality has been erased by a neutral account, re-imposing the dehumanization of contemporary human mobility, that treats those who have emerged from the ordeal as statistics.

Ndione's narrative has been supplemented, over the past decade, with a growing number of documentary accounts that recount attempted journeys from the Global South to Europe. Central to the reception of these have been questions of voice. Some, such as Mahmoud Traoré's *"Dem ak xabaar"/ partir et reconter* (2012),[30] have been co-written with French journalists. The epigraph to Traoré's account is from Fatou Diome: "When Africans recount their own experiences as inhabitants and explorers of the world, that will be the end of exoticism," and the implication is that the narrative that follows will challenge Western traditions of travel writing. The journey recounted in this text lasts three years, and follows an itinerary using multiple modes of transport across Mali, Burkina Faso, and Niger, up through Libya and across the Maghreb, finally gaining access to Spain via the Moroccan enclave of Ceuta. Given Le Dantec's paratextual additions and his overall (re)writing of Traoré's account, the authenticity of the text has been called into question, but the strategy of ghost-writing migrant journeys is not uncommon, as Olivier Favier's *Chroniques d'exil et d'hospitalité* (2016), a collection of narratives recounted orally and then retold, makes clear.[31] Another narrative of journeys, periods of detention, and the negotiation of asylum procedures supposedly authored by a *clandestin*, Omar Ba's *Soif d'Europe* (2008), was subsequently revealed to be a fictionalization of a number of different narratives, in which the author's own experiences were blended with others he had been told.[32]

This growing body of narratives recounting journeys of contemporary migration raises questions about narrative voice, as well as about authenticity and (mis)trust that link back to the earlier twentieth-century text by Bakary Diallo discussed at the opening of this chapter. Far from suggesting any break with previous traditions of the travelogue, it could be argued that such issues in fact imply clear continuities that can be tracked back to what many see at the first French-language travel narrative, Marco Polo's *Divisament dou monde* (known in English simply as *Travels*), transcribed in Old French by Rustichello da Pisa on the basis of stories of Polo's journey he had been told when the two men were imprisoned together in Genoa in 1298. For some critics of travel writing, the extent to which accounts of contemporary clandestine and undocumented journeys can be read as travel writing remains unclear, not least because the equation with "travel" of hazardous migration, whether economically or politically motivated, may seem trivializing. The travelogue has always, however, been an elastic genre, and this chapter has argued that, in the French-language tradition, the practices it is permitted to recount have often been progressively restricted and policed. Although the task of elaborating and extending a genealogy of Francophone postcolonial travel writing is an urgent one, it is equally important to explore the ways in which such a tradition coexists with, interrogates, and ultimately challenges an exclusively French history and practice of the genre. For too long, nonmetropolitan characters have been denied agency and mobility, and reduced to the status of static travelee. The chapter has followed earlier critics such as Romuald Fonkoua and Aedín Ní Loingsigh in outlining the beginnings of a corpus of the Francophone postcolonial travelogue. The clear foundations described at the opening of the chapter suggest the existence of an increasingly well-established tradition in which new directions are increasingly apparent: The *bande dessinée* author Jean-Philippe Stassen has, for instance, recently deployed the potential of the *carnet de voyage* to document the complexity of migrant journeys,[33] and cinema also serves as a medium in which alternative travel narratives are recounted;[34] at the same time, as Abdourahman A. Waberi makes clear in his satirical, counterfactual, dystopian narrative *In the United States of Africa* (2006) – a text in which migrants from a disaster-struck "Euramerica" risk their lives to access the African continent – travel accounts can also continue to serve as a biting form of postcolonial critique.[35]

This chapter was written while Charles Forsdick was Arts and Humanities Research Council Theme Leadership Fellow for 'Translating Cultures' (AH/N504476/1). He records his thanks to the AHRC for its support.

NOTES

1 Tété-Michel Kpomassie, *L'Africain du Groenland* (Paris: Arthaud, [1981] 2015).
2 See Nathalie Carré, *De la Côte aux confins: récits de voyageurs swahili* (Paris: CNRS, 2014).
3 James Kirkup, "An equatorial among the Eskimos," *Times Literary Supplement*, July 3, 1981, 749.
4 Kpomassie, *An African in Greenland* (New York: New York Review of Books, 2001).
5 Edwidge Danticat, *After the Dance: A Walk through Carnival in Jacmel Haiti* (New York: Crown Journeys, 2002).
6 Romuald Fonkoua, *Les Discours de voyages: Afrique-Antilles* (Paris: Karthala, 2001).
7 Aedín Ní Loingsigh, *Postcolonial Eyes: Intercontinental Travel in Francophone African Literature* (Liverpool: Liverpool University Press, 2009).
8 Madeleine Borgomano, "Le voyage "à l'africaine" et ses transformations selon Amkoullel, l'enfant peul," in *Les Discours de voyages*, ed. Fonkoua, 207–16 (208); Johannes Fabian, *Time and the Other: How Anthropology Makes Its Object* (New York: Columbia University Press, 1983).

9 Mildred Mortimer, *Journeys through the French African Novel* (Portsmouth, NH: Heinemann; London: J. Currey, 1990).

10 Alain Borer, et al. *Pour une littérature voyageuse* (Brussels: Complexe, 1992).

11 Edouard Glissant, *Soleil de la Conscience* (Paris: Falaize, 1956).

12 "Pour une 'littérature-monde' en français," *Le Monde*, 16 March, 2007, www .lemonde.fr/livres/article/2007/03/15/des-ecrivains-plaident-pour-un-roman-en-francais-ouvert-sur-le-monde_883572_3260.html.

13 P. Fligneau, *L'Haïtien expatrié: comédie en trois actes et en prose* (Les Cayes: [n. pub.], 1804).

14 A number of different editions exist. See *Mémoires du général Toussaint-Louverture*, ed. Jacques de Cauna (Guitalens-l'Albarède: Editions la Girandole, 2009); *Mémoires du général Toussaint Louverture*, ed. Daniel Désormeaux (Paris: Classiques Garnier, 2011); and *The Memoir of General Toussaint Louverture*, ed. Philippe Girard (Oxford: Oxford University Press, 2014).

15 Bakary Diallo, *Force-Bonté* (Paris: Les Nouvelles Éditions Africaines; Agence de Coópération Culturelle et Technique, [1926] 1985).

16 Percy G. Adams, *Travelers and Travel Liars, 1660–1800* (Berkeley: University of California Press, 1962).

17 Janós Riesz, "The *Tirailleur Sénégalais* who did not want to be a *Grand Enfant*: Bakary Diallo's *Force Bonté* (1926) reconsidered," *Research in African Literatures*, 27, no. 4 (1996): 157–79.

18 Ousmane Socé Diop, *Mirages de Paris* (Paris: Nouvelles Editions Latines, [1937] 1977).

19 Ní Loingsigh, *Postcolonial Eyes*, 34–35.

20 Bernard Dadié, *Un nègre à Paris* (Paris: Présence africaine, 1959); *Patron de New York* (Paris: Présence africaine, 1964); and *La Ville où nul ne meurt* (Paris: Présence africaine, 1968).

21 Ní Loingsigh, *Postcolonial Eyes*, 75.

22 Michael Syrotinski, *Singular Performances: Reinscribing the Subject in Francophone African Writing* (Charlottesville: University of Virginia Press, 2002), 82.

23 Robert Gessain, *Les Esquimaux du Groenland à l'Alaska* (Paris: Bourrelier, 1947).

24 Frances Bartkowski, *Travelers, Immigrants, Inmates: Essays in Estrangement* (Minneapolis: University of Minnesota Press, 1995), 81.

25 Edward Said, *Culture and Imperialism* (New York: Knopf, 1993).

26 Kim Lefèvre, *Retour à la saison des pluies* (Paris: Barrault, 1990).

27 Dany Laferrière, *L'Enigme du retour* (Paris: Grasset, 2009).

28 Motility is understood as "the manner in which an individual or group appropriates the field of possibilities relative to movement and uses them"; see V. Kaufmann and B. Montulet, "Between Social and Spatial Mobilities: The Issue of Social Fluidity," in *Tracing Mobilities: Towards a Cosmopolitan Perspective*, ed. W. Canzler, V. Kaufmann, and S. Kesselring (Farnham: Ashgate, 2008), 37–56 (45).

29 Abasse Ndione, *Mbëkë mi: à l'assaut des vagues de l'Atlantique* (Paris: Gallimard, 2008).

30 Mahmoud Traoré, *"Dem ak xabaar"/partir et reconter: récit d'un clandestin africain en route vers l'Europe* (Paris: Nouvelles Editions Lignes, 2012).

31 Olivier Favier, *Chroniques d'exil et d'hospitalité* (Neuvy-en-Champagne: Passager clandestin, 2016).

32 Omar Ba, *Soif d'Europe* (Paris: Cygne, 2008).

33 Jean-Philippe Stassen, *I Comb Jesus et autres reportages africains* (Paris: Futuropolis, 2014).

34 On this subject, see Carrie Tarr, "The Porosity of the Hexagon: Border Crossings in Contemporary French Cinema," *Studies in European Cinema*, 4, no.1 (2007): 7–20; and Sylvie Blum-Reid, *Traveling in French Cinema* (Basingstoke: Palgrave Macmillan, 2016), 103–24.

35 Abdourahman A. Waberi, *Aux États-Unis d'Afrique* (Paris: Lattès, 2006).

8

TIM YOUNGS

African American Travel Writing

The Postcolonial United States

Although it declared independence on July 4, 1776, and fought its Revolutionary War from 1775 to 1783, the United States of America is rarely thought of as a postcolonial nation. Nor, some discussions of the Black Atlantic and of Pan-Africanism notwithstanding, is the writing of African Americans considered in postcolonial studies as much as one would expect.[1] This is despite the fact that in the sense that "post-colonialism refers historically to writings produced in a previously colonized nation after its independence from colonial control [...] all literature produced in the United States after the War of Independence could be called post-colonial."[2] The main reasons for this relative gap between US and postcolonial studies include the ongoing plight of Native Americans, the continuing legacy of slavery, and the global impact of US foreign policy and military adventures, covert and otherwise, since 1945. These factors help explain how it is that the US may be seen as "the world's first postcolonial and neocolonial country."[3]

The writings – creative and critical – that emerge from the Western superpower are consequently seen by some as tainted or at least as representative of a harmful domination. For example, the editors of a collection of essays on postcolonial travel writing announce that their contributors "examine how postcolonial travel texts resist the gravitational pull of metropolitan centrality and cosmopolitanism by articulating experiences and ontologies that are often removed from dominant European or North American productions of knowledge."[4] Yet as Deborah L. Madsen observes, "Post-colonial theory provides a powerful approach to ethnic literatures of the United States and of those [...] regions significantly influenced by U.S. political or cultural imperialism."[5] Similarly, John Cullen Gruesser notes the "formidable similarities between postcolonial and African American literary criticism," pronouncing it "both surprising and regrettable that only a handful of postcolonial theorists have sufficiently accounted for black American literature and that African Americanists have in general been resistant to postcolonial theoretical concepts."[6] The case for including the writings of African Americans as postcolonial is in fact strong. African American travel accounts in particular have thematic and formal affinities with texts that are more readily labeled postcolonial.[7]

Definitions, Inclusion, and Adaptation

Before proceeding, it is important to point out that the three key terms in this chapter (postcolonial, African American, and travel writing) are all subject to various definitions. The difficulties of defining the postcolonial have long exercised critics. Amritjit Singh and Peter Schmidt observe that "most critics concur that the term 'postcolonial' describes the combination of material, economic, social, and cultural practices an indigenous (and/or creolized) population engages with after the removal of the physical presence of a colonizing nation,"[8] yet in the words of Justin Edwards and Rune Graulund, it "has always been – and will continue to be – an unstable and contested critical term."[9] Introducing an edited collection of essays on American Literature and postcolonial theory, Madsen notes that the term postcolonial "has been employed in a range of diverse readings and interpretations" and that each of her contributors

> argues from their own perspective about what they call the 'post-colonial', calling upon those contexts that are most relevant to the body of literary work and the particular theoretical approaches they address. [...] A number of recurring post-colonial themes do emerge: displacement or diaspora, exile, migration, nationhood, and hybridity.[10]

It is significant that four of the recurring postcolonial themes identified by Madsen involve travel and that the other two may be consequences of it.

As for the second key term, the terminology used to describe members of the African diaspora in the United States is historically, and remains, contentious. During and since the Civil Rights struggles of the 1950s and 1960s in particular, different preferences for self-naming have emerged. Furthermore, the now widely accepted appellation of African American, popularly assumed to apply to those in the north of the continent, risks distracting from the fact that more Africans were transported to Brazil than to what is now the United States. This assumption that African American refers only or predominantly to the United States is a symptom of the politically charged fact that "America" itself is widely used to denote only the United States of America rather than to the landmass and associated islands of which it is a part or to include the islands of the Caribbean. That said, for the purposes of the present chapter, with its geographical and linguistic focus, African American will designate members of the black African diaspora in the United States.

Our third key term is travel writing. Most overviews of and introductions to this genre begin with the difficulty of defining it, including questioning whether it is even a genre at all. One of the two main reasons for this is that travel writing appears to be a composite of several genres, raising the question of how discrete it is. The other arises from the vast number of imaginary travels that have been published, and from the affinity that travel narratives often show with the novel. The second cause of the debates over what constitutes travel writing, then, is whether it encompasses fictional journeys.[11] The present chapter adheres to the view that there are clear differences between fiction and accounts of actual travel – doubts (usually soon resolved) about the veracity of certain accounts, and some similarities of technique notwithstanding. The discussion that follows focuses on first-person narratives of travel authored by the person who undertook the journey. These may take various forms, including letters, diaries, journals, memoirs, essays, poems, reportage, and book-length narratives.

The arguments, uncertainties, and ambiguities surrounding our three core terms complement the subject matter, for African American literature is built on a generic admixture. R. J. Ellis, introducing his edition of Harriet E. Wilson's *Our Nig*, the first African American novel published in the United States, describes

> the problem, *one facing all African American writers*, of how to discover a workable genre within which to explore [the] dilemmas encountered by African Americans in the United States – a process [...] resulting in the creation of writing residing in no single literary genre (novel, autobiography, documentary, popular fiction), but bridging between several genres.[12]

Ellis's identification of a composite form is in keeping with the mixture of genres at play in travel writing. It is appropriate, therefore, that Griffin and Fish announce that their anthology of African American travel narratives includes "autobiographical materials and selections from books, pamphlets, personal letters, notes, diaries, dispatches, travel guides, official reports, lectures, and ethnographies."[13] Appropriately, Griffin and Fish's selections display (as do other African American travel writings) a "complex range of racial and national identities, unfixing and relocating narrow or set notions of black objectivity" (xv).

African American travel writers utilize and experiment with the elements of this blend to aid their efforts at escaping classification and achieving self-definition.[14] Like other African American authors, they take existing literary forms and mold them for their own expression. As Gary Totten puts it, for African Americans, "[t]he travel narrative offers an important and unique form in which writers can enlist a variety of narrative strategies to resist Jim Crow."[15] The editor of a modern edition of David Dorr's 1858 *A Colored Man round the World*, which describes the slave's travels with his master, hails Dorr's "use and manipulation of the forms of Anglo-American travel writing."[16]

At the same time, as Alasdair Pettinger has cautioned, "Every attempt to subvert the tradition runs the risk – it seems – of being co-opted by it."[17] According to Pettinger:

> the situation of slaves and their descendants in the United States is not readily amenable to a colonial or post-colonial analysis. As an oppressed minority, their travel writings might be expected to be oppositional in some way; yet, when describing journeys overseas, it would not be surprising if they began to resemble those of white Americans visiting those parts of the world over which the United States exerts formidable economic, political and cultural influence. (79)

This double-edged character is noted by Griffin and Fish, who observe that many of the writers in their anthology "tend to reproduce at least some values of Western superiority despite a desire to challenge white supremacy and classist, nationalist, or gendered barriers."[18] Likewise, Schueller refers to what she states is Dorr's "decision to write his narrative through a complete and wholesale usage of genteel Anglo forms," though she suggests that Dorr "appropriates the forms and structures of Anglo-American travel writing so completely that what we have is a superb case of literary double-speak: the blackest of texts in whiteface."[19] So, although Pettinger warns that "the usual parameters of 'postcolonial' theory might not be entirely adequate to deal with African American travel writing," one notes the qualification: "might not be entirely," which suggests limitation rather than inappropriateness, as though African American travel narratives cannot be contained by the theory.[20]

Travel and Double-Consciousness

Travel is fundamental to African American identity. The trauma of the so-called middle passage that saw the forcible removal of Africans to the Americas involved a rupture from geographical, cultural, and family roots. Its consequences are still being felt. The experience continues to generate narratives of travel, both imaginative and factual, though it is the latter that are our concern here. Pettinger suggests that "African American travel writing remains haunted by the ancestral memory" of the passage and that "Every subsequent journey is liable to be measured against it, a gauge of how much 'the race' has progressed since" (81). Subsequent tales of escape northward from slavery in the South may be read as the first African American travel narratives. Virginia Whatley Smith, for example, states that "African American travel writing draws its expression from the slave experience and the genre known as the slave narrative."[21] These texts testify to their subjects' oppression and help set up what Robert B. Stepto calls a symbolic geography.[22] Stepto terms these accounts of flight from slavery in the South to freedom in the North narratives of ascent; he labels later generations' tales of journeys south in order to familiarize themselves with the landscape and cultural environment of their ancestors narratives of immersion. An example of the latter is Eddy L. Harris's *South of Haunted Dreams* (1993). In it, Harris pronounces that:

> the South, not Africa, is home to Blackamericans, and Blackamericans as a race are essentially southerners. Only in the South could I discover where my beginnings as a Blackamerican have gone. Without realizing it at the time, I was going home.[23]

Harris travels from his residence in St. Louis to the South in order to confront the source of his anger, which has been provoked by the subservience his father adopted as a survival strategy when visiting the South. Harris senior, a hero to his son, received death threats from white men for seeing a 'high yellow' girl.

Initially, Harris had "no desire, no intention whatsoever, to travel the Deep South" (28), but then he asks:

> How could I not have been drawn to the South, magnetized as my bones were, the dreaded South? The South which defines us [...]. The South that has been saturated in fear and in monumental hatefulness white toward black. (31)

The ambivalence expressed here echoes the mixture of attraction and repulsion voiced in Langston Hughes's 1922 poem, "The South," whose opening reads, "The lazy, laughing South/With blood on its mouth," and which ends with the speaker, after being spurned by the "Honey-lipped, syphilitic" South, resolving to seek the "kinder" but "cold-faced North" in whose "house my children/May escape the spell of the South."[24] The enchantment is delightful *and* sinister, and the more dangerous for being both.

Harris himself comments of the "dual identity" that it is "almost [foisted] on us as part of American society, because that society won't allow us to just be American."[25] His reference to this dual identity echoes the influential

diagnosis by W. E. B. Du Bois in *Souls of Black Folk* (1903) of how the
American world:

> yields [the 'Negro'] no true self-consciousness, but only lets him see himself
> through the revelation of the other world. It is a peculiar sensation, this double-
> consciousness, this sense of always looking at oneself through the eyes of
> others, of measuring one's soul by the tape of a world that looks on in amused
> contempt and pity. One ever feels his two-ness,- an American, a Negro; two
> souls, two thoughts, two unreconciled strivings; two warring ideals in one dark
> body, whose dogged strength alone keeps it from being torn asunder.[26]

Du Bois's much-quoted remarks underpin many discussions of the situation of
African Americans in the United States. They clearly apply also to the colonized in other societies. There is a correspondence with the psychological and
cultural effects of colonialism noted by Frantz Fanon in *Black Skin, White
Masks* ([1952], trans.1967) and *The Wretched of the Earth*, the latter of
which was much cited by leaders of the Black Panthers and Black Power
movements as an influence.[27] The double-consciousness articulated by Du
Bois has clear implications for Black travelers, many of whom use travel to
gain greater self-consciousness and who as well as doing the looking know
they may be looked at by others. This awareness may make them more
conscious than most whites of the effects of the tourist gaze on those who
are subject to it. Some of the travels of Colleen J. McElroy, the great-
granddaughter of a slave, for example, are as much about being gazed at as
they are about looking. "Overseas," she exclaims, "I am always the sight to
see."[28] In a number of her travel essays and her poems McElroy records the
stares and comments directed at her by locals. Their and her reactions affirm
both her resemblance to and difference from other Black people. The physical
similarities that imply kinship are countered by the cultural distance and
economic privilege of her life in the United States. McElroy makes use of this
space to reject claims of a shared identity that overrides material difference
and her relative privilege as a middle-class American. Thus she writes that in
the eyes of the residents of Belgrade, "I may be African, American even."[29]
Probably as a result of her feelings at being looked at and commented on
herself, McElroy displays a sensitivity to others when she travels, eschewing
the "New Age business of [. . .] wear[ing] the spiritual cloak of another culture,
or even worse, of cruising through a country as if browsing the shelves of a
convenience store."[30] Du Bois's idea of double-consciousness, then, may
readily be adapted to the situation of the Black traveler who sees himself or
herself through the eyes of others, within or beyond the borders of the United
States. Travel affords a pivotal point from which one can survey the destination, departure point, and oneself in relation to each.

In words that point to the similarities and distinctions between African American and (other) postcolonial writing, Harris complains that "To be black is to always be reminded that you are a stranger in your native land."[31] The feeling of not belonging that results from being denied full acceptance and equality is common to African Americans and to colonized subjects in other societies.[32] In the case of the former, though, the sense of estrangement is particularly acute because the oppressor is not an external force governing through proxies. As James Baldwin, in an essay on US protest writing, reminds us, "the oppressed and the oppressor are bound together within the same society."[33]

Consequently, the question of home is frequently posed, as it is in much of the literature of other postcolonial societies, especially in diasporic and migrant writing. In the African American case, it impels not only a critical examination of one's environment but, for those going into exile, a quest for alternative homes, and for those on shorter sojourns, a passing comparison with others' homes. Claude McKay, who was born in Jamaica in 1889, migrated to the United States in 1912, and spent several years abroad, including in North Africa, describes himself as having always been a "troubadour wanderer."[34] He explains that in Paris and Berlin he felt differently from white expatriates:

> Color-consciousness was the fundamental of my restlessness. And it was something with which my white fellow-expatriates could sympathize but which they could not altogether understand. For they were not black like me. (189)

While still known as LeRoi Jones, Amiri Baraka (as he renamed himself in 1968), gave *Home* as the title of a collection of his essays from 1960 to 1965. In the short piece that introduces it, he writes:

> I have been a lot of places in my time, and done a lot of things. [. . .] But one truth anyone reading these pieces ought to get is the sense of movement—the struggle, in myself, to understand where and who I am, and to move with that understanding.[35]

Included in the volume is his now famous essay "Cuba Libre," in which he recounts being a member of an organized trip to Cuba. A Spanish-speaker, he joins the huge crowds of people who have journeyed to Oriente to hear Fidel Castro speak. He finds it a transformative experience. He is awakened to the lies he has been told in the United States that have made the "idea of a 'revolution' [. . .] foreign to me" and to most of his compatriots. He thinks of the lies he has been told in writing and of how his own writing might challenge these. In the United States, he reflects, there is no alternative; nothing "not inextricably bound up in a lie" or "part of liberal stupidity or the actual filth of vested interest."[36] "It's much too late" in the States, he concludes, capturing the excitement of many at the time for revolutionary struggles and independence elsewhere:

> We [in the US] are an *old* people already [...]
> But the Cubans, and the other *new* peoples (in Asia, Africa, South America) don't need us, and we had better stay out of their way. (61–62)

Jones tells us that he has arranged his essays chronologically "to show just how my mind and my place in America have changed since the 'Cuba Libre' essay," a statement that only underlines the importance of movement and identity to African Americans in particular.[37] His trip to Cuba and the effect on him of hearing and meeting Castro are in line with the long history of African Americans' contact with radical networks abroad. These extend from the days of slavery when a number of fugitive slaves, such as Frederick Douglass and William Wells Brown, journeyed to and within Europe, talked about their experiences as slaves, and reported back to Americans on the lack of discrimination they encountered compared to their treatment in the United States. The connections continued, by way of links with socialist, Black nationalist, anti-colonial, and Pan-African activists, throughout the twentieth century and into the twenty-first, with international support for the Black Lives Matter network (founded in 2012) gathering momentum.[38]

Between the wars, a number of African Americans visited the Soviet Union. They included artists, intellectuals, and agricultural and skilled workers. There, they "discovered a country that welcomed them and their talents when the United States did not."[39] Joy Carew suggests that to the Soviet leadership the visitors were potential recruits "in the struggle against colonialism and imperial domination" who might help "'organize other disaffected blacks and workers in the United States" and aid "the Soviets [to] reach other populations of color elsewhere" (1).

The artists and thinkers included Claude McKay, Paul Robeson, Du Bois, and Langston Hughes. Du Bois first went in 1926 and then revisited every ten years or so. Carew describes his first trip as a "revelation": like other African Americans, "[i]n the Soviet Union, he felt he was a part of humanity rather than separate from it" (49). As Carew reminds us, Du Bois, who undertook graduate work in Berlin before completing his PhD at Harvard, had long-lived and extensive international contacts, convening a series of Pan-African congresses between 1919 and 1927 and one in 1945, which drew delegates from around the world (55). Despite Du Bois and Robeson having their passports revoked by the United States government from 1951–58 (57, 58), both men maintained their radical stance and transnational networks. They were "thrilled with Khrushchev's call for the freedom of all colonial and dependent nations at the fifteenth session of the General Assembly of the United Nations [in October 1960]" (202),[40] the year in which "on the initiative of the Soviet Union [...], more than 30 African colonies would be granted their independence."[41] During his "latter years, Du Bois continued to press for alliances with socialist nations" (62).

Revolutionary Russia was a source of self-realization for many Black intellectuals and manual workers alike. In the USSR of the 1920s and 1930s, before Stalin's purges disillusioned several of them, African Americans found social and economic opportunities that were denied them in the United States and claimed to experience an absence of racial prejudice. Writing in *The Crisis* in 1923, Claude McKay hailed Lenin's proclamation soon after the Revolution in which he "greet[ed] all the oppressed peoples throughout the world, exhorting them to organize and unite against the common international oppressor – Private Capitalism."[42] Besides the superior job and social opportunities and the lack of racism, the internationalism of the USSR was part of its appeal to African Americans.

Travel Words

For many African Americans, travel is not simply a matter of a journey through space but an opportunity to escape, if only temporarily, from fixity and classification. Elaine Lee, editor of *Go Girl!*, an anthology of travel writing by African American women,[43] proclaims in the first decade of the twenty-first century: "It's great to step outside the United States and its pigmentocracy to be treated like a human being and not as a second class citizen."[44] There is more to it than a stepping away from discrimination, however important that in itself is. The travel demonstrates agency, even if circumstances have left its actors with little choice. It provides a space for a degree of self-determination. Schueller claims that for African Americans journeying to Europe in the nineteenth century, "It was almost the birth of a new identity."[45] In the late twentieth century, McElroy expresses the dynamics of movement, fixity, and identity when, telling us that "The identification of myself and my country has not been an easy task," she explains:

> Partly, I travel to discover more about myself. My journeys have taught me that a definition of who I am cannot be mapped on the simple black-and-white limits of state lines and borders.[46]

The stories of travel are as important as the act of travel, however, for they are the linguistic vehicle through which a repositioning is accomplished. The writing, like the travel itself, is a process through which the self moves. The confluence of travel and writing is nicely illustrated by the title of Langston Hughes's *I Wonder as I Wander* (1956), his second volume of autobiography. Begun while he was still in the Soviet Union, the book "foregrounds his journeying to such an extent that it [...] actually is his life."[47]

The importance of employing language to assert some control over one's life has long been explicit in African American culture. In their manifesto *Black Power*, Stokely Carmichael and Charles V. Hamilton declare:

> We shall have to struggle for the right to create our own terms through which to define ourselves and our relationship to the society, and to have these terms recognized.[48]

Carmichael's acts of redefinition included changing his name to Kwame Ture in honor of Kwame Nkrumah and Ahmed Sekou Toure, leaders of Ghana and Guinea (where he settled in 1969), respectively.

Several African American essays, speeches, and autobiographies, especially during the 1960s and 1970s, testify to the power of words in gaining control over one's identity and environment.[49] But for those who relate their travel stories in writing, there is the question of what precedents one can follow. McElroy remarks that "Accounts of great travels never included black people, so I had no role models."[50] The suggestion that she had to find her own way mirrors not only the predicament of African American writing (turned into advantage), but is similar to statements by postcolonial writers from other societies who have testified to the problems as well as to the liberation involved in charting one's own course. This matter has long been a topic of discussion in postcolonial writing outside the United States, including the debate over whether to write in the language of the colonizer.[51]

Black but Western

It is difficult to think of an exact model for Richard Wright's *Black Power* (1954), a text Wright describes as "a first-person, subjective narrative on the life and conditions of the Colony and Ashanti areas of the Gold Coast."[52] Onto this subjective account he announces that: "In presenting this picture of a part of Africa, I openly use, to a limited degree, [a] Marxist analysis of historic events to explain what has happened in this part of the world for the past five hundred years or more" (xxxvii–xxxviii). This combination of the subjective and scientific is by no means new to travel writing, but Wright's use of it is striking. From the viewpoint of an African American who expresses his difference from Africans and from African Americans, he explores a country in Africa that is on the cusp of independence. The sense of self-exploration is reinforced by the fluidity of the international situation that Wright outlines: he tells us that in his lifetime he has "witnessed a radical change engulf more than half of human society; some nations have disappeared and new ones have risen to take their places; some social classes have vanished and others have come into being" (xxxv).

Black Power describes Wright's journey from Paris, where he is living in exile, to the Gold Coast, whose Prime Minister, Kwame Nkrumah, is about to apply for self-government (4). (The country will become Ghana, a destination later for Maya Angelou, among others.) Wright wonders before his trip, "am I African?" (4, italics in the original) and, during it, laments: "I'm of African descent and I'm in the midst of Africans, yet I cannot tell what they are thinking and feeling" (151). African Americans who write of their travels to Africa tend to examine their own identity in relationship to either side of the Atlantic. Such trips tend either to ease a sense of fracture or to affirm a feeling of estrangement. The latter often results in an uncomfortable recognition that their authors' home really is in the United States. For example, Harris realizes on his African journey in *Native Stranger* (1992) that he cannot feel at home in Africa but that the hold of the continent upon him induces a sensation of doubleness that makes him feel trapped between the "blackness of my skin and the whiteness of my culture."[53] Wright's and Harris's profession of distance from black Africans complicates straightforward identifications of kinship, and their remarks are a reminder that "Africa has served historically as one of the chief terrains on which African Americans have negotiated their relationship to American society."[54] Wright appears aware of this, commenting: "One does not react to Africa as Africa is [...] One reacts to Africa as one is, as one lives" (175).

Wright sums up his and other African Americans' predicament when he converses with Gold Coast Ghanaian chief Nana Kwame Dua Awere II, "an intelligent man, an ex-schoolteacher" (321), about the introduction and effects of modern technology and communications:

> I'm black, Nana, but I'm Western; and you must never forget that we of the West brought you to this pass. We invaded your country and shattered your culture in the name of conquest and progress. And we didn't quite know what we were doing when we did it. (322)

Black but Western signifies the limits of Wright's identification with Africa. At the same time, several passages in the book testify to the difference he feels from other African Americans. On the one hand, this has him using the travel narrative to construct an individual identity in ways characteristic of postwar, white-authored travel writing. On the other hand, it speaks in typically African American ways of a self that is symbolic and yet concerned with finding the parameters of its own freedom. The travel book is well suited to Wright's shifts as he moves between colonial and postcolonial societies. In the conclusion, a letter to Prime Minister Kwame Nkrumah, Wright states: "Your fight has been fought before. I am an American and my country too was once a colony of England" (393).

Conclusion

Singh and Schmidt maintain that "U.S. studies and postcolonial studies have much to teach each other" if scholars and students in each field "cross and question the borders constantly being erected to keep them separate."[55] The same is true of those working on African American and postcolonial travel writing. Whatever degrees of distinction one sees between them, the corpuses have many features in common. This is not to say that their differences should be downplayed. Indeed, although African American writing itself is strongly intertextual, it is important to remember that, in Gary Totten's words, "not all African American travelers share the same ideological agendas or enact the same cultural interventions."[56] Any attempt to group or generalize about them may omit or distort instances that do not fit. Nevertheless, just as the United States may be regarded as both postcolonial and neocolonial, so African American travel writing displays, often within a single text, both the legacy of repression and reactions against it. Totten writes of the cases he examines in his study of travels from Ida B. Wells to Zora Neale Hurston that they "provide models for the cultural work and narrative strategies through which writers might resist the continuing legacies of Jim Crow and assert African American authority and identity" (135). That legacy is still violently apparent, as is the resistance to it. "Have proper ID on you at / All times / There is no right / To travel," writes Reginald Harris in "New Rules of the Road," his poem about Black people being stopped by white police officers.[57] The lines of the poem are set out in columns slanting downward as they move across the page, as though they are trying to avoid constraint but are contained by the regularity of the arrangement and by the width of the page.

Mindful of Totten's caveat, we may conclude nonetheless that African American travel is rooted in restraint, defiance, flight, and remaking. Travel writing, long a deeply political genre, often radical in its politics and form, remains in these circumstances an apt and adaptable vehicle for the self in motion. "[W]hich am I more," Harris wonders as he journeys: "black or American?"[58]

NOTES

1 The key work on the Black Atlantic is Paul Gilroy, *The Black Atlantic: Modernity and Double Consciousness* (Cambridge, MA: Harvard University Press, 1993). Also see the travel writing anthology, Alasdair Pettinger, ed., *Always Elsewhere: Travels of the Black Atlantic* (London: Cassell, 1998).

2 Deborah L. Madsen, "Introduction: American Literature and Post-Colonial Theory," in *Beyond the Borders: American Literature and Post-Colonial Theory*, ed. Deborah L. Madsen (London: Pluto, 2003), 1–11 (2).

3 Amritjit Singh and Peter Schmidt, "On the Borders between U.S. Studies and Postcolonial Theory," in *Postcolonial Theory and the United States: Race, Ethnicity, and Literature*, ed. Singh and Schmidt (Jackson: University Press of Mississippi, 2000), 3–70 (5).

4 Justin D. Edwards and Rune Graulund, "Introduction: Reading Postcolonial Travel Writing," in *Postcolonial Travel Writing: Critical Explorations*, ed. Edwards and Graulund (Basingstoke: Palgrave Macmillan, 2010), 1–16 (2).

5 Madsen, "Introduction," 1.

6 John Cullen Gruesser, *Confluences: Postcolonialism, African American Literary Studies, and the Black Atlantic* (Athens: The University of Georgia Press, [2005] 2007), 2.

7 On this, see for example Glen Winfield, "Dream of an Elsewhere: Contemporary African American Travel Writing," Ph.D. thesis, Nottingham Trent University, 2013, especially the conclusion.

8 Singh and Schmidt, "On the Borders," 18.

9 Edwards and Graulund, "Introduction," 5. For more on defining the postcolonial, see Robert Clarke's Introduction to the present volume.

10 Madsen, "Introduction," 1.

11 For more on the problems of definition, see for example Tim Youngs, *The Cambridge Introduction to Travel Writing* (New York: Cambridge University Press, 2013), 1–7.

12 R. J. Ellis, "Introduction," in *Our Nig, or Sketches from the Life of a Free Black, in a Two-Story White House, North. Showing That Slavery's Shadow Falls Even There*, by Harriet E. Wilson, ed. R. J. Ellis (Nottingham: Trent Editions, 1998), vii–xxxvii (viii, my emphasis).

13 Farah J. Griffin and Cheryl J. Fish, "Introduction," in *A Stranger in the Village: Two Centuries of African-American Travel Writing*, ed. Griffin and Fish (Boston: Beacon Press, 1998), xiv.

14 For more on this argument, see Tim Youngs, "Pushing against the Black/White Limits of Maps: African American Writings of Travel," *English Studies in Africa*, 53, no. 2 (2010): 71–85.

15 Gary Totten, *African American Travel Narratives from Abroad: Mobility and Cultural Work in the Age of Jim Crow* (Amherst: University of Massachusetts Press, 2015), 134.

16 Malini Johar Schueller, "Introduction," in *A Colored Man Round the World*, by David F. Dorr [1858], ed. Schueller (Ann Arbor: The University of Michigan Press, 1999), ix–xliii (xxi).

17 Alasdair Pettinger, "'At Least One Negro Everywhere': African American Travel Writing," in *Beyond the Borders*, ed. Madsen, 77–91 (79).

18 Griffin and Fish, "Introduction," xiii–xvii (xvi).
19 Schueller, "Introduction," xxvii.
20 Pettinger, "One Negro Everywhere," 80.
21 Virginia Whatley Smith, "African American Travel Literature," in *The Cambridge Companion to American Travel Writing*, ed. Alfred Bendixen and Judith Hamera (Cambridge: Cambridge University Press, 2009), 197–213 (213). Similarly, Pettinger states that slave narratives "herald the emergence of African American travel writing" and claims that "Subsequent African American travel writing has inherited [their] frame of reference." Pettinger, "One Negro Everywhere," 80.
22 See Robert B. Stepto, *From Behind the Veil: A Study of Afro-American Narrative* (Urbana: University of Illinois Press, 1979), esp. ch.3.
23 Eddy L. Harris, *South of Haunted Dreams: A Ride through Slavery's Old Back Yard* (New York: Simon and Schuster, 1993), 36.
24 In Arnold Rampersad and David Roessel, eds., *The Collected Poems of Langston Hughes* (New York: Vintage, 1995), 26. The poem was first published in June 1922 in *Crisis*, whose editor was W. E. B. Du Bois.
25 Nicklas Hållén, "'Can't Seem to Live without It Somehow': An Interview with Eddy L. Harris," *Studies in Travel Writing*, 18, no. 3 (2014): 279–94 (288).
26 W. E. B. Du Bois, "The Souls of Black Folk," in *The Norton Anthology of African American Literature*, eds. Henry Louis Gates, Jr. and Nellie Y. McKay, 2nd edn. (New York: W.W. Norton, 2004), 692–766 (694).
27 Kenneth Mostern goes so far as to say that "the theoretical discourse [Homi] Bhabha now calls 'postcolonial critique' existed as early as 1903": that is, with the publication of *The Souls of Black Folk*. Kenneth Mostern, "Postcolonialism After W.E. B. Du Bois," in *Postcolonial Theory and the United States*, ed. Singh and Schmidt, 258–76 (259).
28 Colleen J. McElroy, *A Long Way from St. Louie* (Minneapolis: Coffee House Press, 1997), 7. For more on McElroy, see Alasdair Pettinger, "African Americans on Africa: Colleen J. McElroy and the Rhetoric of Kinship," *Journal of Transatlantic Studies*, 7, no. 3 (2009): 317–28; and Tim Youngs, "'A daughter Come Home?' The Travel Writings of Colleen J. McElroy," *New Literatures Review*, 42 (2004): 57–74.
29 Colleen J. McElroy, "A Skardalija Walk in Three-Quarter Time," in *Traveling Music* (Ashland, OR: Storyline Press, 1998), 22–23 (22).
30 McElroy, *A Long Way from St. Louie*, vi.
31 Harris, *South of Haunted Dreams*, 102. There seem to be nods here to James Baldwin's essay "A Stranger in the Village" (published in 1953, then in the collection *Notes of a Native Son* in 1955) and to Richard Wright's novel *Native Son* (1940).
32 See for example the Jamaican-British author Joan Riley's novel *The Unbelonging* (1985).
33 James Baldwin, "Everybody's Protest Novel," in *Notes of a Native Son* with a new introduction by Edward P. Jones (Boston: Beacon Press, 2012), 13–23 (21).
34 Claude McKay, *A Long Way from Home*, ed. and with an introduction by Gene Andrew Jarrett (New Brunswick: Rutgers University Press, [1937] 2007), 270.
35 LeRoi Jones, "Home," in *Home: Social Essays* (London: MacGibbon and Kee, [1966] 1968), 9–10 (9).

36 LeRoi Jones, "Cuba Libre," in *Home: Social Essays* (London: MacGibbon and Kee, [1966] 1968), 11–62 (61).
37 LeRoi Jones, "Home," 9.
38 See for example, Sean L. Molloy, *Out of Oakland: Black Panther Party Internationalism during the Cold War* (Ithaca: Cornell University Press, 2017).
39 Joy Gleason Carew, *Blacks, Reds, and Russians: Sojourners in Search of the Soviet Promise* (New Brunswick: Rutgers University Press, 2008), 1.
40 Du Bois also visited China in 1936 and 1959. See Carew, 61–62.
41 Lily Golden, quoted in Carew, *Blacks, Reds, and Russians*, 200.
42 Claude McKay, "Soviet Russia and the Negro," in *Stranger in the Village*, ed. Griffin and Fish, 206–14 (206).
43 Elaine Lee, ed., *Go Girl! The Black Woman's Book of Travel and Adventure* (Portland: The Eighth Mountain Press, 1997).
44 Daiyyah A. Edwards Abdullah, "Interview with Elaine Lee," *Studies in Travel Writing*, 10, no. 1 (2006): 57–70 (60).
45 Schueller, "Introduction," xxiv.
46 McElroy, *A Long Way from St. Louie*, ii.
47 Pettinger, "One Negro Everywhere," 84.
48 Stokely Carmichael and Charles V. Hamilton, *Black Power: The Politics of Liberation in America* (London: Jonathan Cape, 1968), 34–35.
49 See for example Huey P. Newton, with the assistance of J. Herman Blake, *Revolutionary Suicide* (New York: Harcourt Brace Jovanovich, 1973), 163.
50 McElroy, *A Long Way from St. Louie*, iv.
51 See especially Ngũgĩ wa Thiong'o, *Decolonising the Mind: The Politics of Language in African Literature* (London: James Currey, 1986).
52 Richard Wright, *Black Power: A Record of Reactions in a Land of Pathos* (New York: Harper Perennial, [1954] 1995), xxxix.
53 Eddy L. Harris, *Native Stranger: A Blackamerican's Journey into the Heart of Africa* (London: Viking, [1992] 1993), 108.
54 James T. Campbell, *Middle Passages: African American Journeys to Africa, 1787–2005* (New York: Penguin, 2007), xxii.
55 Singh and Schmidt, "On the Borders," 44–45.
56 Totten, *African American Travel Narratives*, 5.
57 Reginald Harris, "New Rules of the Road," in *Autogeography* (Evanston: Northwestern University Press, 2013), 49–50 (49).
58 Harris, *South of Haunted Dreams*, 179.

9

ASHA SEN

Postcolonial Travel Writing
and Spirituality

Mapping a story of postcoloniality, travel, and spirituality is a humbling endeavor. There is no simple way to capture the nuances embedded in these concepts let alone the overlap between each. With that caveat, what follows in the first part of this chapter is a brief history of the search for the sacred in medieval, early modern, colonial, and postcolonial travel writing. More specifically, I examine the narrative structures and symbology that define this search, and their reconfiguration in contemporary postcolonial travel writing. From there, this chapter examines the role of spirituality in select postcolonial travel texts: Pico Iyer's *The Art of Stillness* (2014), William Dalrymple's *Nine Lives: In Search of the Sacred in India* (2009), Fatema Mernissi's *Scheherazade Goes West* (2001), Pankaj Mishra's *An End to Suffering: The Buddha in the World* (1995), and Leila Ahmed's *A Border Passage: A Woman's Journey from Cairo to America* (2000). The analysis addresses emerging trends centered on spiritual discourse in contemporary, specifically postcolonial, travel writing. Central to this chapter is the key question as to whether spiritual aesthetics can reshape the conventions of the travel genre or whether they must always be confined by them.

From Ancient Pilgrims to New Age Travelers

Travel has long been determined to be the province of the European male subject. Underlying this perception is the importance given to the concept of "exploration," which privileges "the European age of expansion and colonization stretching from the fifteenth century to the twentieth."[1] The spirit of inquiry that defined this period was related to the reallocation of resources, data collection, and economic expansion, and the consequent prioritizing of a secular vision that continues to influence contemporary discourses on travel writing. Intervening in such secular modes of analysis, Tabish Khair emphasizes the often overlooked intimate relationship between religion and travel, pointing out that "travel seems to mark the beginning of all major religions" from the epic exiles of *The Ramayana* and *The Mahabharata* to the wanderings of Jesus, and Mohammed's journey before revelation.[2] A similar refashioning of secular travel is presented by Jan Elsner and Joan-Pau Rubiés who suggest that "the cultural history of travel is best seen as a dialectic of dominant paradigms between two poles [sacred and secular] that mark every period of Western travel history."[3] By juxtaposing the dominant narrative of the time against the peripheral or emergent one they too attempt to move beyond the secular bias present in contemporary cultural critique and provide a useful model for theorizing the role of the sacred in travel writing.

In premodern times, religious travel found expression in the pilgrimage or haj, almost always taking "place within the institutionalized boundaries of religious tradition."[4] This influenced the narrative structure of accounts such as the Christian *Pilgrimage of Egeria* (circa fourth century CE), where the travelogue is subordinated to spiritual concerns and offers little space for self-reflection. Another important model closely related to the pilgrimage is the chivalric quest romance, which details the spiritually successful journeys of medieval knights.

Columbus inaugurated an era of European travel, which was driven by an awareness of the opportunities available for trade, conquest, and colonization, and the religious desire for conversion. His voyages mark the transition from medieval to early modern European travel, and "a new emphasis on the act of eye-witnessing, of seeing for oneself and establishing facts through empirical enquiry."[5] Subsequent travel to the Middle East and Africa prepared the way for Western European domination, as travel stories became "recognized as a way for attracting investment and of encouraging settlers."[6] Mary Louise Pratt notes, "the apparently strict object-orientated description of 'manners and customs,' that is the anthropological component of these accounts, is a strategy which allows the writers to avoid the portrayal of culture *contact*: the text constructs an 'other' with whom the European traveler does not establish a genuine interpersonal relationship."[7] Under this secular gaze local practice is alienated from precept and translated into barbaric and/or exotic custom.

Christian belief systems also played a significant role in othering non-Western cosmology from the Age of Exploration on. The Evangelical revival of the eighteenth and nineteenth centuries led to the establishment of missionary societies and accounts of missions to "heathen" tribes reinforced the progress narrative of Western civilization. On occasion, evangelical travelers or missionaries even "stood in for imperial institutions and authority" helping to "codify and control local practices."[8]

Significantly, the era of European capitalist colonization marks a difference in the reception of African and Asian travel writers and European ones. The few non-Western texts published during this period came to be stripped of their philosophical and scientific value and presented as anthropological accounts instead. Moreover, as these writers had little access to the leisure market or to colonial resources, they could not compete with the promotion of mass tourism by travel agencies like Thomas Cook. The impetus toward the colonial center also resulted in the neglect of precolonial travel accounts by Africans and Asians, resulting in the overdetermined influence of colonial travelogues on postcolonial travel writing today.[9]

However, even as the age of empire saw diminishing importance given to non-Western travel accounts, it also witnessed a fascination with the East and its "spiritual traditions" on the part of European travelers like Madame Blavatsky, who journeyed to Tibet, Egypt, and India as part of her search for a universal religion. To that end, Blavatsky can be seen as the forerunner of what Alex Norman calls "spiritual tourism," a contemporary phenomenon whose practitioners unlike their early modern counterparts are not aligned with a specific religion but craft individualized models of spirituality in a search for solutions to their problems.[10] Mick Brown, author of *The Spiritual Tourist* (1998), points out that Blavatsky "emerged at a critical juncture, a time not so unlike our own, when traditional certainties were subject to question. The rise of scientific rationalism, and Darwin's theory of evolution appeared fatally to undermine the authority of Christian teachings."[11] A similar sense of uncertainty plagued Europe in the aftermath of World War II and the collapse of once great colonial empires. Postwar fascination with the mystic East came to be popularized by celebrities like the Beatles and Allen Ginsberg, who started the ashram culture associated with controversial gurus Maharishi Mahesh Yogi, Rajneesh, and Putta Putti's Sai Baba.

Today's New Age culture, which valorizes the spiritual power of the individual against conformity to institutional norms, draws inspiration from the counter-culture movements of the sixties.[12] Its practitioners' embrace of everyday spirituality presents a rejection of secular values and a refusal to allow religious space to be cordoned off by the state. However, the logic of late capitalism also necessitates that New Age freedom of choice produces a consumer-driven marketplace where spirituality is turned into an easily purchased commodity. A quick Internet search will produce a plethora of travel blogs by spiritual tourists, travel websites full of tips for the savvy, spiritual traveler, and travel agencies and government websites dedicated to the promotion of spiritual tourism. In addition, books like Sarah Macdonald's *Holy Cow* (2002),[13] William Sutcliffe's *Are You Experienced?* (1998),[14] and Elizabeth Gilbert's best-selling *Eat, Pray, Love* (2006)[15] contribute to the commodification of spirituality in the marketing of the "postcolonial exotic," a space marked by

> the intersection between contending regimes of value: one regime that posits itself as anti-colonial, and that works toward the dissolution of imperial epistemologies and institutional structures; and another – postcoloniality – that is more closely tied to the global market, and that capitalises both on the widespread circulation of ideas about cultural otherness and on the world-wide trafficking of culturally 'othered' artefacts and goods.[16]

This space is fraught for the postcolonial writer dependent on metropolitan marketplaces whose "realities have been shaped, for centuries, according to others' dictates tailored to the requirements of a European exoticist imaginary" (27). Even those travel writers who embody a self-reflexive, post-imperialist consciousness, may intentionally or inadvertently reinforce an ordering of things, a *form*, that is still western in origin.[17] This in turn begs the question whether it is possible for these authors to adopt an "ethics of travel writing" critical of the hegemonic power relations that define today's world.[18]

Spiritual Travel, Pico Iyer and the Cultural Status Quo

The controversial status of cosmopolitan writer Pico Iyer is a case in point. Iyer believes that in today's fast-paced world the international airport becomes "the spiritual center of the double life; you get on as one person and get off as another."[19] But the question of who gets to travel and under what terms and conditions makes this spiritual re-centering the privilege of relatively few. Even though Iyer admits his idea of a "global soul" suggests a surface unity that belies the increasing discrepancy between have and have nots, in his world "globalization is a generally benign process" and a "fait accompli."[20] Consequently, the travels of the global soul can occasionally rearticulate "the logic of empire through new networks, structures and boundaries" without directly addressing the structural inequities that make possible its itinerary (4).

Against this backdrop the author's transition from movement to contemplation in his most recent work, *The Art of Stillness: Adventures in Going Nowhere*, appears all the more significant. While his earlier travelogue *Video Nights in Kathmandu and Other Reports from the Not So Far East* (1989) presents a variety of national responses to US culture and *The Global Soul: Jet Lag, Shopping Malls, and the Search for Home* (2001) examines sites of international congregation, in his most recent travelogue the author makes a compelling case for the pleasures of stillness and introspection.

The Art of Stillness brings to fruition the relation between travel and self-reflection found in Iyer's other writing. In *Sun after Dark* he writes, "travel remains a journey into whatever we can't explain, or explain away,"[21] and in *Video Nights* "home is, finally, not the physical place, but the role and the self that we choose to occupy."[22] However, while Iyer's self-reflexivity is typical of the self-consciousness of the post-imperial travel writer, a travelogue committed solely to the inner workings of the mind presents a significant departure for the genre.

Designed as a talk for the nonprofit organization TED (Technology, Entertainment and Design), the book is written for a world audience that "believe[s] passionately in the power of ideas to change attitudes, lives, and ultimately our future."[23] As a "how to" guide for meaningful living, it embodies the open-ended quality of a life lived in the present with all its ups and downs, which makes it amenable to a diversity of interpretations. Like New age spirituality, it "is at once movement and marketplace, materialist and spiritual, individualist and bent on collective transformation."[24]

On the one hand, it can be accused of a quietist acceptance of a capitalist status quo where "stillness" is conceived of as a resource, which maximizes our productivity, making the author a better writer, Leonard Cohen a finer musician, and contributing to the spiritual betterment of Thomas Merton and Matthieu Ricard. As per this reading, the art of stillness helps social workers with their clients and Marines with PTSD and transforms Google headquarters into a more efficient workplace. However, it is just as easy to debunk these quietist claims, for, as Iyer shows us, every life is closely linked to others; when after years of meditation seventy-three-year old Leonard Cohen comes out with a best-selling album called *Old Ideas* Iyer writes, "Why were people across the planet reaching out for such a funeral album? [...] Maybe they were finding a clarity and wisdom in the words of someone who'd gone nowhere, sitting still to look at the truth of the world and himself, that they didn't get from any other recording artist."[25] And although Iyer is quick to disavow any spiritual affiliation, like Cohen the idea he promotes is an old one; "the poets of East Asia, the philosophers of ancient Greece and Rome" have long presented "sitting still as a way of falling in love with the world and everything in it" (4–5).

As with his previous works *The Lady and the Monk* (1991) and *Abandon: A Romance* (1993), Iyer invokes the *idea* of the monk as a point of self-identification to facilitate the production of his spiritual narrative.[26] Women like Merton's caregiver, Cohen's wife, and Emily Dickinson are referenced as love objects but denied their own voice. In addition, the narration and consumption of Dickinson's innermost thoughts by the author and the Trappist monk he visits turn her into an artefact for their inspiration.

To that end, *The Art of Stillness* does not break with colonial travelogues where gendered bodies are controlled by larger ideological intentions. However, its uniqueness lies in its rejection of earlier models of spiritually triumphant pilgrimage and quest narratives. The author renounces spiritual closure to embrace the truth of living in the moment in all its splendor and horror. Meditation may be the "real feast" for Leonard Cohen, but it can also lead to "doubt or dereliction."[27] As Iyer's spiritual mentor Thomas Merton said, "The way of contemplation is not even a way [...] and if one follows it, what he finds is nothing" (35) or in the words of Emily Dickinson, "The Brain – is wider than the Sky – For – put them side by side – /The one the other will contain/With ease – and You – beside –" (33). By focusing on the truth process rather than on the final product, *The Art of Stillness* does in fact unsettle if not transcend its commodification within the postcolonial marketplace.

William Dalrymple and "Mystic India"

Celebrity author William Dalrymple's spiritual journeys present yet another case study of a postcolonial travel writer's conflicted engagement with the postcolonial exotic. Even as Dalrymple disarmingly admits, "as far as a curiosity in England and America about India and Hinduism is concerned, I feel thankful that it exists because it gives me a job,"[28] he simultaneously adopts the anti-imperialist attitude of the typical postcolonial author. In his introduction to his "collection of linked non-fiction stories" *Nine Lives: In Search of the Sacred in Secular India* he writes:

> By rooting many of the stories in the darker and less romantic sides of modern Indian life, with each of the characters telling his or her own story, and with only the frame created by the narrator; I hope to have avoided many of the clichés about "Mystic India" that blight so much Western writing on Indian religion.[29]

Positioning his subjects as historical artefacts rather than spiritual beings initially places Dalrymple firmly in the tradition of post-sixteenth century European travel writing, where the spirit of empirical inquiry reinforces an uninterrupted secular vision with little room for narrative self-reflection. Even as Dalrymple updates this tradition by bringing "a literary consciousness to ethnographic practice"[30] and labeling his text a collection of "non-fiction stories," whose subjects have the "freedom" to speak for themselves, their agency is severely undermined by the narrative editorializing that takes place in each story.

In the first piece of the collection, "The Nun's Story," the author interviews a Jain nun who has decided to commit *sallekhana*, a ritual fast unto death. Dalrymple is clearly disconcerted by his subject's decision, and her youth and beauty only increase his discomfort. His description of Mataji as, "a surprisingly young and striking woman [...] with large, wide-apart eyes, olive skin and an air of self-contained confidence that expressed itself in vigour and ease in the way she held her body,"[31] is reminiscent of accounts by British administrators who were both attracted and repelled by the "choice" of young Hindu widows to burn on their husband's funeral pyres.[32] Dalrymple's description of Mataji's physical body subtly pushes the reader toward a rejection of her spiritual rationale for *sallekhana* while Mataji's affirmation of the process as peaceful and voluntary is negated by her own horrific description of her best friend Prayogamati's ordeal with the practice. So even as the story ends with Mataji saying: "it is a good way – the very best way – to breathe your last, and leave the body. It is no more than leaving one house to enter another,"[33] her words remain mere rhetoric unable to provide the spiritual closure she intended them to have. In another short account "The Daughters of Yellamma," Dalrymple counters his protagonist devadasi Rani's pride in her profession with the words of her social worker, who informs him that she has contracted HIV and will soon die of AIDS (59, 75).

Moreover, while the earlier stories in the collection focus on the individual interviewee, the later ones introduce different characters and more commentary, which in turn drowns out the voices of the subjects interviewed and provides more authorial opinion. The absence of any major change between the voice of the narrator and his subjects, due in part to the fact that the interviews are translated from eight different languages, creates a seamless narrative where each life is more a glimpse into India's rapidly changing religious landscape and less an articulation of spiritual subjectivity.

The tremendous success of *Nine Lives* in India, where it went to the number one slot on the Indian nonfiction section best-seller list, does, however, extend the parameters of the author's intended audience, creating a more public arena along with the potential to trouble the book's codification of the sacred. Some of Dalrymple's interviewees appear at the world famous Jaipur literary festival and their performances help transform European-style panel discussions into hybrid spaces where sacred song can flow into secular performance and vice versa. Some of these artists have also traveled with the author around the world on promotional tours for *Nine Lives*, and, as the experiences of Fatema Mernissi indicate, even the most tightly regulated book tours can facilitate unexpected learning and transformation.

Spirituality, Performativity, and the Postcolonial Intellectual

Like *Nine Lives*, *Scheherazade Goes West* illustrates the tensions between the mystical impulse and the secular frames of knowledge that represent it. On the one hand, Mernissi's narrative takes on the performative aspect of the medieval storyteller's voice, making it more aligned with Dalrymple's musical productions than with the printed words of his book; on the other, in an attempt to talk back to racist discourses about women and Islam, she falls prey to the wounder/wounded binary found in much postcolonial travel writing,[34] reversing the Orientalist opposition between self and other and reinforcing the very oppositions she seeks to deny.

The history of *Scheherazade Goes West* exemplifies the predicament of the postcolonial intellectual described by Graham Huggan when he writes, "For every aspiring writer at the 'periphery,' there is a publisher at the 'center,' eager to seize upon their work as a source of marketable 'otherness.'"[35] Provoked by Orientalist stereotypes of the Middle East and Islam that she encountered while on a European book tour promoting her memoir *Dreams of Trespass: Tales of a Harem Childhood* (1994), Mernissi wrote *Scheherazade Goes West* as a corrective to Western Islamophobia. In it she ponders the changing representation of the feminist heroine of the Arab folktale *The Thousand and One Nights* as she travels across continents and time zones in an attempt to draw conclusions about Christian and Islamic cultures.

Mernissi bases her philosophy on the Sufi belief that "travel is the best way to learn and empower yourself."[36] The Sufis believe that one must always be in a state of *isti'dad*, or readiness, in order to be entirely receptive to the divine flashes of insight called *lawami* acquired through travel. While Islam insists on a divide between divine and human, Sufis believe that if you concentrate on loving God without intermediaries, these boundaries become indistinct. Aware of the persecution faced by those adhering to the Sufi faith, Mernissi's grandmother Yasmina warns her to conceal any insights she receives by practicing the Sufi art of *teqiyeh*, or secrecy.

Lawami, isti'dad, and *teqiyeh* are key concepts that frame Mernissi's travel narrative; however, by embedding these concepts in the story of Scheherazade, the young Persian bride who reforms her vengeful spouse through one thousand and one nights of storytelling, Mernissi adds a feminist layer to her Sufi aesthetic. As she points out, the stories that Scheherazade tells are ones of female empowerment through travel. Thus, the oral version of one of her stories, "The Tale of the Lady with the Feather Dress," ends with the protagonist finding the wings that her husband had stolen from her and flying away with their two sons. Needless to say, the feminist impulse to this story is eliminated in the authorized Arabic print version, where the captured woman lives happily ever after with her husband and sons. In her journey across the Atlantic, Mernissi is aghast to find even further misrepresentations of Scheherazade – as a passive nude in post-Impressionist art, as the Renaissance French court's model for harem pants, as sex itself in twentieth-century Russian ballet, as complicit in her own execution in American writer Edgar Allan Poe's retelling of her story – and counters such representations with detailed descriptions of the border-crossing icon she grew up with.

Mernissi's Scheherazade constantly crosses the divide between truth and fiction upheld by Islam. Not only does she have all the credentials of an accomplished Muslim religious authority, she combines these with night-time forays into fiction. And she is adept in *samar*, the art of words, which she uses to transform King Shahryar into a benevolent ruler who can give them both "the bliss of living in a world free of anxiety" (50). This, according to Mernissi, is what makes Scheherazade so threatening to the Arab elite, who for many centuries resisted putting her words into print, and the author begins to wonder whether this might also be responsible for the passive Scheherazade of Western art and literature. And then, in a New York department store, she has a flash of *lawami* when the sales woman tells her that she is "too big." Astounded when she hears that "Many women working in highly paid fashion-related jobs could lose their positions if they didn't keep to a strict diet" (213), Mernissi realizes "for the first time that maybe 'size 6' is a more violent restriction imposed on women than is the Muslim veil" (213). And so she concludes:

> Unlike the Muslim man, who uses space to establish male domination by excluding women from the public arena, the Western man manipulates time and light [...] By putting the spotlight on the female child and framing her as the ideal of beauty, he condemns the mature woman to invisibility. (213)

However, even as Mernissi's final chapter provides an answer to the Western colonization of Scheherazade it also reinforces colonial and Islamic binaries between West and non-West, body and mind, reason and fantasy that Sufi precept and Sheherazadian storytelling seek to dismantle. Thus, even as the spiritual content of her book strains against the Orientalist parameters of its form, it is ultimately the latter's secular aesthetic that wins. Devoid of mysticism, spiritual insight becomes intellectual investigation, and *tequiya* a form of sanctioned lying rather than a mystical belief in divine otherness. In trying to educate a Western readership about Islamic feminism, Fatema Mernissi inadvertently reproduces Western secular modes of knowledge production and consumption.

Travel, Innovative Textualities, and the Spiritual

The case studies of Pico Iyer, William Dalrymple, and Fatema Mernissi highlight the challenges embedded in unsettling Eurocentric travel conventions and underline the need to complicate "the travel book," or "first-person, ostensibly non-fictional narrative of travel."[37] As Justin Edwards and Rune Grauland put it, "the expression of progressive political content in contemporary travel writing is vital, but not enough; it must be combined with innovative writing techniques to produce new textualities of travel for a new politics of mobility."[38] To that end, it is worth considering how combining travel writing with other genres like autobiography and memoir might produce a new creative space for spiritual expression.

While "autobiography is primarily concerned with the individual," memoirs "concentrate on communal history"[39] and are consequently more conducive to a spiritual aesthetics of transformation. My final case studies examine the merging of travel conventions with the use of autobiography in travel writer Pankaj Mishra's *An End to Suffering: The Buddha in the World* (2004) and memoir in Islamic scholar Leila Ahmed's *A Border Passage: A Woman's Journey from Cairo to America* (2000).

Although *An End to Suffering* presents "a subtle mix of history, philosophy and autobiography"[40] clearly intended for an academic audience, the intellectual concerns that shape academia are not very different from those of the trade or commercial book. In fact, as Amy Hollywood, Professor of Christian Studies at Harvard Divinity School, points out, the tendency within the academy is to believe "that there is no intellectual life in religious traditions and that reason always stands in a critical relation to putatively irrational belief."[41] Consequently, the reader who picks up Mishra's book will find in it a secular vision not unlike that shared by the previous writers under discussion.

Like Dalrymple, Mishra situates himself within the secular tradition of storytelling, presenting himself as a follower of the Victorian botanist Jacquemont, whose pursuit of scientific knowledge brought him to India. *An End to Suffering* follows the postcolonial trajectory of writing back to empire by reversing Jacquemont's journey via an anonymous narrator whose quest for meaning takes him from small town India to Delhi to London. Even after the narrator experiences a gradual disillusion with the seductions of Victorian empiricism he turns for guidance to the Buddha as a political figure, a psychiatrist, and a philosopher. The book's ending appears to effect the author's successful transformation of the Buddha into an inspirational political leader as the newly awakened narrative voice calls for a transformation of contemporary social order based on Buddhist principles of interdependence.[42] However, there is something about the abruptness of the conclusion that deconstructs the very secular vision it propounds. After four hundred pages of archival research and physical travel, in the last two pages of his narrative the narrator experiences the Buddha in the temporariness of the living moment, and finds "the awareness, suddenly liberating, with which [he] finally began to write about the Buddha" (404). This movement from verbosity to silence mirrors Buddhist scholar Walpola Rahula's belief that "Human language is too poor to express the real nature of the Absolute Truth or Ultimate Reality which is Nirvana."[43] In its conclusion the book leaves us with a sense of a "sublime" "freedom from suffering, hard won and irrevocable,"[44] an appropriate prequel to the spiritual restructuring of narrative found in Leila Ahmed's *A Border Passage*.

A Border Passage chronicles the story of Ahmed's childhood years in Egypt in the 1950s followed by her academic careers in the UK, Abu Dhabi, and the United States. Her physical travels provide the template for her intellectual and spiritual journeys as she moves from a colonial to a post-colonial understanding of her history and from the spirit of empirical inquiry to the wisdom of the Sufis. This movement involves an unlearning and relearning of different ways of being, transforming her memoir from a *bildungsroman* to a historical study to a Sufi parable of how to be in the world.

While *An End to Suffering*'s overarching emphasis on the need for social transformation makes it easy to overlook moments of epiphany tucked away in the book, Sufi references at the beginning and end of *A Border Passage* create a deliberate framing of the author's own spiritual journey. In an interview with Faiza Shereen, Leila Ahmed comments that "when she set out to write [her] memoir, she thought she 'had nothing to say' about the subject and came to realize that 'in order to make sense of [...] her own feelings, she needed to understand the history of the time.'"[45] This concept of emotional interdependence paves the way for her understanding of the pacifist faith found in her mother and aunts' Sufi inspired women's Islam. As Shereen points out, *A Border Passage* "is marked by its spiritual power ... but a formal manipulation of distance and a shifting between different narrative voices keeps the memoir from defining itself in terms of sentimental nostalgia or quasi-religious mysticism" (119).

At the conclusion of her narrative, in words that echo Rahula's comments on the inadequacy of human language, Ahmed quotes Rumi: "This is how it always is/when I finish a poem [...] A great silence overcomes me,/And I wonder why I ever thought to use language."[46] The concluding paragraphs of her memoir stress the Sufi idea of interdependence. Unable to locate her parents' graves in Egypt, she finds instead "a small open-sided mosque and beside it a beautiful, delicate-leaved tree," crowds of beggars "invoking god's mercy on our dead," and the Sufi words "'*nur 'ala nur*' (light upon light)," which the priests chant from the Quran (305). Her final passage invokes Rumi one last time as she reflects upon the crowds of Jews, Christians, Buddhists, Hindus, and Muslims who mourned his passing (307).

Thus, personal memory turns into collective memory, which, in turn, sublimates into a spiritual consciousness transcending the spatial and temporal limits of the form that contains it. To that end, Ahmed's memoir pushes us toward a new direction in postcolonial travel writing, moving us a step closer to the spiritual concerns expressed in indigenous travel narratives of the dispossessed. Reconciliation writing from Australia, for instance, seeks to extend "the idea of spatial narratives, organized according to place and landscape, working through and across space and memory rather than time and history and avoiding the temporal order of linearity and closure."[47] To that end it complements other forms of indigenous writing such as Hmong American author Kao Kalia Yang's *The Latehomecomer: A Hmong Family Memoir* (2008)[48] and the poems of Diné poet Esther Belin. Shamanist principles reframe the physical relocation of the Hmong people in *The Latehomecomer*, adding a spiritual dimension to the psycho-spatial restructuring of their lives in the United States, while in her collection of poems *From the Belly of My Beauty*, Esther Belin documents the temporal and spatial relocation of her people, reminding us that "the physical is easier to achieve/a boundary drawn to separate people/Navajo say no word exists/establishing form to the air we breathe."[49]

Conclusion

The post-imperial self-reflexivity of the last few decades of travel writing has opened up a space for new developments in the genre. To fully understand the transitions taking place we need to shift focus to the politics of reading: to create a space between the oppositional politics of postcolonial theory and the global marketplace of postcoloniality and to focus on "the contingencies of the journey described and translated into narrative and of the reception of that narrative, with an understanding of the limitations of the narrative as a mode of representation and as a force for political and ethical change."[50] The creation of such a space can and will dismantle (post) colonial binaries of secular and sacred, moving postcolonial travel writing from a politics of spiritual inclusion toward the possibility of spiritual transformation.

NOTES

1 Carl Thompson, *Travel Writing* (London: Routledge, 2011), 5.
2 Tabish Khair, "African and Asian Texts in the Light of Europe," in *Other Routes: 1500 Years of African and Asian Travel Writing*, ed. Tabish Khair, Justin D. Edwards, Martin Leer, and Hannah Ziadeh (Bloomington: Indiana University Press, 2005), 1–27 (1).
3 Jan Elsner and Joan-Pau Rubiés, "Introduction," in *Voyages and Visions: Towards a Cultural History of Travel* (London: Reaktion Books, 1994), 7.
4 Alex Norman, *Spiritual Tourism: Travel and Religious Practice in Western Society* (London: Continuum, 2011), 93.
5 Thompson, *Travel Writing*, 40.
6 Norman, *Spiritual* Tourism, 72.
7 Mary Louise Pratt, *Imperial Eyes: Travel Writing and Transculturation* (London: Routledge, 1992), 82.
8 Anna Johnston, "'Tahiti, 'the desire of our eyes'': Missionary Travel Narratives and Imperial Surveillance," in *In Transit: Travel, Text, Empire*, ed. Helen Gilbert and Anna Johnston (New York: Peter Lang, 2002), 65–83 (14).
9 Khair, "African and Asian Texts," 27.
10 Norman, *Spiritual Tourism*, 93.
11 Mick Brown, *The Spiritual Tourist: A Personal Odyssey through the Outer Reaches of Belief* (London: Bloomsbury, 1998), 207.
12 Guy Redden, "The New Agents: Personal Transfiguration and Radical Privatization in New Age Self-Help," *Journal of Consumer Culture*, 2, no. 1 (2002): 33–52 (47).
13 Sarah MacDonald, *Holy Cow: An Indian Adventure* (New York: Broadway Books, 2004).
14 William Sutcliffe, *Are You Experienced?* (New York: Penguin, 1999).
15 Elizabeth Gilbert, *Eat Pray Love: One Woman's Search for Everything across Italy, India and Indonesia* (New York: Viking, 2006).
16 Graham Huggan, *The Postcolonial Exotic: Marketing the Margins* (London: Routledge, 2001), 28.
17 Paul Smethurst, "Introduction," in *Travel Writing, Form, and Empire*, ed. Julia Kuehn and Paul Smethurst (New York: Routledge, 2009), 1–18 (16).
18 Graham Huggan and Patrick Holland, *Tourists with Typewriters: Critical Reflections on Contemporary Travel Writing* (Ann Arbor: University of Michigan Press, 1998); Debbie Lisle, *The Global Politics of Contemporary Travel Writing* (Cambridge: Cambridge University Press, 2006).
19 Pico Iyer, *The Global Soul: Jet Lag, Shopping Malls, and the Search for Home* (New York: Vintage, 2001).
20 Lisle, *Global Politics of Contemporary Travel Writing*, 4.
21 Pico Iyer, *Sun After Dark: Flight into the Foreign* (New York: Vintage, 2004), 7.
22 Pico Iyer, *Video Nights in Kathmandu and Other Reports from the Not So Far East* (New York: Vintage, 1989), 9.
23 Pico Iyer, *The Art of Stillness: Adventures in Going Nowhere* (New York: TED Books, 2014).
24 Guy Redden, "Religion, Cultural Studies and New Age Sacralization of Everyday Life," *European Journal of Cultural Studies*, 14, no. 6 (2011): 649–63.

25 Iyer, *Art of Stillness*, 65.

26 Huggan and Holland, *Tourists with Typewriters*, 84.

27 Iyer, *Art of Stillness*, 32.

28 William Dalrymple, "I'm No Westerner Shopping in the Divine Supermarket," (*Outlook*, October 12, 2003).

29 William Dalrymple, *Nine Lives: In Search of the Sacred in India* (London: Bloomsbury, 2009), xiv–xv.

30 James Clifford and George Marcus ed., *Writing Culture: The Poetics and Politics of Ethnography* (Berkeley: University of California Press, 1986), 62. For a more in-depth discussion of *Nine Lives*, see Asha Sen, *Postcolonial Yearning: Reshaping Spiritual and Secular Discourses in Contemporary Literature* (New York: Palgrave MacMillan, 2013), 18–29.

31 Dalrymple, *Nine Lives*, 3.

32 Lata Mani, *Contentious Traditions* (Berkeley: University of California Press, 1998).

33 Dalrymple, *Nine Lives*, 27.

34 Peter Bishop, "To Witness and Remember: Mapping Reconciliation Travel," in *Travel Writing, Form, and Empire*, ed. Kuehn and Smethurst, 180–98 (194).

35 Graham Huggan, "The Postcolonial Exotic," *Transition*, 64 (1994): 22–29 (29).

36 Fatema Mernissi, *Scheherazade Goes West* (New York: Washington Square Press, 2001), 4.

37 Thompson, *Travel Writing*, 26.

38 Justin Edwards and Rune Graulund, *Mobility at Large: Globalization, Textuality, and Innovative Travel Writing* (Liverpool: Liverpool University Press, 2012), 4.

39 Geoffrey Nash, "From Harem to Harvard: Cross-Cultural Memoir in Leila Ahmed's *A Border Passage*," in *Arab Voices in Diaspora: Critical Perspectives on Anglophone Arab Literature*, ed. Layla Al Malal (Amsterdam: Rodopi, 2009), 351–69 (354).

40 Tim Adams, "Pankaj Mishra: *An End to Suffering: The Buddha in the World*," *The Observer*, 23 October, 2004. For a more in-depth discussion of *An End to Suffering*, see Sen, *Postcolonial Yearning*, 29–32.

41 Amy Hollywood, "On Understanding Everything: General Education, Liberal Education, and the Study of Religion," *PMLA*, 126, no. 2 (2011): 460–66 (461).

42 Pankaj Mishra, *An End to Suffering: The Buddha in the World* (New York: Picador, 1995), 404.

43 Walpola Rahula, *What the Buddha Taught* (New York: Grove Weidenfeld, 1959), 3.

44 Mishra, *An End to Suffering*, 3

45 Faiza Shereen, "The Diasporic Memoirist as Saidian Itinerant Intellectual: A Reading of Leila Ahmed's *A Border Passage*," *Studies in the Humanities*, 30, nos.1–2 (2003): 108–30 (113). For a more in-depth discussion of *A Border Passage*, see Sen, *Postcolonial Yearning*, 50–67.

46 Leila Ahmed, *A Border Passage: A Woman's Journey for Cairo to America* (London: Penguin, 2000), 306.

47 Paul Smethurst, "Introduction," in *Travel Writing, Form, and Empire*, ed. Smethurst and Kuehn, 1–18 (16); Bishop, "To Witness and Remember," 194.

48 Kao Kalia Yang, *The Late homecomer: A Hmong Family Memoir* (Minneapolis: Coffee House Press, 2008).
49 Esther Belin, "On Relocation," *From the Belly of My Beauty* (Tucson: University of Arizona Press, 1999), 68.
50 Robert Clarke, *Travel Writing from Black Australia: Utopia, Melancholia, and Aboriginality* (New York: Routledge, 2016), 15.

10

CHRISTOPHER M. KEIRSTEAD

Contemporary Postcolonial Journeys on the Trails of Colonial Travelers

Footsteps travel writing involves authors' attempts to retrace paths laid out by previous travelers: explorers, family members, more distant ancestors, or other writers. It is a subgenre of travel writing that has attracted numerous popular and influential travel writers, including Jonathan Raban, V. S. Naipaul, Caroline Alexander, Paul Theroux, and Caryl Phillips. The contemporary postcolonial footsteps journey, however, begins in many ways with Henry Morton Stanley's 1871–72 expedition to find David Livingstone. In the popular imagination, the colonial encounter that produced travel writing's most famous single line – "Dr. Livingstone, I presume" – still conjures images of intrepid Victorian explorers risking safety for higher aims.[1] If contemporary footsteps travel writing no longer sets out with the implicit mission of reassuring domestic readers of the nobility of colonial and imperial enterprises, such narratives do risk rewriting history in ways that exploit the landscapes and peoples they cross as backdrops to an essentially Western drama. Just as in *How I Found Livingstone*, where the African guides and escorts, along with the Arab traders in Livingstone's camp, were relegated to the role of spectators as the two men greeted each other under a waving American flag, some contemporary footsteps narratives, including the still active vein of following in Livingstone's and Stanley's footsteps, work to sustain nostalgia for colonial-era travel by removing such ventures from their historic and political contexts.[2] The footsteps genre may be subject to other, more aesthetic liabilities, Tim Youngs observes, being "as predictable in content as it is unadventurous in form."[3]

Such, then, is the case against footsteps travel writing. Yet as Youngs adds, citing Raban, the form includes some "honourable exceptions" that serve to "create a distance between ourselves and earlier values with which we are uncomfortable or suspect that we should be" (185). Such repeat or "second journeys," as Maria Lindgren Leavenworth terms them, also lend expression to a "postmodern desire to trans-contextualise the past, to rewrite it in the present context," whereby the "gap between the past and the present is reduced."⁴ The potential to mediate between the two kinds of historical hindsight Youngs and Leavenworth allude to – one stressing critical distance, the other skeptical of that same effort at distancing – may explain why the footsteps form thrives especially well in postcolonial contexts, where history and living cultural memory are often in uneasy proximity to each other. At their best, postcolonial footsteps journeys open themselves to unpredictable encounters with places and people alike, often invoking a deep affective response even as they scrutinize the limits of travel and travel writing's ability to transcend historically generated boundaries of culture, class, and politics. If easy to exploit for the purposes of "imperialist nostalgia," in Renato Rosaldo's definition,⁵ footsteps journeys may also respond just as readily to a critical impulse to continue to pursue travel routes that remain unsettled and fractured – sites of ongoing debate politically and culturally. This chapter provides a critical taxonomy for this diverse genre giving closest attention to contemporary texts that exhibit what the genre has to afford scholars of postcolonial travel writing.

Footsteps travel writing can be divided into three broad, overlapping categories that embody particular aims. *Forensic footsteps*, the category that is most invested in colonial-era exploration, is defined by an investigative or biographical interest in the fate, methods, and points of geographic and cultural contact of previous travelers. Typically, the subject of such repeat journeys is removed a good deal historically from the present, although an important subset of forensic footsteps includes journalistic travelogues seeking to understand the fate or disappearance of more recent travelers within postcolonial settings. *Foliated footsteps*, perhaps the most rhetorically complex category of footsteps travel writing, follows literary or travel texts as much as actual people or expeditions. These journeys pay tribute to the already deeply intertextual nature of travel writing, following spaces previously mapped by authors who may have never actually visited the destination in question but have nonetheless chartered it, in some sense, in the popular imagination. *Familial/ancestral footsteps* responds more readily to postcolonial travel writers' simultaneous interest in the places and mobilities of ancestral pasts. Such texts may have the most to offer readers in terms of critical reflection on travel writing's role in understanding broader processes of cultural migration and renegotiation.

Forensic Footsteps

Forensic footsteps journeys range in purpose from close investigative or even archaeological efforts to semi-comic or quixotic quests for which the previous journey forms a loose guide or map. Into this latter category falls

William Dalrymple's *In Xanadu* (1989), a fitting starting point for examining the development of the footsteps genre for several reasons. Dalrymple's subject, Marco Polo, is a founding voice in Western travel writing, and his route through the Middle East and China represents a historic ground-zero for footsteps narratives. Another Polo recreation launched the career of Tim Severin in 1964, who has since crafted his own unique brand of mythic and literary forensic investigations with titles such as *The Ulysses Voyage: Sea Search for the Odyssey* (1987), *In Search of Moby Dick* (2000), and *Seeking Robinson Crusoe* (2002). With its satirical, irreverent take on its subject, *In Xanadu* mirrors other late twentieth-century footsteps narratives, especially Stuart Stevens's *Night Train to Turkistan* (1988), which covers similar ground to Dalrymple in China as it retraces the journey that inspired Peter Fleming's *News from Tartary* (1936). Dalrymple's brief encounters with local people, usually played for humorous effect, and his struggles to find reliable transportation, make his book, like Stevens's, emblematic of a kind of global "roadtrip" narrative (an effect enhanced by the presence of other college-age companions on their trips). Dalrymple's climatic arrival at the ruins of Kubla Khan's former "pleasure dome" at Xanadu, where he and a friend recite Coleridge's poem together as they mimic Polo's gesture of emptying a phial of holy water on the ground, underscores the equal opportunity cultural satire *In Xanadu* aims to provide: Returning to the bus, they overhear a Mongolian tourist observe, "Bonkers [...]. English people, very, very bonkers."[6] At the same time, the scene illustrates the limits of the type of cultural conversation that ensues from footsteps narratives that dwell more in the author's own sense of the absurdity or belatedness of the journey. A deeper interest in the history and culture of the locations traversed – the very same "determined studiousness" that Paul Smethurst locates in Dalrymple's later travel books – is missing here from Dalrymple's first effort at the form.[7]

If lacking the literary flair of *In Xanadu*, Tim Mackintosh-Smith's *Travels with a Tangerine: From Morocco to Turkey in the Footsteps of Islam's Greatest Traveler* (2001) reveals how much can be gained by "studious" footstepping efforts at historical and cultural understanding. A scholar of Arabic, Mackintosh-Smith dwells more comfortably in the region, introducing his Western audience to the "Arabic Marco Polo." If it's a comparison, he says, that makes him uncomfortable, it's a necessary translation for a book that represents an important act of reverse cultural missionary work.[8] Offering a Westerner's expert knowledge of the Middle East, *Travels with a Tangerine* may on the surface appear to follow some beaten paths of orientalism. In substance, however, Mackintosh-Smith's book works in subtle ways against familiar orientalist tropes – as does the very structure of his journey, allowing himself to be guided by an important non-Western traveler. Mackintosh-Smith also makes a point of interviewing Arabic Ibn Battuta experts, so extending the book's narrative authority across cultures. Consciously or not, Mackintosh-Smith largely avoids sites of contemporary political unrest, like Jerusalem, that were part of Ibn's extensive travels. At the same time, these omissions aid his effort to remap the region in Western eyes, inaugurating a new, less antagonistic kind of cultural conversation.

Forensic footsteps travel begins to enter more ideologically charged territory as it ventures out of the Middle Ages into the era of global European exploration and colonization. Unsurprisingly, the quest for El Dorado, precisely because it enveloped elements of idealism and fantasy with some of the most ruthless efforts of imperial conquest, forms the subject of two notable books from two decades ago: Stephen Minta's *Aguirre* (1994) and Charles Nicholl's *The Creature in the Map* (1995). At the spot on the Orinoco river where Walter Raleigh and his expedition in 1595 began to encounter traces of gold but were forced to turn around due to lack of supplies, Nicholl finds a new assortment of international prospectors working indifferently alongside the corporate remnants of nineteenth-century mining interests. These contemporary activities, he concludes, seem "not to displace the legend so much as continue it."[9] The conquistador Lope de Aguirre (1510–61), by all historical accounts, was opportunistic and brutal even for his time. Minta makes no effort to rehabilitate Aguirre's image, content to render him as a complex symbol or prophet of future imperial and economic exploitation Minta encounters in the region: "Men like Aguirre came to the New World in search of freedoms denied them by the Old World; mobilities of class, of social and economic expectation. The modern world was made largely in their image, a world that implicitly rejected stability, in favor of unlimited opportunity for all who could seize it."[10]

Tony Horwitz's *Blue Latitudes: Boldly Going Where Captain Cook Has Gone Before* (2002) perhaps best exemplifies the sort of ideological balancing act many postcolonial forensic footsteps narratives endeavor to perform. Written with a mostly American audience in mind, for whom Cook is a fairly unfamiliar figure, Horowitz's book pays homage to its subject while simultaneously aiming to "turn the spyglass around" and consider how Pacific peoples would have interpreted the explorer's purposes and how "their descendants remember Cook now."[11] Horwitz wades into present-day cultural debates over Cook's legacies. As one New Zealander suggests for a plaque on a statue of Cook, "Here's where the first murderer stood. Sanctified by the queen. He died of syphilis" (124). Horowitz's presentation of extremes at times seems calculated to steer readers toward an admittedly "squishy" neutral historical and ideological ground – mirroring other efforts, as one Maori tour guide at the Cook landing site puts it, to tell the same story "from different perspectives" (113). Horwitz's book is characterized by this dual aim to carefully historicize Cook even as it casts him as a universal embodiment of a spirit of adventure.

Traversing an Antarctic landscape that did not host permanent human settlements until the mid-twentieth century, Sara Wheeler's *Terra Incognita* (1996) would seem at first to inhabit a much less charged ideological contact zone than Horwitz's. But as she stresses repeatedly in regard to the turn-of-the-century explorers whose traces she seeks in the landscape, "conquest of the last white spaces became a metaphor for the triumph of imperialism."[12] While being a homage to explorers such as Scott and Shackleton, a wider sense of history and cultural politics is never far from Wheeler's text, especially the gender politics in this largely male preserve. To her surprise, Wheeler develops a sense of camaraderie with the "beards" living in self-imposed exile as she fuels their interest in the history she explores. This history, uncannily preserved by the cold in many of the early explorers' shelters, down to tins of food and other personal effects, makes for a particularly evocative sense of the time-crossing that many footsteps narratives strive for. Sleeping in Scott's, Wheeler admits to a strong affective, even spiritual response. Finely attuned to landscape, history, and the presence of fellow travelers, past and present, *Terra Incognita* also evidences a fully developed sense of the emotional and imaginative longing to connect that motivates footsteps travel.

Footsteps journeys that aim to understand the motives of more recent "extreme travellers," as Graham Huggan has described those "thriving on the awareness of danger and energetically courting extreme risk,"[13] form another compelling subgenre of forensic footsteps travel. Jon Krakauer's *Into the Wild* (1996) investigates the fatal journey of Chris McCandless, who died while traveling alone in Denali National Park in Alaska and where Krakauer himself goes to, among other destinations where McCandless backpacked and made temporary homes. If still remote and dangerous, McCandless's final destination was hardly undiscovered country, and it is in large part Krakauer's unearthing of the cultural myths that guided McCandless that make this book of such strong interest to postcolonial and eco-critics alike. As Krakauer shows, McCandless's insistence on not using a map typifies his commitment to a heavily masculinized, solitary, and Romantic engagement with a "pure" natural world that was nonetheless deeply mediated by his reading of Henry David Thoreau and others. McCandless's Alaska was in a way just as imaginary as the El Dorado that lured explorers centuries before. Carl Hoffman's more recent *Savage Harvest: A Tale of Cannibals, Colonialism, and Michael Rockefeller's Tragic Quest for Primitive Art* (2014) examines the fate of another young American traveler who disappeared a generation earlier in what was then Dutch New Guinea. As its title indicates, Hoffman's book attempts to straddle a difficult line between colonialism and cannibalism, one of the most sensitive and, of course, overindulged topics in all of Western travel writing (the book opens, perhaps unfortunately, with an imagined scene of Rockefeller's murder and dismemberment). Like *Into the Wild*, Hoffman's book is of equal interest for the way it dissects the cultural myths and misunderstandings that drove Rockefeller and may have contributed to his demise, accidental or not. Commenting on Rockefeller's journal, Hoffman writes, "It's clear he likes to be in the wild, but he also seems oblivious to parts of that experience. There's not a single account of friendship with any individual Asmat. He needs and wants the objects [...] less so the Asmat themselves."[14]

Foliated Footsteps

Early in *Passage to Juneau: A Sea and Its Meanings* (1999), Jonathan Raban lavishes attention on the books lining the walls of his boat's saloon:

> When the boat was underway, my still very incomplete library took on a shuffling, drunken life of its own [...] After a rough passage, I'd find Edmund Leach, Evelyn Waugh, George Vancouver, *Kwakiutl Art*, Anthony Trollope, *The 12-Volt Bible*, Homer, and *Oceanography and Seamanship* in an unlikely tangle on the saloon floor, their pages gaping, their jackets half-off.[15]

Raban's book is primarily guided by Vancouver's account of his 1796 voyage up the Inside Passage of the North American Pacific coastline, but as this excerpt attests here, his "narrative vehicle" (14) is one shaped by a diverse array of texts passing in and out of his narrative consciousness. Raban's sailboat serves as an apt metaphor for the deeply intertextual nature of the specific kind of footsteps project he undertakes – one that follows authors as much as explorers or travelers *per se* – although careful attention to the discursive space of travel is something that distinguishes the best footsteps travel writing more generally. Wheeler's skillful use of literary epigraphs in *Terra Incognita*, for instance, underscores the subtle ways in which all travel essentially follows foliated paths laid out well in advance, including fictional and poetic ones. Coleridge's "Kubla Khan" (1816), recall, inspires Dalrymple's *In Xanadu* as much as Polo – an inspiration Caroline Alexander would take a good deal further in *The Way to Xanadu* (1994), which visits locations in Mongolia, Kashmir, Florida, and Ethiopia in an effort to trace the poem's unique intersections of place, history, and imagination.

Journeys on the trail of literary authors associated more closely with specific colonial or postcolonial settings, most notably Joseph Conrad and Robert Louis Stevenson, form one particularly visible subset of these foliated quests. These kinds of traveling literary biographies find their origins in nineteenth-century guides to places such as "Dickens's London" or "Brontë Country," which produced "in aggregate a mapping of national literary heritage onto a national mythic geography."[16] Even when grounded abroad in "Browning's Italy," for instance, such literary guidebooks often serve to testify to the author's cultural ownership of foreign spaces. These books' postcolonial heirs, it should be pointed out, are not typically written as "guides" or with the sense the author will be followed by other travelers, but they still bear witness to an ethical or ideological competition of sorts between insular cultural impulses and a desire to engage global and postcolonial settings on their own contemporary terms. Such is the case with Gavin Young's *In Search of Conrad* (1991), which frames the author's travels in Indonesia with a homecoming to Rugby, where he first became devoted to Conrad and now reads from his works to contemporary students, thus relocating Conrad within a distinctively English literary and cultural heritage. Young's comment as well that "the East will never be the same since he [Conrad] wrote about it" stages the region much in the same way as Conrad famously pointed to an empty space on the map of Africa and declared his intention to go there and make that space his own.[17] The East becomes a blank canvas upon which the West enjoys the authority to craft the global literary landscape in its own image. In turn, literary footsteps travel becomes a kind of pilgrimage to that imaginary space.

Even a more circumspect or more recognizably *post*-colonial footsteps journey such as Paul Hyland's *The Black Heart: A Voyage into Central Africa* (1988) shows the difficulty of charting new ideological paths in such culturally fraught spaces. Searching for the burial place of Georges Klein, one of several potential inspirations for Kurtz, Hyland is gratified to find little local memory of him, pointing to the possibilities of a kind of cultural renewal: "It is well that all white myths and histories for which the people have no use should vanish, as if flushed away by the rains."[18] But Hyland's journey is also motivated by a personal interest in finding traces of his great-uncle Dan Crawford, "extraordinary Scots missionary and explorer" (12), who on another level refills the space Kurtz had vacated. Overcome by his welcome from villagers in the area where his great uncle had made his mission, Hyland writes, "I hadn't dared to hope that Crawford's moments and years here would still be so vivid. I had no idea that the house would be so full of him" (245).

For Hyland, the need to uphold one dimension of the colonial legacy in Africa pushes against a critical impulse to unearth some of the cultural and literary myths that accrue to *Heart of Darkness*. His book illustrates the broader difficulty of staging a kind of critical cosmopolitanism in footsteps travel writing, where more personal moments of connection and hospitality sometimes undermine attention to historical patterns of exploitation (and, which, somewhat ironically, demands the kind of intellectual "distancing" travel seeks to overcome). Gavin Bell's *In Search of Tusitala: Travels in the Pacific after Robert Louis Stevenson* (1994) affords another example of this dilemma, since it is a book distinguished in many ways by a cosmopolitan impulse that seeks to engage Stevenson in new modes of cross-cultural conversation: he wants to read and discuss Stevenson with those he encounters, not just visit landmarks associated with the author. In Tahiti, for instance, while trying to uncover more information about places where Stevenson may have stayed, he meets a great-grandchild of one of the author's closest companions. Bell later sends him a French translation of *In the South Seas*, reflecting, "I like to think of him sitting by the lagoon, his old spectacles perched on his nose, smiling at the stories his great-grandfather related to Stevenson."[19] Bell's gesture of hospitality, in some ways, remains clouded by familiar tropes of exoticization that also serve to make Stevenson, in essence, the literary custodian of Tahitian culture.

Caroline Alexander's *One Dry Season: In the Footsteps of Mary Kingsley* (1990) copes more easily, as it were, with the failure to connect to its predecessor. An example of what Steve Glassman dubs "a travel book about a travel book,"[20] Alexander opens with the familiar footsteps trope of stumbling upon her subject by chance in a library and being overcome with excitement: "Breezy, ironic, bantering, the passages of brilliant hilarity mixed with informative discussion and descriptive beauty – the author's voice sparkled from the pages."[21] Her journey in Kingsley's footsteps, however, is as much about the difficulty of getting landscape, history, and culture all, so to speak, on the same page. After a disappointing meeting with someone she had been led to believe had direct knowledge of Kingsley's travels in the area, Alexander begins to reflect more critically on the vicissitudes of reaching into the past through travel, re-historicizing her subject as "a woman of a specific, bygone era, a fact that one can overlook while reading the *Travels* themselves" (272). In turn, *One Dry Season* channels its narrative energies toward the stories of the people encountered during the trip, with a particular emphasis on women. "I suspect that Kingsley and I learned the same lesson, namely that it is one's choice of guides that determines one's itinerary" (244), Alexander writes, and it is precisely this willingness to let herself be guided more by the chances and accidents of her journey that allows her to complete or creatively remap Kingsley's own.

Familial/Ancestral Footsteps

Though engaged with issues important to postcolonial criticism, forensic and foliated footsteps travel writing features few authors who are themselves postcolonial subjects – the descendants of those displaced by slavery, colonial expansion, or other forced migrations. That absence changes dramatically, however, when the genre is expanded to encompass familial and ancestral footsteps travel that charges itself with retracing the specific means, routes, networks, and geographic centers of diasporic travel. For M. G. Vassanji, for instance, India is less a point of recovery than the beginning of an identity that was always already in transit – symbolized by the dhows he sees that continue to move goods between his ancestral home in Gujarat and East Africa: "In such a dhow my paternal-great grandfather [. . .] went to Mombasa, then proceeded to the interior of what is now Kenya."[22] This interest into inquiring more deeply into historical *mobilities* mirrors a similar shift within postcolonial studies away from efforts to theorize fixed, essentialist notions of identity of the kind critiqued in Paul Gilroy's *The Black Atlantic*.[23] Narratives of "dark return," for instance, as Srilata Ravi describes contemporary Francophone footsteps travel to sites traumatized by poverty or political unrest, pay tribute to how such sites "themselves resist any kind of objectification, remain constantly out of focus and are almost impossible to capture in one master narrative."[24] This critical self-awareness in many ways is the hallmark of the most evocative examples of familial and ancestral footsteps travel.

Journeys inspired by forced relocations of Native Americans offer one potential starting point for investigating contemporary ancestral footsteps travel writing, a subgenre that includes N. Scott Momaday's classic *The Way to Rainy Mountain* (1969). Momaday retraces the long migration south of the Kiowa that began in the seventeenth century, but he dwells less on what he calls the "mean and ordinary agonies of human history" than on the "nomadic soul" itself of the Kiowa – its histories of travel and how travel has always informed their culture and livelihood.[25] The hope that such journeys allow one to connect healingly to the past also informs Janet Campbell Hale's *Bloodlines: Odyssey of a Native Daughter* (1993). Hale's quest is fueled in part by stories about a grandmother who as a young girl had become caught up in Chief Joseph's (1840–1904) attempt to flee from US troops into Canada. Gazing for the first time at the battle site where a defeated Chief Joseph had famously said, "I will fight no more forever," Hale writes, "I was with those people, was part of them. I felt the presence of my grandmother [...] the part of her that lives on in me, in inherited memories of her, in my blood and in my spirit."[26]

Jerry Ellis's *Walking the Trail of Tears* (1991) undertakes to retrace entirely by foot what is undoubtedly the single worst of these forced migrations in terms of scale, hardship, and lives lost along the way: the 1838 Cherokee Removal. Ellis, however, makes the interesting decision to reverse the route in his case, beginning in Oklahoma and ending at the home of his parents in northeast Alabama, thus exchanging a journey of exile for an Odyssean nostos that underscores precisely the "luxury taken away from the Cherokee."[27] Ellis's journey is indeed as much a personal one about recreating a sense of home or connection to others in his life: "it's one-on-one human contact I seek," he writes. "I want to hear secrets and see emotions" (29). Ellis encounters unexpected hospitality at almost every turn and a sense of respect for the journey he undertakes, recalling in some ways William Least Heat-Moon's *Blue Highways* (1982), another "slow travel" journey through more isolated parts of the American landscape. Capturing the essential contradictions of American collective identity, Ellis observes at one point, "Most of the folks I've met have been warm and kind, but they keep telling me to be careful of the next guy. The next guy tells me the same thing" (133). Near the end of his journey, a reunion with a cousin who seems more preoccupied with describing a new computer dampens the otherwise affirmative tone of Ellis's homecoming, causing him to question whether he has truly crafted a more tightly knit sense of community through his long walk or whether he has merely stepped momentarily off the grid (243).

Luci Tapahonso's travel poem "In 1864" (1993) reflects more on the ambivalence one feels attempting to connect with the past through revisiting historically charged sites of Native American forced migration and resistance. The poem recounts a visit with her daughter to Fort Sumner in southern New Mexico, the final destination of some 8,000 Navajo after a 300-mile forced march. "The center lines were a blurred guide," Tapahonso writes of their journey by car, a metaphor for the ease of modern travel and the inevitably limited or "blurred" vision of the past that one can at best hope to achieve in a world so thoroughly reconditioned by modern transportation technologies and infrastructures.[28] This more accelerated journey frames Tapahonso's recollection of stories about how her great-grandmother "walked steadily each day,/stopping only when the soldiers wanted to eat or rest" (9). As the poem moves back into the present, the "car hums steadily, and my daughter is crying softly," capturing both the enduring power and emotion of this painful history but also its competition with the "noise" of the modern world (10). Hale, in an interesting contrast, notes as she looks upon the battlefield, "how quiet it was now that the car's engine no longer ran,"[29] a silence, in some ways, that allows her to transport herself more smoothly into the past.

Travel writing by authors of Caribbean descent offers some of the most visible and influential examples of more global "return" journeys, with V. S. Naipaul perhaps at the forefront. Commenting on the multiple points of racial and ethnic reference in Caribbean writing, Mimi Sheller observes, "to become truly Caribbean you must first go elsewhere; migration, exile, and return have become grounds for forging a pan-Caribbean identity."[30] While they might deny any attempt at crafting a larger pan-Caribbean identity, two other British travel writers with familial roots in the Caribbean, Caryl Phillips and Gary Younge, have authored very different footsteps narratives that nonetheless hinge upon the same question, or "*the* question," as Phillips puts it in *The Atlantic Sound* (1999): "Where are you from. [...] The problem question for those of us who have grown up in societies which define themselves by excluding others."[31]

Phillips's book in some sense follows naturally from his earlier *The European Tribe* (1987), another effort to reverse the directional flows that dominate most contemporary Western travel writing. Unlike the typical footsteps narrative, Phillips does not announce whom he is following or why he is taking the unusual means of a merchant ship returning from the Caribbean to England: *Atlantic Sound* begins literally at sea, with no clear directions or signposts – other than the difficulty itself of finding one's bearings geographically and historically. As they approach the English coast, Phillips recalls once asking his mother about what she did on her own journey there from the Caribbean in 1958: "she looked blankly at me. [...] I now know how she and all the other emigrants felt as they crossed the Atlantic; they felt lonely" (20). Phillips's book could be regarded as an effort to repopulate that lonely historical stage with specific names as he revisits the slave forts and other littoral contact zones associated with the slave trading "triangle" between Europe, Africa, and the Americas. In the process, Phillips crafts a particular kind of *critical* footsteps narrative, one that seeks to engage history in personal, deeply felt ways but which also stresses appreciation for the complexities and more troubling ideological cross-currents of the past. His visit to Elmina Castle during the Ghanaian celebration of Panafest, for instance, finds itself haunted by the historical narrative he interweaves of Phillip Quaque, an African missionary in the early nineteenth century in the waning days of the slave trade. By all evidence, a kind, devout, and widely respected man in his time, what is most remarkable to us now is the utter silence in his letters regarding "his feelings about his 'brothers and sisters' in the dungeons beneath his feet" (179, 222, 228). If ancestral footsteps travel is a kind of spiritual pilgrimage, it is one that must nonetheless be carefully grounded in a critical understanding of history.

Younge's *No Place Like Home: A Black Briton's Journey through the American South* (1999) is not a familial or ancestral footsteps narrative in a direct sense, following instead the routes taken by the "Freedom Riders" of the early 1960s seeking to test court-mandated desegregation of interstate busing lines. Like Phillips, however, Younge uses his journey as a way of arriving at a critical and historically informed sense of transatlantic black British identity. The book's introduction stresses the sense of displacement Younge felt as the son of Barbadian immigrants – neither fully a citizen of Britain nor able to find shelter in a cohesive sense of black identity. Seeking some of that cohesiveness in what he admits is a "dream image" of the American South patched together from various strands of literature and pop culture, Younge writes, "I longed for the heartfelt affinity that both blacks and whites in the South seemed to have with their environment. They were Southerners and, whatever that meant to them, they were proud of it."[32] Younge's book is less a forensic investigation into the details of the Freedom Riders' journey than a broader examination of the legacy of the Civil Rights movement in the American South and a critical comparison of British and American ways of confronting problems of race (or not confronting, in the former case, he suggests). Younge's book is also of particular interest for what the method of his journey teaches him about a side of American society often ignored in travel writing. If bus travel in the 1960s was still an important and vibrant part of American mass transit, interstate bus travel is favored now primarily by those on the outside of the middle-class, suburban car culture that dominates the interstate highway exits and their "discordant symphony of standardized garishness" (128). These people dwelling on the margins of American traveling and class mobilities form a significant part of Younge's narrative, testifying to other, more class-based inequalities lingering from the American past.

Conclusion

At its most evocative, postcolonial footsteps travel may offer models of return or renewal, but it is also something that must push forward and against nostalgia, an idea Phillips emphasizes at the close of *Atlantic Sound* in an epilogue entitled "Exodus." Visiting the Israeli compound of a group of black American emigres who identify themselves with the lost tribes of Israel, Phillips empathizes on one level with this longing for simpler historical narratives and teleologies, but he is also careful to emphasize the essential misdirection they enfold. Addressing them as fellow travelers, Phillips cautions: "You dressed your memory in the new words of this new country. Remember. There were no round-trip tickets in your part of the ship. Exodus. It is futile to walk into the face of history."[33] Footsteps travel writing, whether of the forensic, foliated, or familial and ancestral variety, at its core embodies a kind of "walking into the face of history" – an attempt to recover lost times and travelers or reverse patterns of travel that were once forced upon the disempowered. As such, it is a critical endeavor as well as a creative one that must dwell as productively upon the fractures, impossibilities, and even illusions that travel affords as a way of connecting to people, places, and cultural memory. As Tony Horwitz remarks of Cook's voyages in the Pacific, and his own struggle to develop a critical perspective on that history, "with hindsight, the line between exploration and exploitation, between investigation and imperialism, seems perilously thin."[34] It is this thin, precarious margin that the most insightful and intrepid postcolonial footsteps travel narratives ultimately traverse.

NOTES

1 Henry Morton Stanley, *How I Found Livingstone* (New York: Scribner, Armstrong, 1872), 412.
2 Stanley, *How I Found Livingstone*, 413. See, for instance, Kingsley Holgate's *Africa: In the Footsteps of the Great Explorers* (2013); Tim Butcher's *Blood River: A Journey to Africa's Broken Heart* (2008); Martin Dugard's *Into Africa: The Epic Adventures of Stanley and Livingstone* (2004); and, Jeffrey Tayler's *Facing the Congo* (2000), which partially retraces Stanley's route down the Congo.
3 Tim Youngs, *The Cambridge Introduction to Travel Writing* (Cambridge: Cambridge University Press, 2011), 185.
4 Maria Lindgren Leavenworth, *The Second Journey: Traveling in Literary Footsteps*, 2nd edn. (Umeå: Umeå University, 2010), 189.
5 Imperialist nostalgia, Rosaldo writes, "uses a pose of 'innocent yearning' both to capture people's imaginations and to conceal its complicity" in processes of cultural domination: Renato Rosaldo, "Imperialist Nostalgia," *Representations*, 26 (1989): 107–22 (108).
6 William Dalyrmple, *In Xanadu: A Quest* (New York: Vintage, 1989), 300.
7 Paul Smethurst, "Post-Orientalism and the Past-Colonial in William Dalrymple's Travel Histories," in *Postcolonial Travel Writing: Critical Explorations*, ed. Justin D. Edwards and Rune Graulund (Basingstoke: Palgrave Macmillan, 2010), 156–72 (161).
8 Tim Mackintosh-Smith, *Travels with a Tangerine: From Morocco to Turkey in the Footsteps of Islam's Greatest Traveler* (New York: Random House, 2001), 32.
9 Charles Nicholl, *The Creature in the Map: A Journey to El Dorado* (New York: William Morrow, 1995), 211. Nicholl followed this effort with another notable footsteps narrative, *Somebody Else: Arthur Rimbaud in Africa* (1997).

10 Stephen Minta, *Aguirre: The Re-Creation of a Sixteenth-Century Journey across South America* (New York: Henry Holt, 1994), 149.

11 Tony Horwitz, *Blue Latitudes: Boldly Going Where Captain Cook Has Gone Before* (New York: Picador, 2002), 6.

12 Sara Wheeler, *Terra Incognita: Travels in Antarctica* (New York: Random House, 1996), 16. Wheeler's book is just one example of "frozen footsteps" writing tracing historic journeys to the poles, a subgenre that also includes Roger Mear and Robert Swan's *In the Footsteps of Scott* (1987).

13 Graham Huggan, *Extreme Pursuits: Travel/Writing in an Age of Globalization* (Ann Arbor: University of Michigan Press, 2009), 100.

14 Carl Hoffman, *Savage Harvest: A Tale of Cannibals, Colonialism, and Michael Rockefeller's Quest for Primitive Art* (New York: William Morrow, 2014), 145–46.

15 Jonathan Raban, *Passage to Juneau: A Sea and Its Meanings* (New York: Pantheon, 1999), 33.

16 Nicola J. Watson, "Introduction," in *Literary Tourism and Nineteenth-Century Culture*, ed. Nicola J. Watson (Basingstoke: Palgrave Macmillan, 2009), 1–12 (7).

17 Gavin Young, *In Search of Conrad* (London: Penguin, 1991), 3.

18 Paul Hyland, *The Black Heart: A Voyage into Central Africa* (London: Victor Gollancz, 1988), 136.

19 Gavin Bell, *In Search of Tusitala: Travels in the Pacific After Robert Louis Stevenson* (London: Picador, 1994), 100.

20 Steve Glassman, *On the Trail of the Maya Explorer: Tracing the Epic Journey of John Lloyd Stephens* (Tuscaloosa: University of Alabama Press, 2003), 5.

21 Caroline Alexander, *One Dry Season: In the Footsteps of Mary Kingsley* (New York: Knopf, 1990), 6.

22 M. G. Vassanji, *A Place Within: Rediscovering India* (Toronto: Anchor Canada, 2008), 350. Vassanji revisits Mombasa, the city of his birth, in a later travel book, *And Home Was Kariakoo: A Memoir of East Africa* (2014).

23 In *The Black Atlantic: Modernity and Double Consciousness* (Cambridge: Harvard University Press, 1993), Gilroy warns against a "mystical and ruthlessly positive notion of Africa that is indifferent to intraracial variation and is frozen at the point where blacks boarded the ships that would carry them into the woes and horrors of the middle passage" (189).

24 Srilata Ravi, "Home and the 'Failed' City in Postcolonial Narratives of 'Dark Return,'" *Postcolonial Studies*, 17, no. 3 (2014): 296–306 (298). In *Travel Writing from Black Australia: Utopia, Melancholia, and Aboriginality* (New York: Routledge, 2016), Robert Clarke writes in similar terms of Australian "journey to country" narratives, where "destinations and consequences are apt to be unpredictable and ambivalent [...] a challenge for narrators and readers" (116).

25 N. Scott Momaday, *The Way to Rainy Mountain* (Albuquerque: University of New Mexico Press, 1969), 3, 4.

26 Janet Campbell Hale, *Bloodlines: Odyssey of a Native Daughter* (New York: Random House, 1993), 158.

27 Jerry Ellis, *Walking the Trail: One Man's Journey along the Cherokee Trail of Tears* (New York: Delacorte Press, 1991), 6.

28 Luci Tapahonso, *Sáanii Dahataal: The Women Are Singing* (Tucson: University of Arizona Press, 1993), 7.

29 Campbell Hale, *Bloodlines*, 156.

30 Mimi Sheller, "Demobilizing and Remobilizing Caribbean Paradise," in *Tourism Mobilities: Places to Play, Places in Play*, ed. Mimi Sheller and John Urry (London and New York: Routledge, 2004), 13–21 (15).

31 Caryl Phillips, *The Atlantic Sound* (New York: Vintage, 2000), 124–25.

32 Gary Younge, *No Place Like Home: A Black Briton's Journey through the American South* (Jackson: University of Mississippi Press, 2002), 24.

33 Phillips, *Atlantic Sound*, 275.

34 Horwitz, *Blue Latitudes*, 135.

Peripheries

11

BRIAN CREECH

Postcolonial Travel Journalism and the New Media

Travel journalism has long had an unsteady relationship with both travel writing and the journalism industry. As an industrialized form of writing, it has often been derided as never reaching the literary ambitions of travelogues written by Jack London, Evelyn Waugh, or Joseph Conrad, to name a few. As Mary Louise Pratt notes, these are the writers and forms of literature that are often canonized and analyzed (for better or worse) for the pictures of the world they portray.[1] As a form of journalism, travel journalism has long been derided as less serious, intended for consumers of frivolous experiences.[2]

The distinction between travel writing as a form of either "high" or "middle-brow" literary culture and travel journalism as disposable mass culture is not always a useful one. Ben Cocking argues that, despite tensions around travel journalism's status, there is a "discursive trajectory" from nineteenth-century European travel writing to the more consumption-oriented forms of travel journalism found today.[3] Carla Almeida Santos says of newspaper travelogues from the early twentieth century that travel articles appearing in mass market publications "offer what has not been experienced before by representing it through transforming the moment with extravagant vocabulary and details in order to seduce readers."[4] Concerns over representation and ethical engagement with cultural others provide a rich ground of postcolonial critique, regardless of the economic or institutional arrangements that presage the production of travel texts. Compounded with an explosion of digital content and the fact that the economic sustainability of journalism in North America and certain parts of Western Europe appears to be in perpetual crisis, changes in travel journalism's industrial structure portend changes in the way in which the broader world is represented.[5] As major news organizations close foreign reporting bureaus, more international news content takes the form of travel writing and reporting, often subsidized by the tourism industry.

While the understanding of travel journalism as a representational practice implicated in the spread of tourism as a consumption practice merits critical attention, there is also the potential to consider travel journalism, with its ostensible ethical commitment to accuracy and truth, as a form of representation that complicates the discursive construction of foreign bodies and locales as existing for the consumption of interested travelers.[6] Furthermore, many of the digital changes disrupting journalism have led to a seeming explosion of voices within travel journalism, as amateur writers, local guides, environmental activists, and other nonprofessionals take the reins of representation.

Blogging, tweeting, social media sharing, photo-sharing, and other forms of user-generated content have aggregated into a mass of tourist representations that form an alternative field of representation separate from the consumption-oriented travel texts that appear in newspapers, magazines, and on television. However, unequal representations persist even as technologies offer new possibilities. With this tension in mind, the following chapter examines digital trends in travel journalism and argues that while representations of travel across new media may not fully escape an understanding of tourism as a form of globalized leisure consumption, when considered from a postcolonial perspective, they complicate notions of travel representation and rearrange the conditions that constitute textual authority in travel journalism.

Travel Journalism and the Consumption of Postcolonial Experience

As tourism has become a major global industry, bringing with its expansion much-needed capital and development money into the so-called Global South, the commercial and cultural imperatives of travel journalism have become intertwined in increasingly inseparable ways. The study of travel journalism is a relatively new field, but as international travel grows as a leisure experience, so too have the forms of journalism and media production that abet its expansion. Anandam Kavoori and Elfriede Fürsich argue "international travel is no longer a one-way stream from the West to other countries [...] this makes international person-to-person contact more likely and generates audiences for travel-related journalism and information as a global media topic."[7]

Tourism, as an economic and cultural activity, may flow through paths trodden by colonial history, but this history is neither totalizing nor completely erased. Given the economic development tourism portends for many countries, it is perhaps best to think of the relationship between tourism and the postcolonial condition as an ambivalent one, comprising divergent histories, politics, and economics often flattened beneath the overt commodification of place.[8] Parsing this ambivalence requires attention to representations and the authority upon which those representations are built, and as such, travel journalism has become a site for studying the often complex and competing "ideological dimensions of tourism and transcultural encounters."[9]

This, of course, was not always the case. David Spurr argues that travel journalism, as a particular mode of representation and rhetorical form engaged in telling Western audiences about the rest of the world, has traditionally been the repository of ideological tropes that construct the global other as subservient to Western consumption.[10] As a part of the broader discourse of colonialism, Spurr historically implicates travel journalism as one of the mundane, mass audience practices that sets the terms for understanding European and American encounters with the rest of the world. He singles out *National Geographic* as a particular publication of concern, noting how editorial policies and preferences, while possibly benign in their intention and factually accurate in their execution, worked to aestheticize travel in a way that rendered global experiences ready for mass audience consumption (43–61).

Journalism, as an industrialized form of mass cultural production and consumption, is easily critiqued for rendering all experience consumable. Audience demand, deadlines, and market pressures push journalists to write accurate, compelling stories that will sell papers. Television, as a format, is often critiqued for offering little more than a style of representation primarily used to celebrate travel as a mode of consumption, a means for encountering exotic products, foods, and experiences that can be replicated for other travelers.[11] These limits, though, do not overdetermine the interpretations an audience might make. Santos, for instance, argues that travel writers structure a variety of possible audience engagements with a place, "by giving readers the necessary tools to extend, visualize, and daydream."[12] Vivid imagery, compelling narrative, and rich context all give audiences the textual clues they need to guide their own imagined engagement with the locales travel journalists encounter.

The ability for travel texts to guide audiences' understanding of a place they might not be familiar with otherwise often operates as a useful, redemptive locus for scholars of travel journalism. When done carefully, travel journalists create a sense of critical distance and thoughtful engagement in their work, developing discursive tools that they then "invite audiences to use as their own."[13] In Timothy Brennan's terms, these texts operate "phenomenologically – that is, to speak of a perception that acquires the status of a truth within a bracketed reality."[14] This phenomenological aspect is perhaps best emblematized in Anthony Bourdain's assertion that the best travel journalism reveals the topography of an internal, rather than external, journey, yet it must be noted that such formulations risk construing international experience and engagement with the other as an important part of the traveler's own personal development.[15]

Underscoring this phenomenological experience is a normative ethic of travel as cosmopolitan consumption, where an informed understanding of the destination plays "a key role in facilitating social reflexivity," ultimately leading to a more enlightening experience for the individual.[16] A concept borrowed from John Stuart Mill, cosmopolitanism denotes a sense of belonging to all parts of the world, not privileging one location and its inhabitants over another.[17] Within the context of contemporary global exchange and mobility, cosmopolitanism can be taken to mean "an ability to make one's way into other cultures."[18] In its ideal form, travel journalism may constitute a new global public sphere and fuel a sense of global identity that promotes a mode of cross-cultural engagement as an alternative to the expansion of a global capitalism that flattens all experience beneath the impetus to consume.[19]

However, as a philosophy of engagement, cosmopolitanism struggles to escape a dialectic that positions the broader world as subject to the individual's intellectual growth and moral and ethical development. Ulrich Beck argues these ideals, once mediatized through cultural forms like travel journalism, can crystallize into the consumption of locations as the interchangeable backdrops of an increasingly Western experience of the world.[20] Travel and travel journalism operate as forms of "banal globalism" that construct much of the postcolonial world as not just a realm of material goods ready to be consumed, but also the setting where a narrative of ideological dominance continues to be written.[21]

This is the backdrop that digital technologies in the international journalism industry operate against, reinforce, and potentially disrupt. As digital publishing has lowered the costs of media production, the field of possible representations within travel journalism has greatly expanded, offering a potential mode of agency that does not adhere to the conventions, economies, conditions, and ideological assumptions that undergird traditional forms of travel journalism.

New Media and the Chronicling of Travel Experience

The digital changes that have occurred across journalism and media industries in recent years have brought with them serious economic disruptions and challenges to journalism's authority over the truth.[22] Digital platforms like blogging, social media, web publishing, photo sharing, and content aggregation have made the collection and distribution of information much less expensive. Empowered with these tools, new content producers, like citizen journalists, activist bloggers, and amateur travelers, create their own representations, simultaneously conforming to and challenging traditional modes of journalistic representation.[23] Stuart Allan argues that digital networks abet a form of distant witnessing, where the geographic flattening that has been ascribed to new media technologies grants representations from across the globe the legitimacy accorded to first-person journalistic observation.[24]

In much of the discourse about digital technologies' impact on global forms of media production, there is often an implicit assumption that primarily American and European values dictate cultural dynamics. Fabienne Darling-Wolf, among others, argues against this assumption and states that all media practices, not just the digital, are evidence of "the highly hybrid nature of global culture," and that it is incumbent upon scholars to attend to the "multiple ways in which the global/national/local are mutually constitutive elements of our contemporary era."[25] Digital technologies expand the discursive and imaginative work of media representation, so that it is no longer just Westerners experiencing the rest of the world and representing their experiences. For example, Lena Karlsson finds that blog-based diaries allowed Asian Americans to discursively construct a shared "ancestral homeland" that reflected their identities as part of a broader diaspora, yet a diaspora constructed among particularly local conditions.[26]

Thanks to a growing global middle class, travelers are no longer primarily Western, though it can and has been argued that travelers' tastes are influenced by a global capitalism whose values trace their origin toward Europe and America.[27] That being said, new technologies have been used in a broad variety of ways to chronicle the types of international experience traditional modes of travel journalism preclude. The following examples draw attention to the possibilities of digital technologies while also accounting for lingering colonial tensions that are often expressed in new ways.

Blogging

Blogging platforms and web publishing tools have been credited with lowering costs of content production. Fragmentary in nature, blogs have often been used to bring audiences into the news process, thus challenging the unified authority of representation journalism has enjoyed throughout modernity.[28]

In a travel journalism context, this means that blogs offer opportunities to represent locations that fall outside typical tourist experiences. As Bryan Pirolli shows, travelers often turn to blogs as a more authentic form of information about a location, as bloggers "become akin to travel companions" and "local word of mouth sources."[29] Blogs often claim to offer the authenticity that seasoned travelers seek, as bloggers posit their expertise, experience, and unvarnished opinions as a distinct alternative to the conventions of mainstream travel journalism. On its surface, this authenticity appears genuine. Yet as Hanno Hardt argues, the search for the authentic is just as much a construction of contemporary capitalist relations as any other form of mediated representation.[30]

As others have noted, the construction of the authentic may serve a strategic impulse amid a global system of commodity exchange.[31] A cursory survey of tourism and hospitality research shows growing attention to the use of blogs as a means of marketing not just individual businesses but also entire destinations as a means of capturing the capital travelers embody.[32] This research reveals the proliferation of a market-oriented strategy that uses blogs as evidence of potential traveler interest in new experiences and destinations yet to be commoditized as part of standard travel agendas.

Such is the dynamic of representation that travel blogs typify: They represent places outside the standard itineraries and may lend power to marginalized people and places, but they are also part and parcel of a tourism industry driven by a growing global middle class's taste for new things. Though blogs may offer routes for an international economy of taste to travel, they also offer means of engagement with destinations that are not wholly overdetermined by the dynamics of global capital.

Blogging also offers individuals an ability to experience new cultures while also embodying reflexive engagement. For instance, students who travel abroad often use blogs to document their travels and in the process demonstrate a style of phenomenological engagement that demonstrates a growing awareness of the global forces shaping their experience.[33] Examples abound of travel blogs existing as class documents, but in their totality they demonstrate a growing engagement with a place over time. Take, for instance, the blog *Travel Writing in Cambodia*, a product of the University of Georgia's Travel Writing in Cambodia class, taught by UGA faculty traveling with students in Siem Reap.[34] Containing writing from several semesters' worth of students, the blog stands as a document of growing student skill and empathy when encountering a new culture. Many of the posts deal with landmarks of Cambodia's violent past, but the student authors show care when developing context and focusing on details that emblematized their experience. This is a form of journalism that demonstrates little concern for an audience, and so the blog stands as evidence of attempted empathy by aspiring travel journalists. It offers a space for developing the modes of humane engagement that often do not appear in more commoditized forms of contemporary travel journalism

Blogs also offer a means for identity fashioning among certain travelers and communities of travelers. As Usha Raman and Divya Choudary observe of Indian bloggers writing about their travels, blogs offer these groups a means to "position themselves as global citizens who have the freedom and ability to give themselves the experience of different places and cultures."[35] Blogs, then, offer a mode of representation that allows postcolonial subjects to position themselves as part of global modernity and postmodernity, often in ways that do not compromise their ethnic identity or foreclose the possibilities of political and social critique those identities embody. Blogs allow individuals to engage in the form of hybridity envisioned by Homi Bhabha – one "that entertains difference without an assumed or imposed hierarchy" – often by embodying conflicting strategies of identity formation.[36]

Free from print publications' limited space, travel blogging offers sustained engagement with a destination over time. This engagement transforms a blog away from a consumer-oriented style of travel to a broader engagement with the destination. Taking the example of Cambodia again, several Western and Southeast Asian bloggers have developed blogs that cover not only cultural festivals and destinations, but also report on politics, economics, and social issues, while also offering commentary on the complicated relationship between travel, economic development, and Cambodian history.[37] These blogs often link to each other, revealing a community structure that expands beyond tourism and displays a shared concern about the consequences of political corruption and fights over economic development that a swelling tourist population has brought to the country. Though these blogs may catalyze attention around particular businesses, sites, or tour operators, they also provide a source of news and information beyond the reach of the international press, creating a vision of Cambodia that is much more complex than the notions of historical catastrophe that characterize other travel reporting from the country.

Social Media Platforms

While blogging represents a more traditionally text-based form of representation, often grounded in narrative authority, other forms of new media have been used to develop audiences around platforms of interaction. For example, as eco-tourism has gained growing currency among travelers, activists and eco-tour operators have begun utilizing social media tools to distribute and publicize stories about environmental issues, building an international audience around what could otherwise be construed as strictly local interests. Activists have used social media strategies to develop audience-centric and consumer-centric narratives around issues of environmental concern.[38] Social media becomes integral to a discursive strategy that casts travelers as implicated in the environmental risks they encounter while traveling.

Activists, tour operators, and nontraditional travel journalists convene communities of interest around particular issues by using social media to communicate with travelers after they have left. Not only do they convene an audience, but they can also use these tools to garner the kind of attention that pushes certain localized environmental issues into the popular media. Take, for instance, the Nature seekers of Matura, Trinidad, who bring travelers into Trinidad to spend a week tagging and protecting endangered leatherback sea turtles. Currently in its twenty-fifth year, the group has hitherto relied on international nongovernmental organizations and foundations to attract tourist and media attention, as well as the philanthropic support necessary to support its operations.[39] While international partners offer logistical and financial support for the organization, the Nature seekers use Facebook to mobilize attention around the organization and prolong tourist engagement with the issue of sea turtle conservation.[40]

The platform offers a style of engagement that is not limited to the distribution of information. The organization also engages with user-comments, shares GIFS of hologram whales breaching the floor of a gym, promotes online stores selling handcrafted goods from Matura, shares photos of visitors tagging turtles, and offers opportunities to connect with other ecotourism and environmental conservation agencies. Using these tools, international organizations marshal attention outside the gatekeeping function of the mass media.[41] This attention can then be used reflexively to frame an organization as worthy of international media attention, like when the Nature seekers leveraged their Facebook fans and international network of former visitors into a CNN story and "heroes" award from the network.[42]

Though social media's dissolution of journalistic authority is a common refrain in research about journalism, for the study of travel journalism, it has created the conditions where individual tour operators, government agencies, or activists can gather their own discursive capital to draw in an audience engaged around particular local issues.[43] As organizations master the rhetoric and styles of communication that occur across these platforms, they create viable modes of representation that fall outside of the authority exercised by news institutions. Organizations become part of travelers' social networks and engagements are sustained. Jenny Molz and Cody Paris argue that, thanks to social media and digital infrastructures, travelers have the ability to carry their social world with them, "blurring [the distinction] between home and away," thus encapsulating the use of social media to extend an individual's connection with a place beyond the single tourist experience.[44]

These tools also represent a vast marketing potential, which has been readily exploited by the tourism industry.[45] As such, the tension between commodification and representation inherent in travel and tourism persists, driven by the structures of attention social media technologies make quantifiable. Despite this overt capitalization of tourist attention, alternative visions and modes of collective engagement exist across social media outlets. Furthermore, social media has offered the means for groups to challenge news institutions' authority to represent them, which Nancy Morris and Andrew Mendelson found when looking at the history of *National Geographic*'s coverage of Puerto Rico.[46] By offering a means to collectivize audiences, social media offers organizations and individuals a series of channels for turning a critical mass of audience engagement into productive discursive power.

Photo and Video Sharing

While this chapter has dealt primarily with text and language, control over the visual representation of people and places has been equally disrupted by the increase of digital technologies. Visuals inform an important part of Edward Said's critique of orientalism, as it is through the visual that the imperial imagination constructs and reifies agency-limiting portrayals of the postcolonial world, and this critique of the visual extends into contemporary scholarship about travel journalism.[47] Rhadika Parameswaran has noted the various ways that visual discourses overdetermine the gendered presentation of Asian and Latin American women in American magazines, as well as the way symbols of global capitalism, such as logos and advertisements, subtly mark those same bodies as sites of exchange, even as they appear within seemingly benign outlets such as *National Geographic*.[48] Caitlin Bruce has argued, though, that even the concerned, humanitarian gaze of the Western traveler, embodied by issue-oriented documentaries and highly publicized appeals for humanitarian aid, can construct images of global poverty in ways that absolve viewers of their implication in the systems of exchange that allow that poverty to persist.[49]

While the critiques of the visual construction of the Global South are far too numerous to recount here, digital photo- and video-sharing technologies have offered a means for creating and distributing alternative visions of the sites tourists encounter. For instance, as Brian Ekdale and David Tuwei have argued, digital video sites like YouTube have allowed the easy distribution of videos that critique the conventions of visually representing poverty in global cities by engaging in a form of discourse they call "ironic encounters."[50] Partly because the visual lexicon of humanitarian discourse and Western interest is so pervasive, it offers a visual idiom that can be satirized and used to critique unacknowledged tendencies toward objectification.[51]

Alternative image production practices make little sense without an audience gathered to view them, and so part of their power extends from the networked relations of social media outlined above. Digital videos and images flow across social media networks and become objects that audiences' discursive power can coalesce around. A growing visual critique of travel journalism's institutionalized ways of seeing is presaged upon the uptake of camera-equipped mobile phones and cellphone networks in the developing world, an infrastructure that grants access to systems of image distribution and circulation.[52] As Paolo Favero has argued, these networks bring into sharp relief the materiality of representations, and thus the contexts that they occur within and the power relations that extend from these contexts.[53]

User-Review Sites

While other forms of new media offer a means to challenge the modes of representation inherent in travel journalism, user-review sites like Yelp and TripAdvisor exemplify platforms that merge consumption with localized and seemingly democratized systems of representation.[54] These sites traffic in authenticity of experience, a reliability based upon first-person accounts. As "experience replaces expertise," the market conditions surrounding tourism continue to impinge upon the presumed authority of journalistic representation, as discussed elsewhere in this chapter.[55] For the postcolonial study of travel journalism, the challenges to journalistic authority user-review sites symbolize is indicative of a reordering of global representation toward the consumption of international experience.

User-review sites' platforms are developed in ways to encourage users to write about their travel experiences as something they had consumed and would recommend to others. The aggregated activity across sites like Yelp and TripAdvisor creates what one recent study calls "discursive investment" around trendy sites.[56] The sheer mass of consumer opinions these sites contain, and the positive/negative review structures they afford, encourages "changes to the cultural landscape" by offering a social and data-driven means for identifying "potential sites of capital reinvestment" (4). Ultimately, as cultural texts presenting the collected opinions and individual experiences of thousands of travelers, the sites represent a "cognitive map of homologous consumer choice, in an effort to make social and geographic space coincide" (4).

As such, these sites are deeply implicated in the unequal distribution of capital across space by tapping into a leisure economy driven by "taste," a term that masks historical and often racialized constructions of what counts as a quality experience.[57] These technologies shift the political economy of travel consumption, often by foregrounding traveler expectations and creating an accountability structure where local businesses and travel authorities are expected to cohere with travelers' preconceived notions or face the redistribution of capital and opportunity a negative review may imply.[58] Finally, these sites also offer a structure where the individual's phenomenological experience with another culture is commoditized. An individual review serves not only to evaluate an experience, but also becomes part of a useful corpus of individual experiences where a collective evaluation of a site and its attractions may develop.

These sites embody a flattening of human experience enabled by the Internet, offering a means by which the logic of capital further infiltrates the culture of international travel, commoditizing even the problematic phenomenological consumption of cultural exchange.[59] Though it should be noted that user-review sites should not be confused as the logical end point of all travel representation on the Internet, they do offer a structure of symbolic consumption that makes apparent the deepest impulses toward commodification that postcolonial critics of globalization have long been warning against.

Conclusion: Toward a Postcolonial Critique of Travel Journalism and New Media

While the notion that travel journalism is practiced mostly by dispassionate observers has long been critiqued by scholars, it still offers a useful normative, professional standard to evaluate shifting trends against. As this chapter has argued, many digital and new media tools have been used in ways that call into question travel journalism's authority over the representation of international experience. Still, these tools do not offer an absolute escape from the regimes of global exchange and commodification that travel journalism is bound up within.

Travel journalism has long been a practice implicated in the international expansion of capital from the West into the colonial world and it is possible to see how new technologies continue and accelerate these trends. Hearkening back to Arjun Appadurai's notion that the movement of people, culture, media, finance, and ideologies can be conceived of as a topography of co-constitutive practices, digital modes of media representation create new paths of cultural commodification and exchange and deepen old ones, often in service to an expanding global capitalism.[60] As such, travel journalism and its changing digital pressures act as a cultural form that "creates the conditions of the production of locality."[61]

Yet it is also worth noting that the structural conditions symbolized by the expansion of digital technologies by no means overdetermine the possibilities of agency from within this field of representation. While also delineating the structuring forces of global modernity, Appadurai turns to the imagination as the human ability to synthesize experience and give form to new possibilities as agency's potential repository, arguing that as modes of cultural expression have been granted a unique form of discursive and representational capital, "The imagination is now central to all forms of agency, is itself a social fact."[62]

This reassertion of imagination is important for the consideration of cultural forms like travel journalism because, through acts of representation, an imaginative reconsideration of agency may allow individuals to put forward alternative visions of travel and global experience that escape the seemingly overbearing demands of global capitalism. I would take Appadurai's argument a step further and argue that creative acts reveal possible critical and ethical engagements with the world despite one's implication in the systems of exchange, historical difference, and domination that surround travel and travel journalism. To return nominally to Spurr, digital tools can be used to open up spaces in the practice of travel journalism where individual practitioners may take stock of the conditions they are enmeshed within and hopefully escape "the rhetorics of empire," no matter how they might manifest among contemporary trends of digital exchange and hypermobility.

NOTES

1 Mary Louise Pratt, *Imperial Eyes: Travel Writing and Transculturation* (London: Routledge, 1992), 1–2.
2 Folker Hanusch, "The Dimensions of Travel Journalism: Exploring New Fields for Journalism Research Beyond the News," *Journalism Studies*, 11, no. 1 (2010): 68–82 (70).
3 Ben Cocking, "Travel Journalism: Europe Imagining the Middle East," *Journalism Studies*, 10, no. 1 (2009): 54–68 (66).
4 Carla Almeida Santos, "Cultural Politics in Contemporary Travel Writing," *Annals of Tourism Research*, 33, no. 3 (2006): 624–44 (624).
5 Folker Hanusch and Elfriede Fürsich, "On the Relevance of Travel Journalism: An Introduction," in *Travel Journalism: Exploring Production, Impact, and*

Culture, ed. Folker Hanusch and Elfriede Fürsich (New York: Palgrave Macmillan, 2014), 1–18 (8).

6 John Urry and Jonas Larsen, *The Tourist Gaze 3.0* (London: SAGE, 2011).

7 Elfriede Fürsich and Anandam Kavoori, "Travel Journalism and the Logics of Globalization," in *The Logics of Globalization: Studies in International Communication*, ed. Anandam Kavoori (New York: Lexington, 2009), 189–209 (191–192).

8 C. Michael Hall and Hazel Tucker, "Conclusion," in *Tourism and Postcolonialism: Contested Discourses, Identities, Representations*, ed. C. Michael Hall and Hazel Tucker (New York: Routledge, 2004), 184–90 (189).

9 Elfriede Fürsich and Anandam Kavoori, "Mapping a Critical Framework for the Study of Travel Journalism," *International Journal of Cultural Studies*, 4, no. 2 (2001): 149–71 (150).

10 David Spurr, *The Rhetoric of Empire: Colonial Discourse in Journalism, Travel Writing, and Imperial Administration* (Durham: Duke University Press, 1992).

11 Elfriede Fürsich, "Packaging Culture: The Potential and Limitations of Travel Programs on Global Television," *Communication Quarterly*, 50, no. 2 (2002): 204–23; Reaz Mahmood, "Traveling away from Culture: The Dominance of Consumerism on the Travel Channel," *Global Media Journal*, 4, no. 6 (2005): 2–23.

12 Carla Almeida Santos, "Framing Portugal: Representational Dynamics," *Annals of Tourism Research*, 31, no. 1 (2004): 122–38 (133–34).

13 Brian Creech, "The Spectacle of Past Violence: Travel Journalism and Dark Tourism," in Hanusch and Fürsich, *Travel Journalism*, 249–66 (263).

14 Timothy Brennan, "Postcolonial Studies between the European Wars: An Intellectual History," in *Marxism, Modernity and Postcolonial Studies*, ed. Crystal Bartolovich and Neil Lazarus (Cambridge: Cambridge University Press, 2002), 185–203 (185).

15 Anthony Bourdain, "Introduction," in *America's Best Travel Writing 2008*, ed. Anthony Bourdain (New York: Houghton Mifflin, 2008), xiii–xvi (xiii).

16 Lyn McGaurr, "Travel Journalism and Environmental Conflict: A Cosmopolitan Perspective," *Journalism Studies*, 11, no. 1 (2010): 50–67 (60).

17 John Stuart Mill, *The Principles of Political Economy* (London: John W. Parker, 1848).

18 Ulf Hannersz, "Cosmopolitans and Locals in World Cultures," *Theory, Culture, and Society*, 7, no. 1 (1990): 237–51 (239).

19 Craig Calhoun, "Imagining Solidarity: Cosmopolitanism, Constitutional Patriotism, and the Public Sphere," *Public Culture*, 14, no. 1 (2002): 147–71.

20 Ulrich Beck, *What Is Globalization?*, trans. Patrick Camiller (Malden: Polity Press, 2000).

21 Bronislaw Szerszynski and John Urry, "Cultures of Cosmopolitanism," *The Sociological Review*, 50, no. 4 (2002): 461–81 (461).

22 Digital disruption in the journalism industry is its own vast field of scholarly research but the following books offer a wide-ranging view of recent changes, both in the American context and internationally: Robert McChesney and Victor Pickard, eds. *Will the Last Reporter Please Turn Out the Lights* (New York: The New Press, 2011); David Ryfe, *Can Journalism Survive?: An Inside Look at American Newsrooms* (Malden: Polity Press, 2012); and Joel Simon, *The New*

Censorship: Inside the Global Battle for Media Freedom (New York: Columbia University Press, 2015).

23 For an overview of the state of research on citizen journalism, see James F. Hamilton, "Citizen Journalism: Emergence and Theoretical Perspectives," in *Oxford Bibliographies in Communication*, ed. Patricia Moy (New York: Oxford University Press, 2015), digital resource, DOI: 10.1093/obo/9780199756841-0169, accessed June 1, 2015. www.oxfordbibliographies.com/view/document/obo-9780199756841/obo-9780199756841-0169.xml.

24 Stuart Allan, *Citizen Witnessing: Revisioning Journalism in Times of Crisis* (Malden: Polity Press, 2013).

25 Fabienne Darling-Wolf, *Imagining the Global: Transnational Media and Popular Culture Beyond East and West* (Ann Arbor: University of Michigan Press, 2014), 142.

26 Lena Karlsson, "The Diary Weblog and the Traveling tales of Diasporic Tourists," *Journal of Intercultural Studies*, 27, no. 3 (2006): 299–312 (299).

27 Arjun Appadurai, "Disjuncture and Difference in the Global Cultural Economy," *Theory, Culture, and Society*, 7, no. 2 (1990): 295–310.

28 Melissa Wall, "Blogs of War: Weblogs as News," *Journalism*, 6, no. 2 (2005): 153–72.

29 Bryan Pirolli, "Travel Journalism in Flux: New Practices in the Blogosphere," in Hanusch and Fürsich, *Travel Journalism*, 83–98 (88).

30 Hanno Hardt, "Authenticity, Communication, and Critical Theory," *Critical Studies in Media Communication*, 10, no. 1 (1993): 49–69.

31 Juan-Carlos Molleda and Marilyn Roberts, "The Value of 'Authenticity' in New 'Glocal' Strategic Campaigns: the New Juan Valdez Campaign," *International Journal of Strategic Communication*, 2, no. 3 (2008): 154–74.

32 Bing Pan, Tanya MacLaurin, and John Crotts, "Travel Blogs and the Implications for Destination Marketing," *Journal of Travel Research*, 46, no. 1 (2007): 35–45; Leo Huang, Chi-Yen Yung, and Eonne Yang, "How do Travel Agencies Obtain a Competitive Advantage?: Through a Travel Blog Marketing Channel," *Journal of Vacation Marketing*, 17, no. 2 (2011): 139–49; Vincent P. Magnini, John Crotts, and Anita Zehrer, "Understanding Customer Delight: An Application of Travel Blog Analysis," *Journal of Travel Research*, 50, no. 5 (2011): 535–45.

33 Andrew Duffy, "First-Person Singular: Teaching Travel Journalism in the Age of Trip Advisor," in Hanusch and Fürsich, *Travel Journalism*, 99–116.

34 "Travel Writing in Cambodia," University of Georgia's Grady College of Journalism and Mass Communication, last modified June 2011, https://travelwritingincambodia.wordpress.com/.

35 Usha Raman and Divya Choudary, "Have Traveled, Will Write: User-Generated Content and New Travel Journalism," in Hanusch and Fürsich, *Travel Journalism*, 116–33 (129).

36 Homi K. Bhabha, *The Location of Culture* (New York: Routledge, 1995), 4.

37 Andy Brouwer, *Andy's Cambodia* (blog) http://blog.andybrouwer.co.uk/; Sopheap Chak, *Sopheap Chak: Riding the Wave of Change in Cambodia* (blog) http://sopheapfocus.com/; Adventurous Kate, *Adventurous Kate: Solo Female Travel Blog* (blog), www.adventurouskate.com/tag/cambodia-2/; Simon Oliver, *Tales from an Ex-Pat* (blog), www.talesfromanexpat.com/ blogsite no longer available; see www.facebook.com/talesfromanexpat/; Casey Nelson (pseud.), *LTO Cambodia* (blog), http://ltocambodia.blogspot.com.au/.

38 Lyn McGaurr, *Environmental Communication and Travel Journalism: Consumerism, Conflict and Concern* (New York: Routledge, 2015).

39 Nature seekers annual report. "Trinidad's Leatherback Sea Turtles, 2013," Boston, MA: Earthwatch Institute, 2013: http://earthwatch.org/briefings/sammy_briefing.pdf.

40 Nature Seekers Facebook page, accessed 4 June 2015, www.facebook.com/NatureSeekers/.

41 Kristian A. Hvass and Ana M. Munar, "The Takeoff of Social Media in Tourism," *Journal of Vacation Marketing*, 18, no. 2 (2012): 93–103.

42 "'Crazy Turtle Woman' Transforms Graveyard into Maternity Ward," CNN, May 29, 2009: www.cnn.com/2009/TECH/05/28/cnnheroes.suzan.lakhan.baptiste/index.html?iref=24hours.

43 David Domingo, Thorsten Quandt, Ari Heinonen, Steve Paulussen, Jane Singer, and Marina Vujnovic, "Participatory Journalism Practices in the Media and Beyond," *Journalism Practice*, 2, no. 3 (2008): 326–42.

44 Jennie Germann Molz and Cody Morris Paris, "The Social Affordances of Flashpacking: Exploring the Mobility Nexus of Travel and Communication," *Mobilities*, 10, no. 2 (2015): 173–92 (190).

45 Stephanie Hays, Stephen John Page, Dimitrios Buhalis, "Social Media as a Destination Marketing Tool: Its Use by National Tourism Organizations," *Current Issues in Tourism*, 16, no. 3 (2013): 211–30.

46 Nancy Morris and Andrew Mendelson, "National Geographic and Puerto Rico: A Case Study of Journalistic Authority and Collective Identity in the Digital Age," *Communication, Culture, and Critique*, (2015): doi: 10.1111/cccr.12118. http://onlinelibrary.wiley.com/doi/10.1111/cccr.12118/abstract.

47 Edward Said, *Orientalism* (New York: Vintage, 1978).

48 Radhika Parameswaran, "Local Culture in Global Media: Excavating Colonial and Material Discourses in the National Geographic," *Communication Theory*, 12, no. 3 (2002): 287–315.

49 Caitlin Bruce, "*Episode III: Enjoy Poverty*: An Aesthetic Virus of Political Discomfort," *Communication, Culture, and Critique*, 9, no. 2 (2016): 284–302, doi: 10.1111/cccr/12109.

50 Brian Ekdale and David Tuwei, "Ironic Encounters: Posthumanitarian Storytelling in Slum Tourist Media," *Communication, Culture, and Critique*, 9 no. 1 (2016): 49–67, doi: 10.1111/cccr.12127.

51 Nancy A. VanHouse, "Personal Photography, Digital Technology, and the Uses of the Visual," *Visual Studies*, 26, no. 2 (2011): 125–34.

52 Jonathan Donner, "Research Approaches to Mobile Use in the Developing World: A Review of the Literature," *The Information Society*, 24, no. 3 (2008): 140–59.

53 Paolo Favero, "Learning to Look Beyond the Frame: Reflections on the Changing Meaning of Images in the Age of Digital Media Practices," *Visual Studies*, 29, no. 2 (2014): 166–79.

54 Kathleen Kuehn, "'There's Got to be a Review Democracy': Communicative Capitalism, Neoliberal Citizenship and the Politics of Participation on the Consumer Evaluation website Yelp.com," *International Journal of Communication*, 7 (2013): 607–25.

55 Duffy, "First-Person Singular," 107.

56 Sharon Zulkin, Scarlett Lindeman, and Laurie Hurson, "The Omnivore's Neighborhood? Online Restaurant Reviews, Race, and Gentrification," *Journal of Consumer Culture*, (2015): 1–21, doi: 10.1177/1469540515611203.

57 Sandra Ponzanesi, *The Postcolonial Culture Industry: Icons, Markets, Mythologies* (New York: Palgrave Macmillan, 2014).

58 Susan Scott and Wanda Orlikowski, "Reconfiguring Relations of Accountability: Materialization of Social Media in the Travel Sector," *Accounting, Organizations, and Society*, 37, no. 1 (2012): 26–40.

59 Tiziana Terranova, "Free Labor: Producing Culture for the Digital Economy," *Social Text*, 18, no. 2 (2000): 33–38.

60 Appadurai, "Disjuncture and Difference."

61 Arjun Appadurai, *The Future as Cultural Fact: Essays on the Global Condition* (New York: Verso, 2013), 69.

62 Appadurai, "Disjuncture and Difference," 299.

12

ANNA JOHNSTON

Travel Magazines and Settler (Post) Colonialism

In early 2016, the Australian Broadcasting Corporation (ABC) online news website featured brilliantly colored photographs of Papua New Guinean men in elaborate tribal costume.[1] French photographer Marc Dozier's stunning images celebrate the ingenuity of traditional crafts, the ongoing role of customary practices, and the performative masculinity of Papua New Guineans. Australian readers on their summer breaks found these images on Facebook and other online sources: formats that made the most of the exquisitely colored images. The photographs were undoubtedly exotic, yet for older Australian readers they would also have been strangely familiar. From the 1930s onward, Australian magazines often featured costumes and people from Papua New Guinea (PNG),[2] alongside stories about a wide variety of Pacific crafts and cultures. Mid-century travel magazines such as *Walkabout* – produced between the 1930s and 1970s by the Australian National Travel Association – showcased images with high production values alongside travel narratives written by leading Australian writers. These took armchair travelers deep into the PNG Highlands, for example, providing a privileged view into communities in Australia's geopolitical neighborhood. In so doing, publications helped project Australian soft power in the region, especially after the Pacific Theatre in World War II.

Exotically dressed Papua New Guineans may recall their mid-century precursors, but Dozier's photographic settings are deliberately disjunctive. Mundiya Kepanga traveled to Washington, New York, and other US cities. Dozier juxtaposes the southern highland chief in full traditional dress against iconic backdrops – such as the Statue of Liberty or brilliant yellow New York taxi cabs – or among subcultural groups such as bikies in Tucson, Arizona, LGBTI parade participants in Manhattan, and young Navajos dressed traditionally for the Arizona Festival Navajo Nation Fair. Here the Papua New Guinean is a tourist. Kepanga sees the sights, takes selfie shots, and finds unexpected commonalities while meeting the locals: tattoos, body piercings, flamboyant costuming, and indigenous cultural maintenance.

Dozier's photographic essays have been published in a range of international travel magazines, including *National Geographic, Grand Reportage*, and *El Sur Travel* as well as newspapers such as *Le Monde*. Like Australian readers, global audiences would situate this striking contemporary photography within the context of earlier mass entertainment sources.[3] Dozier's work both continues and questions nineteenth- and twentieth-century traditions, whereby media and literary texts naturalize exotic parts of the world for metropolitan readers, entertaining and educating their consumers while encouraging either armchair or actual travel.[4] Magazines also inculcate particular ideologies and world views, establishing relationships of seeming intimacy between the reader/traveler and other cultures and peoples.

Dozier's photographic studies and *Walkabout* magazine embody the fascination with the exotic regularly featured in travel magazines. Through accessible cultural forms – including film and television, novels, the Internet, and music – dominant social groups regularly explore complex geopolitical ideas. Christina Klein analyzes how intellectuals, texts, and institutions sought to educate Americans about Asia in the Cold War period, by using forms that 1940s–50s critics dismissed as "middlebrow": that is, accessible, educational, and self-improving forms of culture, rather than aesthetically oriented "highbrow" or frankly commercial "lowbrow" forms.[5] Focusing on cultural artefacts that had wide influence – magazines such as *Reader's Digest* and *Saturday Review*, best-selling novels, nonfiction, travel essays, musicals, and Hollywood films – Klein demonstrates how these brought about new kinds of affiliations "by translating them into personal terms and imbuing them with sentiment, so that they became emotionally rich relationships that Americans could inhabit imaginatively in their everyday lives."[6] Although such relationships are imbued with unequal power and access – such that Klein adapts Edward Said's term to identify "cold war orientalism" (10–11, 15–17) – they are also open to diverse opportunities and responses: curiosity, desire, identification, and objectification, among others. These may be characterized by power and privilege, in some instances, but should not be assumed to be exclusive of other potentially progressive possibilities. So too the "exotic" may be closer than expected. James Clifford describes how contemporary media and travel cultures have evacuated otherness of its distinctiveness: "there seem no distant places left on the planet where the presence of 'modern' products, media and power cannot be felt. An older topography and experience of travel is exploded. One no longer leaves home confident of finding something radically new, another time or space."[7] In such ways, we can read travel magazines as part of an imperial or neo-imperial archive, but also as opening new vistas on complex and sometimes subtle cross-cultural encounters.

Settler colonial cultures such as Australia, New Zealand, and Canada – among others, including the United States – formed a distinctive part of the British Empire.[8] Advantaged by their majority status, settlers displaced indigenous communities through colonization and violence, even if they later sanitized such population shifts as settlement rather than invasion. Settlement always involved staking a claim, in terms of ownership of land and the occupation of disputed space, and as a consequence land and politics remain contested between settler and indigenous populations.[9] Settler neocolonialism – such as Australian interests in the Pacific, including PNG – expanded these issues regionally, projecting power over adjacent territories that were sometimes "gifted" to settler polities by imperial powers as part of a gradual decolonization process.[10] The occupation of contested land has strongly influenced the cultural politics of representation.

Travel and settlement are powerful tropes in settler discourse, making travel writing as a form particularly resonant. Productive tensions between knowledge generated by travel and the kinds of knowledge required for settlement characterize Australian travel writing from the colonial period onward, for instance, with some critics speculating that "Australia has always been a land more travelled than settled."[11] Certainly, a vast amount of travel writing about Australia has been produced, and this has conditioned the perspectives of visitors and residents alike on white Australian identity, especially questions of power and relationships between the settler postcolonial nation and both indigenous Australian subjects and Pacific Islanders.[12] This chapter uses early to mid-twentieth-century travel magazines to trace some distinctive features of settler colonialism and magazine culture, with a focus on Australia balanced by comparison with Canada and the United States.

Travel Writing and Magazine Cultures

Travel magazines provide important insights into the way that readers and writers imagined travel and the insights it could provide. Nineteenth-century print culture created a proliferation of venues through which increasingly literate populations accessed information and educated themselves. Reading about exotic cultures from those who had traveled afar was a central part of such cultural practices. For example, stories of missionary adventure among the "heathen" in Africa, India, and the Pacific dominated the voluminous evangelical periodical press from the late eighteenth-century onward.[13] David Spurr's analysis of nineteenth-century travel writing, journalism, and other forms of nonfiction reveals how colonial discourses move across diverse types of texts and in so doing "produce knowledge about other cultures."[14] Travel writing and its ambiguous engagement with both fictional and nonfictional modes provides particular insight into colonial discourse and its relationship with governance and administration. On the one hand, we can see writing produced under the aegis of empire as a direct expression of imperial power: the power to name, to rule, and to record. Yet Spurr and others emphasize that just as imperial theories were carried out imperfectly and unevenly in various locations, so too the characteristic ambiguity and anxiety of colonial cultures can be read in discourse.[15] Colonial authority depends on the presence, and to some extent the complicity, of colonized populations: "Hence the uneasiness, the instability, the frequent hysteria of colonial discourse."[16] Following Michel Foucault, then, colonial (and postcolonial) discourses of travel can be productively mined not for simplistic oppositions between power and resistance, but for their complex and tactical engagements with power in its multiple forms in cross-cultural environments (11).

Recent scholarship in periodical studies emphasizes the role of magazines in print culture. Magazine publications boomed in the early to mid-twentieth century, as publishing industries adopted modern technologies and benefited from increased education, literacy, and leisure in the West to bring about new mass markets for cultural products. Literary modernism made great use of small magazines to explore new forms and literary experiments, and commercial mass culture, too, found periodicals ideal for new markets and produced new readerships.[17] Periodical studies argue, first, for the importance of magazines as sources of pleasure, knowledge acquisition, and the formation of identity. While they have frequently been overlooked in scholarship as ephemeral or trivial, magazines are "vectors for the transmission, for better or worse, of political power, cultural signification and social change."[18] Second, it has become increasingly important to account for magazines in their entirety, rather than mining them for a narrow range of material relating to particular topics. Sean Latham and Robert Scholes argue that scholars, anthology compilers, and even recent digitizing projects have tended to extract the periodical publications of well-known writers for analysis, rather than understanding the periodical as a whole: "we have often been too quick to see magazines merely as containers of discrete bits of information rather than autonomous objects of study."[19] Magazines, they suggest, are textual formations requiring study across their diverse contents and contributions.

The 1920s represented a peak in the volume and cultural influence of magazines, prior to the widespread availability of cinema, radio, and (later) television. In the United States and the UK, magazines flourished from the 1890s: American titles such as *Munsey's Magazine* (1889), *Vanity Fair*

(1913), and *McClure's Magazine* (1893), alongside cognate UK publications such as *Strand Magazine* (1890), *New Statesman* (1913), and *Tatler* (1709; 1901), for example. These magazines themselves traveled and were read across transatlantic spaces, mutually influencing the magazine cultures of the United States and the UK. They were also imported by settler colonies as part of their keen participation in transnational Anglophone culture. Roger Osborne notes that if the literary critic Q. D. Leavis – who famously derided the decline in English taste and literary discernment in the late 1920s as a direct consequence of magazine popularity[20] – had visited Australia, she would have found many of the same titles in local retail outlets.[21] This was also true of Canada, where, as Faye Hamill notes, high culture was imported from Britain, France, and the United States and mass culture from the States.[22] Simultaneously, national magazines emerged, shaped by global market trends: Australia's *The Bulletin* (1880), the *Lone Hand* (1907, modelled on the UK *Strand*), and *Smith's Weekly* (1919);[23] in Anglophone Canada, titles such as *Maclean's* (1911), the *Canadian Home Journal* (1905), *Mayfair* (1927), and *Chatelaine* (1928);[24] and, in New Zealand, the *Triad* (1893), the *Mirror* (1922), and the *New Zealand Listener* (1939).[25] Within these settler colonial markets, travel magazines played important roles.

National Geographic (1888) is perhaps the best-known and longest-lived example of a modern travel magazine. Like its competitors, *National Geographic* is a classic middlebrow institution. Travel writing in general is a quintessentially middlebrow form, as Steve Clark argues, in that it is a democratic genre that accommodates professional and amateur writers, it often has a commercial motivation, and its contribution to literature is "collective and incremental rather than singular and aesthetic." [26] In the early to mid-twentieth century, travel technologies, new cultural forms reflecting the interests of burgeoning middle classes, and commercial periodical publication coalesced. Travel magazines, Faye Hammill and Michelle Smith argue, were "instrumental in forging a link between geographical mobility and upward mobility."[27] Magazines increasingly used travel as a status symbol that could be achieved by their readers, and used narratives of travel to inculcate both the desire for travel and a set of acceptable practices based around tourism (18). Middle-class patterns of consumption converged, bringing together reading, leisure, and tourism, all of which were featured in travel magazines in vibrant and engaging text and images.

National Geographic established itself from the outset as a scientific and educational institution. It had roots in an imperial tradition of the travelogue, whereby intrepid adventurers sought exotic foreign cultures and transformed their travel experiences into narratives that were both thrilling and informative. Such narratives were exotic in the traditional sense in that they identified and classified cultural difference from an Anglocentric norm. They encouraged American readers to view other people and their culture through such a lens. Roger Célestin defines desire as central to exoticism: a compulsion to leave or escape one's home culture that brings about an inevitable change in the self as a consequence of both the desire for and the encounter with difference. Texts of exoticism, then, *"contain both the voyage out and the return."*²⁸ Catherine A. Lutz and Jane L. Collins's *Reading National Geographic* (1993) focuses on the magazine's photographs, and critically appraises the appropriative gaze established between reader and subject. They argue that thematic similarities unite all *National Geographic* photographs of the non-Western world: the people are exoticized, idealized, naturalized, and sexualized.²⁹ Older readers anecdotally recall reading *National Geographic* as much for the pictures of non-Western naked bodies as for the articles, in an era when pornography was difficult to access. Even contemporary issues carry this ideological baggage of both exoticism and eroticism, and the magazine remains vulnerable to such criticisms. The magazine's worldview – of "happy, classless people outside of history but evolving into it, edged with exoticism and sexuality, but knowable to some degree as individuals" – is distinctive in its mass market form but it also continues existing imperial ideologies (116).

Advertising provides a complement to articles and photography featuring non-Western peoples. William O'Barr analyzes advertisements in the 1929 *National Geographic* and concludes that images of exotic people and their cultures were pervasive in advertisements for travel to foreign countries, and that the promotion of goods and services both appropriated and generated images and ideas about otherness.³⁰ Sometimes such advertisements pertained to the practices of travel directly. Those featuring photographic equipment and products often focus on foreign peoples and cultures. Kodak's assiduous marketing of its cameras, film, and later movie cameras sought to democratize the process of photography: their advertisements educated potential travelers about the kinds of amateur representations they could create, which would benefit from familiarity with professional images featured in the magazine. Collecting photographic souvenirs became central to modern travel practices. O'Barr concludes that behind the marketing claims the relationship between the traveler and the people visited was carefully constructed through Kodak advertisements. Terming this "photographic colonialism," O'Barr notes that authority over photographic subjects' lives and experiences rests in the hands of the visitor/photographer: "The frozen scene in the advertisement is but one moment in a larger travel narrative about the relationship of the visitor to the visited" (41, 21). Island cultures were particularly vulnerable to such constructions as remote, time-less, and unchanging.[31]

In their advertisements for transport routes, travel companies themselves mirrored this relationship between the mobile traveler and the static scenes of non-Western others who might be evident outside the window of a train, or who might greet ocean liner passengers when they stopped at various locations: in *National Geographic*, Native Americans featured widely in the former, and Pacific and Asian figures in the latter. Similarly, the major tourist shipping lines regularly placed advertisements in *Walkabout*. Visually linking Australia with overseas locations, they sought to entice readers to travel beyond national borders. P&O, for example, often featured its various routes; so too did the Eastern and Australian Steamship Company (E&A). In each issue in the 1930s, E&A Line encouraged Australians to undertake a round trip to China and Japan. In common with *National Geographic* in the same period, 1930s and 1940s advertisements could be crudely instrumen-talist in their construction of relationships between traveling (white) Austra-lians and the Asian and Pacific peoples they would encounter on their travels.

Other advertisements in *National Geographic* bore little intrinsic relation-ship to foreign travel or indigenous cultures: radios that used images of African drummers to promote their sound quality or fountain pens illus-trated in jungle camp settings because they might have been used "on the page of an explorer's diary, an officer's notebook, [whose] velvet touch has helped write the history of an Empire."[32] The associations were slight, but marketers used such images to promote mundane products that accrued cultural value alongside the text and images of the magazine.

Exotic representations of other places and peoples could work simul-taneously to mark settler colonial whiteness in contrast to non-Western others, and as continuous with European ethnicity. Importantly for settler colonial readers, travel to Europe also figured in middlebrow magazines. Here, ideological associations were made with major European cities figured as centers of settler nostalgia and origin, or sites of modernity and urban glamour: for Canadian readers, Hammill and Smith argue, these brought about "a racially and linguistically exclusive version of Canadian identity," which elided both First Nations and ethnically diverse immigrants.[33]

Australian Settler Colonialism and *Walkabout* Magazine: A Case Study

Writing, mobility, and modernity were key components in cultural and geopolitical reorientations from the mid-1930s onward in the Australasian region, as Australians shifted their emotional and strategic focus from Britain to the United States, with a new awareness of both the threat and opportunity provided by the geographical proximity of the Asia-Pacific region. Travel operated as a way to imagine an idealized space of settler modernity.[34]

Walkabout was an incredibly popular magazine (circulation figures began at 20,000 copies, reaching a one-time maximum of 65,000 in December 1965); it was read in family living rooms, on trains, in dentists' and doctors' waiting rooms, in holiday houses, and in public libraries. Its readership was primarily Australian, although copies were sent officially to overseas embassies and agencies by the publisher, and unofficially by readers to international friends and family: by 1966 there were subscribers in one hundred countries.[35] Readers remember the magazine with incredible fondness, as do those writers, journalists, and editors who worked on it. *Walkabout* paid well for articles and for photographs, supporting a raft of writers and photographers. It made a significant contribution to Australia's sense of itself, by addressing a diverse range of topics: geology; distinctive native flora and fauna; remote Australian regions ("the Outback") and people; the Pacific region; and a distinctively Australian modernity. *Walkabout* was an integral component of what David Carter calls Australia's long overlooked and neglected middlebrow literature.[36]

The magazine provides important insights into debates about Australian identity, during the mid-twentieth century, and the ways in which these were played out in accessible forms. Key to these debates were settler Australian attachments to place, and *Walkabout*'s middlebrow writing provides insights into the ways in which white Australians negotiated their relationships to landscapes, both literal and emotional, including those marked by Aboriginal occupation and belonging. The magazine's title invokes Australian Aboriginal travel within country – as Deborah Bird Rose defines it, country is "a living entity with a yesterday, today and tomorrow, with a consciousness, and a will toward life" – for customary, religious, and practical purposes.[37] As an Anglicized term for indigenous practices, "walkabout" was understood by settlers from early colonial times as a characteristic form of interior travel specific to Aborigines. The term was often used derogatively to indicate fecklessness, particularly in labor relationships, as part of a generalized discourse about presumed "nomadism" that could be used strategically to deny Aboriginal claims to land and to facilitate settler possession.[38] The use of the term to brand the 1930s travel magazine marks both increased interest in, and positive valuation of, Aboriginal culture by some settler Australians of the time; yet it was also, arguably, an appropriation.[39]

Charles Lloyd Jones declared in the first issue:

we have embarked on an educational crusade which will enable Australians and the people of other lands to learn more of the romantic Australia that exists beyond the cities and the enchanted South Sea Islands and New Zealand.[40]

Walkabout's managing editor, Charles Holmes, extolled the positive benefits of travel:

Travel is the most successful of outdoor sports. It conditions the body, informs the mind, inspires the heart, and imparts a grace to our social intercourse. It is a university of experience. It teaches that the bigger drama of life is played in the open – out where ships speak as they pass in the night – where the glory of the mountain, plain, and desert awe us with a mystery that is forever new to the responsive traveller.[41]

Here travel promised not just to support a nascent tourist industry but also to inculcate a set of cultural practices that would perfect the (white) Australian body and mind. In such ways, *Walkabout* sought to bring about the modern Australian citizen and the modern nation. Travel as a peculiarly modern practice was posited as a means by which unique Australian subjectivities would emerge: specifically, the idealized modernity of the settler Australian. This is the kind of "virtuous citizenship and 'nationed' modernity" that middlebrow culture offered.[42]

Tourism and culture were shared concerns for the magazine, and the author Eleanor Dark's article for *Walkabout* succinctly assessed the benefits and limitations of a tourist industry. Writing about Central Australia, Dark traveled the North-South Road (renamed the Stuart Highway in 1944) the wartime development of which was eulogized elsewhere in the magazine. "That road! It is impossible to say whether one loves or loathes it. It performs all that is desirable and necessary from a practical point of view. It has 'opened up' the country; it facilitates transport, defence and the tourist trade."[43] Yet the cost of such industrialized travel comes at the detriment of understanding the country, its temporality, and its distinctiveness. She notes that traveling by coach – as most tourists would – changes the experience of the Center, and negates its nature:

So the traveller by tourist coach is left with the nagging thought that he himself has introduced the one jarring note into this symphony of newly discovered beauty; he has committed the extreme solecism of being in a hurry. And he pays for it. A landscape in which he should be still to feel its stillness is branded forever on his memory as a straight ribbon of road endlessly unrolling, and on either side of it a whizzing streak of colour in which the aboriginal reds,

browns and ochres of the earth and the dull greens of the low-growing vegeta-
tion run together in a blur. A scene whose essence is its remoteness is hurled at
him in chunks at a velocity of almost a mile a minute. (20)

Dark's evocations of place here are mixed with concerns that had troubled
travel writers since at least the nineteenth century. Railways transformed
European landscapes and changed how people understood their environment, marking an industrialized vision of time and space that eroded older
notions of countryside and its use value.[44] Dark's subtle reference to "aboriginal reds, browns and ochres" reminds us that many settler Australians
were well aware that country was integral to indigenous identity; indeed,
that the two were intimately linked. Such articles in *Walkabout* provide
compelling evidence that settler Australians were told about Aboriginal
culture in accessible forms, and that they were interested. This provides
something of a corrective to thin readings of the past that intimate that
white Australians were willfully ignorant of the Aboriginal cultures that
pre-dated European occupation, or that magazines such as *Walkabout* were
inherently racist and derogatory.

Of course, not all representations of race and difference in *Walkabout*
were as subtle as Dark's. It is possible to mine the magazine to find crass,
derogatory, dated, and frankly racist representations of Aborigines, or
Pacific Islanders, or Papua New Guineans.[45] There are stereotypical photographs that portray Aborigines as primitive and debased; images are rou-
tinely and loosely used to illustrate a general point about indigenous cultures
rather than taking into account the specificity of their original setting and
means of production; and some articles use the term "primitive" repeatedly
to demean and diminish non-Western cultural groups. Some articles make
for challenging reading, in light of recent and more politically sensitive
discussions about race and representation, and their potential influence on
the vast body of readers should be cause for reflection about the ongoing
legacy of colonial discourses. But even these dated denigratory representations reveal the intense curiosity that middlebrow readers experienced about
traditional tribal cultures, and about modernizing indigenous communities
at home and in the region.

Walkabout's readers shared with international modernists more generally
a belief that non-Western cultures had something important to contribute to
new ways of understanding the self, society, and the future.[46] We need to
take that interest seriously because it complicates stories about binary
cultural divides and presumed ignorance of difference. It also reintroduces
complex questions about exoticism and its role in negotiating cultural
difference. Charles Forsdick reminds us that it is essential to consider

non-Anglocentric attitudes toward exoticism – now customarily condemned by postcolonial critics – to build more nuanced understandings that encompass "the potential reflexivity or reciprocity within exoticism, but also the implicit challenge it may pose" to reductive analysis.[47] So too, settler cultures require analytical models that do not see them simply as derivative of Europe, but as generating vernacular modernisms with their own local strains and character.[48] Reading about Papua New Guineans, their art, and culture, for example, taught white Australian readers in the mid-century something important about their selves, their nation (including its neocolonial interests in the Pacific), and its place in the world: Dozier's photographs of Mundiya Kepanga continue to do so, albeit in twenty-first-century media forms.

Writing about *National Geographic*, Stephen Greenblatt argues against Lutz and Collins's analysis of the magazine.[49] Greenblatt suggests that the magazine did include signs of non-Western subjects' accommodation to modernity, thus contradicting a key argument of *Reading National Geographic*, and he proposes an alternative analytical path less tied to presentist censure of dated ideology. So too, *Walkabout* taps into a reader's sense of curiosity: akin to the feelings of wonder – "thrilling, potentially dangerous, momentarily immobilising, charged at once with desire, ignorance and fear" – associated with first encounters in colonial spaces.[50] Travel and its writing enable these crucial affective maneuvers that work powerfully to mark some peoples as modern, and some as primitive: this is especially acute in settler colonial locations, where both white and indigenous identities are reworked in conditions marked by asymmetrical power as well as mutual dependence. Greenblatt's work on Renaissance travel writing demonstrates that representations need to be taken seriously, not only because they reflect or produce social realities, but because they are in themselves social relations. That is, representations "are not only products but producers, capable of decisively altering the very forces that brought them into being" (6). Working to link individual experiences to collective understandings, to outline hierarchies of society and cultures, and to reveal the resistances and conflicts that operated through modern culture, travel magazines sought to bring about new national imaginings and complex senses of place for their readers. Settler Australians undoubtedly benefitted from dispossessive colonialism, and it has become a truism that they suffered, as a consequence, from a correlative sense of dislocation from the landscapes in which they dwelt. Reading *Walkabout* reveals another side to national and regional debates about place, identity, and race during this period, and a rich archive of evidence that many writers and their readers considered these issues in accessible forms.

Conclusion

Travel magazines allow us to think about the longevity of imperial travel traditions and their influence upon twentieth- and twenty-first-century modes of mass communication: as Anthony Carrigan suggests, "mass travel practices frequently exploit uneven distributions of wealth, remapping colonial travel patterns."[51] Magazines also enable us to situate travel writing within particularly influential spheres of literary debate in the early to mid-twentieth century. Understanding these texts requires us to read carefully for the ideologies embedded in their very form: through comparative, historicized reading practices that help us unpack colonial practices, discourses, and their ongoing influence in perpetuating structural inequality.

But travel magazines also provide opportunities to read around obvious stereotypes, language, and ideologies to build complex pictures of the past and its aftermath. This is what Ann Laura Stoler terms "reading along the [. . .] grain." Thinking specifically about colonial archives, Stoler argues that, rather than a traditional oppositional reading practice that identifies "imperial" representations and condemns them, critics might productively read along the textual grain to develop thick cultural histories of how representations were constructed and had multiple effects, often exceeding the intentions of their authors. This enables us "to track the production and consumption of facticities as the contingent coordinates of particular times and temperaments, places and purposes."[52] Travel writing provides an ideal mechanism through which to raise serious questions about society, politics, and history in an accessible form, aimed at a general educated reader. As a genre, it carries the taint of histories of racial and class privilege. Yet by association with authorial personalities, travel writing also humanizes and personalizes larger social, political, and historical issues. When readers engage with middlebrow travel writing, they experience an emotional and empathic response that brings them into an intimate form of relationship within the text's author and subject. In doing so, middlebrow travel writing inculcates particular kinds of interpretative and imaginative communities, characterized by engagement and a sense of the opportunities available in the world. Thinking through representations of travel and tourism allows us to take James Clifford's dictum to "rethink cultures as sites of dwelling *and* travel, to take traveling knowledges seriously."[53]

NOTES

1 Catherine Graue, "A Unique Pictorial Story as a PNG Tribal Chief Travels across the US," *Pacific Beat, Australian Broadcasting Commission (ABC) News Online,* accessed January 4, 2016, www.abc.net.au/news/2016-01-04/a-unique-pictorial-story-as-a-png-tribal-chief/7066142.

2 Two of many examples include: Australian Museum, "New Guinea Native," *Walkabout*, May 1936; and, Leigh G. Vial, "New Guinea Warrior," *Walkabout*, November 1942.

3 French audiences would be well aware of Pierre-Dominique Gaisseau's 1961 award-winning documentary *Le Ciel et la boue* (*Sky Above and Mud Beneath*). This documentary about Gaisseau's 1959–60 expedition to Dutch New Guinea continues to be broadcast on French television. In many ways it repeats the imperial tropes mobilized by the 1931 Paris Colonial Exposition. See Pierre Lemonnier, "Sous Le Regard De Saint Pataugas: À Propos d'âge de Pierre, de Globalisation et de la Responsabilité de l'ethnologue," *ethnographiques.org* 5 (April 2004).

4 Dozier's 2008 documentary film *L'exploration inverse* (*Reverse Exploration*) took Mundiya and his compatriot, Polobi, to France, in an ironic inversion of the exploration trope.

5 For definitions and discussions of middlebrow writing and culture, see Joan Shelley Rubin, *The Making of Middlebrow Culture* (Chapel Hill: University of North Carolina Press, 1992); Kate Macdonald, ed., *The Masculine Middlebrow, 1880–1950: What Mr Miniver Read* (Basingstoke: Palgrave Macmillan, 2011); Beth Driscoll, *New Literary Middlebrow: Tastemakers and Reading in the Twenty-First Century* (Basingstoke: Palgrave Macmillan, 2014).

6 Christina Klein, *Cold War Orientalism: Asia in the Middlebrow Imagination, 1945-1961* (Berkeley and Los Angeles: University of California Press, 2003), 7–8.

7 James Clifford, *The Predicament of Culture: Twentieth-Century Ethnography, Literature, and Art* (Cambridge: Harvard University Press, 1988), 13–14.

8 See Alan Lawson and Anna Johnston, "Settler Colonies," in *A Companion to Postcolonial Studies*, ed. Sangeeta Ray and Henry Schwarz (Malden: Blackwell, 2000), 360–76; see also Jenny Sharpe "Is the United States Postcolonial?: Trans-nationalism, Immigration, and Race," *Diaspora*, 4, no. 2 (1995): 181–99; see also *Possible Pasts: Becoming Colonial in Early America*, ed. Robert Blair St George (Ithaca: Cornell University Press, 2000).

9 On Israel and South Africa, see Lorenzo Veracini, *Israel and Settler Society* (London: Pluto Press, 2006); see also Veracini, *Settler Colonialism: A Theoretical Overview* (Basingstoke: Palgrave Macmillan, 2010).

10 Britain transferred the colony of Papua to Australia from 1902. In 1920, the Australian Commonwealth acquired a League of Nations mandate for governing the former German territory of New Guinea. Following the Japanese occupation during World War II, Australia administered the territory, until PNG achieved self-government in 1972. Other settler nations shared similar neocolonial histories.

11 Richard White, "Travel, Writing and Australia," *Studies in Travel Writing*, 11, no. 1 (2010): 1–14 (1).

12 On the centrality of settler-Aboriginal relationships in travel writing, see Robert Clarke, *Travel Writing from Black Australia: Utopia, Melancholia, and Aboriginality* (New York: Routledge, 2015).

13 See Richard D. Altick, *The English Common Reader: A Social History of the Mass Reading Public 1800–1900* (Chicago: University of Chicago Press, 1957); Susan Thorne, *Congregational Missions and the Making of an Imperial Culture in Nineteenth-Century England* (Stanford: Stanford University Press, 1999).

14 David Spurr, *The Rhetoric of Empire: Colonial Discourse in Journalism, Travel Writing, and Imperial Administration* (Durham: Duke University Press, 1993), 11.

15 Nicholas Thomas, *Colonialism's Culture: Anthropology, Travel and Government* (Carlton: Melbourne University Press, 1994).

16 Spurr, *Rhetoric of Empire*, 11.

17 See Richard Ohmann, *Selling Culture: Magazines, Markets and Class at the Turn of the Century* (London: Verso, 1996); David Reed, *The Popular Magazine in Britain and the United States of America, 1880–1960* (London: British Library, 1997); Ann Ardis and Patrick Collier, eds., *Transatlantic Print Culture, 1880–1940: Emerging Media, Emerging Modernisms* (Basingstoke: Palgrave Macmillan, 2008); Peter Brooker and Andrew Thacker, *The Oxford Critical and Cultural History of Modernist Magazines* (Oxford: Oxford University Press, [2009] 2013).

18 Tim Holmes, "Mapping the Magazine: An Introduction," *Journalism Studies*, 8, no. 4 (2007): 510–21 (511).

19 Sean Latham and Robert Scholes, "The Rise of Periodical Studies," *PMLA*, 121, no. 2 (2006): 517–31 (517–18).

20 Q. D. Leavis, *Fiction and the Reading Public* (London: Pimlico, [1932] 2000).

21 Roger Osborne, "A National Interest in an International Market: The Circulation of Magazines in Australia during the 1920s," *History Australia*, 5, no. 3 (2008): 75.1–75.16 (75.6).

22 Faye Hammill, *Women, Celebrity, and Literary Culture between the Wars* (Austin: University of Texas Press, 2007), 19.

23 See David Carter, *Always almost Modern: Australian Print Cultures and Modernity* (North Melbourne: Australian Scholarly Publishing, 2013), 20–21, 135.

24 See the excellent website *Magazines, Travel and Middlebrow Culture in Canada 1925–1960*, University of Strathclyde 2011, accessed June 7, 2016, www.middlebrowcanada.org/Home/tabid/262/language/en-GB/Default.aspx.

25 See Ben Schrader, "Magazines and Periodicals," *Te Ara: The Encyclopedia of New Zealand*, Manatū Taonga Ministry for Culture and Heritage, last modified October 21, 2014, accessed June 22, 2016, www.TeAra.govt.nz/en/magazines-and-periodicals/; Hilliard argues that middlebrow culture was not a dominant force in New Zealand literature: Christopher Hilliard, "'Mind's Middle Distance': Men of Letters in Interwar New Zealand," in *The Masculine Middlebrow* ed. Macdonald, 150–61.

26 Steve Clark, ed., *Travel Writing and Empire: Postcolonial Theory in Transit* (London: Zed, 1999), 3.

27 Faye Hammill and Michelle Smith, *Magazines, Travel, and Middlebrow Culture: Canadian Periodicals in English and French, 1925–1960* (Alberta: University of Alberta Press, 2015), 1.

28 Roger Célestin, *From Cannibals to Radicals: Figures and Limits of Exoticism* (Minneapolis: University of Minnesota Press, 1996), 3, original emphasis.

29 Catherine A. Lutz and Jane L. Collins, *Reading National Geographic* (Chicago: University of Chicago Press, 1993), 89.

30 William O'Barr, *Culture and the Ad: Exploring Otherness in the World of Advertising* (Boulder: Westulew Press, 1994).

31 Anthony Carrigan, *Postcolonial Tourism: Literature, Culture, and Environment* (New York: Routledge, 2011), 11.
32 O'Barr, *Culture and the Ad*, 45, 61.
33 Hammill and Smith, *Magazines, Travel, and Middlebrow Culture*, 18.
34 For a longer discussion of *Walkabout*, see Mitchell Rolls and Anna Johnston, *Traveling Home, Walkabout Magazine and Modern Australia* (London: Anthem Press, 2016).
35 Australian National Travel Association Annual Report 1965/66, State Library of New South Wales, ML550/05 Beresford Box 4 (43).
36 Carter, *Always Almost Modern*, 128, 143.
37 Deborah Bird Rose, *Nourishing Terrains: Australian Aboriginal Views of Landscape and Wilderness* (Canberra: Australian Heritage Commission, 1996), 7.
38 Gillian Cowlishaw, *Rednecks, Eggheads and Blackfellas: A Study of Racial Power and Intimacy in Australia* (Sydney: Allen & Unwin, [1999] 2014), 38–42.
39 This was a common concern: see Mitchell Rolls, "Painting the Dreaming White," *Australian Cultural History*, 24 (2006): 3–28.
40 Charles Lloyd Jones, "The Why and Wherefore," *Walkabout*, November 1934, 7.
41 Charles Holmes, Editorial, *Walkabout*, March 1935, 9.
42 Carter, *Always Almost Modern*, 139.
43 Eleanor Dark, "They All Come Back," *Walkabout*, January 1951, 19–20.
44 Wolfgang Schivelbusch, *The Railway Journey: The Industrialization of Time and Space in the Nineteenth Century* (Oakland: University of California Press, [1986] 2014).
45 See, for example, Jillian Barnes, "Tourism's Role in the Struggle for the Intellectual and Material Possession of 'The Centre' of Australia at Uluru, 1929–2011," *Journal of Tourism History*, 3, no. 2 (2011): 147–76; Max Quanchi, "Contrary Images: Photographing the New Pacific in *Walkabout* Magazine," *Journal of Australian Studies*, 27, no. 79 (2003): 77–92.
46 Marianna Torgovnick, *Gone Primitive: Savage Intellects, Modern Lives* (Chicago: University of Chicago Press, 1990); Susan Hegeman, *Patterns for America: Modernism and the Concept of Culture* (Princeton: Princeton University Press, 1999).
47 Charles Forsdick, *Travel in Twentieth-Century French and Francophone Cultures: The Persistence of Diversity* (Oxford: Oxford University Press, 2005), 33.
48 See Dipesh Chakrabarty, *Habitations of Modernity: Essays in the Wake of Subaltern Studies* (Chicago: University of Chicago Press, 2002); Ellen Smith, "Local Moderns: The Jindyworobak Movement and Australian Modernism," *Australian Literary Studies*, 27, no. 1 (2012): 1–17.
49 Stephen Greenblatt, "Kindly Visions," review of *Reading National Geographic*, by Catherine A. Lutz and Jane L. Collins, *New Yorker*, October 11, 1993, 112–20.
50 Stephen Greenblatt, *Marvellous Possessions: The Wonder of the New World* (Oxford: Clarendon, 1991), 20.
51 Carrigan, *Postcolonial Tourism*, xi.
52 Ann Laura Stoler, *Along the Archival Grain: Epistemic Anxieties and Colonial Common Sense* (Princeton: Princeton University Press, 2009), 53, 33.
53 James Clifford, *Routes: Travel and Translation in the Late Twentieth Century* (Cambridge: Harvard University Press, 1997), 31.

13

APRIL SHEMAK

Refugee and Asylum Seeker Narratives as Postcolonial Travel Writing

This chapter addresses refugee and asylum seeker narratives in English as forms of contemporary postcolonial travel writing. These narratives differ from Eurocentric conventions of travel writing, especially those styles of travel writing that developed simultaneously with European colonialism and were told from the point of view of writers coming from the colonial metropole.[1] Refugee and asylum seeker migration represents one of the most significant forms of contemporary travel. The lives of refugees and asylum seekers are marked by distinct modes of travel that are characterized by escape and flight. Narratives of their journeys are also distinct in that they are some of the most urgent and most politicized. This is travel writing largely focused on obtaining justice, raising awareness, producing empathy for refugees and asylum seekers, or gaining asylum in a host nation.

Although the practice of giving refuge to the stranger dates back millennia, "refugee" is a term that was first used to describe French Huguenots who fled religious persecution in seventeenth-century France. Today, it is a legal designation under international law that was established by the United Nations High Commission for Refugees (UNHCR) following World War II. The 1951 United Nations Refugee Convention defines "refugee" as someone with a "well-founded fear" of persecution based on "race, religion, nationality, membership of a particular social group or political opinion, is outside the country of his nationality, and is unable to, or owing to such fear, is unwilling to avail himself of the protection of that country."[2] However, the official definition of "refugee" does not encompass all of the conditions that contribute to forced migration. Thus, "refugee" is also a general term used to describe those people fleeing life-threatening conditions in their nations of origin. The UNHCR distinguishes between asylum seeker and refugee, stating that "an asylum-seeker is someone who says he or she is a refugee, but whose claim has not yet been definitively evaluated."[3] An asylum seeker narrative must become officially sanctioned by the laws of a nation state in order to qualify an applicant for asylum, and the criteria for granting can vary from nation to nation.

The number of refugees and asylum seekers is at its highest since World War II. The UNHCR notes that as of June 2015, the number of registered refugees was over 20 million. During the same time, the UNHCR notes that the total number of forcibly displaced people worldwide was nearly 60 million.[4] This number does not include those displaced people who did not qualify as refugees because they did not meet the UNHCR's criteria, but nevertheless were forced to leave their countries of origin due to life-threatening circumstances (e.g., economic or environmental factors).[5] The majority of contemporary refugees and asylum seekers are in the "third world" and many end up in refugee camps in neighboring countries or elsewhere in the Global South, although a small number are granted asylum in Western nations.

Refugee and asylum seeker narratives push the limits of travel writing. Tim Youngs defines travel writing as "predominantly, factual, first-person prose accounts of travels that have been undertaken by the author-narrator."[6] Refugee and asylum seekers disrupt the idea of individual travel, since their experience often includes mass migration. Although they may be narrated as individual eyewitness, first-person accounts, these narratives are often mediated by a third party. Youngs notes that travel writing generally signals a blurring of the boundaries of genre: "A near-consensus [among scholars] has developed that travel writing is a mixed form that feeds off other genres" (6). The same is true of refugee and asylum seeker narratives, which may take the form of nonfiction essays and books, historical documents, letters, and diaries, as well as human rights reports, public media reportage, and the UNHCR website.

This chapter expands the definition of travel writing while revising the focus of postcolonial studies. I examine narratives of post-World War II refugees and asylum seekers who come from areas that have been fundamentally shaped by colonialism, whether it be European or other forms of colonialism. There are also new forms of colonialism and imperialism that shape refugee identities and movements. This raises some questions: What *is* a "legitimate" refugee identity? How do states attempt to shape, legitimize, or delegitimize refugee identities? What role does narrative play in these processes? How can postcolonial studies account for this type of urgent traveling? The chapter is divided into three sections: refugee and asylum seeker travel; seeking asylum; and the refugee/writer. It ends by further considering the intersections between postcolonial studies and refugees and asylum seeker travel writing.

Refugee and Asylum Seeker Travel

Much refugee and asylum seeker travel is clandestine or not officially sanctioned. Among the many issues that refugees and asylum seekers face is the urgent journey marked by escape; they are not travelers who plan and plot journeys in the same way as travelers whose lives are not in danger. Refugees and asylum seekers may travel without official documents that legitimize their movements; or they may carry forged documents. Their journeys are often perilous – they often walk vast distances, take precarious water vessels, stowaway on airplanes, and endure a lack of shelter and food insecurity. Smugglers prey upon those who are desperate to flee, so that human trafficking is often a part of the refugee and asylum seeker travel experience. Refugee and asylum seeker travelers may be stalled or halted by legal systems or border patrol. They may end up in camps, in detention, or with asylum in host nations, lacking a sense of belonging, often living for years in limbo. While they may have an outsider's view of their new surroundings, they do not have the leisure to take in a place as would an exile, as they are often consumed with survival. For Western readers, two of the most recognizable forms of refugee and asylum seeker travel include mass forced migration on foot and by boat. I will address both of these forms in the rest of this section.

The partition of the Indian subcontinent in 1947 is considered the largest refugee migration of the modern age. This forced migration took place overland, with many refugees migrating on foot. Nearly fifteen million people were displaced and it is estimated that between one and two million died in the upheaval. The initial displacement and migration occurred in the summer and fall of 1947 when British colonial authorities withdrew and the subcontinent was divided into India as a Hindu-majority nation, and Pakistan (and later Bangladesh) as a Muslim-majority nation.[7] Millions of people became refugees as they fled their ancestral lands and relocated to areas demarcated along ethno-religious lines. As Ravinder Kaur shows, Indian newspaper articles and eyewitness accounts at the time emphasized the otherness of refugees, while a legal framework for refugees had not yet been established. These accounts often emphasized male experiences, while women, thousands of whom had been targeted during Partition through sexual violence, largely remained unrepresented.[8] In *The Other Side of Silence: Voices from the Partition* (2000 [1998]), Urvashi Butalia examines her family's and others' experiences with Partition decades after the turmoil.[9] She explains that, although there was an awareness in her family that some members had migrated because of Partition, the family's history of displacement was never openly discussed. She travels across the border to visit an uncle who had stayed behind with her grandmother in Lahore (now Pakistan) while the rest of the Hindu family migrated to India. She learns that her uncle converted from Hinduism to Islam and married a Muslim woman with whom he had a family. Butalia's travel reverses the refugee migratory route taken decades earlier by members of her family when she visits him at the familial home in Lahore and later brings her mother back to the home for the first time in decades. Butalia's narrative reveals the complexities and ongoing effects of refugee migration as her mother had always been suspicious of her brother's motivations for remaining in Lahore, wondering whether it was because of the violence that he did not want to flee, or that he wanted the family property in Lahore. In addition to interviewing her family members, Butalia interviews other people who lived through Partition, including Rajinder Singh, who describes how he and others expanded the size of their *kafila*[10] for protection from attacks and other forms violence (80–81). These foot caravans extended for miles. Those who walked in *kafilas* were more destitute than those who hired cars or took trains to migrate.

Butalia's ethnographic work dovetails nicely with Bapsi Sidhwa's novel *Cracking India* (1991), which explores the impact of the partition on a nanny (Ayah) and her diverse group of admirers in Lahore. Once the violence begins, the multicultural group of friends becomes fractured and suspicious of each other. Ayah, a Hindu, suffers sexual violence as she is abducted by a group of Muslim men. Sidhwa portrays how, for women, sexual exploitation hung over them as a possibility during Partition. Indeed, refugee migration included the abduction of thousands of Hindu and Muslim women.[11]

Some of the most popular refugee narratives of travel by foot are those by and about the "lost boys," a term used to describe the approximately twenty thousand children who walked across Sudan during its civil war to refugee camps in Kenya. Some of these "lost boys" were eventually resettled in the United States. Dave Eggers's *What is the What: The Autobiography of Valentino Achak Deng* (2006) is a fictionalization of the life of Deng, one of the "lost boys." Eggers's collaboration with Deng raises issues surrounding the narrative authority of refugees. There is an asymmetrical relationship between Eggers as a white man from the "First World" and Deng the Sudanese refugee. Yogita Goyal notes the way that the novel mimics the antebellum slave narrative.[12] The danger of what Goyal refers to as "literary blackface" is that the Sudanese "lost boy" becomes yet another narrative trope for othering Africa, disavowing the specific political and historical circumstances that led to refugee migration.[13] Indeed, the antecedents to many contemporary refugee and asylum seeker narratives are eighteenth- and nineteenth-century slave narratives that attempted to gain the sympathy of white readers. For example, Benjamin Drew's *The Refugee: Narratives of Fugitive Slaves in Canada* configures the fugitive slave as a refugee.[14]

Boat People

The term "boat people" came to prominence in the 1970s with the exodus of over one million refugees who left Vietnam on overcrowded wooden boats to escape the communist government and gain asylum in other nations. The term has since been used to refer to any refugees who journey by sea, although it also has derogatory connotations, as it renders all refugees who travel on the seas in the same category – as destitute victims without agency. The configuration of the maritime refugee has become so ubiquitous that the UNHCR website includes a section devoted to journeys by boat: "Refugee Stories: Life-Threatening Sea Journeys."[15]

Published in 2013, and edited by Carina Hoang, a Vietnamese refugee who now lives in Australia, *Boat People: Personal Stories from the Vietnamese Exodus 1975–1996* contains a collection of photographs and first person accounts from Vietnamese refugees, UNHCR employees, a journalist, and a member of the US government in Vietnam in 1975. The refugees tell of their horrific boat journeys involving overcrowding, hunger, thirst, and other health hazards, as well as encounters with pirates that resulted in theft, rape, and death. The volume also depicts the difficulties that Vietnamese boat refugees faced in finding nations that would allow their vessels to dock and disembark. The book attempts to document the Vietnamese "boat people" exodus, but there is also a facile sense of closure to many of the narratives that end with a photo of the refugee with his or her family and a "where are they now" paragraph listing his or her achievements. Yet the stories presented offer a complex array of voices and conflicting interests that deserve further exploration. A narrative of Hoang's assistance for families to find the graves of their loved ones who were left behind in Vietnam, or those who died on their refugee journeys, points to the lasting impact of refugee experiences.

In the United States, "boat people" came to describe those Cubans and Haitians who left their nations of origin via boat or raft (or *balsas*), hoping to make it to the United States. The official US policy toward these groups has been starkly different. For decades following the 1959 Cuban revolution, Cubans were welcomed "with open arms" since they were fleeing a communist nation. After 1959, the US government established the Cuban Refugee Center to assist resettlement. Indeed, the United States Coast Guard would assist Cuban boat refugees by transporting them to US shores.[16] Unlike most refugees in the United States, there has been a concerted effort to collect the oral histories of Cuban refugees.[17] Haitians, on the other hand, have been considered "economic" rather than "political" asylum seekers and they have been systematically denied asylum, even when fleeing the brutal Duvalier dictatorship.[18]

Haitian American writer Edwidge Danticat has written much fiction and nonfiction about the status of Haitian boat refugees in the United States. In "The Other Side of the Water" from her essay collection *Create Dangerously: The Immigrant Artist at Work* (2010), Danticat writes of her travel to Haiti by plane. Her mobility as a US citizen is vastly different from the Haitian deportee who sits across the aisle from her, and from her deceased cousin Marius, whose body she must return to Haiti.[19] Readers learn that Marius had arrived in the United States clandestinely by boat and he remained undocumented there, which poses a problem when he dies and Danticat is tasked with getting his body back to Haiti for the funeral. The United States would not release his body until they had his "papers" from the Haitian consulate; the Haitian government would not accept his body until he had "papers." In death as in life, a body's movement across national borders requires written documentation to make the body and its journey legitimate. The difficulty that Danticat encounters in getting Marius's body back to Haiti speaks to the partially known and fragmented experience of an undocumented Haitian refugee.

Like the United States, Australia is notoriously harsh in its treatment of boat refugees. At various times, governmental measures have authorized the navy to intercept boat refugees and subsequently detain them on its territory, Christmas Island, or send them to detention on Papua New Guinea or Nauru to await review of their asylum cases. The majority of these asylum cases have been found to be legitimate and the asylum seekers have been resettled in Australia, but only after most have spent months or years in detention. Since the implementation of Operation Sovereign Borders in 2013, the navy is authorized to intercept and turn back refugees on the seas.[20] "The Dream Boat" by Luke Mogelson is a *New York Times Magazine* article that charts the journey of Afghan, Iraqi, and Iranian asylum seekers who hope to make it to Christmas Island and then to asylum on the Australian mainland.[21] Mogelson and his cameraman, Joel Van Houdt, accompany the group, who, by paying smugglers, journey two hundred miles by boat from Indonesia to Christmas Island. For Mogelson and Van Houdt, there is the quality of adventure to their story as they pose as asylum seekers and join the "real" asylum seekers on their journey, who do not know that they are journalists. The story features text, photos, and video of the journey, including dramatic video footage of the boat at sea. When the boat is eventually intercepted by the Australian navy, Mogelson and Van Houdt "out" themselves as journalists to the authorities while the asylum seekers are taken to detention where they will likely remain for months or years. The story raises ethical questions since the journalists pose as destitute asylum seekers but are in positions of privilege that allow them to easily reclaim their freedom to travel.

From Nothing to Zero: Letters from Refugees in Australia's Detention Centres (2003) offers edited fragments of letters written by refugees to Australian citizens who participated in a letter-writing campaign. Many names and other identifying markers have been changed to protect refugees and family members who remain in the nation of origin. The volume progresses thematically through the conditions in the nation of origin, the refugee's journey to asylum (which often takes place by boat), to travel that ends in Australian detention. Significantly, the epistolary form highlights the distance between refugees and Australian citizens, as the refugees are detained on an island without contact with the Australian mainland. *From Nothing to Zero* includes a preface written by the lawyer Julian Burnside, in which he writes, "Every letter is genuine."[22] The introduction to the collection was written by Simon Westcott, the publisher for Lonely Planet, which is known for its travelers' guidebook series. Refugees gain a certain credibility as travelers through this publication venue, but it ultimately results in exoticizing refugee and asylum seeker narratives.

Seeking Asylum

The asylum interview is its own kind of travel narrative, which an immigration officer assesses when deciding whether to grant asylum to an applicant. In many countries, asylum hearings are closed by law; the public does not have access to them. Testimony is the foundation of asylum seeker narratives. Asylum seekers must testify to trauma in the nation of origin to demonstrate "credible fear" to gain asylum. Yet, as I have discussed elsewhere, the "truth" of testimony is always already in question.[23] Refugee and asylum seeker narratives demonstrate that relying on testimony as authentic or representative of an asylum seeker's "real" experience denies the very systems of power that contribute to the construction of these narratives. Refugee and asylum seeker narratives can throw the whole idea of what is "factual" into disarray.

The audiences for these narratives, especially if they are linked to international or national legal systems, typically require a linear narrative that is free of gaps, something that may not reflect a refugee's fragmented and traumatic experience. As Cathy Caruth states, "trauma is not locatable in the simple violent or original event in an individual's past, but rather in the way that its very unassimilated nature – the way it was precisely *not known* in the first instance – returns to haunt the survivor later on."[24]

Gillian Whitlock notes the fraught nature of asylum seeker testimony: "Refugees bring to light uncertainties about who can be understood and felt to be human that set the limits of humanitarian storytelling and its capacity to reach 'distant' others."[25] In her fiction and nonfiction, Edwidge Danticat has addressed the difficulties Haitians have had in seeking and receiving asylum. Piecing together US government documents and the testimony of her cousin Maxo, Danticat's memoir *Brother, I'm Dying* (2007) portrays the death of her eighty-one-year old uncle Joseph Dantica in detention after he had applied for asylum and fell ill during his asylum interview and did not receive immediate medical attention. She writes of Joseph's subsequent death as he was shackled in the Jackson Memorial Hospital in Miami. Joseph Dantica's disastrous asylum interview is indicative of the systematic denial of Haitian asylum applications and the limits of Haitian asylum seeker testimony.

There is a moral value associated with asylum seeker testimonies; any embellishment or fabrication of their stories is seen as a breach on the host nation.[26] In an August 1, 2011 story published in *The New Yorker*, Suketu Mehta follows an African woman who uses the pseudonym "Caroline" as she works her way through the US asylum process, chronicling how she embellishes her story with the assistance of another African refugee, "Laurent," in order to gain asylum. Despite the fact that her family had been persecuted as part of the political opposition in her home nation – one of the factors which can qualify a person for refugee status under the UN Refugee Convention – "Caroline" concludes that her story will not be convincing enough to immigration authorities unless she says that she was raped as part of her asylum narrative. Mehta writes, "She had pangs about lying: 'Telling that story makes me sad, because I know it's true for someone.'"[27] In a podcast interview about the article, Mehta asserts that such stories reflect the "inflation of atrocity" that applicants can use to construct "stories that the system understands."[28] Mehta states, "[Laurent] wasn't doing it to make a buck, but that it would help people who had a well-founded fear to stay in the country." Indeed "Laurent," while having survived the Rwandan genocide, made up his own asylum story, saying he fled strife in Burundi, because he "didn't want to compromise [his] family in Rwanda."[29] While some might see the change in stories as a "betrayal of the American system," it reflects what Didier Fassin refers to as "political subjectivation," which "is the production of subjects and subjectivities possessed of political meanings within social interactions."[30] Refugees must produce themselves as subjects that conform to the political structures of the nation in which they seek asylum, structures which cast them as without agency and deem testimony to a particular kind of trauma as the basis for establishing a claim. "Laurent" understands how producing a refugee narrative means being aware of political subjectivation in the United States *and* Rwanda. His work with "Caroline" indicates the varied literacies asylum seekers must have in order to navigate cultural, bureaucratic, and psychological borders and checkpoints.

"Laurent" is aware of the exchange value of trauma in an asylum narrative. In their book *The Empire of Trauma*, Didier Fassin and Richard Rechtman argue that the idea of trauma is a construction and a very recent phenomenon. Far from being an evident reality, they assert that what constitutes trauma in contemporary psychological medical discourse (and public discourse) has been a construction dependent upon political and social events over the last century. This is not to suggest that atrocity and other acts of violence do not have a significant psychological and physical impact, but that the way that we think of this impact has been shaped by historical, social, and political forces. As Fassin and Rechtman state, "while trauma is a language that appears both neutral and universal in its account of victims, it significantly fails to throw light on certain signifieds and certain agents."[31] Asylum seekers can only be recognized as refugees when they can testify to some sort of trauma (that qualifies for refugee status by the UN definition of "refugee") in the nation of origin. Refugees who operate outside of these parameters of victimhood are rendered suspect and untruthful, which reflects part of a historical legacy of delegitimizing refugee testimony in the West. Those who are discovered to have manipulated a system that is stacked against them are perceived as violating the core of a moral economy of trauma.

In his novel *How to Read the Air* (2010), Dinaw Mengestu represents the cynicism of the asylum process when the narrator, Jonas, who is the child of a refugee and is employed at a refugee agency in the United States, writes, edits, and embellishes asylum seeker narratives. Jonas is acutely aware that asylum seeker narratives must offer traumatic experiences if they are to persuade immigration authorities to grant the applicant asylum. Jonas and the agency that he works for facilitate the means through which the idea of trauma "reinvents 'good' and 'bad' victims, or at least a ranking of legitimacy among victims" (282). He continues to explain that the "persecuted" narratives shared similar formulaic statements:

> The village, city, town, country I came from, was born in, lived in, for forty-five, sixty years was taken over, occupied, bombed, burned, destroyed, slaughtered, and I, my family, my sister, cousin, aunt, uncle, grandparents were arrested, shot, raped, detained, forced to say, tortured to say, threatened if we did not say that we would vote, not vote, believed in, did not believe in, supported or denounced the government, or movement, or religion of X. In the end the consequences were always the same, and each ended with a similar emphatic note: We, I can't, won't, will never be able to go back.[32]

Mengestu's novel suggests the complicity of the system with the fabrication of stories; it is a political system based on the construction of trauma for political purposes.

The novel challenges the conventions of refugee testimony and the notion of the witness as Jonas is neither a survivor of persecution, nor a witness to it, yet his life revolves around constructing traumatic refugee narratives. *How to Read the Air* and Mengestu's other novels (*The Beautiful Things That Heaven Bears* [2008] and *All Our Names* [2015]) reveal deep skepticism toward any kind of solidarity-building that narrating a refugee story might appear to offer. The refugee story becomes one of an endless deferral of meaning. This begs the question: What kind of literacies are necessary for reading and interpreting refugee experience?

However, one cannot underestimate the role of the political climate in recognizing and legitimizing refugees and asylum seekers, even if they are discovered to have lied on their asylum application. In *Infidel* (2008), Ayaan Hirsi Ali offers a first person account of her experience as a Somali refugee woman. She sought and received asylum in the Netherlands. After she became a member of the Dutch Parliament, she admitted that she had lied on her asylum application when she sought asylum in the Netherlands. Yet, Hirsi Ali's story has been widely popular in some circles because her strong critiques of Islam fit an ideology that demonizes Muslims as terrorists.[33]

Refugee/Writer

Writers who are refugees occupy a unique position through which to explore narrative voice and the fragmentation of refugee journeys. Albino Ochero-Okello's "Arrival" (2011 [1999]) charts his journey through the asylum process in Britain upon his arrival by airplane at Gatwick Airport from Uganda, his nation of origin. The essay begins by foregrounding the significance of testimony at the point of entry, where he must persuade an immigration officer to allow him into the country: "As I stood in front of the immigration officer, I was already worrying about my answers to the questions he might ask."[34] The self-questioning that begins the story signals that the essay takes place in a space of uncertainty. The essay documents both the physical travel that Ochero-Okello undertakes as a refugee as well as his psychic travel as he remembers the torture and death of family members in Uganda while awaiting his asylum interview. After immigration authorities send him to the "Beehive," a detention center for asylum seekers, Ochero-Okello and a fellow Ugandan asylum seeker are eventually released and granted entrance into Britain while they await decisions on their asylum cases. They are confronted with the difficulties of having to negotiate the systems of a new country. The only travel assistance given to them are tickets for a train to London. Ochero-Okello attempts to reconcile British trains with the trains that he traveled on in Uganda. The London train becomes a signifier of first world modernity: "The first impression was marvellous. The seats were smart. There was no overcrowding" (14). He remembers the "hazards" of the Ugandan railway system that included riding alongside livestock. Notably, the Ugandan railway system is a vestige of the colonial era when Britain ruled Uganda and brought workers from British India to aid in its construction. The train is thus an ironic signifier of the legacy of British colonialism and the arrival of Britain's former subjects to the metropole.

Whereas "Arrival" represents the confrontation of the writer-as-refugee with the immigration interview, the writer becomes the interviewer of refugees in Nuruddin Farah's *Yesterday, Tomorrow: Voices of the Somali Diaspora* (2000). In it, Farah attempts to chart the circuitous journeys and unstable conditions facing Somali refugees in the early 1990s after the collapse of the Somali government in 1991. He interviews Somali refugee communities throughout Africa and Europe, making for a complex portrait of this group of refugees. The book is as much a travelogue of various refugee communities as it is a record of the difficulties of travel that Somali refugees face. Farah renders Somali refugee experience through partiality, fragmentation, contradiction, and nonlinearity. What's more, throughout the book, Farah searches for a definition of "refugee," repeatedly asking his interviewees to define the term. In doing so, he challenges official definitions of the term, signalling its ambiguity.

Farah not only traces the routes of Somali refugees, but he simultaneously charts his own travels to interview refugees. He remarks on his own privilege in carrying "legitimate" documents such as a passport, visas, and other identity information, but authorities often assume that these documents are forgeries *because* he is Somali. He is stopped, detained, and harassed by immigration officials at airports and by soldiers at various checkpoints. His travel, while vastly different from that of the refugees that he interviews, is also circumscribed by the fact that he is an African traveler.

Farah notes the parallel between the end of empire after World War II and the surge in refugees from former colonies. The response from former colonizers has been one of racism; they do not want refugees, especially those from the Global South in "their" countries.[35] For example, once the fleeing Somalis arrive in Italy, most will not be given the status of "refugee," but instead that of "visitor," allowing the Italian government to forego providing the protections that would be required by them with the classification under the UN Refugee Convention (63).

As David Farrier points out, asylum seekers signal the limits of postcolonial studies. They are diasporic and move beyond national boundaries, but they rely upon nation-states to provide them with protections, and thus, do not fit into an antinationalist framework that upholds the diasporic, the migrant, and the cosmopolitan as ideal agents of postcoloniality. Instead Farrier, quoting Gayatri Spivak, argues that the refugee represents a "new subaltern" that cannot be conceptualized through the existing frameworks of postcolonial studies.[36] One way of expanding the theoretical possibilities for considering refugees and asylum seekers is through Jacques Derrida's theorization of "hospitality," which considers the obligation that states have to take in refugees. Derrida highlights the tension between "unconditional hospitality," which requires granting the stranger welcome without question and the "laws of hospitality," which comprise the restrictions of border control and legislation.[37] Refugees and asylum seekers disrupt existing configurations of identity and citizenship in the contemporary world. Such configurations demonstrate that colonialism has not ended, but has taken on new forms for which postcolonial studies, in its focus on the aftermath of European colonialism, has not accounted. For example, Syrian, Tibetan, Hmong, Armenian, and Kurdish refugees speak to a range of (neo)colonial dynamics. A disruption occurs where the native and the stranger encounter one another, at the threshold of the nation where the stranger/refugee seeks entrance. This disruption calls for a reconsideration of how and when the refugee and asylum seeker can be heard within social and political discourse. As Derrida states, "Language *is* hospitality" (135). Thus, it is necessary to consider how refugee and asylum seeker narratives function in an increasingly inhospitable world.

Conclusion

Given the exorbitant numbers of displaced people who continue to flee their nations of origin, refugee and asylum seeker narratives will continue to be written and disseminated. As this chapter demonstrates, postcolonial travel writing requires that we consider the ethical demands of travel writing when people's lives are fundamentally shaped by forced migration. Writings about these journeys are fraught with social, political, linguistic, and ideological complexities, but it is clear that the study of travel writing is being transformed by it.[38]

NOTES

1 On this point see the Introduction to this volume.
2 "Asylum Seekers," *UNHCR*, accessed April 10, 2016, www.unhcr.org/pages/ 49c3646c137.html. See also, *The 1951 Convention Relating to the Status of Refugees and Its 1967 Protocol* (UNHCR: Geneva, 2011). Available online at www.unhcr.org/4ec262df9.html.

3 "Asylum Seekers."

4 "Worldwide displacement hits all-time high as war and persecution increase," UNHCR, accessed May 2, 2016, www.unhcr.org/558193896.html. It is important to note that only a small percentage of refugees end up in the West, where an even smaller number are granted asylum. The majority of asylum seekers languish in camps in the "Third World."

5 "Figures at a Glance," *UNHCR*, accessed May 2, 2016, www.unhcr.org/pages/49c3646c11.html.

6 Tim Youngs, *The Cambridge Introduction to Travel Writing* (Cambridge: Cambridge University Press, 2013), 3.

7 The date of Partition was August 15, 1947.

8 Ravinder Kaur, "Distinctive Citizenship: Refugees, Subjects and the Post-Colonial State in India's Partition," *Cultural and Social History*, 6, no. 4 (2009): 429–46.

9 Urvashi Butalia, *The Other Side of Silence: Voices from the Partition of India* (Durham: Duke University Press, 2000).

10 In the glossary, Butalia defines *kafila* as "a foot-column of people, usually refugees" (297).

11 See Ritu Menon and Kamla Bhasin, *Borders and Boundaries: How Women Experienced the Partition of India* (New Brunswick: Rutgers University Press, 1998); Urvashi Butalia, "Questions of Sexuality and Citizenship during Partition," in *Embodiment: Essays on Gender and Identity*, ed. Meenakshi Thapan (New Delhi: Oxford University Press India, 1997), 90–106.

12 Yogita Goyal, "African Atrocity, American Humanity: Slavery and Its Transnational Afterlives," *Research in African Literatures*, 45, no. 3 (Fall 2014): 48–71 (50).

13 Other "lost boy" refugee narratives include the 2003 film *Lost Boys of Sudan* and the memoir *They Poured Fire on Us From the Sky: The True Story of Three Lost Boys of Sudan* (2005), written by three "lost boys" who were resettled in the United States, Alphonsian Deng, Benson Deng, and Benjamin Ajak, in collaboration with Judy A. Bernstein.

14 Other well-known slave narratives that testify to the escape from slavery include Harriet Jacobs's *Incidents in the Life of a Slave Girl* (1861) and Frederick Douglass's *Narrative of the Life of Frederick Douglass, an American Slave* (1845).

15 See "Refugee Stories: Life-Threatening Sea Journeys," *UNHCR Stories*, accessed May 2, 2016, http://stories.unhcr.org.

16 Decades later, this policy was changed so that Cuban refugees had to reach American shores on their own before being granted asylum. This became known as the Wetfoot / Dryfoot policy.

17 The Cuban Heritage Collection at the University of Miami contains oral histories with Cuban exiles in Miami who came in the 1960s.

18 For more on the discrepancy in the treatment of Haitian versus Cuban refugees, see April Shemak, *Asylum Speakers: Caribbean Refugees and Testimonial Discourse* (New York: Fordham University Press, 2011), 49–54.

19 Edwidge Danticat, "The Other Side of the Water," in *Create Dangerously: The Immigrant Artist at Work* (Princeton: Princeton University Press, 2010), 87–96 (87).

20 See "Operation Sovereign Borders," *Australian Government: Department of Immigration and Border Protection,* accessed October 28, 2017, www.osb .border.gov.au/Outside-Australia/Outside-Australia-fact-sheet.

21 Luke Mogelson, "The Dream Boat," *New York Times Magazine,* November 15, 2013, www.nytimes.com/2013/11/17/magazine/the-impossible-refugee-boat-lift-to-christmas-island.html?pagewanted=all&_r=0.

22 Julian Burnside, "Preface," in *From Nothing to Zero: Letters from Refugees in Australia's Detention Centres,* ed. Janet Austin (Oakland: Lonely Planet, 2003), v–vii (v).

23 Shemak, *Asylum Speakers,* 29.

24 Cathy Caruth, *Unclaimed Experience: Trauma, Narrative, and History* (Baltimore: Johns Hopkins University Press, 1996), 4.

25 Gillian Whitlock, *Postcolonial Life Narrative: Testimonial Transactions* (Oxford: Oxford University Press, 2015), 179.

26 For more on the requirements of "authenticity" in asylum narratives, see Agnes Woolley, *Contemporary Asylum Narratives: Representing Refugees in the Twenty-First Century* (Basingstoke: Palgrave Macmillan, 2014), 12.

27 Suketu Mehta, "The Asylum Seeker," *The New Yorker,* August 1, 2011, www .newyorker.com/magazine/2011/08/01/the-asylum-seeker, n.p.

28 Suketu Mehta, "Out Loud Podcast: Suketu Mehta on Illegal Immigrants," podcast audio, July 26, 2011, accessed April 8, 2016, www.newyorker.com/podcast/ out-loud/suketu-mehta-on-illegal-immigrants. African immigrants make up a tiny fraction of the total number of immigrants in the United States; however, their numbers have significantly increased since the 1990s.

29 Suketu Mehta, "Out Loud Podcast."

30 Didier Fassin, *Humanitarian Reason: A Moral History of the Present* (Berkeley: University of California Press, 2012), 202.

31 Didier Fassin and Richard Rechtman, *The Empire of Trauma: An Inquiry into the Condition of Victimhood* (Princeton: Princeton University Press, 2009), 281.

32 Dinaw Mengestu, *How to Read the Air* (New York: Riverhead Books, 2010), 22.

33 Indeed, the current discourse surrounding whether Syrian refugees should be allowed to enter Europe and the United States centers on the potential "terrorist threat" Muslim refugees pose to host nations.

34 Albino Ochero-Okello, "Arrival," in *The New Granta Book of Travel,* ed. Liz Jobey (London: Granta Books, 2011), 1–14 (1).

35 Nuruddin Farah, *Yesterday, Tomorrow: Voices from the Somali Diaspora* (London: Cassell, 2000), 54–55.

36 David Farrier, *Postcolonial Asylum: Seeking Sanctuary before the Law* (Liverpool: Liverpool University Press, 2011), 5.

37 Jacques Derrida, *Of Hospitality* (Stanford: Stanford University Press, 2000), 77–81.

38 For further reading: Katrina Powell, *Identity and Power in Narratives of Displacement* (New York: Routledge, 2015).

14

STEPHEN M. LEVIN

Imaginary Tourists
The Fashioning of the Global Traveler in Postcolonial Fiction

The annals of the postcolonial travel novel in the twentieth century begin with the tenacious hold of the *bildungsroman,* a formal dominance that novels of the late twentieth- and early twenty-first centuries seek to subvert.[1] If dramas of selfhood dominate colonial representations of travel – in, for example, E. M. Forster's *A Passage to India,* Joseph Conrad's *Heart of Darkness,* or George Orwell's *Burmese Days* – they also persist within and deeply shape postcolonial travel fictions, including well-known examples by Graham Greene, D. H. Lawrence, V. S. Naipaul, and Paul Theroux. One might assert that the presence or absence of the self – and the prospects of its articulation through practices of travel – constitutes the central preoccupation of colonial and postcolonial travel novels. To some extent, these fictions are haunted by a foundational irony. Although voluntary travel might be expected to produce narratives of emancipation from national, cultural, and epistemological boundaries, and celebrations of the fluid and flexible identities that are made possible when a subject is unmoored from the constraints of place, colonial and postcolonial depictions of travel frequently focus on the shattering dislocation of selfhood that accompanies the traveler's journey outside of Europe where the violence of colonialism becomes exposed and the sentimental fantasies of reciprocity more difficult to sustain. These travel fictions build upon themes of heroic struggle that Mary Louise Pratt identifies in the genre of sentimental travel writing that matures into a confessional form by the 1870s.[2] Yet the novel departs from the confessional travel narrative as it comes to be suffused with modernism's more ambivalent interest in the private recuperation of selfhood from the turbulent civilizational crises of the early twentieth century. The twentieth-century travel novel, then, pushes the *bildungsroman* toward contested terrain. On one hand, the self may be newly integrated as travel enables new modes of fulfillment and self-development, such as when experience enables new modes of aesthetic pleasure or when travel allows the social order to be comfortably reproduced. On the other hand, the determined focus on the connective tissue between self and world also leads to an exploration of new idioms of selfhood that move beyond the model of the stabilized, anchored, and individuated subject. While the representation of travel once functioned as a register of the colonist's anxious efforts to maintain the boundary between colonizer and colonized, travel later comes to index new presentations of selfhood that gesture toward new epistemologies and ontologies, and to a worlding sensibility that opens new paths for the novel form.

Nervous Conditions and the Colonial Traveler

In light of the defining conflicts of the early twentieth century, it is not surprising that travel becomes associated with the depiction of nervous conditions attendant to colonialism and decolonization. The global traveler's descent into madness reaches its nadir in Conrad's *Heart of Darkness* and Forster's *A Passage to India*, and extends to Paul Bowles's *The Sheltering Sky* and later narratives such as Alex Garland's *The Beach*. It may be surprising, given his focus on the epistemic continuity of orientalism as a field of ideas, that Edward Said also addressed the conditions of precarity for the European traveler in a colonial setting: "Every European traveler or resident in the Orient has had to protect himself from its unsettling influences."[3] Said attributes the perils of colonial travel to the association of the Orient with libidinal excess and the challenges of translating "its hopelessly strange languages, its seeming perverse morality" to the normative prose style of European writers. This encounter with the Orient, Said continues, "wore away the European discreteness and rationality of time, space, and personal identity" (167). Said's statements resonate with the escalation of colonialism's extractive enterprises undertaken by Kurtz in *Heart of Darkness*, where any veneer of a civilizational idiom becomes impossible to sustain, and in the echo heard by Adela Quested in *A Passage to India*. That echo disorients not only Quested as she tours the Marabar caves, but also the formal status of the realist novel. Pericles Lewis contends that Forster insists on the ambiguous origins of the echo.[4] Although Lewis reads this ceding of narrative authority as a transitional sign marking modernism's skepticism toward the sovereignty of the individual, the travelers themselves, unlike the novel form, prove much less adept at making this transition. The emphasis on the precarity of European selfhood, as has been pointed out, for example, in Chinua Achebe's well-known critique of *Heart of Darkness*,[5] relies on an encounter with what Achille Mbembe describes as an "absolute otherness" in the context of the colonial dyad. If the postcolony serves as an emblem for "all that is incomplete, mutilated, and unfinished," then the European subject strives for completion, wholeness, and totality – that is, the perspicuity of the *bildung*.[6]

The modernist portrayal of a bourgeois self in crisis constitutes, as Michael Valdez Moses contends, a kind of "prototype of the postcolonial novel" insofar as these narratives convey a loss of faith in the subject of bourgeois humanism.[7] These depictions also underscore that orientalism carries an epistemic burden for the European traveler in the colonial setting. For instance, Kurtz is trapped within the instrumental enterprise of resource extraction at all human and ecological costs, and Adela Quested is fated to reassert herself within the limited parameters of the *memsahib*.[8] And yet postmodernist narratives of travel that revisit the themes of Conrad and Forster frequently illustrate the heroic efforts entailed in authorizing and symbolizing a form of more "authentic" travel that, to the traveler at least, appears to circumvent colonial or neocolonial lineaments. In Alex Garland's *The Beach*, for example, when Daffy appears to Richard on the Khao San Road in Bangkok and shows him a map of a secret island accessible only to a select group of determined travelers, he manifests as the spectral presence of Kurtz. Daffy possesses a secret knowledge of the horror that permeates the structure of the beach paradise whose location he has disclosed, and yet his gesture enables this horror to be suppressed beneath fantasies of authentic self-development, social exclusivity, and geopolitical neutrality. Eventually, the reassertion of the real serves to expose the fragile lie of the virtual, as the specter of Daffy indeed returns, revealing the horrific underlying structure of the beach: its internal hierarchies and divisions, and its contingency on the protection of a local drug trafficking paramilitary group.

In focusing on travel as a causal factor and symptom of a crisis of European identity in colonial settings, modernist and postmodernist narratives neglect the alternative figurations of travel that emanate from non-European contexts. An example of a counter-idiom of modernist travel may be found in the writings of Rabindranath Tagore, who, in the course of his journeys to Europe, North America, China, Iran, Latin America, and Indo-China, insisted on the virtues of traveling without the encumbrance of preordained goals. Tagore objected to the excessive rationalization of the Western self. Just as he advocated for a view of India as "a land without a centre,"[9] so he adhered to an orientation of the self that acknowledged, as Jorge Luis Borges wrote of Tagore, the "unlimited possibilities of the soul."[10] Inverting Mbembe's imagery of dismemberment, he expresses his concern that "man's personality is mutilated in the western world and [...] is reduced to a machine."[11] Tagore supplements Conrad's and Forster's focus on the crisis of European selfhood by suggesting that the dissolution of selfhood constitutes the goal of travel instead of the self's "oedipal" completion. As with the figure of the *flâneur* depicted by Walter Benjamin, this view of travel stresses performance and enunciation rather than the formation of the *bildung*. Arrival is deferred, and yet out of these deferrals the *flâneur* "wrenches heroism from defeat" by securing the compensatory pleasures derived from immersive mobilities and the arts of aesthetic assemblage. Commentaries on the *flâneur* often underscore a paradox: On one hand, the *flâneur* relies on a decidedly masculinist subject endowed with the capacity to wander invisibly through the city and to take "possession" of the environment, and yet the *flâneur* also exhibits a melancholic structure that derives from its basis in deferred action and estrangement.[12] As the example of Tagore affirms, these two views of the *flâneur* may be reconciled: Artistic production, enabled by the freedoms afforded by unrestricted mobility, seeks its inspiration in the melancholy of indeterminacy.

In his insistence on a model of selfhood that stresses nomadism and deterritorialization rather than individuation, Tagore anticipates later interventions from such figures as V. S. Naipaul and Salman Rushdie. In portraying the self as an *aporia* that cannot be easily recuperated to stand in for figures of fluidity and translation, these writers chart a transition away from the European modernists. Whether the depiction of such a fractured self, composed as it is of disparate and incommensurable elements, constitutes a critique of the liberal humanist subject or a symptom of a toxic and overdetermined colonial attachment is a question that yields multiple and contradictory perspectives in the works of Naipaul and Rushdie. In some instances, again, the work of assemblage acts to restore the wonder of travel and the security of a stable subject position. In the field of Rushdie criticism, scholars have at times foregrounded the theme of *bricolage* and focused attention on cultural hybridity and the creative labor entailed in composing a self from its richly variable influences and inheritances. Other readings stress the seemingly opposed thematic of the melancholic traveler who hangs in the balance of a gap that cannot be traduced or translated across, and who reflects a nontraversable split between a self and its others: a discussion I return to below.

Emergent Postcolonial Travelers: Deterritorializing the Self

If the journeys of Marlowe and Adela Quested herald the crisis of European selfhood caught in the repetitions of asserting colonial dominance, Naipaul refigures this crisis as a dialectics of being and becoming. As the empire recedes, so the postcolonial traveler emerges, and yet, as Naipaul vividly underscores, this figure comes into being marked, following Stuart Hall's gloss on Fanon, by a "traumatic character of the colonial experience."[13]

Naipaul's postcolonial travelers are constituted out of the "formative dislocation" and "epistemic fractures" of empire,[14] and they must therefore reckon with the composition of a self that is fashioned in historical conditions marked by death and decay. For Timothy Brennan, exile represents the horizon at which the postcolonial subject comes into being, and hence the self-fashioning of the postcolonial traveler reflects the "simultaneous recognition of nationhood and an alienation from it."[15] Yet in the postcolonial state, the demise of empire, evoked in figures of decay and ruins, becomes an occasion for the postcolonial traveler to reflect on the disjunctive worlds that constitute the self. Naipaul's long literary career converges on this tension between narrating the deformation of selfhood and recognizing the capacious worlds contained in hybridized cultural forms. His most dystopian portrait of a postcolonial state, the 1979 novel *A Bend in the River*, opens by linking the emergence of the state with the erasure of the subject: "The world is what it is; men who are nothing, who allow themselves to become nothing, have no place in it."[16] Although his 1987 novel *The Enigma of Arrival* in many respects repeats the melancholic tone of the earlier work, death in this narrative becomes paradoxically linked to epiphanic recognition, as the narrator comes to realize that his "subject was not my sensibility, my inward development, but the worlds I contained within myself, the worlds I lived in."[17] Although Naipaul's rejection of large-scale revolutionary movements has sometimes led detractors to regard him an apologist for colonialism, Naipaul may better be understood as a critic of the European *bildungsroman*. He returns again and again to the figure of a postcolonial traveler who anticipates a plenitude to be yielded from the sedimented remains of the postcolonial state, but who comes to recognize that a self may be fashioned only through an encounter with empire's remnants.

In *A Bend in the River*, for example, Naipaul presents a vision of selfhood that prioritizes processes of self-creation over the "telos" of the fully individuated self. And yet, as has been pointed out by a number of commentators on the novel, the world of *Bend* has been drained of all prospects for enchantment. As the cycle of empires progresses from one despotic formation to the next, yielding ever-familiar hierarchies of domination and subjection, so does self-creation prove to be a metaphysical dead end. Amit Chaudhuri has written that Naipaul's middle period owes much to Conrad in that law and bourgeois hierarchy recede as forms of authority: "the father-figure disappears, and what we have then is the metaphor of travel, the lone figure moving through what is, on one level, a metaphysical landscape."[18] Naipaul, Chaudhuri continues, takes up the trope of the "disengaged observer, traversing, in Dantesque manner, the disintegrating 'half-formed societies' around him" (238). In *Bend*, this shift in narrative focus manifests most dramatically in a long monologue by Indar, cousin to Salim, the Muslim Indian merchant who has settled in a newly independent African state in a trading town near the river. Salim refers to Indar's "depression" – an assessment repeated by Indar himself as he recounts his education in Britain and his desire to "trample on the past" and to "win and win and win" in the scheme of the emergent postcolonial order.[19] Indar's narrative is suffused with instances of thwarted action and the painful consequences of the cruel optimism that led him to believe, upon his initial arrival in Britain, that his hard work and business acumen would lead to social inclusion and material success. Thus foiled, Indar aims to unmoor himself from the past and to turn his profound feelings of loss and homelessness into a virtue – "I'm a lucky man. I carry the world within me. You see, Salim, in this world beggars are the only people who can be choosers" (155). Rather than cede history to "great men," he wants to "be a man [himself]" (152). Yet we learn by the novel's end that Indar's efforts have been obstructed once again, and his view – of the postcolonial subject who can escape the traumatic wound of history and become "re-manned" – is not the one that becomes the novel's narrative focus. Instead, the main narrative centers on Salim, who clings to his outpost by the river without attachments, or even hope, and who can only bear witness to the perpetual cycles of disorder and violence until he himself is eventually swept up in these events. The apocalyptic transition of the postcolonial state to autocratic rule is mirrored in the annihilation of the postcolonial self as it succumbs to the surrounding disorder. In this pessimistic vision, a fragmentation of selfhood is signified in the affective gloss of shame, rage, and impotence.

As a revision of Conrad and Forster, then, Naipaul's fatalistic portrayal in *Bend* of the decrepitude of postcolonial nationalism, and his focus on figures of capture and dislocation rather than of resistance (in its nationalistic or Marxist forms) and self-realization, may seem a paltry intervention – and not one that substantiates the historicity of postcolonial subjects. If the earlier travel fictions of Forster and Conrad focused predominantly on the precarious subjectivities of European travelers, Naipaul, arguably, repeats the gesture of that erasure by way of a melancholic realism that portrays subjects fated to be trapped in the conditions of their history. Figuring the shift from colonial to neocolonial modes of governance, the assumption of power in the African state by the "Big Man" acts to extend the despotic tendencies of the European colonizers and the social unrest it provokes. And yet out of this view of travel as a kind of pure negation – as we see in the portrayal of forms that yield to disintegration and ruin – emerges a kind of ethics of the ruin itself. What I wish to stress is that Naipaul refuses the Hegelian gesture of ascribing a linear totality to history.[20] Instead he offers a

mode of realism without the underlying commitment to totality that typically holds realism together; his realism works decidedly through the presentation of fissures, derangements, and implosions of colonial history. This
mode of representation is figured quite directly in the title of his 2001 novel
Half a Life, which Michael Gorra describes as a "meditation on the difficulties of building a coherent self, suggesting that there is always an unrealized
and true self that remains separate from the conditions under which we
live."[21] In refusing the Hegelian gesture, Naipaul also rejects the messianic
one: The narrative, Gorra continues, becomes a "novel sawed off and
finished, half a life with no promise of any more to come."

As with *Bend*, *Enigma*'s use of a paratactic structure, combined with its
narrative oscillation between the protagonist's childhood upbringing in
Trinidad and his present-day residence in the Wiltshire countryside, links
the arrival of the self decidedly to the loss of the certitudes that shaped
colonial narratives of the English landscape. Departing from its modernist
predecessors, the novel portrays a narrator who relinquishes any anticipa-
tion of becoming oriented within narratives of place and national identity,
even though he expresses a nostalgic wish for a time when such narrative
frames were possible. Whereas Conrad and Forster expose the connection
between dreams of the self's realization and sentimental fantasies of the
other, Naipaul, by contrast, elegiacally explores the simultaneous decay of
both the bourgeois state and bourgeois interiority, and shows that the
postcolonial self, constituted as it is from processes of historical derange-
ment, surrenders the European fantasy of being fully constituted.[22] Yet
despite this recognition, *The Enigma of Arrival* suggests a redemptive function for art. Writing becomes a site, like travel, that enables capacities for
self-invention and makes possible the expression of the subject's desire. The
act of narration emerges as a locus for constructing the self in the context of
the death of the colonial order.

In many respects the central conflict depicted in Naipaul's work recalls
many of the founding themes in postcolonial studies, such as the opposition
between tropes of settlement and travel (roots and routes, or nation and
diaspora), but I wish to suggest here that it may also be helpful to frame this
conflict in terms of the poetic figure of prosopopoeia. In *Half a Life*, the
protagonist, Willie Chandran, laments that everyone around him appears to
be following a script and is diminished by their longing to conform to
idealized notions of cultural identity. He decries that his fellow inhabitants
of East Africa reside in a "half-and-half world,"[23] whose part-object status
derives from an excessive identification with an external referent, such as a
former colonizing power. Subjects perform roles and exist only as fascias:
"They became like people in a play we might have been studying at school,

with everyone a 'character', and every character reduced to a few points" (151). In *The Enigma of Arrival*, we see glimpses of prosopopoeia assuming a more generative form, in which the act of narration functions to give the subject a face, and in so doing constitutes a playful gesture in the poetics of self-creation. What I want to stress in these examples is the distinction between a representation of postcolonial travel that dramatizes the deterritorialized or nomadic subject who recognizes and works through the impossibility of being "located," and a postmodern one that fashions a "hybrid" self as a pastiche of cultural influences. The significant departure in this phase of postcolonial writing from its modernist predecessors lies not in its idealization of a hybrid subject, but in posing a model of selfhood that emerges from an impossible act of translation – that is, one that is necessarily partial – across epistemic fractures, ideological boundaries, and cultural dislocations.

Although Salman Rushdie has frequently been evoked as a prototype for postcolonial theorizations of hybridity, I want to conclude this section by suggesting a perhaps unlikely consonance between Rushdie and Naipaul. Rushdie's *The Satanic Verses* is in many respects an exemplary postcolonial travel novel, with a rhizomic narrative structure in which themes of travel surface in the airplane journeys of Gibreel Farishta and Saladin Chamcha, Ayesha's pilgrimage, Allie Cone's mountain climbing, Rosa Diamond's migration to Argentina, and Gibreel's wandering through the streets of London. Much attention has been paid to the framing queries that open the novel as Gibreel and Saladin are falling from the sky: "How does newness come into the world? How is it born? Of what fusions, translations, conjoinings is it made?"[24] These lines underscore the precarious conditions out of which this newness might achieve some personal or cultural articulation: Gibreel and Saladin wonder how it could survive and "stave off the wrecking crew, the exterminating angel, the guillotine" (8). Indeed, the novel may be read as being deeply pessimistic on the prospects for its survival. Gibreel and Saladin are both actors – again calling to mind the figure of prosopopoeia – but the dominance of the fascias that guide their performances (for Gibreel, the portrayal of sacred figures in theologicals, and for Saladin, the discourse of orientalism in British secular television) overwhelm their own capacity for narrative play and self-creation. In the end, the novel concludes with figures of unrequited love, the demise of religious pluralism, Gibreel's suicide, and Saladin's return to his childhood home after enduring the brutal racism of the London police and being treated as an exotic token by his television producers. As with Naipaul, the picture that emerges has less to do with the benign formation of hybrid cultural forms and more to do with travel as a practice that struggles against, and may frequently succumb to, any number of powerful hegemons – secular and sacred – that circulate and vie for dominance in the postcolonial state. Rushdie's centrality in the postcolonial canon may largely stem from the delicate balance he achieves in his representations of postcolonial selfhood, as his protagonists oscillate between the inventive potential of prosopopoeia – engaging in modes of play made possible by travel across cultural and epistemic boundaries – and a melancholic acknowledgment that such capacities for play and convention are frequently suppressed within histories of power and domination. In the latter instance, the fate of the part-object recalls the "guillotine" evoked in the opening pages, as it never gains a face and so remains truncated, denied the opportunity to display its full expressive potential, analogous to signifiers that remain entrapped in enclosures of denotation without the animating figures of metaphor and catachresis.

From Nomadism to Worlding: Postcolonial Travel Fictions and the Global Novel

In the foregoing sections I described two readings of the depictions of the noncentered subject of liberal humanism that appear in postcolonial travel fiction. In the examples of Forster and Conrad, the prospect of the dissolution of the subject precipitates a crisis and a move toward the recuperation of form, and in the instances of Naipaul and Rushdie, the subject refracts the trauma of splintered histories and acquires form only through the expressive practice of narration. In this final section, I wish to consider a genre of postcolonial travel fictions that regard "half a life" to be a figure not for the deterritorialized self that resists translation and emerges as a symptom for a disintegrated imperial order, but rather for a self that depends on the other for its own sense of being. I am using the term "worlding" to refer to travel fictions that extend the critique of the subject's autonomy by underscoring its relational structure, examples of which include multi-site novels that depict globalization as a maze of interconnected plots and uncanny correspondences; explicit engagements in the networked politics of global capitalism; or fictions that challenge the ontology of selfhood altogether and argue for a transformed ethical relationship to the world. These representations of travel shift their focus away from the ubiquitous thematic of self-development and toward sites of translation and exchange in a globalized world, and suggest that such an outward turn holds the potential to impart to subjects more robust capacities for empathy and critical self-perception.

Recent work in postcolonial theory, drawing, for example, on Dipesh Chakrabarty's insistence on "provincializing Europe," underscores the risks of reading world history within the frameworks of abstract and universal categories.[25] Similar concerns pervade recent debates regarding the status of world literature and caution against a reified logic of center and periphery as a model for understanding the production and circulation of texts.[26] Barbara Herrnstein-Smith notes that such models may reinscribe imperial hierarchies by "seeing in every horizon of difference new peripheries of its own centrality, new pathologies through which its own normativity may be defined and must be asserted."[27] The notion of "worlding" represents an attempt to restore our attention to the dynamic production of world-making, as a challenge to the view of global culture as a normative monolith defined by a particular version of European modernity. As Pheng Cheah has observed, a "world" is produced as a result of a fluid and active process of narration, and should not be assumed to have an *a priori* character. Worlding compels a recognition that the relation between cultural forms often proves to be incommensurate and therefore resistant to translation. Although travel practices may promote the comparison of heterogeneous spaces, a critical postcolonial travel practice approaches the cultural encounter as a problem of comparing the incomparable.[28] Worlding alludes to an ethics resonant with Goethe's view that world literature is "found in the intervals, mediations, passages, and crossing between national borders" rather than in the coalescence of a uniform global culture.[29]

In postcolonial travel writing, worlding practices may follow different modalities and assume a wide range of forms. Here I am only able to offer brief sketches of some of the strategies employed. What these texts have in common is an attempt to reframe the estrangement brought on by the self's demise – a condition, I have suggested, exemplified in Naipaul and consonant with notions of nomadism and deterritorialization – into a relational perspective that in fact de-emphasizes the drama of the self's formation. For instance, in his 2007 novel *What is the What*, Dave Eggers focalizes the narrative around the story of Valentino Achak Deng, a Dinka child who is separated from his family during the Sudanese Civil War of the 1980s. Achak manages to flee to a refugee camp in Ethiopia, and then, when Mengistu is overthrown in Ethiopia, to another refugee camp in Kenya. Achak eventually emigrates to the United States through the "Lost Boys of Sudan" resettlement program. In some respects, we might view this exercise as raising questions that recur in the postcolonial canon: Does Eggers enable the subaltern to speak, or does the novel risk an act of expropriation in its attempt to write a "fictionalized autobiography"?[30] What I wish to foreground are the questions pertaining to genre that arise in this attempt to travel across the subject's experience, and to view narration, and indeed the publication of a book, as collaborative act.

Another strategy of postcolonial worlding narratives builds upon the earlier interventions of authors such as Naipaul and Rushdie by challenging the ontology of the self's contiguous formation and alluding to new frameworks for reading the self's constitutive fragments. An illustrative example may be found in a 1996 short story collection by Hafid Bouazza, entitled "Abdullah's Feet" and set in an imaginary Moroccan village. In the titular story, the narrator's brother returns home in 1977 after having left to fight in a holy war, but only his disembodied feet remain. The more conspicuous significations of the feet may refer to the impact of violent struggle writ on the body, and to the symbolic reduction of the figure of the migrant to the signs of his mobility. Yet, as Anke Gilleir notes in her reading of the story, the narrative also remarks upon the status of synecdochic logic itself and the expansive capacities of figurative language in the postcolonial text.[31] The arrival of the feet of Abdullah gestures toward the unknowable dimensions of his experience and, more generally, to the epistemic limits of the self's modes of fashioning knowledge about the world. Provoked by the unsettling appearance of Abdullah as an insoluble remainder, Bouazza's story engages in a practice of worlding that overthrows existing ontologies and calls for modes of reading that open up new valences of the metaphor of the fragment. Additional models of worlding in recent travel narratives further contest the ontological status of the individual by asserting the connectivity of nature, culture, and capital. Examples of such narratives, to cite just a few, include Leslie Marmon Silko's *Gardens of the Dunes* (1999), Ruth Ozeki's *My Year of Meats* (1999), and Karen Tei Yamashita's *Through the Arc of the Rainforest* (1990).

These interventions raise questions regarding the very form of the global novel and the repetition of travel as a central metaphor. The multi-sited novels of David Mitchell have perhaps most self-consciously explored the ethical implications of the self's effacement as it becomes possible to envision new modes of connectivity, often enabled by technology. Throughout his corpus, Mitchell's writing reflects a formal effort to render the flows of globalization as entailing a wandering consciousness that surpasses the perceptual limits of the body.[32] As Rita Barnard notes, his novels tend to deploy "not a stable omniscient point of view [...] but a kind of multiple, mobile optic, both internal and external to its successive narrators."[33] Yet Mitchell's primary concern lies with both the emancipatory promise and the potentially troubling consequences of this fragmentation of the self into what might be described as its "quantum" particles. When Quasar, the narrator of the opening chapter of his 1999 novel *Ghostwritten*, recalls his induction into a faction led by a figure referred to as "His Serendipity," he recounts the appeal of the bonds of kinship against the isolation he felt when trapped in his more earthly natal identity: His Serendipity tells him "Today you have joined a new family. You have transcended your old family of the skin, and you have joined a new family of the spirit. This family [...] will grow, and grow, with roots in all nations."[34] The reader eventually learns that Quasar has planted a bomb on a Tokyo subway. In the concluding chapter when he reappears, the novel vividly illustrates the fallacy of the notion of transcending the self, as the promise of a disembodied (i.e. traveling) consciousness is linked to a disavowal of the ethical obligation of engaging in the material world, and shown to deny the affective vitality of the subject altogether. Alone on the subway platform, Quasar asks "What is real and what is not?" (426).

This theme, of the tension between the emergent capacities for virtual travel enabled by technology and globalization and the ethical foundations of the subject, persists as the action of *Ghostwritten* unfolds. In a chapter entitled "Mongolia," the narrator is a disembodied consciousness called a "noncorpum" that travels from body to body in pursuit of the story of its origins. The trajectory of the story uncovers a dual nature to the narrator's travels. On one hand, the narrator's wandering consciousness allows traumatic histories to gain visibility, culminating in the revelation that he was executed as a young boy, along with his master, during a purge of Buddhist monks by the occupying Communist regime. And yet elsewhere, the noncorpum exhibits a decidedly authoritarian character, such as when he boasts: "I learned how to read my hosts' memories, to erase them, and replace them. I learned how to control my hosts. Humanity was my toy" (157). The point I wish to underscore is that a theory of the ethics of worlding in the context of an historical trauma – such as the postcolonial traumas imagined vividly in the examples of Naipaul's "Big Man" or Rushdie's airplane explosion – cannot be reduced simply to figures of self-fashioning and modes of connectivity that transcend the self. In the examples I cite here, worlding instead presents itself in metaphors of travel that gesture toward empathy and to critiques of ontology that disclose new modes of connection between human and nonhuman agencies. Travel that facilitates transcendence of the self does not guarantee an ethics of worlding.

Conclusion: The Rhetoric of the Fragment

In "Culture and Finance Capital," Fredric Jameson offers up a view of capital that has become deterritorialized, a condition marked by the separation of money capital from productive spaces and into the arena of speculation and abstraction. It is not an incidental connection to make, I think, between the dematerialization of capital and Mitchell's ambivalent portrayal of the noncorpum. Jameson turns his attention to what he describes as "a logic of extreme fragmentation"[35] as capital subjects all objects to the arbitrary dynamics of exchange value, and then goes on to describe two ways of periodizing the "rhetoric of the fragment" (257). In the earlier phase, exemplified by the filmmaker Luis Buñuel, the shattering of the old orders leaves in its wake only signs of the meaningless of the modern era: "image fragments" that are "forever incomplete, markers of incomprehensible psychic catastrophe, obsessions and eruptions, the symptom in its pure form as an incomprehensible language that cannot be translated into any other" (263). In the later phase, one that could be described as postmodern and represented in the work of filmmakers Stan Brakhage and Derek Jarman, the narrative attempts to organize these fragments into some aesthetic whole, but the result is "autonomized." The contexts for the fragmented images remain lost, and their assemblage into a montage can only affirm their abstract meaninglessness. This essay has sought to oppose a rhetoric of the fragment in postcolonial travel writing to the traditional dominance of the *bildung*, and to allude to aesthetic strategies that seek to go beyond the presentation of the fragment as a *mere* symptom and toward imagining new modes of relatedness and ontologies of the global.

NOTES

1 Bruce Robbins, "The Worlding of the American Novel," in *The Cambridge History of the American Novel*, ed. Leonard Cassuto (Cambridge: Cambridge University Press, 2011), 1096–1106 (1099). See also Caren Irr, "Toward the World Novel: Genre Shifts in Twenty-First-Century Expatriate Fiction," *American Literary History*, 23, no. 3 (Fall 2011): 660–79 (662).
2 Mary Louise Pratt, *Imperial Eyes: Travel Writing and Transculturation* (London: Routledge, 1992), esp. 77–85.
3 Edward Said, *Orientalism* (New York: Vintage Books, 1979), 166.
4 Pericles Lewis, *Cambridge Introduction to Modernism* (Cambridge: Cambridge University Press, 2007), 68–69.
5 Chinua Achebe, "An Image of Africa: Racism in Conrad's *Heart of Darkness*," in *Heart of Darkness*, 3rd edn., ed. Robert Kimbrough (London: W. W. Norton, 1988), 251–61.
6 Achille Mbembe, *On the Postcolony* (Berkeley: University of California Press, 2001), 2, 1.
7 Michael Valdez Moses, *The Novel and the Globalization of Culture* (Oxford: Oxford University Press, 1995), 67.
8 See Fanon's formulation: "The Negro enslaved by his inferiority, the white man enslaved by his superiority alike behave in accordance with a neurotic orientation." Frantz Fanon, *Black Skin, White Masks* (New York: Grove Press, 1967), 60.

9 Tanika Sarkar, quoted in Ramachandra Guha, "Traveling with Tagore," in *Nationalism*, ed. Rabindranath Tagore (Gurgaon: Penguin Books India, 2009), vii–lx (l).

10 These remarks are from a 1961 essay by Borges and quoted in Guha, "Traveling with Tagore," lviii.

11 Rabindranath Tagore, Letter to CF Andrews, January 14, 1921. Cited in Ramachandra Guha, "Traveling with Tagore," xxix.

12 See Elizabeth Wilson, "The Invisible Flâneur," *New Left Review*, 191 (1992): 108–9.

13 Stuart Hall, "Cultural Identity and Diaspora," in *Identity, Community, Culture, Difference*, ed. Jonathan Rutherford (London: Lawrence and Wishart, 1990), 222–37 (225–26).

14 Sanjay Krishnan, "Formative Dislocation in V. S. Naipaul's *The Enigma of Arrival*," *MFS: Modern Fiction Studies*, 59, no. 3 (2013): 610–27 (617, 620).

15 Timothy Brennan, "The National Longing for Form," in *Nation and Narration*, ed. Homi Bhabha (London: Routledge 1990), 44–70 (63).

16 V. S. Naipaul, *A Bend in the River* (New York: Vintage, 1979), 3.

17 V. S. Naipaul, *The Enigma of Arrival* (New York: Vintage, 1987), 147.

18 Amit Chaudhuri, *Clearing a Space: Reflections on India, Literature and Culture* (Oxford: Peter Lang, 2008), 238.

19 Naipaul, *Bend in the River*, 141, 155.

20 See also Erica Johnson, "Provincializing Europe: The Postcolonial Urban Uncanny in V. S. Naipaul *A Bend in the River*," *Journal of Narrative Theory*, 40, no. 2 (2010): 209–30 (211).

21 Michael Gorra, "Postcolonial Studies," *The New York Times*, Book Review, October 28, 2001, www.nytimes.com/2001/10/28/books/postcolonial-studies .html.

22 As Sanjay Krishnan states, Naipaul shows that the postcolonial self cannot be "adequately inventoried." See "Formative Dislocation," 616.

23 V. S. Naipaul, *Half a Life* (New York: Vintage Books, 2002), 150.

24 Salman Rushdie, *The Satanic Verses* (New York: Random House, 1988), 8–9.

25 Dipesh Chakrabarty, *Provincializing Europe: Postcolonial Thought and Historical Difference* (Princeton: Princeton University Press, 2007).

26 A recent example that has been at the center of debates on world literature is Pascale Casanova, *The World Republic of Letters* (Cambridge, MA: Harvard University Press, 2007).

27 Barbara Herrnstein-Smith, *Contingencies of Value: Alternative Perspectives for Critical Theory* (Cambridge, MA: Harvard University Press, 1991), 54.

28 See Robert Young, "The Postcolonial Comparative," *PMLA*, 23, no.3 (2013): 683–89 (688).

29 Pheng Cheah, "What is a World? On World Literature as World-Making Activity," *Daedalus*, 137, no. 30 (2008): 26–38 (30).

30 Eggers invokes this self-description of the novel in an interview. www.vadfounda tion.org/interview-with-the-creators/

31 Anke Gilleir, "Figurations of Travel in Minority Literature: A Reading of Hafid Bouazza, Salman Rushdie, and Feridun Zaimoglu," *Comparative Critical Studies*, 4, no. 2 (2007): 255–67 (258–59).

32 David Mitchell has repeatedly made use of disembodied and dislocated narrators in his multi-stranded novels, including a novel composed of a hybrid of genres that begins in 1850 and ends in a post-apocalyptic future (*Cloud Atlas*, 2004), a historical novel chronicling late eighteenth-century exchange between the Dutch East India Company and a Japanese trading post (*The Thousand Autumns of Jacob de Zoet*, 2010), and a more fantastical novel that, like *Cloud Atlas*, traverses time periods and narrators and concludes in a dystopian future shaped by climate change (*The Bone Clocks*, 2014).

33 Rita Barnard, "Fictions of the Global," *Novel: A Forum on Fiction*, 42, no. 2 (2009), 207–15 (212–13).

34 David Mitchell, *Ghostwritten* (New York: Vintage, 1999), 9.

35 Fredric Jameson, "Culture and Finance Capital," *Critical Inquiry*, 24, no. 1 (1997): 246–65 (257).

15

Afterword

I

In 1498, when Christopher Columbus was making his third voyage to what in his mind was still the kingdom of the Great Khan of China, he found himself sailing in a strait south of the island that he had previously named, and we still know as, Trinidad. He knows there is land to his left and to his right. He notes extraordinarily strong currents, hears a sound of roaring water, and discovers, though he is far from shore, that the water he is sailing in is fresh. All this can mean only one thing: the estuary of a river immense enough to send fresh water miles out into the sea, which in turn means a land mass to the south large enough to create such a river. The land mass was of course the continent we now call South America, the river is the Orinoco. In his letter to the King and Queen of Spain, however, Columbus raises two possibilities to explain the fresh, roaring water: either this is a marvel such as none have never heard of, or he is approaching the site of the Garden of Eden, where the four great rivers of the world intersect.[1] Citing his detailed measurements and calculations, his deep knowledge of Ptolemaic geography, and navigation, Columbus concludes that unquestionably, he has located the Garden of Eden, which he is delighted to place in their majesties' possession. A year or so later the Florentine navigator Amerigo Vespucci would confirm the other hypothesis, declaring Columbus's discovery a *terra nova*, and that is how, through the intervention of the German mapmaker Martin Waldseemuller, the continents came to be known as the Americas and not the Colombias.[2]

Nothing was more inconvenient to the Spanish Crown or more embarrassing to Columbus himself than the prospect that a continental land mass, vast enough to produce a river that could propel fresh water miles into the ocean, lay between Europe and Asia. Economically, the Spanish crown was interested in trade routes, not land masses; it wanted China to be nearer, not farther. The discovery meant that Columbus's navigational calculations,

Ptolemaic geography, and Christian cosmogony were all wrong. It set in motion an unsought revolution in knowledge and belief.

Ironically, Columbus arrives at the correct hypothesis, and fails to choose it. He is doing what people do as they live change. Humans have a horror of semantic vacuums. Familiar paradigms orchestrate desires, interests, relations that hold the world together at the level of human interaction, imagination, and belief. Who would not prefer the earthly paradise whose very details we know so well (though none of us has seen it) over something unimagined and unimaginable? It takes a leap of faith, courage, and ambition to opt, as Vespucci did, for the unfamiliar, unwelcome, unlovable possibility that changes everything. Such leaps do get taken, however. Just after Columbus and Vespucci came another such pair, Nicolaus Copernicus and Galileo Galilei.

Columbus and Vespucci were inaugurating one of the most consequential changes in human and planetary history, the development of contact between Europe and the Americas, and with it the unfolding of global capitalism. Postcolonialism arises at a later point in the history of that order, following the wave of decolonizations in Africa, Asia, and Oceania in the decades after World War II. This was another moment of radical change, when vast orderings of familiarity, relations of power, webs of desire, interest, and belief, visions of plenitude as gorgeous as paradise were faced with earthshaking alternative analyses of the world. For those who did not live the change it can be hard to imagine how little the workings of empire, colonialism, and coloniality were thought about or understood as late as the 1970s, or how thoroughly, as Edward Said put it, "the literary-cultural establishment" had "declared the serious study of imperialism and culture off limits."[3] As one who did live that change, I can perhaps best illustrate it with an anecdote.

In 1977, shortly after I arrived at Stanford University as an assistant professor of Comparative Literature, I was invited to give a talk about my research. I presented a paper focused on Gide's novel *L'Immoraliste* (*The Immoralist*, 1902) and Albert Camus's short story collection *L'Exil et le royaume* (*Exile and the Kingdom*, 1957). Using detailed close readings, I discussed these works as explorations of Franco-North African colonial relations. I analyzed Camus's story "La femme adultère" ("The Adulterous Woman") as an attempt to rewrite and partially decolonize Gide's text, while retaining a *parti-pris* with Europe and with whiteness.[4] The reception of the talk surprised me. The colleagues who studied English and European literatures understood what I was saying but simply did not believe it. It was to them just not plausible that these French texts were in any way "about" colonialism or Algeria. They were existential parables about the homelessness of modern man; they could not be illuminated in any way by facts about French imperialism in North Africa. The real or "historical" Africa had no relevance at all to the interpretation of either text; misled perhaps by my interest in language, I had simply failed to grasp the philosophical nature of the texts. That was the pre-postcolonial moment. The omnipresence of empire and coloniality in the European literary canon was as invisible, unthinkable, and inconvenient as the South American continent was to Columbus. The writings of C. L. R. James, Frantz Fanon, Aimé Césaire, Albert Memmi, Chinua Achebe, Samir Amin, and Kwame Nkrumah were out there, but still beyond the horizons of mainstream literary scholarship.[5]

Things were about to change. A book called Orientalism was in press at the very moment I was giving my talk. Coincidentally, it had been written at Stanford, during Said's year as a fellow at the Center for Advanced Study in the Behavioral Sciences (1975–76). In Orientalism, Said, like Vespucci, insisted on the existence of a vast, unwelcome terra nova: the complicity of European systems of knowledge and representation with its imperial and colonial enterprises. Today few readers would find it implausible to read The Immoralist and Exile and the Kingdom as "about" colonialism. In fact, it is difficult now to read them any other way. It is now normative to see the West as fundamentally constituted by its imperial undertakings as unthinkable apart from them. Like Columbus, Vespucci, and their contemporaries, we have lived a knowledge revolution, involving unfolding historical processes, dramatic and intense struggles over truth and meaning, and earthshaking discoveries.

Since the 1990s, postcolonial inquiry has been an important actor in the decolonization of knowledge inaugurated by the political decolonization struggles of the 1940s, 50s, and 60s. It is both product and agent of the "huge and remarkable adjustment in perspective and understanding"[6] those struggles set in motion. Like all knowledge revolutions, this one has put human minds and imaginations to work at their most ambitious and dynamic pitch. We have seen understandings begin crudely and get more refined, increase in depth, sophistication, and scope. Things written at the beginning come to look heavy handed or oversimplified (as Orientalism inevitably did). People get things wrong and are corrected. Concepts appear, give what they have to give, then cede to others.

It has been a tremendous achievement to come to know what we now know about how empire and colonialism work, how they generate knowledge, orchestrate desires, execute power, and produce subjects, aesthetics, tastes, plenitudes; to know how they enable the enchantment of the world, the projection onto others of beloved things Europe was destroying in itself,

and despised things Europe could not confront in itself; to discover the deep
moral unrest writhing at the heart of it all and surfacing from time to time in
horrible forms. It is genuinely world-changing to discover how these processes continue to mutate and unfold in empire's afterlives.

The process is, of course, not complete; nor will it ever be. The decolonization of knowledge, in my view, should not and cannot be seen as a telos, that
is, a project with a fixed outcome that we will recognize when we get there. It
is common in postcolonial criticism to judge texts according to degrees of
complicity with colonial paradigms, implying an ideal of noncomplicity that
writers approach to greater or lesser degrees. While some, including many
writers in this volume, celebrate writers who "embrace new ways of telling"
(Justin Edwards, this volume [Chapter 2]),[7] others argue that there is "no
outside" to the discourses of empire (Ali Behdad, cited by Edwards, 28),
melancholically imagining a longed-for outside that does not exist. From the
beginning, critics of the concept of the postcolonial have noted that it leaves
the Eurocolonial narrative at the center of modern history. Theorizing
around binaries like colonizer/colonized, self/other leaves the epistemological
center of gravity with the colonizer, even when the project is decolonization.[8]
Many of the texts studied in this volume seek to supersede that episteme.

In *The Critique of Postcolonial Reason*, Gayatri Chakravorty Spivak
observes that eurocentrism, ethnocentrism, and colonialist thinking cannot
simply be set aside; they must be worked through, even as they persist
around us in continuously mutating forms.[9] I regard the work of decolonization as this long and continuous process of working through, a collective
task that is ongoing, arduous, and crucial to the future of humankind. With
respect to this task, "decolonization" and "postcolonial" operate as concepts, in the sense developed by Australian philosopher Elizabeth Grosz. In
Becoming Undone: Darwinian Reflections of Life, Politics, and Art (2011),
Grosz follows up on Gilles Deleuze and Félix Guattari's claim that "all
concepts are connected to problems without which they would have no
meaning, and which can themselves only be understood as their solution
emerges."[10] Concepts, Grosz elaborates, are not solutions to problems, they
are enablers of change, "transforming the givenness of chaos, the pressing
problem, into various forms of order, into possibilities for being otherwise"
(78). They are a means by which "the living add ideality to the world [. . .]
practices we perform, not on things but on events [. . .] to give them consist-
ency, coherence, boundaries, purpose, use" (78). "Decolonization" and
"postcolonialism" do not in any way "solve" the unfolding aftermaths of
Euroimperialism, but they enable the working through. They enable us, in
Grosz's words, "to surround ourselves with possibilities for being otherwise
that the direct impact of events on us does not" (78). Concepts, Grosz

emphasizes, are intangible but they are *not reducible to discourse*. They are brought into existence through bodies and events (78–79). This approach regards postcolonial inquiry as embodied action, texts as events, oriented toward the creation of a future that is unknown and unknowable to us. We produce concepts when we need to "address the forces of the present and to transform them into new and different forces that act in the future" (80). We leave them behind when their power to do this is exhausted.

II

The object of Anglophone postcolonial inquiry, scholarly or aesthetic, has primarily been European colonialism and its aftermaths in the nineteenth and twentieth centuries in Europe, Africa, and Asia. This object was constituted through a series of exclusions that have enabled its conversations, but limited their scope. Four of these exclusions in particular stand out. First, postcolonial inquiry excluded from its purview the so-called first wave of European imperial expansion, that is, the Spanish, Portuguese, British, and French colonial enterprises carried out in the fifteenth through eighteenth centuries, all over the planet, but most conspicuously in the Americas. Postcolonial inquiry began with the "second" wave of European incursions, which for some was inaugurated by Napoleon in 1800 and for others by the scramble for Africa in the 1880s, and ended with post-World War II independences.[11]

Second, postcolonial inquiry constructed a bypass around noncolonial forms of empire, such as the militarized control exercised by the United States under the Monroe Doctrine (1823) and the Platt Amendment (1901), or the economic domination France and Britain exercised over Spanish America after it became independent from Spain. This latter form came to be called neocolonialism, meaning the continuing exercise of imperial power in economic form after colonies become politically independent.[12] The separation is artificial, for colonial and noncolonial forms of empire often work hand in hand. In the nineteenth century, Britain and France were colonizing powers in Africa and Asia, and equally aggressive neocolonizers in Latin America. Indeed, they helped Spanish Americans gain independence from Spain in order to gain access to Latin American markets and resources themselves. Joseph Conrad's *Heart of Darkness* (1899), a postcolonial sacred text, ought to be read alongside his other great novel *Nostromo* (1904), which in equal depth explores British neocolonialism in South America. And both should be read alongside Philippine novelist José Rizal's penetrating deconstruction of rising nationalism and waning Spanish colonialism in the Philippines in *Noli me tangere* (1887) and *El Filibusterismo*

(1891).[13] Before the term "postcolonial" established itself, imperialism was the core concept.[14] In his 1992 volume *Culture and Imperialism*, Said wrote: "The real potential of post-colonial liberation is the liberation of all mankind from imperialism" and the "reconceiving of human experience in non-imperialist terms."[15]

Third, as is already apparent, postcolonial studies has focused its inquiry on Europe, Africa, and Asia – the Afroeurasian land mass – to the exclusion of Oceania and especially the Americas. This certainly avoids some inconvenient complications. Chronologically, Spanish America became postcolonial in the 1820s, and the United States in 1776. How does the term apply to them (cf. Tim Youngs, this volume [Chapter 8])? For a long time, neither postcolonial scholars nor Americanists showed much interest in exploring that question. The geographical integrity and historical interconnectedness of the Afroeurasian land mass bounded the field. Interesting parallels were lost in the process. For instance, several authors in this volume identify narratives of return as a subgenre of postcolonial writing (Srilata Ravi [Chapter 5], Christopher Keirstead [Chapter 10], Charles Forsdick [Chapter 7]). These are narratives in which a colonial or ex-colonial subject returns to her or his homeland after a long period living away in the metropole, rediscovering their place of origin in new, usually disturbing, ways. Nineteenth- and early twentieth-century Spanish American literature is also peppered with such narratives of return, and they function in the same postcolonial ways, "working through the trauma of colonialism" (Clarke 66), and searching for viable models of fractured selfhood (cf. Levin, Edwards).[16] The two novels of Rizal mentioned above are also textbook examples of such narratives of colonial return. The postcolonial literary landscape is punctuated by decolonizing rewrites of metropolitan works – V. S. Naipaul rewriting Conrad (cf. Levin), J. M. Coetzee rewriting Defoe, Césaire rewriting Shakespeare, and so on. This manoeuver characterized Latin America's postcolonial moment a century before the post-World War II moment. Examples include a gaucho version of *Faust* written in Argentina in the mid-1800s, and several Mexican take-offs on *Don Quijote*.[17]

Fourth and finally, postcolonialism's elision of the Americas goes hand in hand with an apparent reluctance to engage with the category of the indigenous. Postcolonial scholarship rarely embraces indigenous agency and intellectual authority as forces in the work of decolonizing knowledge and subjectivity.[18] Indeed, one could argue that postcolonialism's foundational concept of hybridity implicitly (and sometimes explicitly) disavows indigeneity as a source of insight on the colonial and ex-colonial condition, or even as a reality. Several authors here (Clarke [Chapter 4], Youngs [Chapter 8],

Keirstead [Chapter 10]) correct this absence. Indigenous scholars experience the exclusion as an imperial gesture in its own right, keeping indigenous ways of knowing in a place of inferior otherness.

Why would postcolonial thought bypass indigeneity as a central dimension of colonialism and an agent of decolonization? Why would it not empower indigenous interlocutors? Perhaps one answer lies in the way postcolonialism mapped out its decolonizing task. Postcolonialism's foundational intervention consisted in superseding binary oppositions of colonist/native, refusing to regard these parties as inhabiting separate and opposing realities. The postcolonial project sought to grasp the colonial condition as interaction, collusion, entanglement, mediation, and interpenetration of subjects positioned in multiple, shifting ways with respect to the colonizer/colonized divide. Hybridity, impurity, ambiguity, fluidity, and ambivalence are the ingredients of colonial relations and experiences that postcolonial thought explores. They are not side effects; they are the thing itself; they are the way it unfolds. Without this approach, colonialism and its afterlives cannot be understood at all. An important goal was to mitigate the militant stance of anticolonial thought, which condemned colonialism unequivocally and viewed the colonized as its victims.

The decolonizing strategy of indigenous thought is different. Indigeneity pivots on a before and after construct and a narrative of unsolicited encounter and dispossession. It claims epistemic authority based on resistance, attachment to land, and continuity with a precolonial history that continues to unfold in the present despite the colonizer's aggression.[19] Indigenous subjectivity grounds itself in place, where sovereignty and the sacred both dwell. Such "placedness," in theorist Sandy Grande's sense of the term, is central to indigenous being, a principle exemplified by the aboriginal "return to country" journeys discussed here by Clarke [Chapter 4] in relation to Australia and Keirstead [Chapter 10] in relation to the United States.[20] As a force, indigeneity decolonizes by retaining and bringing forward ways of being, knowing, and doing that are alternative to the dominating ways of the colonizers and correct their weaknesses and errors. From this perspective, Grande argues, "the concepts of *mestizaje*, hybridity, and border subjectivity dear to both critical pedagogy and postcolonial studies cannot be models for indigenous subjectivity" (117). From the point of view of indigeneity, she says, the idea of *mestizaje* is not emancipatory or revolutionary because its imagined subject is "deplaced," ungrounded. (117). Moreover, the term presupposes the unsolicited colonial encounter rather than addressing it. The postcolonial optic, in other words, comes into play only after colonialism's foundational dispossession has occurred, when indigenous people have already been wiped out or disempowered. It thus cannot offer a model for indigenous being. From an indigenous perspective, she argues, "the seemingly liberatory constructs of fluidity, mobility, and transgression are perceived not only as the language of critical subjectivity but also as part of the fundamental lexicon of Western imperialism" (117). This does not mean that indigenous being does not recognize, and inhabit, the workings of hybridity, entanglement, ambivalence, and the rest. Rather, indigenous emancipatory projects do not begin there, and thus remain invisible or illegible to the postcolonial paradigm.

The concept of indigeneity, I have suggested, is founded in unsolicited encounter. Its logic is most powerful in places where there was no prior history of contact before colonization, where Europeans arrived out of the blue and neither side knew of each other's existence. This was the case in land masses separated from Afroeurasia, like Oceania, and North and South America. Territories within the Afroeurasian landmass had long and varied histories of contact and interaction before the Euroimperial enterprise took shape.[21] The concept of indigeneity has been less generative in this landscape,[22] yet that too may change, as the Western equation of mobility with freedom continues to fade.

III

It was the study of empire that made travel and travel writing objects of academic inquiry. Before that, they were of minor interest. You can't create empires and colonies without large-scale circuits of travel, transport, and reportage. On top of those necessities, imperial expansion generates all kinds of creative energies, curiosities, ambitions, and desires. It sets bodies and imaginations in motion. In Europe after the invention of the printing press, European imperial expansion created travel writing as an industry that still flourishes today – and that, of course, is the subject of this book.

The study of travel writing also became an industry, from the 1990s on; an academic industry that generated an astonishing volume (I think again of Columbus by the roaring waters of the Orinoco) of books, articles, journals, theses and dissertations, conferences, anthologies, encyclopedias, and dictionaries. The study of travel writing became a favored instrument for studying empire and for debating how to study empire, and rightly so. As several authors observe here (Clarke [Chapter 4], Forsdick [Chapter 7], Edwards [Chapter 2], Youngs [Chapter 8]), for all the richness of this outpouring of scholarship across several generations of researchers, it retained a Eurocentric, and even Anglocentric focus, rarely attending to the travels and travel writings of people from other parts of the world. Attempts to break down the exclusion went unheeded. In the main, scholarship on travel writing stayed stuck looking over the shoulders of traveling Europeans, thereby reproducing the imperial relations that were under examination. Despite all that was achieved, I believe we must acknowledge this as a failure of imagination, intellectual ambition, and scholarship. After the initial insight that travel and travel writing were central instruments for constructing imperial knowledge, the project could easily have moved on to the next set of questions: How was Europe depicted by its others? What other kinds of travel and travel writing exist and have existed? How were imperial travelers and their writings received and written over by those they depicted? How do people take over imperial strategies of representation and rework them for their own purposes?[23] Instead, as Edwards observes here, the richness and analytical ease of the Euroimperial optic had the undesirable effect of discouraging (or perhaps delaying) the move to other questions, languages, and corpuses capable as Clarke puts it (quoting Aedín Ní Loingsigh) of "untying travel writing from its Western moorings" (14). Contemporary writing and scholarship, like that represented here, are gradually taking on that work, and the field has moved beyond the European and North American academy.

The essays gathered here, all written for this volume, raise intriguing questions: What makes a travel text postcolonial? What is it to decolonize travel writing? Is that an oxymoron: that is, is travel writing irremediably colonial? What aesthetic projects exemplify the post-colonial moment in travel writing? Is the term postcolonial relevant to them? What about its commercial forms? Is travel writing still a valuable instrument for illuminating the world? Another set of questions has to do with travel itself. What is "travel" in the postcolonial frame? What is it to decolonize travel? What kinds of mobility has capitalist globalization brought into play? Is the term postcolonial relevant to them? Are they travel? Who will record these forms of movement, and how? Do the foundational categories of going and staying, home and away, still work? How can we supersede (decolonize) that equation of mobility and freedom that is built into the Western imagination, and into the concept of travel? Finally, we are called upon to ask what will or does the post-postcolonial look like?

About half the essays here focus on the work, to use Clarke's phrase, of exploring the nature of the "postcolonial condition" (14), using a variety of primary materials. Anna Johnston (Chapter 12) and Eva-Marie Kröller (Chapter 6) examine the construction of national identities in British ex-colonies (Australia and Canada), in one case through national magazines with a strong internal travel theme, in the other, in diplomatic diaries. Jill Didur (Chapter 3) reads ecological travel writing as a decolonizing intervention. Others (Ravi [Chapter 5], Clarke [Chapter 4], Keirstead [Chapter 10],

Forsdick [Chapter 7], Sen [Chapter 9]) examine texts that "work through the trauma of colonialism" (Clarke 66) – pilgrimages to sites of atrocity, diasporic returns to homes known and unknown, reverse migrations to ancestral lands, south to north journeys of self-discovery, and spiritual tourism. In many of these cases, authors find, a decolonizing intervention combines with melancholic nostalgia. Forsdick (Chapter 7) and Levin (Chapter 14) examine fictional corpuses where authors writing from ex-colonies directly intervene in or operate upon colonial configurations, working "across epistemic fractures, ideological boundaries, and cultural dislocation" (Levin 281). Levin records the trajectory from the Anglophone colonial (Conrad, Forster) canon to the postcolonial (Naipaul, Rushdie); Forsdick fruitfully complicates that chronology by finding in the francophone archive a two-hundred-year history of "reverse gaze" writing from the Francophone Caribbean, Vietnam, and Africa toward Europe. Experiments in genre and form appear constantly in these essays. Even more often the postcolonial intervention involves quests to express new forms of subjectivity and epistemic authority. In both nonfiction and fiction, postcolonial travel writers decolonize the self-consistent, authoritative, (white and male) voice of the travel writing convention. They speak from the multiplicitous, fractured, mobile subjectivities of transnational subjects, homeless emigres, disoriented returnees. Mastery and control cease to drive the text. As Didur brilliantly shows, Arundhati Roy deploys ecological understanding as a decolonizing instrument that requires the human subject to cede mastery and invent a different kind of presence.

At other points, these essays press the limits of the field's core concepts. Neoliberal globalization has fostered on a mass scale forms of mobility that break the frame of both travel and the postcolonial: economic migrancy, human trafficking, coerced displacement, the mass flight of refugees and asylum seekers, the coming waves of climate refugees. These forms of displacement couple with related forms of immobilization and entrapment, creating dramas of separation, abandonment, and unfreedom. These geographies of cruelty and coercion, examined for example by Clarke (Chapter 4), Shemak (Chapter 13), and Youngs (Chapter 8), reconfigure everything as soon as they are brought into the frame. Should the transatlantic Middle Passage, the Navajo Long Walk, or the Cherokee Trail of Tears be thought of as travel? Surely not, but is this a conceptual, a political, or a moral question? What about the northward migration of millions of Mexicans after the North American Free Trade Agreement? The cruel and deadly exodus across the Mediterranean that the world has been watching for the last two years? Yet these forms of mobility also generate corpuses of stories and texts. Slave narratives are an early example (Youngs).[24] Asylum seekers and refugees, Shemak observes, are required to produce narratives of fear and suffering that meet legal criteria for admission to receiving states. "Inflation of atrocity" is a standard device of such narratives (Shemak) – one's life is at stake. In recent years, undocumented youth in the United States have developed a form of videotaped personal narrative designed to gain support for their legalization. The Diocese of San Juan de los Lagos in Mexico distributes a *Devocionario del Migrante*, a devotional manual for migrants made up of prayers customized for each moment of the journey – boarding the bus, crossing the desert, under detention, and so on. Its lexicon of travel involves not adventure, discovery, or freedom, but *destierro, amargura, lejania, necesidad, peligro* ("exile, bitterness, distance, necessity, danger"). Involuntary migration generates a literature where the equation of mobility and freedom breaks down.[25] Before Skype, the Mixtecos of southern Mexico sustained communal governance by means of videotapes carried from migrant communities in California to home communities in Oaxaca. How do these vast, strategically devised corpuses impact the concept of travel writing? Does travel writing become a subcategory of a larger "literature of mobility" (Forsdick 127) in which freedom, coercion, self-sacrifice, self-preservation, and self-realization entangle in myriad ways? Or is that term just a place holder until post-postcolonial concepts appear?

The concept of travel begins to dissolve in a different way in the cyberspace examined here by Brian Creech (Chapter 11). The Internet, as Creech demonstrates, has transformed travel. In the tourist industry, online reviewing has the power to make the material world adjust to consumer desires at lightning speed. Blogs, Creech observes, offer uncensored, noninstitutional spaces of expression free from commercial constraints. New lexicons have appeared: "content producers" generate "distant witnessing" (Creech 213) The volume, conventions, and limitations of Internet representation result in "geographical flattening" and "banal globalism" (212). The phenomenon of cyberspace calls on us to figure out not just what the analytical categories should be, but what the questions are.

Social media change the experience of being "away" by conserving uninterrupted verbal and visual contact with those at home. More importantly, the uninterrupted contact – visual and verbal messages, sent through a panoply of channels and forms – remains the same whether one is at home or away. The photo of a lunch is the same sent from down the street, the next room, or across an ocean. The conventions of cyber contact seem to be indifferent to geographical distance. Social media level the home/away dichotomy that structures the concept of travel. They do not, however, level the experience of travel. Corporeal distance (at least for now) remains a real thing.

IV

Travel writing continues to thrive in the contemporary world, as the studies in this book richly demonstrate. In its more strictly commercial forms, it continues to traffic in exoticism and the experience of first world travelers constructed for first world readers. As I wrote this afterword, for example, the *New York Times Book Review* published its 2016 survey of travel books, just in time for holiday gift purchases. All ten books reviewed conformed to that paradigm. Their titles speak of "hidden wonders," "improbable" "adventures," "the world's most unusual corners."[26] This does not mean they are unworthy or trivial books. With imagination and art, this literature carries out the often loving work of re-enchanting the world for those who long after it. The lines of enchantment still run along lines of geopolitical power and imperial history, and perhaps they always will in this market-place. As a serious literary endeavor, travel writing flourishes today as an often urgent search for emergent possibilities of being in the contemporary world. It remains an enabling instrument for interrogating the present through lived, bodily experience, for revealing what must be demanded of life and the world, as well as what can be found there. The essays in this book richly demonstrate the continuing vitality of this work. If the postcolonial dissolves into the ecological, as the new concept of the Anthropocene suggests, travel literature will remain a vehicle for deep reflection on modes of being. As always, the writers will be out in front of us, leading with curiosity and courage. They are our companions, and we are theirs.

NOTES

1 For Columbus's letter see: Christopher Columbus, "Narrative of the Third Voyage of Christopher Columbus to the Indies, in which He Discovered the Mainland, dispatched to the Sovereigns from the Island of Hispaniola," in *The Four Voyages of Christopher Columbus*, ed. and trans. J. M. Cohen (Harmondsworth: Penguin, 1969), 206–26.

2 The *terra nova* term appears in Vespucci's widely read letters whose sensationalist accounts of the land's exotic wonders (notably its lascivious women) eclipsed Columbus's less imaginative prose. Martin Waldseemuller, having read Vespucci's letters, put his name on his famous *mappa mundi* of 1507, though he was later said to have repented of his choice.

3 Edward Said, "Introduction," *Culture and Imperialism* (New York: Vintage, 1994).

4 Mary Louise Pratt, "Un mapa ideológico: Gide, Camus y Argelia," *Escritura*, 7 (1979): 77–92.

5 One plausible starting point for postcolonial criticism is Chinua Achebe's move to the University of Massachusetts in 1972, an encounter that produced his groundbreaking essay on Conrad: "An Image of Africa: Racism in Conrad's Heart of

Darkness," in *Hope and Impediments: Selected Essays* (New York: Knopf, 1988), 1–20. This essay – an amended version of a lecture Achebe gave at the University of Massachusetts in February 1975 – set in motion the first serious dialogue between first world and third world literary critics.

6 Edward Said, *Orientalism* (London: Penguin, [1978] 1992), 243.

7 Further references to *Companion* chapters are given in text.

8 This point was made early on in two influential essays that appeared in a special issue of *Social Text* (31/32, 1992) dedicated to Third World and Postcolonial Issues: see Anne McClintock, "The Angel of History: Pitfalls of the Term 'Postcolonialism,'" *Social Text*, 31/32 (1992): 84–98; and Ella Shohat, "Notes on the 'Post-Colonial'" *Social Text*, 31/32 (1992): 99–113.

9 Gayatri Spivak, *A Critique of Postcolonial Reason: Toward a History of the Vanishing Present* (Cambridge: Harvard University Press, 1999), 110.

10 Gilles Deleuze and Félix Guattari, *What Is Philosophy?* (New York: Columbia University Press, 1994), cited in Elizabeth Grosz, *Becoming Undone: Darwinian Reflections on Life, Politics, and Art* (Durham: Duke University Press, 2011), 78.

11 The field of transatlantic studies has emerged to fill this gap.

12 Kwame Nkrumah, *Neocolonialism: The Last Stage of Imperialism* (London: T. Nelson, 1965).

13 Rizal was a Filipino writer and statesman who wrote in Spanish. The novels were banned by Spanish authorities and unable to circulate widely until after Philippine independence in 1898. Rizal was executed by the Spanish colonial government in 1896 for fomenting rebellion.

14 For example, Bill Ashcroft, Gareth Griffith, and Helen Tiffin, *The Empire Writes Back: Theory and Practice in Post-Colonial Literatures* (London: Routledge, 1989); David Spurr, *The Rhetoric of Empire: Colonial Discourse in Journalism, Travel Writing, and Imperial Administration* (Durham: Duke University Press, 1993); Said, *Culture and Imperialism*; and Pratt *Imperial Eyes: Travel Writing and Transculturation* (London: Routledge, [1992] 2008).

15 Said, *Culture and Imperialism*, 274, 276.

16 See for example: Juana Manuela Gorriti, "Si haces mal no esperes bien" (Peru 1861), Gertrudis Gómez de Avellaneda, "La vuelta a la patria" (Cuba, 1871), Maria Wiesse, "El forastero" (Peru 1926) The returnee story is everywhere in contemporary Latin American literature.

17 See for example: Estanislao del Campos, *Fausto* (1866), José Joaquín Fernández de Lizardi, *La quijotita y su prima* (1818) and *Don Catrín de la fachenda* (1819).

18 This claim can be confirmed by examining the table of contents of the dozens of anthologies of postcolonial scholarship.

19 Anishinaabe critic Gerald Vizenor introduced the concept of *survivance* to capture this indigenous mode of being. Survivance is "an active sense of presence," sustained by stories that "renounce domination, tragedy and victimry": Gerald Vizenor, *Manifest Manners: Narratives on Post-Indian Survivance* (Lincoln: University of Nebraska Press, 1999), vii.

20 Sandy Grande, *Red Pedagogy: Native American Social and Political Thought* (Lanham: Rowen and Littlefield, 2004), 117.

21 This interconnectedness is the object of study of the emerging field of interimperial studies. See Laura Doyle, "Inter-Imperiality: Dialectics in a Postcolonial World History," *Interventions*, 16, no. 2 (2014): 159–96.

22 See Marisol de la Cadena and Orrin Starn, eds., *Indigenous Experience Today.* Wenner Grenn International Symposium Series (Berg: New York, 2007).
23 *Imperial Eyes* made an initial attempt to set such questions in motion by introducing the dynamics of transculturation, especially in the part of the book on the Americas. However, that side of the project did not galvanize other scholars as I hoped it would.
24 Captivity and shipwreck narratives are others, not explored here. For comments on their resurgence in contemporary migration stories see Mary Louise Pratt, "Why the Virgin of Zapopan went to Los Angeles," in *Images of Power: Iconography, Culture and State in Latin America*, ed. Jens Andermann and William Rowe (New York: Berghahn Books, 2005), 271–90.
25 Mary Louise Pratt, "Mobility and the Politics of Belonging: Indigenous Experiments in Creative Citizenship," in *Resistant Strategies*, ed. Diana Taylor (Durham: Duke University Press, forthcoming).
26 Liesl Schillinger, "Itineraries Await in the Season's Best Travel Books," *New York Times Book Review*, 29 Nov. 2016, 18–19.

FURTHER READING

The following materials and guides to further reading include texts that address the heritage of travel writing of specific interest to students, teachers, and researchers in colonial and postcolonial studies.

Anthologies

While there are as yet no anthologies devoted to postcolonial travel writing in English *per se*, readers will find examples of postcolonial travel writing in numerous sources. It is often remarked that travel writing is enjoying a golden period of publishing, and this is reflected in the growth and popularity of anthology series such as *Best American Travel Writing* (published annually since 2000); *Best Women's Travel Writing: True Stories from Around the World* (ten volumes published since 2005), *Best Travel Writing* (eleven volumes since 2004), and *Granta*, the literary magazine that regularly publishes special issues on travel.

Adams, Percy, ed. *Travel Literature through the Ages: An Anthology*. New York: Garland, 1988.

Agosín, Marjorie and Julie H. Leveson, eds. *Magical Sites: Women Travelers in 19th Century Latin America*. Buffalo: White Pine Press, 1999.

Bassett, Jan, ed. *Great Southern Landings: An Anthology of Antipodean Travel*. Melbourne: Oxford University Press, 1995.

Bracewell, Wendy, ed. *Orientations: An Anthology of East European Travel Writing, ca. 1550–2000*. Budapest: Central European University Press, 2009.

Foster, Shirley and Sara Mills, eds. *An Anthology of Women's Travel Writing*. Manchester: Manchester University Press, 2002.

Ghose, Indira, ed. *Memsahibs Abroad: Writings by Women Travellers in Nineteenth Century India*. Dehli: Oxford University Press, 1998

Griffin, Farah J. and Cheryl J. Fish, eds. *A Stranger in the Village: Two Centuries of African-American Travel Writing*. Boston: Beacon Press, 1998.

Hahner, June E., ed. *Women through Women's Eyes: Latin American Women in Nineteenth-Century Travel Accounts*. Wilmington: Scholarly Resources, 1998.

Hooper, Glenn, ed. *The Tourist's Gaze: Travellers to Ireland 1800–2000*. Cork: Cork University Press, 2001.

Khair, Tabish, Martin Leer, Justin D. Edwards, and Hanna Ziadeh, eds. *Other Routes: 1500 Years of African and Asian Travel Writing*. Oxford: Signal, 2006.

Kitson, Peter J, et al., eds. *Nineteenth-Century Travels, Explorations and Empires. Writings from the Era of Imperial Consolidation 1835–1910.* 8 vols. London: Pickering and Chatto, 2003–4.

Lamb, Jonathon, Vanessa Smith, and Nicholas Thomas, eds. *Exploration and Exchange: A South Seas Anthology, 1680–1990.* Chicago: University of Chicago Press, 2001.

Mancall, Peter C., ed. *Travel Narratives from the Age of Discovery: An Anthology.* Oxford: Oxford University Press, 2006.

Nash, Geoffrey, ed. *Travellers to the Middle East from Burckhardt to Thesiger: An Anthology.* London: Anthem, 2009.

Pettinger, Alasdair, ed. *Always Elsewhere: Travels of the Black Atlantic.* London: Cassell, 1998.

Robinson, Jan, ed. *Unsuitable for Ladies: An Anthology of Women Travellers.* Oxford: Oxford University Press, 1995.

Critical Studies Travel Writing: General

Andras, Carmen, ed. *New Directions in Travel Writing and Travel Studies.* Aachen: Shaker Verlag, 2010. Print.

Betteridge, Thomas, ed. *Borders and Travellers in Early Modern Europe.* Aldershot: Ashgate, 2007.

Blanton, Casey. *Travel Writing: The Self and the World.* New York: Routledge, 2002.

Bohls, Elizabeth A. *Women Travel Writers and the Language of Aesthetics, 1716–1818.* Cambridge: Cambridge University Press, 1995.

Burton, Stacy. *Travel Narrative and the Ends of Modernity.* New York: Cambridge University Press, 2014.

Cabañas, Miguel A, Jeanne Dubino, Veronica Salles-Reese, and Gary Totten, eds. *Politics, Identity, and Mobility in Travel Writing.* New York: Routledge, 2015.

Chard, Chloe. *Pleasure and Guilt on the Grand Tour: Travel Writing and Imaginative Geography, 1600–1830.* Manchester: Manchester University Press, 1999.

Cronin, Michael. *Across the Lines: Travel, Language, Translation.* Cork: Cork University Press, 2000.

de Botton, Alain. *The Art of Travel.* London: Hamish Hamilton, 2002.

Duncan, James and Derek Gregory, eds. *Writes of Passage: Reading Travel Writing.* London: Routledge, 1999.

Elsner, Jaś and Joan-Pau Rubiés, eds. *Voyages and Visions: Towards a Cultural History of Travel.* London: Reaktion Books, 1999.

Farley, David G. *Modernist Travel Writing: Intellectuals Abroad.* Columbia: University of Missouri Press, 2010.

Hooper, Glenn and Tim. Youngs, eds. *Perspectives on Travel Writing.* Aldershot: Ashgate, 2004.

Hulme, Peter and Tim Youngs, eds. *The Cambridge Companion to Travel Writing.* Cambridge: Cambridge University Press, 2002.

Kowalewski, Michael, ed. *Temperamental Journeys: Essays on the Modern Literature of Travel.* Athens: University Georgia Press, 1992.

Moroz, Grzegorz and Jolanta Sztachelska, eds. *Metamorphoses of Travel Writing: Across Theories, Genres, Centuries and Literary Traditions.* Newcastle upon Tyne: Cambridge Scholars, 2010.

Robertson, George, Melinda Mash, Lisa Tickner, John Bird, Barry Curtis, and Tim Putnam, eds. *Travellers' Tales: Narratives of Home and Displacement.* London: Routledge, 1994.

Salzani, Carlo and Steven Tötösy de Zepetnek. "Bibliography for Work in Travel Studies," *CLCWeb: Comparative Literature and Culture,* 12 Jan 2016, http://docs.lib.purdue.edu/clcweblibrary/travelstudiesbibliography.

Speake, Jennifer, ed. *Literature of Travel and Exploration: An Encyclopedia.* New York: Fitzroy Dearborn, 2003.

Thompson, Carl, ed. *The Routledge Companion to Travel Writing.* London: Routledge, 2016.

Travel Writing. London: Routledge, 2010.

Youngs, Tim. *The Cambridge Introduction of Travel Writing.* Cambridge: Cambridge University Press, 2013.

Critical Studies on Travel Writing: Colonial and Postcolonial

Arana, R. Victoria, ed. *Black Travel Writing.* Philadelphia: Frenzella Elaine Delancey, 2003.

Behdad, Ali. *Belated Travelers: Orientalism in the Age of Colonial Dissolution.* Durham: Duke University Press, 1994.

Blunt, Alison and Gillian Rose, eds. *Writing Women and Space: Colonial and Postcolonial Geographies.* New York: Guilford Press, 1994.

Brisson, Ulrike and Bernard Schweizer, eds. *Not So Innocent Abroad: The Politics of Travel and Travel Writing.* Newcastle upon Tyne: Cambridge Scholars, 2009.

Brown-Guillory, Elizabeth ed. *Middle Passages and the Healing Place of History: Migration and Identity in Black Women's Literature.* Columbus: Ohio State University Press, 2006.

Cabañas, Miguel A. *The Cultural "Other" in Nineteenth-Century Travel Narratives: How the United States and Latin America Described Each Other.* Lewiston: Edwin Mellen Press, 2008.

Castillo, Susan and David Seed, eds. *American Travel and Empire.* Liverpool: Liverpool University Press, 2009.

Clark, Steve, ed. *Travel Writing and Empire: Postcolonial Theory in Transit.* London: Zed Books, 1999.

Clark, Steve and Paul Smethurst, eds. *Asian Crossings: Travel Writing on China, Japan and Southeast Asia.* Hong Kong: Hong Kong University Press, 2008.

Diedrich, Maria, Henry Louis Gates, and Carl Pedersen, eds. *Black Imagination and the Middle Passage.* Oxford: Oxford University Press, 1999.

Dissanayake, Wimal and Carmen Wickramagemage. *Self and Colonial Desire: Travel Writings of V. S. Naipaul.* New York: Peter Lang, 1993.

Dolan, Brian. *Exploring European Frontiers: British Travellers in the Age of Enlightenment.* London: Macmillan, 2000.

Edwards, Justin D. and Rune Graulund. *Mobility at Large: Globalization, Textuality and Innovative Travel Writing.* Liverpool: Liverpool University Press, 2012.

eds. *Postcolonial Travel Writing: Critical Explorations.* Basingstoke: Palgrave Macmillan, 2010.

Fish, Cheryl J. *Black and White Women's Travel Narratives: Antebellum Explorations.* Gainesville: University of Florida Press, 2004.

Fogel, Joshua A. *The Literature of Travel in the Japanese Rediscovery of China, 1862–1945*. Stanford: Stanford University Press, 1997.

Ghose, Indira. *Women Travellers in Colonial India*. Delhi: Oxford University Press, 1998.

Gilbert, Helen and Anna Johnston, eds. *In Transit: Travel, Text, Empire*. New York: Peter Lang, 2002.

Glage, Liselotte, ed. *Being/s in Transit: Traveling, Migration, Dislocation*. Amsterdam: Rodopi, 2000.

Grenier, Katherine Haldane. *Tourism and Identity in Scotland, 1770–1914: Creating Caledonia*. Aldershot: Ashgate, 2005.

Grewal, Inderpal. *Home and Harem: Nation, Gender, Empire, and the Cultures of Travel*. London: Leicester University Press, 1996.

Griffiths, Gareth. "Postcolonial Travel Writing." In *The Cambridge History of Postcolonial Literature*, edited by Ato Qayson, 58–80. Cambridge: Cambridge University Press, 2012.

Henes, Mary and Brian H. Murray, eds. *Travel Writing, Visual Culture and Form, 1760–1900*. London: Palgrave Macmillan, 2015.

Holland, Patrick. "Travel Literature (Overview)." In *The Encyclopedia of Post-Colonial Literatures in English*, edited by Eugene Benson and L. W. Conolly, 1586–89. vol 2. London: Routledge, 1994.

Hulme, Peter. *Remnants of Conquest: The Island Caribs and Their Visitors, 1877–1998*. Oxford: Oxford University Press, 2000.

Hulme, Peter and Russell McDougall, eds. *Writing, Travel and Empire*. London: I.B. Tauris, 2007.

Johnston, Anna. *Missionary Writing and Empire, 1800–1860*. Cambridge: Cambridge University Press, 2003.

Kerr, Douglas and Julia Kuehn, eds. *A Century of Travels in China: Critical Essays on Travel Writing from the 1840s to the 1940s*. Hong Kong: Hong Kong University Press, 2007.

Kleeman, Faye Yuan. *Under an Imperial Sun: Japanese Colonial Literature of Taiwan and the South*. Honolulu: University of Hawaii Press, 2003.

Knowles, Sam. *Travel Writing and the Transnational Author*. Basingstoke: Palgrave Macmillan, 2014.

Korte, Barbara. *English Travel Writing from Pilgrimages to Postcolonial Explorations*. Trans. Catherine Matthias. London: MacMillan, 2000.

Kuehn, Julia and Paul Smethurst, eds. *New Directions in Travel Writing Studies*. New York: Palgrave Macmillan, 2015.

Leon, Carol E. *Movement and Belonging: Lines, Places, and Spaces of Travel*. New York: Peter Lang, 2009.

Lewis, Reina. *Rethinking Orientalism: Women, Travel and the Ottoman Harem*. New Brunswick: Rutgers University Press, 2004.

Liebersohn, Harry. *The Travelers' World: Europe to the Pacific*. Cambridge: Harvard University Press, 2006.

Lindsay, Claire. *Contemporary Travel Writing of Latin America*. New York: Routledge, 2010.

Lopez Ropero, Maria Lourdes. "Travel Writing and Postcoloniality: Caryl Phillips's *The Atlantic Sound*." *Atlantis* 25, no. 1 (2003): 51–62.

Lorente, Beatriz P., Nicola Piper, and Shen Hsiu-hua, eds. *Asian Migrations: Sojourning, Displacement, Homecoming and Other Travels*. Singapore: Asia Research Institute, 2006.

Mee, Catharine. *Interpersonal Encounters in Contemporary Travel Writing: French and Italian Perspectives*. London: Anthem, 2015.

Mills, Sara. *Discourses of Difference: An Analysis of Women's Travel Writing and Colonialism*. London: Routledge, 1991.

Gender and Colonial Space. Manchester: Manchester University Press, 2005.

Mohanty, Sachidananda, ed. *Travel Writing and the Empire*. New Delhi: Katha, 2003.

Moynagh, Maureen C. *Political Tourism and Its Texts*. Toronto: Toronto University Press, 2008.

Nash, Geoffrey. *From Empire to Orient: Travellers to the Middle East 1830–1926*. London: I.B. Tauris, 2005.

Oboe, Annalisa and Shaul Bassi, eds. *Experiences of Freedom in Postcolonial Literatures and Cultures*. London: Routledge, 2011.

Pettinger, Alasdair. "Travel-Writings by Africans: A Reader's Guide." *Journal of African Travel Writing* nos. 8–9 (2001): 172–81.

Pitman, Thea, "Mexican Travel Writing: the Legacy of Foreign Travel Writers in Mexico, or Why Mexicans Say They Don't Write Travel Books." *Comparative Critical Studies* 4, no. 3 (2007): 209–23.

Schmeller, Erik S. *Perceptions of Race and Nation in English and American Travel Writers, 1833–1914*. New York: Peter Lang, 2004.

Schulz-Forberg, Hagen, ed. *Unravelling Civilisation: European Travel and Travel Writing*. Brussels: Peter Lang, 2005.

Seixo, Maria-Alzira, John Noyes, Graça Abreu, and Isabel Moutinho, eds. *The Paths of Multiculturalism: Travel Writings and Postcolonialism*. Lisbon: Edições Cosmos, 2000.

Siegel, Kristi, ed. *Issues in Travel Writing: Empire, Spectacle, and Displacement*. New York: Peter Lang, 2002.

Gender, Genre, and Identity in Women's Travel Writing. New York: Peter Lang, 2004.

Skinner, Jonathon, ed. *Writing on the Dark Side of Travel*. New York: Berghahn Books, 2012.

Smith, Sidonie. *Moving Lives: Twentieth-Century Women's Travel Writing*. Minneapolis: University of Minnesota Press, 2001.

Steadman, Jennifer Bernhardt. *Traveling Economies: American Women's Travel Writing*. Columbus: Ohio State University Press, 2007.

Talwar, Urmil and Bandana Chakrabarty, eds. *Culture, Transformation and Identity: Travel, Fiction, Autobiography*. Jaipur: Institute for Research in Interdisciplinary Studies and Rawat Publications, 2015.

Teng, Emma Jinhua. *Taiwan's Imagined Geography: Chinese Colonial Travel Writing and Pictures, 1683–1895*. Cambridge: Harvard University Press, 2006.

Totten, Gary. *African American Travel Narratives from Abroad: Mobility and Cultural Work in the Age of Jim Crow*. Amherst: University of Massachusetts Press, 2015.

Wevers, Lydia. *Country of Writing: Travel Writing and New Zealand, 1809–1900*. Auckland: University of Auckland Press, 2002.

Wrobel, David M. *Global West, American Frontier: Travel, Empire, and Exceptionalism from Manifest Destiny to the Great Depression*. Albuquerque: University of New Mexico Press, 2013.

Youngs, Tim, ed. *Travel Writing in the Nineteenth Century: Filling the Blank Spaces*. London: Anthem Press, 2006.

Travellers in Africa: British Travelogues, 1850–1900. Manchester: Manchester University Press, 1994.

Zilcosky, John. *Kafka's Travels: Exoticism, Colonialism, and the Traffic of Writing*. New York: Palgrave Macmillan, 2003.

Postcolonial Travel Writing and its Theory

Campbell, Mary Baine. "Travel Writing and its Theory." In *The Cambridge Companion to Travel Writing*, edited by Peter Hulme and Tim Youngs, 261–78. Cambridge: Cambridge University Press, 2002.

Clark, Steve, ed. *Travel Writing and Empire: Postcolonial Theory in Transit*. London: Zed Books, 1999.

Holland, Patrick and Graham Huggan. *Tourists with Typewriters: Critical Reflections on Contemporary Travel Writing*. Ann Arbor: University of Michigan Press, 1998.

Huggan, Graham. *Extreme Pursuits: Travel Writing in an Age of Globalization*. Ann Arbor: University of Michigan Press, 2010.

Lindsay, Claire. "Travel Writing and Postcolonial Studies." In *The Routledge Companion to Travel Writing*, edited by Carl Thompson, 25–34. London: Routledge, 2016.

Lisle, Debbie. *The Global Politics of Contemporary Travel Writing*. Cambridge: Cambridge University Press, 2006.

Ní Loingsigh, Aedín. *Postcolonial Eyes: Intercontinental Travel in Francophone African Literature*. Liverpool: Liverpool University Press, 2009.

Pratt, Mary Louise. *Imperial Eyes: Travel Writing and Transculturation*. 1992. London: Routledge, 2008.

Said, Edward. *Orientalism*. London: Penguin, 1978.

Spurr, David. *The Rhetoric of Empire: Colonial Discourse in Journalism, Travel Writing, and Imperial Administration*. Durham: Duke University Press, 1993.

Postcolonial Travel Writing and the Environment

Arnold, David. *The Tropics and the Traveling Gaze: India, Landscape, and Science, 1800–1856*. Seattle: University of Washington Press, 2011.

Crane, Kylie. *Myths of Wilderness in Contemporary Narratives: Environmental Postcolonialism in Australia and Canada*. New York: Palgrave Macmillan, 2012.

Crosby, Alfred W. *Ecological Imperialism: The Biological Expansion of Europe, 900–1900*. Cambridge: Cambridge University Press, 1986.

DeLoughrey, Elizabeth, Jill Didur, and Anthony Carrigan. *Global Ecologies and the Environmental Humanities: Postcolonial Approaches*. New York: Routledge, 2015.

Grove, Richard. *Green Imperialism: Colonial Expansion, Tropical Island Edens and the Origins of Environmentalism, 1600–1860*. Cambridge: Cambridge University Press, 1995.

Huggan, Graham and Helen Tiffin. *Postcolonial Ecocriticism: Literature, Animals, Environment*. New York: Routledge, 2010.

Mueggler, Erik, *The Paper Road: Archive and Experience in the Botanical Exploration of West China and Tibet*. Berkeley: University of California Press, 2011.

Nixon, Rob. *Slow Violence and the Environmentalism of the Poor*. Cambridge: Harvard University Press, 2011.

Roos, Bonnie and Alex Hunt, eds., *Postcolonial Green: Environmental Politics and World Narratives*. Charlottesville: University of Virginia Press, 2010.

History, Memory, and Trauma in Postcolonial Travel Writing

Burroughs, Robert M. *Travel Writing and Atrocities: Eyewitness Accounts of Colonialism in the Congo, Angola, and the Putumayo*. London: Routledge, 2011.

Clarke, Robert. *Travel Writing from Black Australia: Utopia, Melancholia, and Aboriginality*. New York: Routledge, 2016.

Clarke, Robert, Jacqueline Dutton, and Anna Johnston. "Dark Travel and Postcolonial Cultures." *Postcolonial Studies*, 17, no. 3 (2014): 221–35.

de Mul, Sarah. *Colonial Memory: Contemporary Women's Travel Writing in Britain and the Netherlands*. Amsterdam: Amsterdam University Press, 2011.

Gregory, Derek. "Colonial Nostalgia and Cultures of Travel: Spaces of Constructed Visibility in Egypt." In *Consuming Tradition, Manufacturing Heritage: Global Norms and Urban Forms in the Age of Tourism*, edited by Nezar Alsayad, 111–51. London: Routledge, [2001] 2013.

Rosaldo, Renato. "Imperialist Nostalgia." *Representations* 28 (1983): 107–22.

Walder, David. *Postcolonial Nostalgias: Writing, Representation and Memory*. New York: Routledge, 2011.

Diasporic Returnees

Forbes, Curdella. "Selling That Caribbean Woman down the River: Diasporic Travel Narratives and the Global Economy." *Journal of West Indian Literature* 13, nos. 1–2 (2005): 1–27.

Gilroy, Paul. *The Black Atlantic: Modernity and Double Consciousness*. London: Verso, 1993.

López, Iraida H. *Impossible Returns: Narratives of the Cuban Diaspora*. Gainesville: University Press of Florida, 2015.

Ravi, Srilata. "Home and the 'Failed' City in Postcolonial Narratives of 'Dark Return.'" *Postcolonial Studies* 17, no. 3 (2014): 296–306.

Safran, William. "Deconstructing and Comparing Diasporas." In *Diaspora, Identity, and Religion: New Directions in Theory and Research*, edited by Waltraud Kokot, Khachig Tölöyan, and Carolin Alfonso, 9–29. London: Routledge, 2004.

Diplomat Travelers

Bosworth, Clifford Edmund. *Eastward Ho! Diplomats, Travellers and Interpreters of the Middle East and Beyond, 1600–1940.* London: East & West, 2012.

Cromwell, Valerie. "'Married to Affairs of State': Memoirs of the Wives and Daughters of British Diplomats." In *Political Memoir: Essays on the Politics of Memory,* edited by George Egerton, 207–24. London: Frank Cass, 1994.

Lambert, David and Alan Lester, ed. *Colonial Lives across the British Empire: Imperial Careering in the Long Nineteenth Century.* Cambridge: Cambridge University Press, 2006.

Lloyd, Lorna. *Diplomacy with a Difference: The Office of High Commissioner, 1880–2006. Diplomatic Studies.* Leiden: Martinus Nijhoff, 2007.

Francophone Postcolonial Travel Writing

Edwards, Natalie and Christopher Hogarth, eds. *Gender and Displacement: "Home" in Contemporary Francophone Women's Autobiography.* Cambridge: Cambridge University Press, 2008.

Forsdick, Charles. *Travel in Twentieth-Century French and Francophone Cultures: The Persistence of Diversity.* Oxford: Oxford University Press, 2005.

Forsdick, Charles, Feroza Basu, and Siobhan Shilton, eds. *New Approaches to Twentieth-Century Travel Literature in French: Genre, History, Theory.* Amsterdam: Peter Lang, 2006.

Mortimer, Mildred. *Journeys through the French African Novel.* Portsmouth: Heinemann; London: J. Currey, 1990.

Ní Loingsigh, Aedín. *Postcolonial Eyes: Intercontinental Travel in Francophone African Literature.* Liverpool: Liverpool University Press, 2009.

Syrotinski, Michael. *Singular Performances: Reinscribing the Subject in Francophone African Writing.* Charlottesville: University of Virginia Press, 2002.

African American Travel Writing

Campbell, James T. *Middle Passages: African American Journeys to Africa, 1787–2005.* New York: Penguin, 2007.

Griffin, Farah J. and Cheryl J. Fish, eds. *A Stranger in the Village: Two Centuries of African-American Travel Writing.* Boston: Beacon Press, 1998.

Gruesser, John Cullen. *Confluences: Postcolonialism, African American Literary Studies, and the Black Atlantic.* Athens: University of Georgia Press, [2005] 2007.

Black on Black: Twentieth-Century African American Writing about Africa. Lexington: University Press of Kentucky, 2000.

Madsen, Deborah L., ed. *Beyond the Borders: American Literature and Post-Colonial Theory.* London: Pluto, 2003.

Pettinger, Alasdair, ed. *Always Elsewhere: Travels of the Black Atlantic.* London: Cassell, 1998.

Totten, Gary. *African American Travel Narratives from Abroad: Mobility and Cultural Work in the Age of Jim Crow.* Amherst: University of Massachusetts Press, 2015.

Whatley Smith, Virginia. "African American Travel Literature." In *The Cambridge Companion to American Travel Writing*, edited by Alfred Bendixen and Judith Hamera, 197–213. Cambridge: Cambridge University Press, 2009.

Youngs, Tim. "Pushing against the Black/White Limits of Maps: African American Writings of Travel," *English Studies in Africa* 53, no. 2 (2010): 71–85.

Postcolonial Travel Writing and Spirituality

Clarke, Robert. "'New Age Trippers': Aboriginality and New Age Australian Travel Books." *Studies in Travel Writing* 13, no. 1 (2009): 25–41.

Norman, Alex. *Spiritual Tourism: Travel and Religious Practice in Western Society.* London: Continuum, 2011.

Ratti, Manav. *The Postsecular Imagination: Postcolonialism, Religion, and Literature.* London: Routledge, 2013.

Sen, Asha. *Postcolonial Yearning: Reshaping Spiritual and Secular Discourses in Contemporary Literature.* New York: Palgrave MacMillan, 2013.

Postcolonial Journeys on the Trails of Colonial Travelers

Keirstead, Christopher. "Convoluted Paths: Mapping Genre in Contemporary Footsteps Travel Writing." *Genre* 46, no. 3 (2013): 285–315.

Leavenworth, Maria Lindgren. *The Second Journey: Traveling in Literary Footsteps.* 2nd edn. Umeå: Umeå University, 2010.

Ravi, Srilata. "Home and the 'Failed' City in Postcolonial Narratives of 'Dark Return." *Postcolonial Studies* 17, no. 3 (2014): 296–306.

Postcolonial Travel Journalism and the New Media

Cocking, Ben. "Travel Journalism: Europe Imagining the Middle East." *Journalism Studies* 10, no. 1 (2009): 54–68.

Creech, Brian. "The Spectacle of Past Violence: Travel Journalism and Dark Tourism." In *Travel Journalism: Exploring Production, Impact, and Culture*, edited by Folker Hanusch and Elfriede Fürsich, 249–66. New York: Palgrave Macmillan, 2014.

Hanusch, Folker and Elfriede Fürsich, eds. *Travel Journalism: Exploring Production, Impact, and Culture.* New York: Palgrave MacMillan, 2014.

McGaurr, Lyn. *Environmental Communication and Travel Journalism: Consumerism, Conflict and Concern.* New York: Routledge, 2015.

Molz, Jennie Germann. *Travel Connections: Tourism, Technology and Togetherness in a Mobile World.* London: Routledge, 2012.

Travel Magazines and Settler (Post)Colonialism

Hammill, Faye and Michelle Smith. *Magazines, Travel, and Middlebrow Culture: Canadian Periodicals in English and French, 1925–1960.* Alberta: University of Alberta Press, 2015.

Klein, Christina. *Cold War Orientalism: Asia in the Middlebrow Imagination, 1945–1961.* Berkeley and Los Angeles: University of California Press, 2003.

Lutz, Catherine A. and Jane L. Collins. *Reading National Geographic*. Chicago: University of Chicago Press, 1993.

O'Barr, William. *Culture and the Ad: Exploring Otherness in the World of Advertising*. Boulder: Westulew Press, 1994.

Rolls, Mitchell and Anna Johnston. *Traveling Home, Walkabout Magazine and Modern Australia*. London: Anthem Press, 2016.

Veracini, Lorenzo. *Settler Colonialism: A Theoretical Overview*. Basingstoke: Palgrave Macmillan, 2010.

Refugee and Asylum Seeker Narratives as Travel Writing

Datema, Jessica and Diane Krumrey, eds. *Wretched Refuge: Immigrants and Itinerants in the Postmodern*. Newcastle upon Tyne: Cambridge Scholars, 2010.

Farrier, David. *Postcolonial Asylum: Seeking Sanctuary before the Law*. Liverpool: Liverpool University Press, 2011.

Menon, Ritu and Kamla Bhasin. *Borders and Boundaries: How Women Experienced the Partition of India*. New Brunswick: Rutgers University Press, 1998.

Powell, Katrina. *Identity and Power in Narratives of Displacement*. New York: Routledge, 2015.

Shemak, April. *Asylum Speakers: Caribbean Refugees and Testimonial Discourse*. New York: Fordham University Press, 2011.

Woolley, Agnes. *Contemporary Asylum Narratives: Representing Refugees in the Twenty-First Century*. Basingstoke: Palgrave Macmillan, 2014.

Travelers in Postcolonial Fiction

Burroughs, Robert, "Weird *farang* thing: Dark Tourism in Alex Garland's *The Beach* (1996)." *Postcolonial Studies* 17, no. 3 (2014): 320–33.

Levin, Stephen M. *The Contemporary Anglophone Travel Novel: The Aesthetics of Self-Fashioning in the Era of Globalization*. New York: Routledge, 2008.

Moses, Michael Valdez. *The Novel and the Globalization of Culture*. Oxford: Oxford University Press, 1995.

Ramsey-Kurz, Helga and Geetha Ganapthy-Doré, eds., *Projections of Paradise: Ideal Elsewheres in Postcolonial Migrant Literatures*. Amsterdam: Rodopi, 2011.

Resources

A number of journals specialize in publishing scholarly articles on travel writing, including postcolonial travel writing. These include *Studies in Travel Writing* and *Journeys: The International Journal of Travel and Travel Writing*. The *Journal of African Travel Writing* was in circulation from 1996 to 2001. Journals that focus specifically on postcolonial studies and that regularly publish articles on travel writing include: *Postcolonial Studies*, the *Journal of Commonwealth and Postcolonial Studies*, and *Interventions: The International Journal of Postcolonial Studies*. Notable journals devoted to travel and tourism research include the *Annals of Tourism Research*, the *Journal of Travel Research*, the *Journal of Tourism and Cultural Change*, and *Tourism, Culture and Communication*.

A number of publishers currently have book series devoted to scholarship on travel writing that include works of relevance to postcolonial travel writing. These include: the Routledge Research in Travel Writing series (www.routledge.com/Routledge-Research-in-Travel-Writing/book-series/RRTW); Parlor Press Writing Travel series (www.parlorpress.com/travel.html); and the Anthem Studies in Travel series (www.anthempress.com/anthem-studies-in-travel).

INDEX

ABC. *See* Australian Broadcasting
    Corporation
"Abdullah's Feet" (Bouazza), 212
Aboriginal peoples, 57–58
    Canadian Aboriginal soldiers, 80, 82
    racist representations of, 182
acculturation, 24–25
Achebe, Chinua, 203–4, 228–29
activists, 164
adivasi peoples, 40
    environment and, 44–45
    erasure of, 41
    liberty for, 46
adventure stories, 81
advertisements, 178–79
Africa. *See also* sub-Saharan Africa
    Asia cultural transactions with, 26
    South Africa, apartheid regime in, 56
    travel writing from, 26–27
Un Africain au Groenland (Kpomassie). *See*
    An African in Greenland
African Americans
    culture, 118
    Soviet Union and, 116
    as subjects of colonialism, 115
    travel writing by, 119
    various definitions around, 110–12
African diaspora, 110
The African Eskimo (BBC documentary),
    93–94
An African in Greenland (Kpomassie), 94
African National Congress, 56
African travel writers (*écrivain-voyageur*), 93
After the Dance (Danticat), 94
Aguirre (Minta), 142
Ahmed, Leila, 133
Alexander, Caroline, 146–47
Ali, Ayaan Hirsi, 197

Allan, Stuart, 161
ancient pilgrims, 124–27
Anglophone literature, 95, 177
Anthropocene, 34
anticolonial sentiments, 51
anti-travelers, 99
apartheid, 56
Appadurai, Arjun, 167–68
appropriation, 11
Arnold, David, 33–34, 37
"Arrival" (Ochero-Okello), 197
Asia
    travel writing from, 26–27
asylum seekers, 188
    interviews for, 194–97
    travel by, 190–91
At Large in Burma (Ghosh), 27–28
The Atlantic Sound (Phillips), 149–50
Aung San Suu Kyi, 28
Australia, 57–58
    Australian identity, 180
    boat people and, 193
    cultural and geopolitical reorientations in,
        179–80
    "journeys to Country," 60
Australian Broadcasting Corporation (ABC),
    173

Ba, Omar, 105
Baldwin, James, 115
Balfour Report on Inter-Imperial Relations,
    85
Baraka, Amiri, 115–16
Bartkowski, Frances, 102–3
Beck, Ulrich, 160
*Becoming Undone: Darwinian Reflections of
    Life, Politics, and Art* (Grosz), 220–21
Behdad, Ali, 23

242